D1571202

ON SEXUALITY

ON SEXUALITY

Psychoanalytic Observations

Edited by

TOKSOZ B. KARASU
and
CHARLES W. SOCARIDES

INTERNATIONAL UNIVERSITIES PRESS, INC.
New York

Library of Congress Cataloging in Publication Data
Main entry under title:

On sexuality.

   Bibliography: p.
   Includes index.
   1.   Sex (Psychology)   2.   Psychoanalysis.   I.   Karasu,
Toksoz B.   II.   Socarides, Charles W.   [DNLM: 1.   Sex
behavior.   2.   Psychoanalytic interpretation.
WM460.5.S3 058]
BF692.05   155.3   78-67478
ISBN 0-8236-3857-X

Manufactured in the United States of America

Contents

Preface

The past decade has witnessed accelerating, even revolutionary, changes in sexual behavior and customs. Concomitant with these changes has been an increasingly wide variety of approaches to the understanding of human sexuality. The resurgence of the neurobiological approach to sexual behavior and its reinforcement by data from biochemistry, pharmacology, genetics, and behavioral theories have tended to lead many away from the motivational approach of psychoanalysis into a more mechanistic, behavior-oriented, and social-engineering framework.

Although sexuality and psychoanalysis have been interrelated from the earliest years of our science, there has been a growing trend toward separating psychoanalytic clinical research from "sex research." This trend seems to be associated with a tendency to eliminate conflict theory and to substitute for it research into physiology, chemistry, and animal and human experiments. The conspicuous feature of human sexuality, however, is that it is not governed by hormonal influence, statistics, changing sex roles, and other factors, no matter how important these may be, but by conscious and/or unconscious psychological events occurring at the level of the cerebral cortex. It is our conviction that sexual behavior is primarily a motivated field, and motivational analysis supplied by psychoanalysis is the only method by which science can reach the whole individual on the behavior level. It is only by combining psychoanalytic findings with those from other disciplines that the intellectual foundations of research into sexual behavior can be preserved and expanded.

Our interest in this volume originated from the need to present to psychoanalysts, psychiatrists, and other behavioral scientists the latest developments in the field of human sexual behavior from the psychoanalytic point of view. The original theoretical contributions, as well as the critiques and surveys of special areas found in this book, provide overwhelming evidence against the popular misconception that psychoanalysis fails to take into account sociocultural factors in its pursuit of intrapsychic causation and mechanisms.

Understanding of the stages in the development of sexuality, the cornerstone of psychoanalytic theory, has been profoundly enriched by the work of a number of psychoanalytic investigators. Direct observational studies of infants has led to monumental formulations of separation-individuation processes and the development of a sense of identity. Eleanor Galenson's and Herman Roiphe's efforts have been in the direction of providing vital data on the beginning awareness of a gender-defined self-identity. Having discovered that infants experience genital awareness considerably earlier than had been thought, they report on sex differences in infants during the second year of life, findings based on direct observation of 70 boys and girls at the Albert Einstein College of Medicine in New York City.

Aaron Esman examines the impact of the ''new'' sexuality on the functioning of adolescents, both sexually and in their total adaptation to the realities confronting them. New patterns of handling guilt and anxiety seem to be emerging in our patients, and the analyst must deal with them against a backdrop of changing expectations regarding sexual behavior, marriage, and childbearing.

Utilizing information from the psychoanalysis of adults, in conjunction with a deep knowledge of child analysis, Irwin Marcus provides us with a lucid chapter on masturbation, drawing particular attention to its constructive and adaptive functions in the formation of an internalized representation of both self and object.

Nathaniel Ross traces the origin of sexuality and love ontogenetically, phylogenetically, and historically. While sex, love, and aggression are necessary for survival and adaptation, it is the affect of love that must fuse with both instinctual drives in order to counteract the destructiveness and self-destructiveness of man.

Edith Buxbaum's chapter on ''Modern Woman and Motherhood'' highlights the vitally important new discoveries with respect to the psychobiological events following birth in both mother and child. Because these events occur independently of social changes, it is essential to carefully evaluate innovative concepts of motherhood introduced by society, in terms of whether they aid the process of integrating the multiple needs of both mother and child or increase the risk of personal maladaptation for both—and disharmony for society.

Paternity has been a relatively neglected subject, compared with that of motherhood. In the forefront of an emerging concentration on this subject is the work of John M. Ross. In a comprehensive and scholarly essay in which the author matches scientific acumen with stylistic elegance, Ross describes the attainment of paternal identity, the nature of fatherhood itself, and traces a developmental line from infancy to fatherhood, beginning with the prospective father's own infancy, continuing through separation-individuation, the oedipal crisis, adolescence, the attainment of true intimacy and love, the desire to have children, and, ultimately, the conflicts attendant on the attainment of fatherhood.

Arno Karlen offers a panoramic view of attitudes toward sex throughout history. Happily, Karlen's sense of humor triumphs over what one feels is his sense of dismay at the human condition.

The chapter by Stuart A. Waltzman and Toksoz B. Karasu is the only article, so far as we know, that spells out the vicissitudes of sexuality in the elderly and gives equal stress to physiological, psychological, and sociocultural factors. We believe the medical profession as well as other health professionals will find it of immeasurable value.

Psychoanalysis has made major advances in the direction of understanding the sexual deviations, these are represented by three chapters in this book.

From psychoanalytic clinical research studies of a variety of fully developed sexual perversions over a twenty-year period, Charles W. Socarides presents a unifying concept of the perversions in an attempt to explain their common core. The genesis of well-structured perversions may well be the result of disturbances that occur earlier than has been generally assumed and accepted. Socarides sees sexual perversion as serving to repress a pivotal nuclear conflict: the urge to regress to a preoedipal fixation in which there is a desire for and dread of merging with the mother in order to reinstate the primitive mother-child unity.

Vamik Volkan presents psychoanalytic research material on more than 25 cases of transsexualism. He provides clinical information derived from the study of the family of a nine-year-old transsexual boy, as well as a six-month analytic study of a man who ultimately underwent surgery, only to fall prey to nightmares of the return of his phallus in horrifying form.

Milton E. Jucovy succinctly reviews the literature on transvestitism, giving special emphasis to gender-identity disturbances and other preoedipal factors in the causation of this disorder. Transvestitism can be seen to serve a particular adaptive function, inasmuch as cross dressing may play a central role in tribal initiation rituals.

Robert Dickes cautions us that advances toward healthy sexuality, largely attained through modern scientific approaches to sex, can still be imperiled by emotional resistances encountered in medical schools and psychiatric residency programs. One of his conclusions is that certification in sex therapy for psychiatric residents may become a necessity if medicine is to stay in the forefront of this area of public health.

Glenn, Bezahler, and Glenn approach the problem of sex education from the vantage point of psychoanalytic theory and clinical experience. They note that Freud's discoveries pointed to the need for the sexual enlightenment of children. This task, however, is fraught with serious theoretical and practical problems. The authors address themselves to these problems, concluding that the best assurance for a sound sex-education program is a sexually enlightened and psychoanalytically informed instructor.

Virginia Clower posits that no adequate psychology of women yet exists, reminding us that Freud himself acknowledged that his theoretical conclusions were tentative, subject to validation and change. It is the task of contemporary analysts to clarify and expand upon his seminal discoveries in this area. Clower provides glimpses into exciting discoveries concerning penis envy, preoedipal castration fear, the "initiators" of feminine behavior, and a correction in the concept of the normality of feminine masochism. In a remarkably eloquent and balanced essay, she meets the objections leveled at a Freudian psychology of women, while posing unexplored questions to be answered by future research.

Frosch, Ginsberg, and Shapiro illustrate how social factors such as changing public attitudes toward sexuality and a widening acceptability of new sexual customs and practices can cause a shift in the delicate balance between satisfactory sexual performance and orgastic failure. Although the roots of such difficulties are shown to be intrapsychic, the authors demonstrate the precipitating effect of certain external factors.

Edward M. Levine provides a sociologist's view of the consequences of accepting perversions as simply alternative life styles.

Finally, Karasu, Maj-Britt Rosenbaum, and Inez Jerrett survey the techniques of sex therapy currently used in this country, ranging from the psychodynamic to a variety of behavioral approaches. Although the current trend, with only rare exceptions, appears to be one in which the knowledge of unconscious dynamic processes is not fully utilized, the psychodynamically trained physician can benefit by being fully informed of these new developments in technique.

We wish to acknowledge our immeasurable debt of gratitude to the authors represented in this volume. Their expertise in their own areas of specialization, as well as their shared conviction of the importance of such a book, has made this project profoundly stimulating and rewarding. We hope the reader will find it equally stimulating and rewarding. Our guiding principle throughout has been that an examination of the many facets of current sexuality from the psychoanalytic perspective will lead to maturation, improvement, and healthy change, both for the individual and for society. As Lawrence Kubie so correctly reminds us: "If the push of society were in the direction of finding ways to rear healthy children, who are capable of change, these children might be able to grow into and work out the creative society of which humanists dream."

The Editors

Acknowledgments

The Editors wish to express their deep gratitude to Natalie Altman whose valuable suggestions, as Manuscript Editor, helped weld this book into an integrated whole. By her encouragement, coupled with perceptive questioning, she challenged the contributors to formulate and express their ideas with greater clarity and incisiveness, thereby enriching each individual contribution.

Our thanks go also to Barbara Bonner Socarides for her editorial assistance in the early phases of the preparation of the book, and to Norma Brooks for her secretarial assistance throughout.

Contributors

Harvey B. Bezahler, M.D.
Clinical Assistant Professor of Psychiatry and Faculty Member, Division of Psychoanalytic Education, State University of New York, Downstate Medical Center.

Edith Buxbaum, Ph.D.
Clinical Professor of Psychiatry, University of Washington (State); Consultant, Ryther Child Center.

Virginia L. Clower, M.D.
Training and Supervising Analyst in Child and Adult Psychoanalysis, Washington, D.C. Psychoanalytic Institute.

Robert Dickes, M.D.
Professor and Chairman of the Department of Psychiatry, State University of New York, Downstate Medical Center.

Aaron H. Esman, M.D.
Chief Psychiatrist, Jewish Board of Family and Children's Services; Faculty Member, New York Psychoanalytic Institute.

William A. Frosch, M.D.
Professor and Vice-Chairman of the Department of Psychiatry, New York Hospital-Cornell Medical Center.

Eleanor Galenson, M.D.
Clinical Professor of Psychiatry, Albert Einstein College of Medicine; Clinical Professor of Psychiatry, Mount Sinai School of Medicine, New York City.

George L. Ginsberg, M.D.
Associate Professor of Clinical Psychiatry, New York University School of Medicine; Director of Residency Training in Psychiatry, NYU-Bellevue Medical Center.

Sylvia Glenn, M.A.
Formerly, Research Assistant, Child Development Center, Jewish Board of Guardians, New York City.

Inez Jerrett
Research Assistant, Department of Psychiatry, Albert Einstein College of Medicine at Bronx Municipal Hospital Center.

Milton E. Jucovy, M.D.
Training and Supervising Analyst, New York Psychoanalytic Institute; Visiting Staff Psychiatrist, Long Island Jewish-Hillside Medical Center.

Toksoz B. Karasu, M.D.
Associate Professor of Psychiatry and Vice-Chairman, Department of Psychiatry, Albert Einstein College of Medicine; Director of Psychiatry, Albert Einstein College of Medicine at Bronx Municipal Hospital Center.

Arno Karlen
Writer and editor. Author of *Sexuality and Homosexuality* and Co-editor of *Sex Education in Medicine.*

Irwin M. Marcus, M.D.
Clinical Professor of Psychiatry, Louisiana State University Medical School, New Orleans; Supervising and Training Analyst in Adult and Child Analysis and Chairman of the Child/Adolescent Division, New Orleans Psychoanalytic Institute.

Edward M. Levine, Ph.D.
Professor, Department of Sociology, Loyola University of Chicago.

Herman Roiphe, M.D.
Associate Clinical Professor of Psychiatry, Mount Sinai School of Medicine, New York City.

Maj-Britt Rosenbaum, M.D.
Associate Clinical Professor of Psychiatry, Albert Einstein College of Medicine.

John M. Ross, Ph.D.
Clinical Assistant Professor of Psychiatry, State University of New York, Downstate Medical Center.

Nathaniel Ross, M.D.
Clinical Professor of Psychiatry, Division of Psychoanalytic Education, State University of New York, Downstate Medical Center. Formerly, Associate Editor of the *Journal of the American Psychoanalytic Association.*

Theodore Shapiro, M.D.
Professor of Psychiatry and Professor of Psychiatry in Pediatrics, New York Hospital-Cornell Medical Center; Director of Child and Adolescent Psychiatry, Payne Whitney Clinic.

Charles W. Socarides, M.D.
Clinical Professor of Psychiatry, Division of Psychoanalytic Education, State University of New York, Downstate Medical Center; Visiting Clinical Professor of Psychiatry, Albert Einstein College of Medicine.

Vamik Volkan, M.D.
Medical Director and Professor of Psychiatry, Blue Ridge Hospital, Division, University of Virginia.

Stuart A. Waltzman, M.D.
Assistant Clinical Professor of Psychiatry, Albert Einstein College of Medicine.

CHAPTER 1

The Development of Sexual Identity: Discoveries and Implications

ELEANOR GALENSON and HERMAN ROIPHE

It has been generally accepted theory that boys and and girls develop sexually in the same way for about the first three years of life. According to Freud's (1933) formulations, both sexes would seem to be little boys until their observation of the anatomical difference (Freud, 1925b). This experience then leads to the development of the castration complex and to divergent lines of sexual development from that time on (Abraham, 1920; Freud, 1931, 1933; Lampl-de Groot, 1927). It was thought that the oedipal constellation was involved in this sexual development from the beginning.

However, Freud (1931, 1933) himself began to question his early concept when he became aware that the girl's preoedipal attachment to the mother continued on into the phallic phase and beyond, an attachment that terminated neither as early nor as decisively as he had originally thought. Freud also mentioned reports by Jones and Melanie Klein of early vaginal sensations in little girls.

The early sexual development of both sexes was again brought into question when Anna Freud (1951) reported instances of early penis envy in girls, occurring sometime between eighteen and 24 months of age. She suggested that the bodily intimacy between boys and girls in the residential nursery where the observations were made

1

may have produced the very violent reactions of penis envy in some of the girls. In 1962, L. Sachs reported a case of severe castration anxiety in an eighteen-month-old boy, but she regarded this as arising from an oedipal conflict.

Greenacre (1950) had also suggested that genital arousal might occur in girls earlier than the usual genital phase. She attributed such arousal to the possible presence of early but vague vaginal arousal, stimulation of vaginal awareness by direct oral and anal stimulation, and by generalized states of increased tension which might then be discharged through prematurely activated genital pathways. Greenacre suggested that the regular sequence of preoedipal development would be disrupted in consequence of this premature and massive stimulation.

The concept of a normally and regularly occurring early genital phase, as proposed by Roiphe, was a departure from these earlier views. Roiphe (1968) described a moderately severe castration reaction observed in a nineteen-month-old girl, a reaction closely resembling in its symptoms the case Sachs had reported. This reaction, which arose after the little girl had been bathed with a little boy playmate, consisted of an initial acknowledgment of the genital difference. This was soon replaced by a forceful and defensive denial and displacement, reactions that pervasively affected her relationships and attitudes. She also developed a number of other symptoms, including severe negativism and a brief period of urinary incontinence. As her defensive denial broke down, her sleep became disturbed, and she developed reparative fantasies that women had a hidden penis. After several more months had elapsed, she also showed evidence of having equated stool and phallus.

Roiphe thought that the disruptive force of the child's reaction to her observation of the genital difference was due to the threat of object loss and the undermining of her body self-representation, stimulated in this particular child because of her separation from her father not too long before her experience of viewing her playmate's genitals.

Pursuing the same line of thought, Roiphe (1973) presented data from his treatment of a three-and-a-half-year-old pseudoautistic psychotic girl. Indications of genital arousal had appeared in this girl subsequent to the establishment of her awareness of bowel and bladder functioning; her open masturbation was then followed by the emergence of curiosity concerning the genital area of dolls; a clear-cut penis-envy syndrome soon developed.

Roiphe pointed out that both Freud (1933) and Jones (1927) had described the existence of a close association between anal and genital sensations. In Roiphe's view, however, the early genital arousal he had found in both of the girls gave evidence of the existence of an early genital phase. He postulated that the genitals were now available as a regular and mature channel for discharge of tension and pleasurable experience; that this was part of a normally occurring early genital phase, a developmental precipitate of the process of sphincter control arising in the course of differentiation of self from object.

Under ordinary circumstances, children pass through this phase with minimal behavioral evidence of disturbance. However, Roiphe anticipated that symptomatic preoedipal castration reactions, of severe violence at times, would ensue when, in the course of traversing this early phase, the child had the opportunity of observing the anatomical difference between the sexes, and if the child had previously had experiences which had interfered with the sense of developing body intactness or with the mother-child relationship.

One of the children Roiphe described had been separated from her father at fifteen months of age, a loss which heightened her anxiety about losing her mother. When this child reached the early genital phase and her own genitals had attained high narcissistic value, her observation of the genital difference then brought about a marked intensification of her concerns about bodily integrity in general, as well as her fears of object loss.

In addition to such conditions as the one described, which tend to undermine the mother-child relationship, Roiphe anticipated that other experiences, such as severe pain, convulsions, or serious illness, would interfere with the sense of the own body, and would similarly predispose the child to develop a preoedipal castration reaction, following the emergence of genital awareness. For it is not until the later phallic phase that the sense of both self and object is stable enough to resist the threat of the oedipal castration reaction. During this earlier era, at the end of the second year, the more massive preoedipal castration reactions which occur under the circumstances already described might be the developmental antecedents of the fetishistic disturbances de-scribed by Greenacre (1953, 1955, 1960b).

Direct Observational Studies of Early Genital Activity

The first important studies of early genital activity, carried out by Spitz and Wolf (1949), concerned mothers and infants living under unusual circumstances. In contrast to these, Kleeman (1965) reported on a mother's direct observation of her infant son's developing genital self-stimulation. Kleeman concluded that this early genital play con-stituted an aspect of the regular establishment of the body image as a whole. Although he noted that a mild to moderate degree of erotic pleasure was present during the genital self-stimulation, neither was the infant self-absorbed nor was there any evidence of mounting ex-citement. By the end of the first year, however, meaningful rather than random genital exploration appeared, as manual-visual coordi-nation improved. Kleeman considered two factors of specific impor-tance in this genital self-stimulation: the general maturational process and the good quality of the mother-infant relationship.

Following up the child in his second year, Kleeman (1966) found that awareness of penile sensation had increased, along with an ob-servable increase in genital sensitivity, which began during the fif-teenth month. Kleeman considered these transitional between the body exploratory genital behavior of the first year and the definitively mas-turbatory stimulation of the oedipal years.

In 1966, we initiated a ten-year research project [1] (Galenson and Roiphe, 1974) with the aim of investigating Roiphe's hypotheses re-lating to early genital development, as well as aspects of the devel-oping symbolic function (Galenson, 1971). In 1967, we established a research nursery modeled on The Master's Children Center devel-oped by Mahler (1963; see also Pine and Furer, 1963). A large room contained an informal grouping of sofas for the mothers at one end and tables and chairs; open shelves with appropriate toys occupied the remainder of the room. Next to this room was a small kitchen and

[1] This research was carried out in the Department of Psychiatry of the Albert Einstein College of Medicine.

bathroom, to which the infants had free access. Next to the bathroom was a diapering table. Adjacent to the toy area was a one-way screen used for videotaping.

A self-selected upper-middle-class group constituted our research population. The parents were told that we were engaged in research, and our nursery was offered as a kind of indoor playground.

Each mother-child pair was assigned to a pair of observers consisting of a senior and a junior staff member, the latter either a psychiatric resident or a child-psychiatry fellow who had elected to work in the nursery during the entire year. Each junior staff observer attended at least one session each week, while the senior staff observers often attended several additional sessions. During the nursery period, the mothers and children were free to interact with one another, as they would in an outdoor playground. Mothers form close friendships in this way, and their children engage in play with one another, with the mother, or on their own.

Developmental data concerning the first year of life were gathered when the prospective babies were visited at home, prior to entrance in our program. The babies, between ten and thirteen months of age when they entered the Nursery in the fall of each year, were equally divided between the sexes. From the larger pool of self-selected families, two babies were deliberately chosen each year on the basis of their having had some prior experience during their first year of life that would be expected to predispose them to the occurrence of the preodipal castration reactions, as hypothesized by Roiphe.

Such prior experience would consist of a threat to the developing body image, such as a severe illness or surgical intervention, or an undue degree of disturbance in the mother-child experience—perhaps prolonged separation from the mother or a serious maternal depression. The remainder of the research group of children was, as far as can be determined by history, free of any such previous experience.

Once the Nursery program began, data were gathered from the mother during the Nursery session as she and the observer assigned to her sat together informally. A number of behavioral categories which had been selected in advance served the observers as a basis for this informal questioning. Following this, the observer observed the child's behavior and, in addition, recorded a ten-minute period of the child's activity. The remaining observational data were dictated after the session in an impressionistic account.

The data for each mother-child pair were summarized every two months, again according to preselected categories, and these summaries were then presented for staff discussions at the weekly staff conference. Formulations of the material already gathered, as well as predictions concerning future development, emerged from these presentations.

Several publications based upon the data from this research project described the development of a number of children who had been selected upon the basis of their untoward experiences during the first year of life. The study of a girl who had a congenital malformation which required a corrective apparatus (Galenson and Roiphe, 1971) and the report of a boy whose father had been absent since the child's earliest months (Roiphe and Galenson, 1973b) provided valuable insights regarding the form and character of the preoedipal castration reactions in such children.

The case of a child who had suffered from severe colic and had worn orthopedic braces during the first few months of her life (Galenson et al., 1976), clarified our understanding of the prevalence of early fetishistic behavior (Roiphe and Galenson, 1973a; Galenson and Roiphe, 1977). Such behavior appears to be far more common than previously thought and probably has a dynamic continuity with the fetishism of later life.[2]

Findings Concerning Sex Differences in Early Normal Genital Development

The studies of our unusual cases have now been compared with the data of 60 normally developing infants and ten with some devia-

___

[2] In addition to the early genital development and its vicissitudes, the individual case studies clarified our understanding of certain aspects of the developing symbolic function, particularly as it pertained to genital awareness. Galenson (1971) had suggested that the infant's play during the first years of life is intimately linked with certain bodily experiences, as well as with many aspects of the parent-child interaction. Thus, this early play would represent not only a sensorimotor experience but a symbolic expression closely related to the semisymbolic play described

tions in development, totaling 35 girls and 35 boys. Cross-sectional analysis of the data of the girls has been completed (Galenson and Roiphe, 1977) and a preliminary study of the data pertaining to the boys offers considerable understanding of the early sexual development of both sexes.

Endocrinological and other biological studies have demonstrated early sex differences in many areas of physical sexual development. Our own studies, however, have been concerned with the psychological rather than with the physical aspects of the sense of sexual identity. Although the biological phenomena undoubtedly influence developing psychological processes, they are not necessarily parallel phenomena. Grossman (1976) has emphasized, in this connection, that psychoanalysis and biology must not be confused with one another, although their mutual influence cannot be disregarded. Grossman suggests that, when the problem of sexual identity is considered primarily with regard to its psychological aspects, it becomes clear that the question of sexual identity is essentially an epistemological matter for the child: that is, how does the child construct his ideas of genital reality, both in relation to himself and to others? The emphasis is thereby shifted from the more superficial matter of the infant's behavior to the underlying question about the nature of the psychological content of the child's concept of his gender and his likeness or difference from those about him.

How does this concept of gender come into being and how early does it take form? Our views are essentially in agreement with those expressed by Kleeman (1977): genital experiences begin very early, probably in connection with feeding and other caretaking experiences. These genital experiences are undoubtedly influenced by the conscious as well as unconscious parental attitudes. It is nevertheless extremely difficult to document the manner in which such attitudes and experiences shape the infant's concept or image of himself. In only one area of our own data could a clear-cut difference between the sexes be

---

by Piaget (1945). We hypothesized that any disturbance in the developing body image, as well as in the area of the child-parent relationship, would be reflected in the content and structure of the developing symbolic function of play. This would be particularly true in relation to the impact of the early genital discovery upon the young child (see Galenson et al., 1976).

identified; this was the area of early genital self-stimulation, and here again our findings agree with Kleeman's.

In girls, sporadic self-stimulation begins near the end of the first year, and gradually increases in frequency unti the middle of the second year. This is interspersed with periods during which genital self-stimulation is entirely absent. Boys begin sporadic genital self-stimulation some months earlier than the girls; that is, between seven and ten months of age, and the activity is more focused, occurs more frequently, and seems to be more intentional in nature. In both sexes, this early genital play seems, under normal circumstances, to be in the service of general body exploration. The difference between the two sexes in early genital play patterns may be related to a variety of factors: The male genitalia are more exposed and therefore apt to receive greater direct stimulation from diapers and cleansing procedures; the penis has been involved in both the urinary process and in the experience of erections since birth; and, of course, differential parental handling probably contributes to the male-female differences as well.

We suspect that these consistently different early genital play patterns both reflect and contribute to increasingly distinctive psychological attributes, particularly since these patterns involve a body area that is so shortly to become a primary erotogenic zone. They very probably play a significant role in the developing sense of sexual identity, along with those male-female differences in play and toy preference, motility, degree of exploratory behavior, and degree of fearfulness and aggressive behavior which have been reported (Kleeman, 1977).

Psychosexual Development During the Second Year

Freud (1905) originally conceptualized the sequence of the emergence of the erotogenic zones as a biologically predestined, regularly occurring process of maturation. Greenacre (1953) offered a modification of this concept, suggesting that all three erotogenic zones may be active to some degree from birth onward; the peaks of ascendancy of each zone, however, would follow a maturational timetable. Furthermore, Greenacre suggested that any zone might be prematurely activated by life experience.

The task of documenting the sequence of psychosexual development through direct observation has emerged as one of the basic problems confronting psychoanalytically oritented researchers during the past decade or more.

Anal-Phase Organization

Mahler's studies of the separation-individuation process (Mahler et al., 1975) have revealed glimpses of anal-phase-related behaviors, along with ample evidence of the emotional ambivalence and negativism so characteristic of object relations during the anal phase. Kestenberg's (1968) technique of studying body rhythms has identified rhythmic body patterns during the second year that are considered characteristic of anal-zone functioning. Observational data from our own research study (Galenson and Roiphe, 1974; Galenson et al., in preparation) have provided us with many behavioral sequences which clearly signal the onset and subsequent elaboration of anal-phase organization. These sequences occur both at the anal zone itself and at a distance from the zone: that is, either at some other site of the child's body or in relation to inanimate objects. The latter group have been identified by virtue of their structural or organizational properties, which resemble those of the anal zone or its function (Galenson, 1971).

At the anal zone itself, anal-phase emergence is marked by variations in bowel patterning, the occurrence of diarrhea or constipation, and behaviors such as squatting, flushing, straining, and grunting during or directly preceding defecation. Directly following defecation, infants begin to signal for or to resist diaper changes and become interested in the stool itself or in exploring the anal area. Anal-derivative behavior has included not only action, gestures, and words, but also those affective states which were identified by Freud (1905) as characteristic aspects of anal-phase organization: aggressiveness, ambivalence, and anxiety over anal loss. Anal curiosity has been demonstrated by the children's investigation of the anal areas in other people and in toy animals and dolls. There have also been many play sequences in which the form, structure, or other attribute (such as an olfactory interest) resembles that of the anal area or the stool: collecting-and-piling games and in-and-out games are typical examples of such play. Interest in the toilet apparatus and in garbage cans and incinerators are other forms of derivative play, while the increase in the level and intensity of motor activity, in general negativity, and in focused angry behavior expresses the underlying typical anal-phase impulses and affects.

The onset of anal-phase organization could be easily identified in the 70 children of our research group through the collection and analysis of the behavioral sequences just described. Anal-phase organization was found to emerge sometime between the twelfth and fourteenth month in most of the children, although toilet training had not yet been initiated. However, two girls showed beginning anal-phase organization at six months of age, while in one boy it was not noted until his nineteenth month. In every instance, anal-derivative behavior appeared only after anal-zone awareness was already present. Similarly, fears of anal loss emerged only after anal-derivative behavior, usually reaching peak intensity near the middle of the second year.

Urinary Organization

Because the onset and elaboration of urinary organization has received relatively little attention in the literature, the richness of this aspect of our research data was particularly rewarding. Direct zonal manifestations included changes in urinary diurnal patterning and behavioral changes immediately before, during, and following urination, such as selective attention to wet diapers, squatting, visual and tactile attentiveness to the urinary stream, and touching puddles of urine. Affective concomitants included shame, excitement, and embarrassment.

Urinary-derivative behaviors were also very commonly observed. The infants were clearly curious about the urinary function in other people—adults as well as children—and there were many play sequences involving pouring, squirting, and other types of manipulation of liquids which were structurally similar to the act of urination itself.

In our group of 70 infants, urinary zonal awareness emerged sometime between the eleventh and fourteenth month in most instances, and usually, although not always, after anal awareness was already present—independent of toilet-training efforts. Urinary-derivative behavior followed soon afterward: most impressive was the intense curiosity seen in almost every infant concerning the parents' urinary functioning. In fact, most of our small subjects succeeded in being admitted to the parents' toileting just at this time, in spite of considerable parental modesty in several families. This intense urinary curiosity then rapidly became enmeshed in the early genital curiosity that soon followed.

The Early Genital Phase

The early genital behavior originally described by Roiphe has now been verified in our research population. We regard this early genital phase as a developmental precipitate of the separation-individuation process. For, with increasing self-object differentiation, the anal and urinary zones become heightened sources of pleasure and, at the same time, sources of anxiety as well; stool and urine are both invested as body parts, and their surrender precipitates considerable anxiety. It is in the midst of the anal-urinary elaboration that genital self-stimulation of a qualitatively different variety emerged for the first time in our 70 children (Galenson and Roiphe, 1974, 1977). Similar observations were made by Kleeman (1975) and more recently by Mahler et al. (1975).

Sometime between the fifteenth and nineteenth month, in all the nontraumatized girls and boys we studied, the heightened genital sensitivity began to serve as a source of focused pleasure which was far more intense than the earlier forms of genital self-stimulation had provided. During the early weeks of this increased genital sensitivity, both boys and girls carried out repetitive and intense genital self-stimulation either manually or by such indirect means as rocking and thigh pressure. Both boys and girls attempted visual exploration as well as the tactile genital contact. There was clear evidence of accompanying erotic arousal, including pleasurable facial expressions and autonomic excitation. In addition, penile erections in the boys were often part of their genital self-stimulation, although these occurred at other times as well. The child often initiated affectionate gestures and bodily contact with the mother either during or following the genital stimulation.

Free access to the genitals is, of course, provided primarily when the infant is bathed or diapered, and these were the times during which genital self-stimulation was most prominent. It does seem probable, however, that an additional factor in this clustering was the infant's earlier genital experiences during the countless caretaking activities carried out by the mother, as Freud (1933) himself pointed out.

In the girls, the new-quality genital self-stimulation observed consisted of manual and repetitive rubbing, squeezing, and pinching of the labia, the mons area, and the clitoral area. Although several mothers noted that their infant girls had introduced their fingers into the vaginal opening itself, the vagina was not the main site of stimulation. Indirect masturbation in the girls frequently took the form of straddling the parents' legs, a rocking horse, or furniture, or perineal rocking and thigh pressure. In boys, the genital self-stimulation was largely manual and, at times, included the testicles as well as the penis itself.

Open affectionate behavior toward the mother began to disappear as an accompaniment of the new genital self-stimulation after the first few weeks, soon to be replaced by the familiar inward gaze and a facial expression indicating self-absorption. From these sequences, we infer that a fantasy feeling-state had now become a regular concomitant of the genital self-stimulation, and that this new type of genital activity is true masturbation (Galenson and Roiphe, 1977). Kleeman (1975), on the other hand, does not regard the qualitatively new type of early genital self-stimulation as masturbation because of the absence of a verbalized form of accompanying fantasy.

The Transitional Object and the Infantile Fetish

In many of the infants, but most frequently in the girls in our group, a variety of inanimate objects became part of the masturbatory sequence. These objects included nursing bottles, favorite blankets, stuffed animals and dolls, and objects that had been a part of the early intimate interaction of mother and infant, the transitional objects described by Winnicott (1953). Winnicott believed that the attachment to these objects provided the infant with an intermediate area of experience neither exactly internal nor the external shared reality—an experience that remained important in life in relation to later creativity, religion, and mythology.

Our observations allowed us to follow the changing role of the transitional object (Roiphe, 1968, 1973; Galenson and Roiphe, 1971; Roiphe and Galenson, 1973a) as the infants coped with the ordinary strains of attaining upright motility (Greenacre, 1969, 1970), the separation-individuation process (Mahler et al., 1975), and the anal, urinary, and early genital psychosexual developmental phase.

In the earlier periods, the transitional objects served to blur the sense of separateness, an awareness that evokes anxiety over threatened object loss and self-dissolution. With the emergence of the early genital phase, these transitional objects were often used in relation to genital curiosity, as well as for masturbation itself, probably providing a bridge between the familiar earlier maternal experiences and the new and somewhat threatening genital differentiation.

Genital Derivative Behavior

Confirming Roiphe's original hypothesis of an early genital phase has been the genital-derivative behavior that has followed upon the emergence of the new type of genital self-stimulation in all the infants we studied. The earliest curiosity concerning the genital area in parents, peers, animals, and dolls leads the infants to intrude upon parental toileting and bathing, to closely attend the diapering table where other children are being diapered, to flock to the bathroom when another child is on the toidy seat, and to constantly undress dolls and toy animals. The toddlers also accompany their investigative actions with gestures and words which indicate without a doubt that they are comparing the genital anatomy and searching for the penis. Concrete references to the genital anatomical difference include the girls' placing phallic-shaped rods and sticks at the pubic area both on themselves and on dolls. During the first weeks of the early genital phase, masturbation is often displaced transiently to the umbilicus, anus, ears, or other body parts. The derivative genital sequences that have been observed to occur in the wake of the emergence of genital awareness give impressive substantiation of the organizing influence of the genital experience: that is, the existence of an early genital phase. The boys showed a sharp increase in their use of toy cars, trucks, airplanes, and other types of inanimate objects that could be set into motion. In the girls, not only did doll play increase in quantity, but the nature of the play itself changed. Dolls were continually undressed and the crotch area examined, phallic-shaped objects were placed just in this area, and the dolls themselves were often used as part of the masturbatory action or were positioned by the little girl underneath her genital area during sleep. Furthermore, for many of the girls we studied, one doll now became the favorite as well as an obligatory companion during both sleeping and waking hours.

The affective reflection of the genital-phase organization included definite pleasure in body exhibitionism in the boys—the strutting body posture, as well as direct phallic pride. The girls were flirtatious and exhibitionistic, with skirt-lifting and genital exposure during the early weeks of their new genital awareness.

Boy/Girl Differences After Eighteen or Nineteen Months: The Preoedipal Castration Reactions

During the early weeks after their initial discovery of the genital anatomical difference, the development of the boys and girls in our group was essentially similar. Then subtle but definite differences began to appear. All the boys gradually became more active physically than the girls, an increase that ranged from mild to intense. We have thought that this may have represented some degree of anxiety experienced by the boys in consequence of their awareness of the genital difference. Their patterns of masturbation remained largely unchanged, however. Only two of the 35 boys showed an important and serious degree of psychological disturbance (Galenson et al., 1975); both of these boys had suffered a serious disturbance in their maternal relationship and developing body-image area during their first year of life.

In contrast to the boys, all 35 of our girls developed some degree of disturbance in the wake of their discovery of the genital anatomical difference. In this group were eight whose disturbance was quite severe, and all of these had experienced an important threat either to the developing body image or to their maternal relationship.

Thus, all those children who developed a severe castration reaction had fulfilled Roiphe's original prediction, namely, that such early untoward experiences would predispose the infants to disturbance at the time of the emergence of the early genital phase. It is evident however, that girls are far more vulnerable to this disturbance. Furthermore, their preoedipal castration reactions involved almost every area of development. At the genital zone itself, manual masturbation was frequently replaced by indirect stimulation through straddling rocking horses, parents' legs or furniture, or through perineal rocking or thigh pressure. Some girls abandoned masturbation entirely, while several continued to masturbate, although without pleasure (Roiphe and Galenson, 1973b, Galenson and Roiphe, 1977).

But it was in the area of genital-derivative behavior that the differences between the two sexes were most impressive. For example, the girls showed a far greater tendency to utilize regressive oral and anal comforting devices, including mouthing and sucking, anal masturbation, and anal and urinary retention. Displacement of masturbation to other body parts frequently was manifest. The concurrent oral- and anal-phase anxieties of object loss and anal loss were reflected in the little girls' newly intensified fear of separation and in their concern over small bodily imperfections (minor bruises and scratches) and their avoidance of broken toys of any kind.

The type of object relatedness appropriate to these earlier psychosexual phases was also revived as the preoedipal castration reactions unfolded, particularly with regard to the heightened ambivalence toward the mother. And there was also a definite change of mood (Galenson and Roiphe, 1971), a temporary loss of zest and enthusiasm in some, while others showed a more serious sadness and "depressive" mood, which, as Mahler (1966b) has pointed out, might be the forerunner of a basic tendency toward a depressive mood in later life.

Symbolic functioning was also affected by the preoedipal castration reactions in many of the girls. Male/female differential labels and pronouns were temporarily lost in several girls who had already acquired them. Furthermore, where the castration reactions were not too intense, semisymbolic play became quite elaborate and there were early attempts at graphic representation. Play, however, became restricted and stereotyped in those girls whose castration reactions were very marked. As a further manifestation of the impact upon the symbolic function, it appeared that new attachments to a great variety of inanimate objects emerged during the period of castration reaction in the girls. These objects were often a special doll or a toy, such as a flute or miniature umbrella, which now replaced the former obligatory soft blanket or cuddly stuffed animal; and these objects were obligatory and often positioned beneath the girls' genitals at bedtime. It is our view that these inanimate objects now served as infantile fetishistic objects (Roiphe and Galenson, 1973a; Galenson and Roiphe, 1971), providing an illusion of the missing penis and preparing the ground for the eventual body-phallus equation. Furthermore, it is possible that the rich repertoire of partially symbolic play that emerged under the impact of the less intense type of castration reaction contributes to a richer inner fantasy life in the little girls at this time than is found in boys of the same age. At any rate, the quality of the developing symbolic function would appear to be influenced by the early genital-phase experience (Galenson et al., 1976).

While both boys and girls begin to develop a special relationship with the father toward the end of the first year, as they are emerging from the symbiotic attachment to the mother, a different quality of erotically tinged and more intense attachment to the father emerged in most of the girls in our study during their preoedipal castration reactions. This attachment, a dyadic one, seems to prepare the way for the triadic relation of the later oedipal period.

However, in those girls who suffered unusually severe early castration reactions, hostile ambivalence to the mother became extremely marked. This was gradually replaced by intense clinging to the mother, and the fear of strangers increased. (It would seem that the maternal image had been divided, with the "good" mother image retained while the "bad" mother was projected onto strangers.) Furthermore, the shift of erotic attachment to the father did not take place.

Theoretical and Clinical Implications

The emergence of genital awareness and special sensitivity, along with the consequent sense of castration and loss, takes place in girls toward the end of the second year, several years earlier than Freud had anticipated. Since both self- and object schematization are still relatively unstable at the time of these reactions, the fears of object loss and of self-dissolution are revived, along with the preoedipal castration reaction. It is likely that all three levels of anxiety remain indissolubly connected from that time.

The erotic shift to the father appears to be facilitated by the milder form of preoedipal castration reaction seen in most of the girls; if the reaction is severe, this shift does not take place and the girls remain ambivalently tied to the mother.

All areas of development are influenced by the events in the psychosexual sphere; mood changes and symbolic elaboration or inhibition of function are among the many consequences of the effects of the early genital phase we have described. From that time on, the development of boys and girls follow different patterns in many sectors of their personalities. The girls who have negotiated the early genital phase with only moderate reactions appear to be on their way toward the development of the usual type of oedipal phase, beginning sometime toward the close of the third year of life. Inasmuch as they have already discovered the genital difference well before the onset of the oedipal phase, the complex of penis envy and castration anxiety does not appear to usher in the oedipal phase, as Freud (1925b) had originally postulated.

Those girls who show unduly severe reactions during the period of early genital discovery appear to be destined for the development of an oedipal attachment of a negative type, in which the ambivalent attachment to the mother remains the primary libidinal tie. Masturbation is inhibited either entirely or to a large degree in these cases, in addition to inhibition in many other areas of development, including the symbolic function.

Boys appear to traverse the period of early genital discovery without distress, except in very unusual instances. Their interest in phallic types of activities and toys increases, and their masturbatory activity continues to be of the same character as during the period of the emergence of genital awareness between sixteen and nineteen months of age. The details of the sexual development of the boys in the research sample await further analysis of the data already accumulated.

CHAPTER 2

Adolescence and "The New Sexuality"

AARON H. ESMAN

For as long in human history as they have been defined as a coherent social group, adolescents have been on the front lines of social change. In our time, particularly, their changing styles of dress, speech, and behavior have been sensitive barometers to the shifting winds of change in values and cultural norms (cf. Esman, 1977). Assuming the existence of a "sexual revolution," we should expect adolescents, experimental in outlook and caught up in the process of adaptation to their newly acquired sexual capacities, to be its shock troops and to be engaged in the energetic formulation of a new sexual morality. We must also expect, however, that many of those who cannot participate in this revolutionary enterprise will experience serious conflict, made the more poignant by the flamboyance of their peers, and that they will themselves develop institutionalized ways of coping with this situation.

The study of adolescent sexuality is fraught with difficulties. The task of distinguishing between overt behavior and inner attitudes is equalled in difficulty only by that of assessing the various meanings that may be expressed by identical behaviors. Offer and his associates (1969) have alerted us to the problem of overgeneralization and extrapolation from clinical phenomena to those of normal development. Clinical study may, however, demonstrate the special stresses imposed by new developments, and some of the defensive and adaptive responses elaborated by those who are vulnerable to such stresses; these may to a lesser degree be characteristic ones for the population at large. A survey of the response of adolescents to the "new sexuality" requires, therefore, a multifaceted approach, employing both social science and clinical methods to arrive at useful conclusions.

Historically, adolescents in our culture have inhabited a narrow and shifting ground defined by their own intense sexual urges, on the one hand, and the constraints imposed upon them by social norms, conventions, and moral judgments, on the other. Prime among these constraints has been the Judeo-Christian tradition which bans or frowns upon all sexual activities other than genital congress in the setting of monogamous marriage. In this context all sexual avenues open to adolescents have been potentially—and often actually—burdened with guilt and/or shame, and every adolescent engaged in them has been obliged to make some accommodation to this burden (cf. Gadpaille, 1976). In an earlier work (Esman, 1972) I described some of the ways in which this was done, in which, that is, the adolescent's superego was reshaped in response to the new needs and possibilities opened to him by his sexual maturation. Mead's study of Samoan adolescents (1928) shows that such conflicts are neither inevitable nor universal, but that they are embedded in a particular cultural matrix.

The "new sexuality" appears to represent a significant, if not quite revolutionary, change in cultural patterns. Many of the values and attitudes characteristic of the older tradition seem to have crumbled along with the institutions that embodied and supported them. The form and content of this "new morality" have been extensively documented. Illustrative is the recent study by Wall and Kaltreider (1977) of adult patients in an outpatient gynecology clinic in California. Comparison with similar studies performed by Kinsey et al. (1953) and Winokur et al. (1959) makes evident striking shifts in attitudes and behavior; Wall and Kaltreider found "a substantial decrease in formal marriage, a reduction in the wish for children, . . . and an attitudinal shift toward acceptance of a bisexual adaptation" (p. 565).

Evidence of the impact of these changes upon adolescents has been increasingly prominent in the social science literature. Sorensen (1973), for example, reports that in his large national sample 19 percent of 13 to 15 year-old girls agreed with the statement "if you really dig a boy it's all right to have sex with him even if you've only known him for a few hours''; 53 percent of all adolescent boys share a similar sentiment regarding girls. He defines what he calls "the new sexual relationship—serial monogamy without marriage" as "a close sexual relationship of uncertain duration between two unmarried adolescents from which either party may depart when he or she desires, often to participate in another such relationship" (p. 219). Twenty-one percent of all American adolescents were at the time of his survey involved in such an arrangement (as were 23 percent of Wall and Kaltreider's subjects). Some 62 percent of all adolescents surveyed said, "So far as sex is concerned, I do what I want to do regardless of what society thinks." However, 30-35 percent of these subjects acknowledged that "sometimes I feel guilty about my sexual behavior." (Interestingly, the highest percentage of these "guilty" ones were boys thirteen to fifteen; presumably their guilt referred largely to masturbation.)

Similar findings have been reported by Schmidt and Sigusch (1972) from West Germany, where the age of first coitus in comparable adolescent populations declined sharply between 1966 and 1970, especially among the more educated (Gymnasium) students. The girls in the 1970 study had a "much greater sexual motivation for their first coitus and correspondingly the first coitus was more often the result of mutual initiative" than had been the case hitherto. Further, they "more often felt happier after the first coitus and less often found [it] unpleasant, repulsive and/or disgusting" (p. 41). Although similar trends obtained among boys, they were much less marked.

Peplau (1977) reported that women appear to determine both the occurrence and timing of intercourse in dating couples; "when a couple does not have intercourse, the woman's attitudes are usually the restraining force. It is clear that in couples not having intercourse the man is often highly desirous . . . the woman is not." "Women in couples who have intercourse are significantly more liberal in their sexual attitudes than are women in couples that abstain. For men there is no difference" (p. 33). For both men and women the double standard has virtually disappeared. The major change underlying the greater frequency and earlier age of onset of sexual intercourse must, then, be the attitudes and behavior of young women.

Further, among middle-class adolescents in the New York Longitudinal Study population (Chess et al., 1976) few of the girls spoke of marriage and family as life goals; this confirms Hendin's (1975) observations in his study of Columbia University students. Finally, Yankelovich (1974) found in his 1973 survey that "fewer unmarried students (61 percent) personally look forward to getting married than in 1968 (66 percent)" (p. 59). Yankelovich's study is of further interest in demonstrating the spread of the "new morality" from the vanguard college population to the noncollege, traditionally more conservative group. In 1969, 43 percent of college students said that they would "welcome more acceptance of sexual freedom" while only 22 percent of the noncollege population echoed this view. By 1973, 47 percent of the noncollege youth took this position. Similar patterns were found in regard to questions about abortion, homosexuality, and premarital intercourse.

From these sociological studies, then, certain conclusions can reasonably be drawn: (1) A "new morality" has developed in the decades of the 60's and 70's, one that sanctions, if it does not encourage, a freer sexuality among adolescents. (2) The predominant shift underlying the "new morality" has been in the values and behavior of adolescent girls who now feel permitted to do what had earlier been forbidden them. It seems clear that this change is in large measure an outgrowth of the "new feminism." (3) The characteristic pattern of "new sexual behavior" is that of "serial monogamy." Promiscuity is not the rule and, indeed, appears to be found only among the more disturbed members of the youth population.

Clinical data may permit us a sharper perspective on these findings, giving us insight into both their extent and their boundaries. For example, Mary, when first seen at fifteen, was a shy, anxious girl who sought treatment because of her inability to relate to boys and to express herself in school. Unusually pretty, she had many girl friends, but had never gone out with a boy and felt paralyzed when approached by them. Further, she was getting mediocre grades in school, although unusually bright, because she couldn't bring herself to speak out in class and was profoundly anxious about examinations. Prim, a bit compulsive in dress and manner, she was shocked by the conduct of her one-year-younger sister who smoked marijuana and engaged in what Mary regarded as promiscuous sex. She soon became aware of her unconscious attachment to her idealized ne'er-do-well father who had left the family when she was nine, had remarried, and was living in another country. Her mother, hard-working, outwardly self-reliant but chronically depressed, represented an ambivalently valued ego-ideal figure for her.

Two years of intensive therapy led to considerable loosening of Mary's too rigid defenses. At seventeen, she met a bachelor neighbor some ten years her senior; in short order she entered into an intense romantic and sexual relationship with him—the first such attachment of her life. Her mother not only offered no objection to this liaison, but openly supported it. That Bill was a father surrogate was obvious. Mary ultimately moved in with him, enjoying for a year or so a part-lover, part-daughter role in which sex, though present, played a secondary part to being cared for, supported, and desired.

Gradually over the next year she became increasingly dissatisfied with Bill. He was too staid and compulsive, not sufficiently romantic, and indifferent to her expanding range of intellectual and cultural interests. Finally, in an act of courage and determination buttressed by feminist ideals of self-realization and autonomy, she broke with him, quickly finding a college classmate with whom she became intensely enamored and with whom she launched into a new and exciting sexual affair. She recognized that the relationship with Bill had perpetuated her preadolescent dependency and had, in fact, served as a defense against age-appropriate involvement and experimentation with her peers. The relative ease with which she had entered a pseudo-mature sexual affair was clearly facilitated by the current ethos (including, of course, the elimination of fears about impregnation), but it also enabled her to avoid uncomfortable social encounters with younger men.

Jonathan was sixteen when he sought treatment because of a series of terrifying LSD "trips." He, like Mary, was the product of a broken home. Though still living together, his parents were completely estranged, and his father moved out and sought a divorce from his alcoholic wife about a year later. Jonathan was an intellectually gifted, asthenic, and rather passive boy who, having done badly at two conventional private schools, was in his senior year at a somewhat "special" school for bright but "different" adolescents, like himself. He had already had a fairly extended sexual relationship with one of his classmates, a girl with a similar school history; they were both fourteen when their affair began and it was still going on, sporadically. Jonathan wanted to detach himself from Jennifer, but she was deeply attached to him, and he, more or less submissively, accepted her favors, along with those of one or two other girls who made themselves available to him until he went off to college.

There he met Cecily, a confused young woman who became dependently attached to him so that, when he dropped out after a year and returned to New York, she left with him and, at her insistence, they moved into an apartment together (Jonathan was now nineteen). Again he submitted to an arrangement that he found unpleasant until he returned to a local university a year later and was with great relief obliged to move back to the family home. During the next two years he was involved in fleeting and loveless sexual contacts with girls he had known in high school and an occasional new acquaintance. Sometimes, during periods when he found girls unavailable, he considered, and occasionally accepted, homosexual overtures; he was clearly uncomfortable in discussing these, but espoused the position that under the circumstances it was better than nothing and that, anyway, homosexuality was "just another sexual option." He longed for a "female lover," but his passivity prevented him from making active efforts to find one. He usually wanted girls to call him and offer themselves, and felt hurt when they didn't. Despite his role as a "sexual adventurer" (Sorensen, 1973), he balked at accepting the overtures of the fourteen- and fifteen-year-olds he met at parties and who made their availability evident to him. He was regularly anxious lest he be impotent, though in fact he never was; he experienced the girls with whom he was involved as sexually demanding and felt sure that when they didn't call him it was because they had found him sexually inadequate or inept.

Jonathan thus exemplified many aspects of the situation of the male adolescent caught up in the "new sexuality." He conformed to the traditional stance of the young male adventurer, but his developmentally determined passivity led him to accept with relief—even to value—the new active stance of the "liberated" young women in his peer group. At the same time, their very aggressiveness and explicitness threatened him with what Ginsberg et al. (1972; see also Chap.

15, this volume) have called "the new impotence," and intensified his tendencies to passive avoidance.

The concern of young men regarding their sexual performance and their tendency to measure their self-esteem thereby is no new phenomenon. It does appear, however, to have been intensified by the increasingly explicit demands of young women for sexual satisfaction and by their new emphasis on orgasm—even multiple orgasm—as the expected outcome of all sexual acts. Unfortunately, some of those young women who do not readily "achieve" this goal experience the same performance anxiety as do their male counterparts. Nancy, just twenty, had been having intercourse since seventeen in a succession of "serially monogamous" relationships. That she never experienced orgasm in intercourse was a source of great shame to her and left her feeling inadequate and defective. Pleasure she had felt, but this did not measure up to her expectations. It did not occur to her that questions of technique and timing might be involved, although she was able to achieve orgasm easily with masturbation. In her view, she was "frigid" and thus deeply inferior.

The current permissive tendencies regarding homosexuality tended to soften the definition of Jonathan's sexual preference. He felt no great pressure to suppress or repress his homosexual wishes, secure in the knowledge that, at least in the milieu in which he lived, no intense stigma would be attached to them. Indeed, he even gave some passing consideration to joining the Gay Liberation group in his university despite his conviction that he was basically heterosexual, as indeed he was. His position was thus akin to that of many of Peplau's female subjects—tolerant toward and even attracted to a bisexual identity because it promised an easier, less tension-laden solution than a rigorously heterosexual one.

Mary and Jonathan have, in their own ways, adapted to the multiple demands of adolescence and the "new sexuality." For a significant number of young people, however, these demands are overwhelming and unmanageable. In this, of course, there is nothing intrinsically new; the sexual pressures of adolescence have always posed a threat to some who have taken refuge from them in a variety of psychological positions and institutional settings such as the monastic and conventual ones provided by traditional religious bodies, and

postures of asceticism and instinctual renunciation of the kind referred
to by Anna Freud (1958). The decline of conventional organized religion and of its appeal to young people has led inevitably to the
emergence of alternative institutions that offer the vulnerable the same
sort of haven. In the past two decades a host of new or exotic religious
groups has appeared on the American scene, each characterized by,
among other things, a puritanical code of morality that sets firm limits
to permissible sexual behavior (cf. Johnson, 1975). The Hare Krishna
group, for instance, limits sexual activity within marriage to purposes
of reproduction and prohibits any sexual congress among its adherents
after the age of 30. Fundamentalist Christian groups assert the validity
of traditional constraints on premarital sexuality and on the sanctity
of virginity and the pure life. Clearly, to adolescents who find themselves troubled by the new permissiveness and the onslaught of media-
born sexual stimulation, such doctrines provide a welcome relief.

The sexual revolution, therefore, whatever its impact upon the
adult population, has introduced nothing truly new to the adolescent
world. Sexual experimentation, intense sexual passion, endless sexual
curiosity, and the longing and search for suitable sexual partners have
always been a part of the adolescent experience. What the new morality has done is to reduce the strength of old constraints and inhibitions so that at least among middle-class adolescents (and increasingly
among working-class youth as well) a relatively guilt-free flowering
of manifest sexual experience is occurring earlier than it did a generation ago. Fears to the contrary of the adult world notwithstanding,
there is no evidence that sexual promiscuity or rampant perverse sexual
behavior has been the consequence of this loosening of old restraints.

I know of no evidence, for instance, of increases in sadomasochistic or other perverse practices among young people despite the
proliferation of pornographic representations and explicit advertise-
ments in the "personal" columns of literary publications. In particular, the bedrock prohibition—the incest taboo—shows no signs of
weakening in the new sexual climate. Indeed, the greater ease of
accessibility of exogamous sexual partners tends in all probability to
reduce the temptations to incestuous alliances, particularly the brother-
sister incest so often portrayed in Romantic literature. Certainly there
is no evidence that the most fundamental taboo—that on mother-son
incest—has been breached.

Anna Freud (Shengold and McLaughlin, 1976) has acknowledged that in contemporary adolescents the battle against incest and incestuous fantasies goes on as before, with the same defenses and with no less success. In her view, however, the "free" sexual behavior of contemporary youth and their sexual exhibitionism reflect the cessation of the old battle against pregenital and genital sexuality and are used in many cases as a way of punishing the parents who still adhere to traditional standards of conduct. Although this tendentious, conflict-related "use" of "the new sexuality" doubtless applies in some cases, the formulation seems to me an illustration of the kind of overgeneralization from the clinical situation against which Offer has warned us. Sorensen's modal adolescents do not report serious conflict with their parents about their sexual behavior. Chess et al. (1976) similarly find a kind of tacit acceptance by parents of their children's sexual activity, in some cases out of resignation, no doubt, but seldom with the sense of being "punished."

> There was . . . little intergenerational discussion of actual sexual behavior [except as] a result of conflict regarding the adolescent's behavior. The parents had a general idea of the extent of their youngster's sexual activity, and in most cases their assumptions appeared correct . . . By the time these youngsters were sixteen, sex was a closed topic between themselves and their parents. The adolescents guarded their privacy carefully, and for the most part parents respected that privacy . . . parents 'did not attempt to impose their own ethical values on their children . . . Most of the youngsters and parents were fairly open and comfortable, however, when talking about sex to . . . interviewers . . . the avoidance of sex discussions by parents and youngsters is a manifestation of the adolescent's drive to establish independence and a way of avoiding the family tensions and conflicts that such discussions might produce [pp. 695-699].

It seems, then, that what has emerged is a new pattern of sexual involvement characterized by premarital monogamous attachments which are maintained with relative fidelity "as long as we dig each other"; i.e., Sorensen's (1973) pattern of "serial monogamy." There is no evidence that this greater sexual freedom has interfered in any significant way with the adaptive success of most of this generation's adolescents. Consistent with the new emphasis on self-realization and career development for girls, however, it does appear that this generation's adolescents look forward with less interest to ultimate marriage and with considerably less anticipation of ultimate childbearing as long-term life goals.

What we have described can scarcely be called a sexual revolution at all. It seems, on the contrary, to be an evolutionary change in the pattern of sexual mores and values with which most adolescents are comfortable. For some, the new freedom does arouse anxiety, especially in relation to sexual performance, generally transitory but occasionally imbricated with a neurotic pattern of inhibition and avoidance. For those even more threatened by the lack of structure and definition in the current sexual atmosphere, however, and who require social and ideological support for maintaining a more restrained approach to sexuality, new institutions have arisen to replace some of the old ones that are no longer effective—old wine in new bottles, perhaps. Only those on the most vulnerable edge of the spectrum of personality development require, as they always have, the ultimate redress of personality disintegration and ego regression as the last resort in coping with the stresses engendered by the ''new sexuality.''

CHAPTER 3

Masturbation

IRWIN M. MARCUS

Sexuality, one facet of which is mastubation, is an inextricable part of human life from infancy to senescence. We are accustomed to tracing adult patterns of masturbation in terms of Freud's (1905) psychosexual phases. I believe that if we include in our considerations Mahler's separation-individuation phases and subphases (Mahler et al., 1975) which occur concomitantly with psychosexual phases, it will enhance our understanding and provide a broader framework from which to evaluate pathological formations and for discerning healthy maturational patterns.

Sexual impulses are part of our biological nature and are observable in other primates and a variety of mammalians. Nevertheless, for over five thousand years, one "establishment" after another has promoted guilt and inhibitions by forcefully insisting that sex was harmful. Contrary to prevailing opinion, the Bible did not refer to masturbation, but only warned against withdrawal (coitus interruptus) as a means of contraception (Gen. 38:9). The latter was termed the "crime of Onan," and, erroneously, masturbation was read into Biblical interpretation and designated as "onanism." Parents in some societies wished to prohibit the sexual activity of their children and adolescents and did so by instilling fear of the consequences of the activity. Unfortunately, physicians, being products of their own cultural upbringing, continued, as recently as the early part of this century, to attribute many physical and mental disorders to masturbation.

Freud, however, shifted the focus onto the damaging effects on character formation when the parents distort and confuse the child's

psychosexual development by instilling fears and guilt about masturbation. The unique position occupied by masturbation in sexual and
personality development led Freud to refer to the subject throughout
his many contributions, both in terms of "normal" developmental
phenomena and in association with mental pathology. (See the extensive bibliography in *Masturbation: From Infancy to Senescence* [Mar-
cus and Francis, 1975].) Freud noted, for example, the connection
between masturbation conflicts and compulsions and addiction-type
character disorders (1887-1902).

Masturbation, herein, refers to volitional, genitally directed,
rhythmic self-stimulation that produces sexual pleasure. Any organ
capable of producing sexual pleasure and thereby arousing genital
excitation may be used for masturbation. In some individuals, secondary erogenous zones may become the primary focus for sexual
excitation. In others, psychic masturbation may take place when fantasies are sufficiently stimulating to produce an orgasm without physical self-stimulation. Kinsey et al. (1953) reported that two percent of
their female sample achieved orgasm with erotic fantasies alone.

Masturbation, as the term is used here, does not include the infant's nonspecific, random exploratory behavior, which may include
the genitals. In the first few months of life, such behavior is one of
various forms of autoerotic activity and can more accurately be termed
genital play.

Kleeman (1965) found that the child's genital touching had little
of the autoerotic aspects at its onset. Genital manipulation during this
early phase is neither age-appropriate autoerotic nor autoaggressive
behavior. When erotization of the genitals does occur in the first year,
it is due either to innate hypersensitivity or, possibly, to overstimulation. In this very early phase the fantasies accompanying the autoerotic activity are likely to be linked with pleasure in general. The
association of fantasies with specific sex objects, initially the mother,
probably occurs later, when the child has matured sufficiently to know
the difference between itself and others. Actual rhythmic manipulation
of the genitals ordinarily does not occur until the second year of life,
or even the third, when individual variability of maturation and co-
ordination of small muscles come into play. On the other hand, such
autoerotic activity as rocking may be seen as early as six months of

age because of the earlier ability to control the large muscles.

In what has become a classic study, Spitz and Wolf (1949) investigated a total of 248 infants through the first year of their lives and continued the observations into the second and third years. One hundred seventy of these infants were housed in a penal nursery with their mothers, 61 were living in a foundling home, and seventeen were living in their parents' houses. Three important observations were made: (1) Where the relation between the mother and child was at its best, development surpassed the average in all respects, and genital play was general in the first year of life. (2) Where the relation between mother and child was a "problematical one," genital play was much rarer, and other autoerotic activities tended to replace it. (3) Where the relation between mother and child was absent, general development dropped far below the average, and genital play was completely missing (see also Panel, 1962).

In view of the significance of genital play in infancy, masturbation may well be said to be at the root level of sexual development. The fantasies associated with masturbation activities are frequently interwoven into sexuality—including interpersonal sexual experiences —throughout development. Moreover, the conscious and/or unconscious fantasies that usually accompany masturbation from childhood onward contribute to personality development and maturation. Masturbation becomes an early means of self-discovery and self-awareness. Basic to the concept the infant forms of itself is the concept it acquires of its own body. As an avenue for discharging tension and/or anxiety associated with conflicts, masturbation has a homeostatic function in re-establishing a degree of psychic equilibrium.

Most people state that they discovered masturbation for themselves, and did so early in life. Some people recall having been told or shown how it is done by their friends in childhood or adolescence. According to Hite (1976), in a nationwide questionnaire survey of 3,000 women from ages fourteen to 78, almost all the women indicated that they were reared in families with attitudes opposed to masturbation. However, of the 1,844 women whose replies about masturbation were analyzed statistically, 82 percent indicated they do masturbate, fifteen percent stated they did not, and three percent did not answer. Some recalled starting in childhood, others in adoles cence, and some only after their sexual experiences with partners began. Hunt (1974) reported findings of the Research Guild from 2,026 questionnaires completed during the first half of 1972. His sample was derived from groups meeting in 24 cities, and consisted of 982 males and 1,044 females, eighteen years and over. The sample closely paralleled the national population for the age grouping. The majority of the women and men, even in the older age group (above 35), had begun to repudiate the traditional moral condemnation of masturbation. In the younger age groups, the accepting attitudes among both sexes were as much as five times greater than the rejecting attitudes. The spread of liberating literature is noticeably influencing the older women (above 35) toward experiencing masturbatory orgasms, within and without the marital relationship. Because of the double standard, they had generally been more conservative in their activities. The data on this subject, when compared to earlier surveys (Kinsey et al., 1953) reflect a continued shift toward more accepting attitudes on masturbation and other sexual experiences by women.

The apparent "liberation" in sexual attitudes and behavior among late adolescents and young adults, as well as gradual modifications in the older group, however, do not imply freedom from ambivalence, conflict, guilt, and anxiety so far as unconscious reactions or even conscious awareness are concerned. The associated fantasies of oedipal origin, now translated into fantasies of teachers, relatives, therapists, and others, may continue to generate emotional problems. Preoedipal fantasies of the mother and her derivatives, or narcissistic objects such as friends of one's own gender may stimulate anxiety and conflict around homosexuality or bisexuality.

A more complete understanding of the significance of masturbation as a modality in sexual maturation and development necessitates that we free ourselves from the pendulum-type movements which in the past have swung from undue degrees of suppression to complete freedom and encouragement.

While the child is undergoing the oral, anal, and phallic psychosexual phases in the first three years of life, it is also undergoing the separation-individuation process described by Mahler and her coworkers (Mahler et al., 1975). In what follows, an attempt will be made to describe the vicissitudes of masturbation during this period and beyond.

For the first month or more, during the autistic phase, the infant does not distinguish between himself and the outer world. From the second month on, the earliest awareness of the mother as a need-satisfying object marks the onset of the phase of symbiosis: The merger of the infant's visual image of the mother's face with his "mouth-hand-labyrinth-skin" provides an experience in which the child senses a dual unity with the mother (Spitz, 1965). The pleasurable body sensations derived from the caretaking mother who holds, feeds, cleans, and lovingly caresses her child during their many hours together is a binding force in their early relationship. The interaction between mother and child is of major significance for the infant in pursuit of pleasurable sensory impressions. The child's ability to reproduce these pleasurable sensations independently of the mother is a significant aid toward permitting him an awareness of being a separate entity. Autoerotic activities thus play a role in the separation-individuation process.

Freud (1920) believed that the infant's need to repeat actively the passive experience with the mother initiates autoerotic activity. Freud (1931) also thought that a relation exists between identification mechanisms, the gradual growth from dependence to independence, and the feeding experiences. The proportions of activity and passivity vary throughout each phase of maturation and development; stereotyped rhythmic activity in infancy might therefore be related to later masturbation only in a peripheral, superficial manner.

During the second year of life, Mahler's practicing and rapprochement subphases, genital manipulation continues to be subordinate to the primary preoccupations of learning toilet control and its associated rhythms. The observable pleasure in urinating, defecating, and watching others in the bathroom, all taking place around the anxiety of toilet training, may be considered a precursor of the later castration anxiety and penis envy. Kleeman observed intermittent genital self-stimulation during this phase and considered the behavior a transition between the exploratory behavior of the first year and the more clearly defined masturbation activity of the following phallic-oedipal period. In general, the drive tensions have become a little more organized during the second year of life. The task of achieving sphincter control during the toilet-training period, and its associated conflicts, may influence later masturbatory behavior and fantasies.

An example of a specific form of masturbation due to trauma and overstimulation during the anal period was seen in a young married female whose exclusive masturbatory pattern was rhythmic anal stimulation to orgasm. For several years in her early childhood, she was forced into accepting enemas administered by her mother. She vividly recalled her feelings of humiliation and pain in being held down by both her mother and her grandmother. Her fantasies during vaginal intercourse with her husband were of receiving an enema, so she had a great deal of ambivalent feeling toward her husband during sex, and frequently inhibited orgasm. She preferred anal intercourse to vaginal, and her fantasies, which brought her to a high pitch of excitement, included giving an enema to a woman, or being given one by the woman. There were also expressions of envy of the male, with fantasies of having her own penis and engaging in anal intercourse with females. When having the fantasy of other men performing anal intercourse on her, she could achieve a masturbatory orgasm. During episodes of feeling inferior and inadequate because of hostile exchanges with her husband or others, she experienced the fantasy of not having her anus. She drew the analogy with castration by referring to these feelings as "deanaltration."

It is during the rapprochement subphase of separation-individuation that the child is discovering the anatomical differences between the sexes. Although the boy may discover his penis as early as the first year of life, the emotional impact of this significant pleasure-producing organ is associated with the beginnings of gender identity only during the second year. The ability to stand upright unquestionably facilitates the visual and sensorimotor exploration of the penis. Although mothers have reported observing their boys masturbating during the practicing subphase, Mahler's group observed the boys holding their penises for reassurance in this third subphase, or the second half of the second year and the beginning of the third year. Girls, on the other hand, when confronted by the penis, displayed a range of reactions including anxiety, anger, and defiance. Mahler's group felt that masturbation in girls occurred earlier and seemed to be a more desperate, aggression-laden activity than masturbation in boys. Their findings substantiate the psychoanalytic concept of penis envy in girls, since the discovery of the sexual difference was often associated with envy and jealousy.

In general, observations suggest that the task of individuation seems more difficult for girls than for boys because of the girls' tendency to revert back to their mothers. They become more demanding of them, experience disappointment, and intensify their ambivalent ties to them. On the other hand, the boys during the second and third years seem capable of utilizing their own bodies for pleasure and satisfaction and also seek the father as a source for identification. Abelin (1975) suggested that the boys are able to cope with their castration anxiety in this phase through a quasi-preoedipal triangulation. Their castration anxiety becomes more of a problem later. The child's developmental task during the rapprochement subphase requires coping with oral, anal, and genital conflicts, along with the increased awareness of his body image and pressures from those erogenous zones. He also must forgo his illusory security from his own fantasied omnipotence and that of his mother. Object loss and abandonment can be coped with more effectively because of increased ego development. There is now the internalization of parental demands, signaling the onset of superego development, but this in turn intensifies the fear of losing the object's love. A sense of security thus becomes intimately involved with awareness of approval or disapproval by the parents.

Mahler's fourth subphase encompasses consolidation of individuality and the beginnings of emotional object constancy. Because it has no clear-cut, single point of termination, this last phase is not a subphase of the same magnitude as the first three. Once the child has developed object constancy, he is capable of having a complete fantasy of the need-satisfying object. This fantasy material is considered the ''true masturbatory fantasy,'' and genital masturbation at this phase may become a primary autoerotic activity. The fantasies can take any direction and deal with any libidinal zone. They may be fantasies concerned with the mother and the father, may involve genital function or oral and anal areas, or may be fantasies of activity or passivity, contain elements of aggression and hostility, and other variations.

Boys masturbate in this phase by direct manual manipulation of their penis, frequently holding the penis or masturbating whenever the impulse seizes them, whether at home or in public. Girls engage in clitoral manipulation, but often use additional means such as rubbing their thighs together, rocking on objects, or rubbing objects with their hand against their genitals. The objects used by young children in masturbation are often true fetishistic substitutes for mother and, later, for the ''mother's phallus'' (Sperling, 1963). In girls, the entire genital and anal area is responsive to stimulation, and the sensations in the vagina, labia, and anus play a part.

During the oedipal period, masturbation may be considered one of the progressive forces that help to defend the child from the ever present tendency to regress to the earlier preoedipal levels in the face of anxiety. It also provides pleasurable release for sexual and genital tension, as well as fantasy wish-fulfillment, and further strengthens the awareness of separateness. The child's fantasies during this phase involve the libidinal objects, and the content may be concerned with fantasies of conquest and success in the competitive struggles with the parent of the same sex, but may also be concerned with guilt reactions and fears of retaliation. Masturbation, both in its actions and fantasies, serves to promote the individuation process and to reinforce the internalized representations of self and objects, a paramount developmental task during this period. The child's ability to generate pleasure from self-stimulation as a separate and distinct experience from the pleasure experienced from the mother's fondling enhances the child's ability to love himself, to be distinguished from loving the mother as a part of himself.

The following shows the part masturbation can play throughout life when a child loses his mother at two and a half years of age and has subsequent traumatic experiences. At age two and a half, the child is reaching toward the object constancy subphase of the separation-individuation process and about to enter the oedipal phase. He should show increased capacity to play separately from his mother, indirectly reflecting more capability of retaining her image in his mind. Achieving object constancy during the third year remains a rather unstable and reversible achievement (Jacobson, 1964).

An adult male who had been married for several years and had two children undertook analysis because he was unhappy in his marriage. He complained that he felt a lack of closeness between himself and his wife. He found that he was usually impatient with people, he could not stand frustration, and whenever he was alone he had the urge to masturbate. His most disturbing symptom was that of chronic severe depression. Although he had always felt inadequate, inferior, helpless, and hopeless and most analytic sessions included crying at one point or another, he was in fact a successful businessman who enjoyed his hobbies of collecting guns and antique lamps. He was a heavy smoker, had a tendency to drink at least four or five cans of beer a night, and often drank in excess of ten cups of coffee with considerable sugar and cream during a day. He was a little overweight, but not excessively obese. In the course of the analysis, he revealed a compulsion to go to pornographic movies during the day or at night. While watching these movies, he usually masturbated through his trousers.

His developmental history included a prolonged period of anorexia following his mother's death. At the age of three and a half, he began to play with matches and caused a small fire. He received extensive burns on his legs and needed hospitalization for several weeks. He recalled feelings of loneliness during that episode, along with pleasurable memories of having his body massaged with soothing lotions for many months.

He continued to use a nursing bottle until he was about five years old. He pretended to have "breathing problems," diagnosed as asthma, which he used as an excuse to remain at home with his stepmother. During this period he seemed to have an allergy. He recalled his Teddy bear being thrown into the fireplace and burned because of the possibility that its covering was causing his allergic reaction. He sometimes slept with his younger brother and recalled placing his penis between his brother's thighs for masturbation.

Although he remembered playing with his penis and practicing fellatio with other children during latency, active masturbation to orgasm began at about the age of fourteen, and he stated that he was taught the activity by an older man. During his adolescence he masturbated a great deal. He made efforts to suck his own penis, then became involved in sucking the penises of other boys and in group masturbation. There were a few experiences during this phase when he had mutual anal intercourse with these friends. He recalled seeing his stepmother lying on top of his father in bed. This became one of his most exciting fantasies, and a preferred content in the pornographic films was seeing women mounting men. His masturbation activities continued almost daily from his adolescence into his marriage, and continued for a considerable period during his psychoanalysis.

He viewed masturbation as "taking care of himself," "being independent," and "relieving his depression." He saw masturbation as an immediate gratification which he could control and as a means of reassuring himself that he had a penis, was a man, and could accept himself. On the other hand, he felt guilty and viewed masturbation as adolescent and unmanly.

His desire to carry a concealed weapon, a hand gun, was clearly associated with having his penis, which defended him from feeling helpless. He enjoyed measuring his guns, and similarly enjoyed measuring his penis. These possessions were a source of comfort and security to him. Along with the chronic feelings of depression was an awareness of anger. He both resented and enjoyed periods of solitude when he felt that things were peaceful and quiet. When he masturbated, he liked feeling that he could cling to himself and was pleased with the size of his penis. He relieved his loneliness by attending pornographic theatres, where he could be "recharged," watching women who appeared to be enjoying their sexual activities and who were seen as ideal women because they enjoyed taking care of the men and wanted to give them pleasure. He felt that the women in the films were accepting of their femininity and had a "loving nature." An additional excitement in attending the pornographic movies was the pleasure he felt in being "sneaky." Sneakiness also entered into the excitement of finding unusual places for masturbation at work, at home, and in the theatre.

His interest in collecting antique lamps served several purposes: sublimating his masturbatory activities, countering his anxiety in the dark, and having a "play thing" which he could polish and rub as he did his guns. These caretaking activities reflected his wish that people take care of him in that way. His hobbies were not only linked with masturbation, but also disguised the repetition compulsion to master the anxiety and narcissistic trauma from his childhood burns, and re-enacted the pleasure when he had been rubbed with oils during the recovery period.

He considered his wife and stepmother "cold." He associated coldness with being dead, which in turn related to his mother. He felt that "good mothers" take care of you, don't abandon you, and don't reject you. He saw his wife as the "bad mother." He felt that she was too aggressive and too controlling and that she was not a "soft woman."

To return to other developmental aspects of maturation: During the latency period, superego activity brings about repression of the Oedipus conflict and its ssociated masturbation fantasies. However, since repression is seldom complete, the defenses are further enhanced by temporary periods of regression to preoedipal levels. The regression generates anxiety and, therefore, a new level of defense, namely, reaction formation, takes place. The defensive structure is fortified by a great increase in acquiring new skills and in new learning experiences; schooling and athletics, hobbies, games, all of which are ego dominated, enhance repression of sexuality.

Latency children may interrupt their pleasurable sexual fantasies and consciously deflect them to nonsexual areas. Erections during this period may generate anxiety and guilt, and subsequent anticipation of punishment. Boys at this age often show considerable embarrassment about erections when they are naked or in the bathroom; in their concern about being observed they are careful to lock the bathroom door. Penis play usually is not continued to the point of orgasm. Inhibitions against masturbation during this period may produce severe insomnia. The aggressive and sexual feelings may be diverted into other activities wherein the child scratches his skin or bites his nails or preoccupies himself with sadomasochistic fantasies.

Modifications in the masturbation fantasy may take the form of daydreams that are concerned with wielding power or performing heroic acts to save the disguised parental figures or others (family romance). Children's compulsive rituals prior to bedtime can become a technique for avoiding contact with the genitals, genital arousal, or

sexual fantasies. Latency-age children, because of their superego reactions to sexual impulses and masturbation, may unconsciously masochistically invite punishment through provocative actions. Children
who struggle with masturbation conflicts may desexualize these
thoughts and develop symptoms of obsessional thinking. Actual masturbatory behavior can also serve as a defense against pregenital regressive impulses and fantasies. Furthermore, a varied symptomatology
can reflect the child's struggles to prevent sexual feelings and fantasies
from breaking through to consciousness. Daydreaming, inattentive-
ness, and lack of concentration at school may be related to such withdrawal techniques. Thus, various behavioral patterns, including
antisocial actions, can be an acting out of unconscious masturbation
fantasies in disguise.

The development toward the latter half of latency (between ages
eight to ten) associated with further maturation of ego and superego
mechanisms permits the child a much more integrated defensive structure against sexual impulses. Ordinarily, sublimation permits the child
to be more cooperative and efficient in learning. A healthy, developing
child is expected some mild expressions of guilt, and if these are not
reinforced, continued ego development will not be inhibited.

The preadolescent period (ten to twelve years) is characterized by
a biological increase in the pregenital and genital impulses. Masturbation activity as well as sexual exploration or related activities with
the peer group become more common. Coping with these challenges
to ego development is considered important for continued ego differentiation and maturation. The preadolescent interest in mechanical
devices further serves to help master the anxieties that have their
origins in learning how to control and integrate body functions. Preadolescent girls begin to show a heightened interest in boys as a means
of resisting the regressive defense of a return to dependency upon the
preoedipal mother. Ordinarily, girls in this phase do not practice mutual masturbation to the extent seen among boys. A number of girls
show an interest in horseback riding, which seems to serve as a disguised genital stimulus, and also as a reassurance of their ability to
control these impulses through mastering the sport.

The adolescent period covers a long span from the onset of puberty
until the beginning of adult life, so it is difficult to make general

statements that apply to the entire phase. Masturbation activity, which ordinarily peaks during early adolescence, can become a problem in later adolescence if masturbation becomes a complete substitute for heterosexual object relations. Therefore, we would expect that at some point during this phase there will be an increased ego-dystonic reaction. Hence, some degree of intrapsychic struggle would be phase-appropriate. In certain adolescents who remain preoccupied with masturbation, it may perpetuate the phase-specific fantasies from early adolescence. When this does occur, preoedipal oral means of expressing impulses can become the vehicle for social patterns, distorting the maturational aspects of phase-appropriate object relations in later adolescence, and beyond, into adulthood.

Blos (1962) described the adolescent struggle in masturbation, wherein the adolescent has to deal with the regressive pulls to his early childhood autoerotic sensations and fantasies. These tendencies are in sharp contrast to the great push toward independence and maturation and a preference for the peer world. Masturbation fantasies usually include a variety of impulse-connected wishes with both preoedipal and oedipal content and their disguises. Masturbation in adolescence has a progressive influence upon development because it aids the integration of earlier impulses and pregenital conflicts, bringing them under the influence of genital-phase-specific function. Earlier autoerotic experiences and fantasies are more appropriately directed, promoting development of mental structures, discrimination between inner and outer reality, stronger self-concept, and, finally, integration of body parts into the new total body image.

Bernstein (1962) and Root (1962) found a close connection between the dreams of the adolescent and the nature of his masturbation fantasies. Both dreaming and masturbation reflect the adolescent's methods of controlling and discharging tension. Masturbation activities during adolescence serve to affirm gender identity—the masculine or feminine self-image—and, as in the clinical example of the patient who lost his mother at age two and a half, to combat feelings of inadequacy, inferiority, and vulnerability. Under healthy circumstances, masturbation, both the act and fantasy, prepares the individual for developing love relationships. In some adolescents, masturbation fantasies intensify feelings of confusion about gender identity and body image, and the narcissistic gratifications become a barrier to the growth of object love. For some adolescents, masturbation does not facilitate maturation if the activity becomes the sole or indispensable means for diminishing tension, or generates an undue degree of superego anxiety, and remains too closely associated with preoedipal or oedipal objects.

Continued masturbation throughout adult life may or may not interfere with object relations. In those instances where it is not an interference, it may contribute significantly to the sexual responsiveness of each partner toward the other, or may be used by a couple as part of their mutual stimulation and thus enhance their sexual pleasures. Finally, it may be used to supplement an individual's own sexual needs.

Each developmental level produces its own characteristic fantasies and behavior; earlier levels of mental life, however, are always available as a reservoir for fantasies in later life. Fantasies during sexual excitement with a partner frequently can be traced to similar fantasies associated with masturbation from earlier experiences. An adult married man had a repetitive fantasy during masturbation and intercourse: An attractive, voluptuous, naked woman smoked a cigarette while holding a balloon in her mouth. The balloon was covered with whipped cream or shaving cream; it burst and smeared her face. The fantasy was traced to a memory of his mother blowing up balloons for him at a childhood birthday party. The fantasy had many levels of unconscious significance: orality, anal smearing, phallic "ejaculation-in-the-face," as well as sadomasochistic humiliation, and subduing and controlling the woman with his phallic power. The enlarging balloon was a fused breast-penis symbol. The patient also concealed beneath his aggressive fantasies his own identification with the female and his wish to be in the passive-submissive role, a derivative of his early oedipal wish to receive his father's penis.

A married woman who was markedly frustrated by a rejecting, hostile husband who rarely had sexual contact with her had a repetitive masturbatory fantasy which she traced back to her adolescence. She was captured by men who tied her on her back and stood around her naked with their erect penises which they forced her to suck. She was a bright, educated, attractive woman whose mother was frequently ill during her childhood. The patient was cared for by other women in the family. She was prone to depressive reactions during her life, aggravated by her marital situation. Her self-esteem was low, and the fantasy served to disguise both her wish to be desired by many men and her oral desires to be fed and cared for by a ''good mothering man.'' The earlier wishes for a mothering woman were later revealed and expressed in more direct homosexual fantasies. I find that the masturbatory fantasies associated with partner-sexuality vary with the events of the individual's life and the levels of regression in certain phases of the analysis or in coping with the life situation. Extraneous self-selected reading material, magazine pictures, or seductive social repartee at cocktail parties may become the stimuli for masturbation fantasies from varying levels of the unconscious.

Although a masturbation fantasy may originally express a conflict or serve as a vehicle for expressing aggression, sexuality, or anxiety, the pleasure attached to it can reinforce its use. The fantasy then may become repetitive and appear to be compulsive and autonomous. I have found these fantasies are not only operative because of ''conditioning,'' but also because of residual frustrations, such as unsatisfied dependency needs or continuing conflicts around sexual identity, guilt, anxiety, anger, and so on.

A behaviorally oriented approach (Marquis, 1970) suggested a ''reconditioning'' procedure for those who seem locked into their childhood or adolescent masturbation fantasies. The technique consists of conscious, deliberate alteration of the fantasy when approaching orgasm, and in time to avoid ever using the older fantasy for arousal. It is conceivable that, if successful, the modified fantasy may diminish conscious guilt, but as an analyst with considerable respect for the power of the unconscious, I would expect the unsolved problems to make their presence known via a new avenue.

Individuals who masturbate excessively in an effort to achieve a quick relief from any degree of tension can diminish the ability of the ego to develop a tolerance for such tension. Because of the anxiety and guilt, they may forgo masturbation and shift their pattern to various types of drug addiction as a means of both relieving tension and avoiding its association with sexual impulses and fantasies. Although many neurotic and psychotic individuals masturbate frequently, it is important to recognize that this behavior is the result of their various conflicts and not the cause. If a pathological degree of guilt or anxiety is associated with masturbation, the ensuing conflicts can produce phobias or inhibit schoolwork or performance in recreational activities. Some compulsive neurotic men have expressed fears that they have damaged their genitals because of masturbation, a concern obviously produced by guilt and magical thinking that they are the victims of self-inflicted punishment. A clinical example: An adult male with castration feelings associated with masturbation had strong inhibitions against relationships with women. He had neither homosexual nor heterosexual experiences, but was preoccupied with fears that if he were to have a heterosexual relationship, the woman would discover that he had a small penis or one that functioned poorly, and that she would then know he had masturbated.

Excessive sexual activity for certain individuals might be a symptom of mental problems but not a cause. It is usually physically impossible for an individual to engage in too much sex because the reactions of the body serve as their own control mechanisms; when there is satiation from orgastic response, whether it be due to masturbation, intercourse, or sexual play, it is unlikely that the individual will engage in further sexual activity. The fantasies associated with adult sexuality may be influenced by one's earlier masturbation fantasies, and, if they do not arouse conflicts or guilt but are used to intensify sexual excitement and pleasure, may be viewed as part of normal human behavior. Many people are aware of fantasies associated with their sexuality which enhance their excitement, whether they are due to stimulation from masturbation or intercourse. For many women stimulation directed to the clitoral area, either manually, orally, or from objects or vibrators, is their primary means of achieving orgasm. Although a number of women have indicated that this direct noncoital method is physiologically more satisfying than that produced by intercourse, others consider intercourse and the closeness in a partner relationship more gratifying emotionally.

Masturbation is only one aspect of sexuality, but it occupies a unique position in human development. It serves as an early organizer for one's identity, and for social attachments. Refuting the misconceptions about masturbation that have been handed down over thousands of years, modern researchers have found that it can hardly be considered a rare, unusual, or abnormal human activity. Males and females are gradually moving toward a common humanity, with each learning more about the other. Perhaps society can finally permit them to share equally their right to enjoy sexual pleasures and live healthy, productive lives.

CHAPTER 4

On the Significance of Infantile Sexuality

NATHANIEL ROSS

Freud's discovery of infantile sexuality contains implications for man's fate the far reaches of which could not possibly have been foreseen at the time. Unfortunately, his use of the word sexuality, however truly accurate in its ultimate meaning, led to much misunderstanding because it was too easily made synonymous with genital sexuality, although Freud himself warned that he specifically did not use the terms synonymously (1910a,b, 1940a). In more recent times, in a personal communication in 1961, George Klein suggested the use of the term sensuality instead, but his definition has not become popular in the psychoanalytic literature because of its implications for meta-psychology. Although it includes the connotation of genital behavior, it is closer to Freud's original concept of infantile experience than the meaning almost automatically associated with the word sexuality.

In this day and age it seems superfluous to underline the importance, if not basic essentiality, that Freud placed upon the central role of sexuality in human experience and of its absolutely necessary relationship to the phenomenon of love. Explicitly, in numerous contributions, he asserted that affection, love, and all experiences related to such phenomena depend absolutely upon infantile pleasure, which he defined as *eroticism* obtained from the subject's own body. The chief source of infantile pleasure, said Freud (1910a), is the appropriate excitation of certain parts of the body that are especially susceptible to stimulation. Apart from the genital, the oral, anal and urethral orifices, these include the organ of hearing, the skin, and other sensory surfaces. The "affectionate current," said Freud (1912b), springs from the earliest years of childhood and is directed to close members of the family. Such affectionate currents "continually carry along with them erotism, which is consequently diverted from its sexual aims" (p. 181). So insistent was he upon the essential derivation of love from sexuality that in his paper on "wild" psychoanalysis (1910b), he cited the case of a woman who was erroneously told by a physician that the anxiety which ensued upon her divorce had been caused by lack of sexual satisfaction. According to Freud, this was "wild" analysis because the physician had interpreted sexual needs as simply those for coitus or analogous acts, whereas in psychoanalysis what is sexual comprises all the activities of the tender feelings that have their source in primitive sexual impulses. Further, said Freud, we prefer to speak of *psychosexuality,* thus stressing the fact that the mental factor in sexual life should not be overlooked or underestimated.

Further to implement Freud's point of view of sexuality and love, in "Group Psychology and the Analysis of the Ego" (1921), he stated that being in love "is based on the simultaneous presence of directly sexual impulsions and of sexual impulsions that are inhibited in their aims" (p. 142). In the history of the development of the family there have been group relations of sexual love, but the more important sexual love became for the family and the more it developed the characteristics of being in love, the more it required to be limited to two people. As a matter of fact, current views in developmental psychology hold that love also *begins* between two people—mother and child.

The thesis of this chapter is that infantile sexuality is more significant for human development than even Freud realized. It has now been amply demonstrated (Hoffer, 1950; Spitz, 1945, 1946a; Bowlby, 1969; Greenacre, 1960a; Mahler et al., 1975; Winnicott, 1965, among others) that sufficient and continuous pleasurable physical contact between the infant and his upbringers is absolutely essential for the infant's optimal development, not only emotionally as such, but in perceptual, motor, intellectual, linguistic, and social dimensions. Naturally, the latter developments depend upon the neutralization of instinctual energies. One may say with certainty today that such repeated contact, which also provides pleasure and gratification to those who rear him and is thus a continuously reciprocal process, is necessary for the infant's very survival. Such reciprocal stimulation between mother and infant has received considerable attention within recent years (Thomas et al., 1972; Klaus et al., 1972, 1975; Ainsworth, 1974). Lichtenstein (1977) has discussed this interaction at great length, and has strongly emphasized the lasting effects of the mother's unconscious attitudes toward her newborn infant in his comprehensive work on problems of human identity. Spitz (1945) has dramatically shown how infants may literally fall sick and die of the lack of love.

Freud's discovery, at first reacted to with horror and distaste, has profound implications for man's survival and for his evolution. It also contains far-reaching implications for the ultimate complexities of the phenomenon of love, the structure of the family, the relationships between affect and cognition, the interplay with aggression, the development of knowledge, religious experience, the scientific pursuit of truth, the arts, music, and literature, and the philosophic search for ultimate meanings. Obviously, too, it is at the core of psychopathological vicissitudes. The evidence continues to accumulate. As stated above, within recent years, observations have been made of mothers and babies immediately and very shortly after birth which reveal, contrary to the prevailing assumption that the infant at first lives in a purely self-contained world, that it definitely and demonstrably responds to the mother very early. It does so in a startlingly rhythmic way. Klaus and Kennell (1976), working with infants and mothers at the Rainbow Babies and Children's Hospital in Cleveland, have taken slow-motion pictures of such reciprocating behavior at this postnatal time. Their films reveal a rhythmic correspondence between the mother's sounds and movements and those of the child. Mothers in contact with their infants immediately after birth seem instinctively to pitch their voices at a higher level, as if they knew that the child would respond more to the higher tones. The authors of this research call the effect "a beautiful linking" of mother and child. Thus, the responses of the infant to the mother may well have to be dated earlier than the "three-month smiling response" (Spitz, 1946b). I myself have observed smiling at two weeks with mothers more than averagely endowed with love for their children.

Although this chapter is specifically concerned with the tactile-sensual modality in infants, i.e., infantile sexuality, it should be stated here that it is generally assumed that the total experience of the infant at the very beginning of its extrauterine existence is "coenesthetic," i.e., nondifferentiated sensory experience. The earliest bonding between mother and child seems to take place in this experiential context, with the specific modalities becoming increasingly differentiated during the course of development.

Klaus and Kennell (1976) studied two separate groups of mothers and infants—one that had "continuous contacts" and the other "brief contacts." When the children were two years old, the mothers of the first group were asking them many more questions and issuing far fewer commands than those in the latter group. At the age of five, the children of the first group had higher IQ's than those of the second and were much more advanced linguistically. Similar findings have been reported by other workers.

Recently, extended studies at the Queens Mental Hygiene Center for Children have brought out, according to a Roche Report in 1976, through controlled observations, that individuals who come from large families, all other factors considered, suffer from a higher incidence of both mental retardation and mental disease than those from small families. This would seem to follow from the effects observed of lack of sufficient loving contact with children at earlier age levels. Clearly, it is hardly possible for a child from a large family to obtain as much loving attention from the mother as one from a small family, even with the best maternal intentions. Obviously, instances of gifted individuals emerging from families with many children will come to mind, but, if the above observations are verified, there would appear to be little doubt of the salutary effect of limiting the size of families.

The findings I have cited will not surprise psychoanalysts, except perhaps to make them re-examine the timetable for the so-called "nondifferentiated" phase, the onset of symbiosis, and the advent of the separation-individuation phase. While this is not the place to recapitulate the recent findings in infantile development (for which, see Mahler et al., 1975), a few observations are worth emphasizing.

In describing the development and growth of the ego, Freud (1923a) remarked that the ego is first and foremost a body ego. This "body ego" or "image" arises from repeated contact with another's body.

Hoffer (1950) asserted that adequate libidinization of the body arising from the mother-infant relationship is important (I should say *necessary*) for the development of the body image. And the formation of the body image is absolutely essential for ego development, with all of the latter's implications for internalization, self- and object relationships, and affective functioning in the real world. Mahler et al. (1975) emphasize the prime importance of the mother's enjoyment in holding the infant as a basic force in the furtherance of its development. They consider such holding, if it is genuinely pleasurable, even more important than breast feeding. The mother who holds the child rigidly while breast-feeding is not particularly effective in enhancing the child's growth. Mahler and her colleagues have observed that bottle-fed children if held and fondled lovingly by their mothers are nevertheless more relaxed, smile sooner, and advance more rapidly in their behavior than those who are breast-fed mechanically.

Considering the work done by Harlow and Harlow (1965) on monkeys, we should not be too surprised by these observations. It is especially striking that Harlow's monkeys with wire-cage mothers were entirely unable to mingle with their peers or to procreate. In a follow-up study, Harlow (cited by Starr, 1971) brought some of his asocial monkeys into frequent and repeated contact with normal monkeys five or six months old, who continually played with the alienated ones. Within a few months to a year, the latter became fully rehabilitated, to the point of engaging in sexual activity as well as other normal monkey behavior.

I think it is a reasonable assumption that the consistent "sensual" contact between mother and child during the course of the earliest months and years is absolutely essential for the latter's maturation, if not survival. This is by no means to overlook other factors in the rearing of children, such as proper weaning, wise toilet training, the gradual setting of limits, the encouragement of healthy aggression and individuation, the provision for adequate educational stimuli, the setting of mature examples, adequate nutrition, and all the other factors which belie the all-too-common assumption that in the upbringing of children one need only blindly follow one's "instincts" and family traditions.

In view of these considerations, it seems logical to assume that an "object relations" rather than "instinct impulsion" approach to sexuality is called for in understanding the course of human development. Here, I cite Lichtenstein's (1977, pp. 49-126) discussion of the increasing importance of nonprocreative sexuality as one ascends the evolutionary scale.

The fate of mankind depends, ultimately, upon the ability to love. Unhappily, there are innumerable pathological forces—social, economic, personal, traditional, ideological, etc.—that interfere with the growth and maturation of this ability to love. But I am here almost (but not quite) entirely confining myself to the core problem of the role of infantile sexuality in the history of mankind. I am also postulating that the primal origin of all love is that of the mother for her offspring; that this love is the basis of the love of man for woman, woman for man, both for their society, love of others, and the passion of the mind, which has given rise to the greatest achievements of mankind in his mastery of the world around him.

It is a sad commentary on the ambivalence and suffering implicit in man's experience that, until the twentieth century, the young of the human race have been treated with so much brutality, contempt, indifference, and downright destructiveness. Only the love arising from the sensual endowment of human beings has served as a counterforce to these mindless assaults upon helpless little victims.

As late as the early twentieth century, infanticide was still being practiced in China (and quite probably elsewhere). The missionary father of a patient of mine had witnessed the results of such a practice.

There is far more evidence of the antithesis of love in prehistoric man than of its affirmation. The crushed skulls of human beings in the caves of Chou-Koutien bear vivid evidence of the cruelty of man to his own kind. This was homo erectus, circa 500,000 years or so ago, but later, Cro-Magnon man, true homo sapiens, was also richly endowed with intense, hostile aggression. In fact, the first Cro-Magnons discovered were a man and woman in a cave with both skulls crushed, evidently by a blunt instrument (Wendt, 1972).

Evidence showing that there was love in prehistoric man is scarce, but it does exist. Recently, a grave was discovered in Carmel in the Near East (Solecki, 1975) which had apparently been strewn with flowers, as evidenced by a concentration of pollen grains too great to be accounted for by mere accident. More surprisingly, most of the pollen came from plants with known medicinal qualities. In addition, bones of Neanderthal man have been unearthed which had been smeared with red ochre (Hawkes, 1976, p. 22). A reasonable speculation is that such findings point to the existence of some crude beliefs that an individual could survive after death and that the survivors cared enough to try to help him to do so. (The red ochre in all likelihood represents blood, with which to bring the dead man to life.)

Before entering into further considerations of the history of love, let us take up some anatomical, neurophysiological, and ethological phenomena bearing upon our subject.

As we pursue the evolutionary sequences in animals and man, we cannot help but observe the increasing elaboration and complexity of the central nervous system. What has been termed the reptilian part of the brain is the lowest part of the brain stem, which is the seat, not only of various vital functions such as respiration, various metabolic rhythms, etc., but also of certain domination-submission and hierarchical tendencies in animals (Sagan, 1977). Above this area is the limbic system, containing the hypothalamus, thalamus, hippocampal gyrus, etc., which are predominantly associated with affect. Then, of course, there is the neocortex, increasing in elaboration and complexity until we reach the brain of homo sapiens. In the australopithecine precursors of man, the volume of the brain case is not much more than 500 cc.—in chimpanzees it is 450 cc. Pithecanthropus erectus, whom we today designate as homo erectus, was more advanced and had a larger brain volume (750 cc.) than australopithecus, but homo neanderthalensis had a brain volume fully equal to that of modern man—1500 cc. Yet it was not until recently that this lowly creature was accorded a relatively human status. Of animals lower than man, the cetaceans have much larger brain volumes in proportion to their size than animals lower in the scale, but the higher primates, of course, begin to approach the 500 cc. level. Without going into the innumerable neurophysiological correlations between man and the lower animals, I wish to state that, considering the evolutionary sequence, it is difficult to deny lower animals similarities in behavior that may well correspond to subjective experiences which cannot as yet be demonstrated by evidence such as is employed in the physical sciences.

What I am specifically referring to is the "emotional experiences" of animals, including those of affection and love. It is customary to dismiss all such claims as anthropomorphizations, yet the similarities are too striking to warrant such total dismissals. Indeed, if we ask ourselves how we "know" how another human being "feels," we cannot adduce the kind of proof demanded in the physical sciences. Yet, there are human beings who seem to be far more "in tune with" their fellow men and others who appear to make little or no such "contact" (sic!) with others, even though such individuals may have extremely high cognitive capacities. There certainly appear to be two different kinds of knowledge—affective and cognitive. I have entered at considerable length into this subject elsewhere (1975). Thus, when we "sense" that an animal has feelings that are analogous to ours, such an experience cannot be dismissed as entirely illusory. It does not seem reasonable to assume that in the evolutionary chain there is a complete dichotomy between man and animals with regard to affective experiences. The sketchy anatomical facts I described above presume that where there are similar vital structures there may well be functions which are at least approximately analogous to them.

There is a wealth of evidence that the phenomena of affection and love can be described on an evolutionary scale. Before I adduce a few ethological phenomena, however, I would like to offer another postulate, which will certainly appear strange. This is that, in effect, affect may well be an earlier and more primitive form of cognition. How does an animal "learn" about the world around it, so as to recognize friend or foe, sources of safety or danger, food or poison, etc., if not through its affective experience with its mother and its affective responses to various stimuli? Indeed, recent work teaching chimpanzees sign language shows that they are capable to some degree of distinguishing between truth and falsehood, can express anger, disgust, and contempt, and are even capable of a certain degree of abstraction (Sagan, 1977). How does an animal "recognize" (note a word that contains the idea of "knowing") danger, if not through an affective response? There are many examples of words in common usage which may have both affective and cognitive meanings. Examples are *understand, mean, know* (in the Bible to *know* may even mean to have intercourse), *feel, sense,* etc. (N. Ross, 1975).

Let us now describe some ethological phenomena bearing upon the subject of love. Konrad Lorenz (1952) describes the behavior of a male kite that had Lorenz "imprinted" upon him at the optimal age. (Is it possible that imprinting also takes place in man in the form of the behavior of the infants described by Klaus and Kennell? Lichtenstein presents such a hypothesis in his book on human identity [1977].) In any event, at mating time the kite built a nest and began to court Lorenz in the most insistent way, attempting to stuff masticated worms into his mouth, nostrils, and ears. It displayed great intensity in this pursuit and signs of what appeared to be distress when Lorenz did not respond to its attentions. Lorenz also reports that when the dominant kite in a flock lost its mate and joined up with a female which had been of the lowest hierarchical order, the latter began to display toward other kites behavior which would be difficult to describe otherwise than as arrogance and contempt.

As for evidences of love in animals, one can cite many instances. Porpoises have been repeatedly observed protecting and sustaining above water injured members of their groups and staying with them until it is no longer possible to do so. Anyone who has ever lived with a pet dog has repeatedly observed what certainly looks like shame, sadness, affection, rebelliousness, etc.

Considerable ethological evidence has accumulated regarding the extensive effects of "handling" early in life among animals. Here is a quotation from R. Chauvin (1977): "One of the greatest discoveries of behavioral science in recent years . . . is the ease with which the equilibrium of the newborn can be upset by stress from seemingly insignificant life experiences. . . . Handling consists of 'gentling' or fondling newborn animals for a few minutes each day and then returning them to the litter. Such handling is enough, however, to induce several months later (which would correspond to several years in man), long after the handling has ceased, very marked behavioral differences as compared to control animals not so handled" (pp. 127-128). Further, "The consequences of early handling are so great that *even the biochemistry of the brain and adrenal glands is modified.*" (p. 129). And "*Sensory stimulation,* especially if it is rich and varied, also modifies the perceptual capacity of subject animals" (pp. 130-131).

According to Chauvin, "Being deprived of the mother or companions at an early age and for prolonged periods causes very serious and sometimes irreversible consequences in most higher animals" (p. 132). Further parallels to human behavior illustrate the fact that the social experiences of the first few months are crucial for later development in numerous aspects of behavior. It is my thesis that the specific contact clearly defined as infantile sexuality by Freud is the decisive factor in producing the long-term effects described. Chauvin summarizes the numerous theories concerning the effects of isolation as follows: (1) "being deprived of sensory excitation causes serious and permanent alterations in the corresponding sense organs; these changes are at the root of later behavioral deficiencies"; (2) to complete the development of a number of under- or undeveloped physiological mechanisms at the time of birth "there must be a series of sensory stimulations at a certain critical period after birth"; (3) isolation causes learning deficiency; (4) isolation causes traumatic effects (pp. 139-140).

Although Chauvin disputes Freud's thesis that infantile attachment and sexuality are interrelated, he does not appear to take into account Freud's broader definition of sexuality; Chauvin considers sexuality synonymous with genital sexuality. While Chauvin's dichotomy may be more valid for the lower animals, it is this writer's opinion that the distinction is not so decisive as that made by Chauvin, especially for the higher animals, and becomes less so as one ascends the evolutionary scale.

Care for and attachment to the young is ubiquitous among many animals, especially those that have formed social groups, such as the baboons and macaques cited above. Further, this is not confined to the females. Male baboons, who are among the fiercest of he primates—clearly an adaptation to life in the open fields—show the strongest affection for infants of their group. They will actually approach females in order to caress and fondle their babies, and meekly give up when the mother, however low in the hierarchical order, demands the return of her infant. If a female is injured and lags behind the troop, the male will fall back to protect her. He will, indeed, attack much larger predators in order to protect his band (Starr, 1971). Wild dogs of Africa will risk their lives in defense of their groups.

Dogs, especially those which Lorenz (1952) postulates as having descended from wolves (German shepherds, Alaskans, chows, dobermans, etc.), have been known to starve themselves to death after the death of a master.

My thesis is that it seems artificial to regard the presence of affects as having suddenly sprung from the brain of man. I think that, just as in all other forms of behavior, there has been a gradual evolution along the animal scale, culminating in the enormously complex phenomena subserved in man under the headings of love and aggression ("healthy" and "unhealthy"). Such a thesis would accord with the increasing size and elaboration of structures in the central nervous system. In man, the assumption of the upright posture, stereoscopic vision, the increasing efficiency of the hand, and, finally, the acquisition of language gave the most enormous impetus to the development of a being who outstrips his predecessors in the evolutionary sequence to such a degree as to make it possible for him to master the world in which he lives—for better *and* for worse.

When the earliest hominid descended from the trees in the Pleistocene era, probably about five million years ago according to the latest estimates, he was precipitated into a far more dangerous environment than the one in which he had hitherto lived. New conditions on earth, following a period of wetness and extreme temperatures, forced these prehominids out of the jungles onto the drier and more open plains. The "naked apes" who survived were called upon to compensate in various ways for the loss of their protected environments. In order to devote themselves to defense against the powerful and dangerous predators they would now encounter in the open, for the individual and the species to survive, it became necessary for both "love" and aggression to be developed to increasingly higher degrees—love to preserve and nurture the most helpless and dependent of newborn animals, and aggression both to protect their young and the females and to seek and find food. With respect to the latter, an omnivorous diet, containing high levels of protein, became essential. The carnivore does not have to eat all day long as does the herbivore. Already in chimpanzees we see the beginnings of an omnivorous diet. Man was given time to develop all sorts of elaborate skills by the nature of his diet and the development of his hands and brain.

We therefore see that both love and aggression were necessary to
the survival and adaptational capacities of man. If there is an endless
battle between them, this was made inevitable by the very nature of
their surroundings. The fact that aggression may become unhealthy,
as it did in the form of cannibalism and war, is not too difficult to
understand.

Such a struggle between these two primal forces is what I call
"bringing the death instinct down to earth." I think it is a far more
rational statement of the battle between Eros and Thanatos than Freud's
(1920) original formulation and that of present-day Kleinians.

Let us return to the concept of infantile sexuality. We now know
that an optimal degree of pleasurable experience of this nature is absolutely essential to the effective functioning of the child—and ultimately of the adult—not only in the development of object relations,
but for the fullest degrees of emotional, intellectual, and social maturation. (I am not overlooking the necessity for certain degrees of
frustration, as well, in the process of growth.) If this appears to be a
simplistic view, it must be borne in mind that, in concentrating upon
a particular facet of human experience, we must do so for purposes
of clarity. It does *not* mean that infantile sexuality is the *sole* force in
personal development. It is also hardly necessary to emphasize the
fact that, with all the best will in the world and with such awareness
at their disposal of the importance of holding and fondling infants,
individuals are dominated by unconscious forces that will make it
difficult or impossible to carry out their good intentions effectively.
But certainly we should put an end once and for all to the notions of
the "original sin" of sexuality, the denial of physical affection for
young children, physical punishment, and severe deprivations as methods of child rearing, and fear of expressing love in words and deeds
toward our progeny. If such injunctions seem outmoded, one has only
to recall the childhood experiences of deprivation we still encounter
every day in listening to our patients. The fear of loving is still a
ubiquitous phenomenon.

To summarize, it appears to me that there is a continuum in the
evolutionary scale of phenomena ultimately subsumed under the headings of affect and cognition, reflected in the increasing size and complexity of the brain. Originally, affect and cognition were fused in

their anatomic origins, the former serving as an approximation of the latter and providing particular animals with the means of adaptation and survival. In effect, these constitute varying degrees of experience, culminating in the successful mastery of the particular environment of individual species. In mammals, the close physical relationship between the mother and offspring, generically reflected in the prolonged existence of the fetus within the mother, must be carried on after birth to insure the survival and ultimate socialization of the individual. In higher mammals and man, this inevitably leads to the elaboration of various effects, particularly that of love, which reveals a continuum in its development and complexity as one ascends the latter of evolution. In man, such a phenomenon as love, based, as Freud repeatedly insisted, upon infantile sexuality, counteracts the destructiveness and self-destructiveness of opposing forces. In variously directed and sublimated forms, it constitutes a necessary force for his survival in a world to which he himself constitutes the main threat.

CHAPTER 5

Modern Woman and Motherhood

EDITH BUXBAUM

A great deal has been written about the bringing up of children; in recent years, the emphasis has been on the bringing up of babies. But as Winnicott (1958) has said, "There is no baby. There is only a baby and a mother." In this chapter, I shall try to bridge the gap and talk about mothers.

Obviously, the baby is not as necessary for the mother as the mother is for the baby. But that does not mean that the baby serves no functions for the mother. If the idea, so prevalent in male-oriented societies, that women existed primarily for the purpose of having babies is open to question, the idea that women have babies only because society expects them to is equally questionable. Procreation is a biological matter, on which the survival of the species depends. The survival of the species rests on the individual mother's commitment to the survival of her offspring. This commitment is viable only when it brings her satisfactions of her innate maternal instincts. The vicissitudes of the mother's psychosexual development may interfere with these satisfactions. Further, the discrepancy between her instinctual wishes and the restrictions imposed upon them by society may leave her in conflict. Our clinical work allows us to see these conflicts more clearly than sociological overviews or statistical data. We can follow the conflicts of the pregnant woman who has to decide whether or not she wants the child. We can penetrate the surface and understand the unconscious forces affecting the mother and child in their relations with each other and with the society in which they live.

Bibring et al. (1961) arrived at the following formulation: "the biophysiological, developmental process in pregnancy has its significant psychological counterpart and equivalent in the specific sequence and alterations of the woman's object-libidinal and narcissistic positions. An intense object relationship to the sexual partner leads to the event of impregnation, by which a significant representation of the love object becomes part of the self. . . . Under the impact of the marked physiological and anatomical changes of the first months of pregnancy, the libidinal concentration on the self increases and leads to the integration of, and merging with, this foreign body, turning it into an integral part of herself'' (p. 15). They also point out that the core of the adjustive task of the pregnant woman "lies in [her] relationship to her own mother, its infantile aspects and its maturational resolution in the daughter's move toward becoming a mother herself'' (p. 18).

Beverly had become pregnant by a man with whom she had an affair but with whom she did not want to live. She decided that she did not want to bring up the child without a father and would have an abortion. She did so, with some apprehension of physical injury but apparently without any conflict about the morality of her action. She had the abortion early in the pregnancy and without any difficulty, but became depressed after it. Her boy friend was helpful and supportive. Although she had not wanted a permanent relationship with him, she now became attached to and dependent on him. At the same time, she was angry with him for having impregnated her, for having caused her to abort and suffer pain, and she insisted that she wanted to have another child. He resented her dependence on him and, in reaction to her hostility, he left her.

Why had the picture changed after the abortion? Beverly needed him, became dependent, and hated him for it. The relationship became similar to her relation to her mother on whom she was deeply dependent, whom she accused of not liking her, and whom she alternately loved and hated. She became the infant which she had aborted, but also the hateful child whom the man, like the mother, rejected. Beverly would have liked to give her mother a grandchild. She thought maybe this would have been the gift which would have won the mother's love. She never told the mother about her pregnancy or the abortion. In this case the woman had a need for the child of which she was not aware. She had to take on the role of the infant herself when she denied herself the role of the mother. She wanted to have a child in order to replace the one she had aborted.

The biophysiological developmental process that started with the pregnancy was interrupted by the abortion; the psychological counterpart, however, the change in libidinal cathexis which was set in motion, continued. Beverly's libidinal concentration on herself increased, but the baby, which should have been the recipient and object of her narcissistic love, was missing. She herself became the baby and regressed instead of progressing toward becoming a mother. The loss of the pregnancy was a narcissistic loss. It was experienced as the loss of a part of herself, and she responded with depression, i.e., mourning her loss of self. The need to replace the lost baby may be perceived as an undoing of a wrongdoing toward the fetus. The aggression against the man whose child was destroyed, against the mother with whom she could not identify, is cause for guilt feelings, which are reinforced by religious feelings to varying degrees. But above all, the reason for the woman to replace the baby is the sense of loss of self she experiences. The loss of the baby is felt as the loss of a part of her body, and, with this, old feelings of inadequacy are revived. The baby seeks independence from the symbiotic relationship with the mother, but also yearns to return to it in order to relive the omnipotent feelings he enjoyed at that time. The woman, during pregnancy, relives these narcissistic omnipotent feelings in reverse. Like the young child who misses his mother as if she were a part of himself, the woman who loses a child misses the union that afforded her these narcissistic omnipotent feelings.

Beverly's reaction is similar to the reactions of women who suffered miscarriages, and also to women who are somewhat depressed before menstruating. They regret every egg that didn't materialize into a baby, aside or on top of all the other reasons why they don't want to menstruate. Also, postpartum depressions are related to the reaction of the case described, insofar as the depressions are to some extent the mourning of the mother for the loss of her baby as if it were a part of her body.

Bonding Between Mother and Child

Normally, the birth of a child takes place under circumstances dictated by the society and its traditions and rituals. In most societies the infant stays with the mother right after birth. In our affluent society mother and child are taken care of in the obstetrics ward in a hospital, and mother and baby are usually separated immediately after birth. This procedure, which is introduced in order to protect the mother and give her a chance to recover from her labors, is an intervention in the process of mother-child bonding which would take place without such interference. Leboyer (1974) is an advocate of immediate skin contact of the baby with the mother after birth in order to make the outside world acceptable for the baby. Klaus (1975) expressed the strong belief in a sensitive period of attachment in the human mother. Mothers who had early and extra contact with their babies in the hospital in a controlled study were more likely to breast feed; they touched their babies in a certain way beginning with the fingers and moving down the trunk; they talked to them, and 80 percent of them referred to the baby's eyes. The mother looks for the baby's open eyes. "In order to develop an attachment, the love object must make love to the lovemaker," (Klaus, 1975, p. 33). *En face* eye contact between infant and mother is one of the important indicators of the mother's attachment to the infant. The mothers' intensive interest in their infants' eyes, matched with the unusual ability of the newborn infant to attend and follow, especially in the first hour of life, suggest that the period immediately after birth may be uniquely important (Klaus et al., 1972).

Equally vital for the bonding between mother and child is breast after an interval. Kauffmann (1970) says that the nursing infant satisfies its hunger while at the same time it stimulates the nipple and the breast of the mother and relieves the tension caused by accummulated milk. He considers the pleasure the mother derives from the infant's touching her of equal importance. Physiological responses in coitus and lactation are allied. Uterine contractions occur during suckling, and sexual excitement brings about nipple erection and even milk ejection. These mutual physical satisfactions are the basis of bonding between mother and infant. They enable the mother to be aware of the infant's needs through reactions in her own body. The nursing mother knows when the infant is hungry by the tensions in her full breasts. She enjoys the nursing because it gives her relief. She is attuned to the baby who satisfies her. The mother who is in touch with her infant by physical closeness and nursing lays the basis for the child's psychosocial behavior. It is the experience of mutuality that affords her the satisfactions which make her devotion a pleasure and reward her for her troubles.

Symbiotic Relations and Their Disturbances

The symbiotic relation between mother and infant is a continuation of the oneness between mother and fetus *in utero*. When the mother does not enjoy her infant, the symbiotic relationship does not develop or is disturbed. This maternal attachment behavior, which is so important for the mother's and the baby's well being, can be influenced by a great many factors. The young mother's relation to the father of the baby, her own experiences as an infant with her mother and her family are of primary importance. Since family relationships and marriages are so frequently broken and breaking up, the atmosphere that favors maternal attachment behavior is frequently not available for the young mother. Just as biophysiological developments influence psychological states, so do psychological states influence the biophysiological states. The young mother who lacks the support of her spouse, who feels estranged from her family, may not welcome the baby and not want to feel attached to this child lest it disappoint her as she was disappointed by people in her past. She may hate the child as she hated her heavy body and her dripping breasts. Ineptitude in nursing the baby may result and make the baby a poor sucker. On the other hand, another young mother under similar circumstances may turn to the infant, look into his eyes, and expect that the infant will satisfy needs that have been left unsatisfied by her husband or her family or her own mother. In both cases, the mother's rejection of the baby or the unrealistic expectation leads to misery for the mothers. As important as it is to allow the biophysiological processes to go on, it is just as important to give the young mother the support she needs in other areas. She needs to be taken care of in a maternal way in order to be able to take care of her child in a maternal way.

Innate Maternal Caretaking Responses

Bowlby (1951) cites five behaviors of the infant which function as innate releases of maternal caretaking responses: crying, smiling, following, clinging, and sucking. A "good enough mother" (Winnicott) responds to the baby's behavior with innate maternal caretaking responses. If the mother is unable to respond, both she and the baby are in trouble. If she provides for the baby to be cared for by some other person than herself, the baby can develop normally. Human females, like some animals, are able to react with maternal behavior even without being mothers, or with children other than their own. Some mothers have a hard time giving up their infants, even if they are not psychologically able to take care of them. The case of Mrs. C. illustrates this point.

Mrs. C. gave birth to Johnny when she had already divorced Johnny's father. She went to work when he was two weeks old, and he was taken care of in daycare. She said he was a good baby. When he was one and a half years old she had another child from another man, who used and pushed drugs and who beat her up. Johnny changed into a difficult, unhappy child when he was two years old. When he was five, she left the second man, and Johnny, who had formed an attachment to him, regressed to wetting the bed. She beat him cruelly, and Children's Protective Services removed him to a foster home. The foster parents wanted to adopt him, but the mother would not release him for adoption. She was jealous of the foster mother and insisted on Johnny's visiting her every weekend—when she did not know what to do with him. Johnny missed his mother and wanted to return to her, although she did not want him. This is not unusual.

Mrs. C. was herself an unwanted child. She was removed from her mother and sisters whom she loved. She grew up unhappily in one foster home after another, but she always returned to her mother. Mrs. C.'s difficulties in becoming a good-enough mother were compounded when she gave birth to Johnny. She was all alone and afraid of the pain, of the responsibility of having a child, and of what the child of the hated man would be like. She dealt with Johnny the same way as her mother had dealt with her. She knew no other way. She was apparently better able to be a mother to her two younger children whom she kept with her. One could see that, too, as a repetition of what her mother had done when she had sent her away and had kept her younger sisters. Harlow et al.'s experiments with rhesus monkeys (1966) show that females who were totally inadequate mothers with their first infants became more adequate mothers with their second offspring, suggesting the possibility of biological innate motivations in these mothers too. The behavior that concerns us is the tie the mother had to this child she could not love and would not allow to leave her. She was tied to him as she had been tied to her own mother, whom she could not relinquish. Her behavior resembles that of a toddler who follows the mother around even if the mother pushes the child away. Bowlby (1951) enumerates following behavior as one of the releasers of maternal caretaking responses, and Mahler (1963) discusses it in her work on separation-individuation. Lorenz (1952) describes following as a sign of imprinting. It seems that identification alone does not account for this unhappy, unsatisfactory ambivalent behavior in Mrs. C. She is developmentally fixated in the phase of the toddler who has to return to his mother. Following is an innate behavior of the baby which this mother has not outgrown. She uses it in reverse with her child.

There are young mothers who get angry when their babies do not nurse well, do not look at them, do not smile, do not play with them, do not cuddle, and cannot be consoled by them. The mother thinks the baby does not love her and feels rejected. She in turn then rejects the baby. These mothers expect something from their babies which they need for themselves but which the infants are unable to give. They want to be loved by their baby. She, the mother, wants to be the receiving infant. Mrs. C. wanted Johnny to love her and her alone, even if she left him, like the toddler who wants to be received with open arms by the mother, even if he runs away. This, I think, is the dilemma of this mother and all the other ones who see in their babies their own rejecting and rejected mothers.

The Needs of Mothers

The need of the mother for the baby matches the need of the child
for the mother. Normally, both diminish as the child grows older.
Ideally they should diminish at the same rate. That is more often not
the case and results in tensions between mother and child. In the case
of abortion or miscarriage, it is most convincing that a biophysiological process is interrupted while the psychological process is still
continuing. Also, when the child is born full term there is a certain
lag between the physiological and psychological processes in the
mother, as we have discussed in regard to postpartum depressions.
From then on, the biophysiological process in the mother changes
gradually into one of mutuality as manifested in the nursing-lactation
relationship. The symbiotic relationship becomes less physiologic and
gradually fades out; the tie becomes increasingly a psychological one,
with the ensuing development toward independence. However, this
easily becomes a struggle between mother and child, one wanting
more independence or dependence from the other at differing times.
As the saying goes, the child is tied to the mother's apron strings. The
child could be tied to another woman's apron strings to their mutual
satisfaction; but it isn't apron strings, it is the mother's heart strings
to which he is tied. And when she tears herself away prematurely, she
hurts.

The separation-individuation process between mother and child
goes on in phases through adolescence. Whenever a new level of
maturity is reached, new adjustments of relationships and adaptations
to changes are necessary. Some mothers feel lonely and become depressed when the child starts going to school. Others feel relieved.
Adolescence is often a time of crisis: youngsters' attempts to make
their own choices threaten the parents, who are afraid of losing whatever control they had over their children. Their childrens' becoming
adults revives old conflicts in them: they question their own choice of
lifestyle in work, family relations, and sex partners. The more insecure
they are, the less tolerant they are to their children. They become
aware of aging. When the children leave home to go to college, to
work, or to live by themselves, the parents frequently find that they,
too, wish to change their ways. For the mothers, it may be the begin-

ning and the end of an era—the end of their responsibility for the children gives them the freedom to do what they want or what they always wanted. Often they do not know what they want and have the same conflicts and indecisions they had when they were young adults and left home. They have to do their growing up all over again.

Mothers have different needs in relation to their children. The ability of the child to separate himself successfully from the mother and to become independent depends to a large degree on the synchrony with the mother's need to separate from her child. There are mothers who love to have an infant in their arms. As soon as the child can move about on his own, they are no longer interested in this child, but long to have another baby. Often, they do have babies at one- to two-year intervals, are good mothers to them as long as they are very young, and then turn away from them. Other mothers like to have their children with them longer than the child needs to be with them. Mrs. D., for example, was an excessively attentive mother. When her little girl reached for something, Mrs. D. got her whatever she wanted. She carried her all the time and did not let her crawl. Consequently, the little girl was late in walking compared to other children. Other mothers feed their children longer than they want to be fed, wipe their behinds when they would like to do it themselves, dress them, and choose their friends and careers for them. Eventually the children, adapting to their mothers, become as attached as the mothers apparently want, refuse to separate from them—and then the mothers feel imprisoned and enslaved.

Sociological Changes and Mother-Child Relations

The mothers I have discussed in their roles as women and mothers are not only individuals with a unique history and development but are also typical in their reactions to a changing culture.

As the man-created culture changes, man has to adapt to it. Old adaptations become obsolete and new ones have to be developed. In these transitional stages, biosocial functions are disturbed, in addition to the disturbances of individuals through developmental and environmental crises. The culture in which we live and of which we are part is our ecosphere.

The cultural changes since the nineteenth century—industrialization, mechanization, transportation, communication—have demanded tremendous adaptations. Even the nuclear family, the building block of nearly all human societies, has undergone changes. The childrearing practices and mother-child relations are changing. Mother's prolonged caretaking is being increasingly transferred to mother substitutes; fathers are participating more than before. These changes affect the child's forms of socialization, his object relations, and, in Wilson's (1975) words, his development of reciprocal altruism. The changes also disturb the woman's functioning in her maternal role, which represents the other side of this reciprocal altruism.

In his monumental book *Sociobiology,* Edward Wilson (1975) discusses social evolution, which has achieved its pinnacle in man. "Man," he says, has not reduced his selfishness, but rather has acquired the intelligence "to consult the past and to plan the future. Human beings establish long-remembered contracts and profitably engage in acts of reciprocal altruism that can be spaced over long periods of time, indeed over generations" (p. 380). Reciprocal altruism is a part of object relations. It is developed through prolonged maternal care, which socializes the child. Wilson quotes Dobzhansky (1963), who says, "Culture is not inherited through genes, it is acquired by learning from other human beings—in a sense, human genes have surrendered their primacy in human evolution to an entirely new, nonbiological or superorganic agent, culture. However, it should not be forgotten that this agent is entirely dependent on the human genotype" (Wilson, p. 550). Through prolonged caretaking, man transmits culture to the child; the mother fulfills this task more than the father who, in our society, takes care of the child only to a limited degree, although the limits are now being extended. Maslow (1954, 1972) postulated that human beings respond to a hierarchy of needs and that the lower levels—i.e., hunger and sleep—must be satisfied before much attention is devoted to the higher ones. Brecht expressed this in the *Threepenny Opera*: "Erst kommt das Fressen und dann kommt die Moral." (First comes the feed and afterward the morals.) But again the caretaking person—mostly the mother, who satisfies the child's vital needs—makes it possible for him to devote his attention to higher needs. Maternal care is the carrier of reciprocal altruism and culture. It is represented in the mother's psyche or in her genes as a need to fulfill this task.

If, however, altered childrearing practices brought about by cultural changes result in a reduction of object relations and reciprocal altruism, an increase in aggression, which is held in check by object relations, will follow. This sounds ominous for the future of mankind; predicting individual fates is, however, still most uncertain, and predicting the development of cultures is even less certain. It is possible that our genes may be working in the direction of preserving and continuing the human species, and it may turn out that this trend in our culture may be temporary and will shift to another direction. The development of the Kibbutz society may be an example of this kind (Buxbaum, 1970). After the infants had been removed from the mothers to the babyhouse for a number of years, the mothers demanded that they be allowed to keep their children with them. Actually, the mothers, who themselves had grown up in the babyhouse, were the ones who decided that they wanted to take care of their babies. It seems that the maternal instinct of these women demanded to be satisfied and reversed the trend. They again became caretaking mothers and transmitters of the essential ingredients for sociocultural behavior.

We have returned to Winnicott and his words: "There is no baby—there is only a baby and a mother." And the baby becomes the carrier of culture and social behavior when he becomes a parent.

CHAPTER 6

Paternal Identity: The Equation of Fatherhood and Manhood

JOHN MUNDER ROSS

Fatherhood and Psychosexuality

Seventy-five years ago, in his "Three Essays on the Theory of Sexuality" (1905), Freud introduced his theory of genital primacy (see also Freud, 1923b) when he detailed the progression and penultimate objectives of infantile sexuality, with its changing libidinal zones and aims. Initially linked to the survival of the self and less tangible narcissistic necessities, slowly becoming invested in others for their own sake, an individual's quest for pleasure eventually became focused on his/her genitals and on intercourse with a person of the opposite sex. Ultimately, Freud added, sex serves and ensures the reproduction of the species.

Implicit, then, in Freud's concept of genitality and its childhood *Anlagen* is a view of a simultaneously evolving "generativity" (Erikson, 1963; J. M. Ross, 1975). The adult individual's potential biological and social parenthood is also foretold in the erotic and sensual activities and sexual identifications of the growing child, destined, as he or she is, to become not only an adult individual but, further, the vehicle of his or her species' "germ plasm" (see Freud, 1914). For the grown man—as much as for the woman—parenthood is both the outcome of his sexual history and a testimony to his masculinity.

73

Actual paternity is an elusive matter, of course, as the proverbs have it (see also Freud, 1909b), as hard to grasp hold of with certainty as is the psychological state of fatherhood itself. Perhaps it is this elusiveness and complexity that have led analysts largely to ignore the matter of a man's fatherhood. But the psychoanalytic investigator should not in fact be deterred from attempting to adumbrate the complex psychosexual currents that enter into a man's paternal identity as well as the contributions a father makes to the psychosexual and psychosocial growth of his children. Paternity and psychosexuality are red threads, intimately interwoven with each other.

An Overview

A man does not come to fatherhood in a vacuum. His paternal identity, expressed in fathering his children, is embedded in a life-historical, intrapsychic, and interpersonal context. Only gradually has the analytic community come to appreciate the complexity, seeds, and consequences of psychological fatherhood (J. M. Ross, 1975, 1977).

Fathers have been sons. They have a stock of experiences with their fathers and mothers from which to draw in synthesizing their own representation of parenthood. In childhood are discovered the prestages of paternity, the successive parental identifications that accrue to the self-representation, preparing the way for the capacity for the active nurturance and generativity of the adult man.

Biological fatherhood and the ongoing responsibilities of child care often precipitate an age-specific crisis. Confronted by a new significant object and new role, a father endeavors to integrate the images of the child and of himself as parent by way of both *assimilation* and *accommodation*. He identifies in part with the baby's infantile needs and modes of expression, experiencing and enacting these for himself; and he translates and interprets these events according to the existing configurations, either current or outmoded, of his representational world, fitting them to fantasies and memories of his own parents and of himself as a child. But in the end, the novelty and immediacy of fatherhood engender a "state of dynamic disequilibrium" which cannot be mastered by assimilation alone, referred to the extant past. An *accommodation* to the actual experience is demanded, an active au-toplastic adjustment, which resonates through and reshapes the man's representational world, altering images of the self and parents, and the relations among them. The adult developmental crisis provoked by the birth and presence of children needs, then, to be elucidated from the vantage point of an object-relations theory and further in-formed by the guiding principles set forth in what could be called the "genetic structuralism" elaborated by Piaget and others. (For notions about the adult developmental phase, see Kestenberg, 1975; Benedek, 1959, 1970a, b; and Erikson, 1963, 1964. For definitions of genetic structuralism, see J. M. Ross, 1977; Piaget, 1970; Klein, 1975; and Kernberg, 1977.)

A new father will influence and in turn be affected by the devel-opment of his child. A unique individual with particular capacities, needs, modes of apprehension and expression—a growing child will nonetheless pass through typical developmental phases. A father will attune to these by seeking an empathic foundation in his own history. As he finds many of his childhood struggles revivified and vicariously re-resolved, he will in turn help determine the further course of his child's psychological growth. Within the *dyad* of father and child there transpire mostly implicit communications which spring from the deep-est and most basic motives of each participant. These require delicate yet profound mutual adjustments that ideally answer at once the needs of both child and man. Under less than optimal conditions, both father and child can make the best of what they have and what is offered—a testimony to human resiliency.

The context in which this dyad is embedded cannot be over-looked—the elaborate network of familial relations among father, mother, and other siblings as individuals, pairs, triads, and so forth. All are further anchored in a culture replete with the myths, proscrip-tions, and workaday routines that order a man's life.

Paternal Identity: A Coming-to-Terms

"Identity," identity of any kind, is one of those "star words" (Pruyser, 1975)—"splitting" is another—which capture a great deal, yet elude specificity and definition and thus invite controversy. Precise-minded analysts argue for a more restricted use of only such delimited concepts as self or self-representation. I do not share this view, believing the sense of identity to be a most valuable and encompassing concept, one at the interface of phenomenological experience and theoretical reflection. I nevertheless agree that such terms must be more explicitly defined.

Phenomenologically speaking, identity may be viewed as an individual's sense of wholeness, sameness, and continuity. In psychosocial language, this is an internal consistency over time, which, in turn, is mirrored, affirmed, facilitated by the demands and opportunities afforded by other people, as well as by the roles, cultural traditions, and institutions that constitute the surrounding social environment. In more developmental and genetic terms, identity unfolds as an "evolving configuration . . . established by syntheses and resyntheses throughout childhood . . . gradually integrating constitutional givens, idiosyncratic libidinal needs, favored capacities, significant identifications, effective defenses, successful sublimations and consistent roles" (Erikson, 1959, p. 116). Compared with character—personal style observed from without (Moore and Fine, 1968)—identity may be articulated as an individual's own sense of the themes and modalities that shape and insure his personal integrity.

Finally, an object-relations perspective might have it that a sense of identity is the reciprocal of object relations proper. Evolving in interdependence with each other, both object relations and identity describe the various configurations of and relations between self- and object representations, with the accent falling in the one instance on the object and in the other on the self. Thus, an identity, in contrast to a role, is fundamentally a private experience, an experience of self in relation to others, one with conscious and unconscious dimensions. But as with object relations, it is realized in the interpersonal and societal realm, others recognizing one for who one is. By "relations" are meant the affects, cognitions, instinctual wishes, attitudes, guiding principles, and felt obligations that link self and others (Kernberg, 1977; Stolorow and Atwood, in press).

The various aspects of identity organize one another. Core gender identity, for instance, Stoller's concept (1968b), which is consolidated prior to the phallic phase, refers to an individual's cognitive and emotional conviction of being male or female in relation to members of the same and opposite sexes. Sexual identity is at once a broader and a more delimited concept, evolving through the course of the life cycle and pertaining to an individual's sense of the particular kind of man or woman he or she is, especially in the sexual arena. It is a sense that derives not only from the certainty of one's given gender but also from transformations of pre-emptive, if most often unconscious, *ambi*sexual and indeed cross-sexual identifications and desires. Generational identity is another pertinent dimension of identity as a whole, describing an individual's appreciation of the place of his life cycle within the generational flow, as it were, or, more concretely, of his or her felt status and attributes as a child, a parent, a grandchild, and so forth.

Generational identity is not quite equivalent to parental or paternal identity, the subject at hand. Parental identity pertains to one's fantasies, ambitions, and actual achievements in the imagined or real role of a generator and nurturer of products, human and otherwise. Paternal identity in particular represents the dovetailing and synthesis of parental, sexual, and male gender identity. For a man, it describes his sense of self as a *masculine procreator, producer, caretaker—a personal equation of parenthood and manhood with fatherhood.*

The Developmental Line Recapitulated

While such an identity can only be actualized with genital maturity and adult responsibility, and then only with luck, its roots, in the form of various would-be identifications and aspirations, unfold early in childhood. Indeed, paternal identity may be seen to evolve along a line of development interwoven with the progressions of selfhood and of sexual identity. But before summarizing this developmental line (A. Freud, 1965), which I have drawn in greater detail elsewhere (J. M. Ross, 1977), I must underline certain caveats.

What I describe here is an ideal progression for an "ideal type" of boy, in Weber's sense (1947), a construct serving heuristic purposes without any direct manifestation in reality. "The boy" depicted is not a norm, not even a reality. Other, real-life boys may pass through the following stages with a different timetable, skipping some sequences, altering or even reversing others. Perhaps most important, in isolating a series of individual steps such as these, one inevitably ignores the impact on a child of his actual caretakers, to whom he must adapt, and does a disservice to the reciprocity between parents and child. Overgeneralized, the "average expectable environment" (Hartmann, 1939) serving as background here may ultimately amount to no environment at all. Yet, these drawbacks notwithstanding, the epigenetic scheme charted below does have a basis in the data of projective and observational research as well as in clinical practice, all of which may in turn be further illumined by reference to it.

Throughout life, procreative and nurturing fantasies will bespeak progressive and active strivings along with regressive, passive longings. Most specifically, the wish to possess a baby will betray both desires to bear or rear a child in the manner of a powerful parent and urges to be an infant, succored and discharged of responsibility. This essay will concentrate primarily on the progressive threads that run through would-be generativity on the part of male children and adolescents and young adults.

Active efforts at self-parenting begin at the beginning. The specific smiling response that ushers the infant out of the relative autism of the first weeks and into symbiotic "dual unity" may be seen to signal a first effort, groping and instinctively patterned to be sure, to "extract maternal supplies" (Spitz, 1965; Mahler et al., 1975). Subsequently, transitional phenomena emerging at the close of symbiosis and easing a child's unfolding individuation from the mother represent prototypical gestures on the toddler's part at serving as a parent to himself. Comforted by his security blanket at the same time as he cradles and comforts it, enacting the roles of mother and child at once, perpetuating an illusion of abiding union with mother while taking upon himself her soothing functions—a little child anticipates unmistakable fantasies of parenthood (Winnicott, 1953; Tolpin, 1971).

Such fantasies require a number of developmental advances, of course. The birth of representational thinking, a delineation of body boundaries, some sense of gender and anatomical differences, relative object constancy, the ascendancy of anal urges in the broad sense of impulses to produce from within the mysterious inner body something live and valuable—all these are required for a child to entertain an image of himself as producing or rearing a baby of his own. It is between roughly eighteen months, the era of anality and of the rapprochement crisis, and two and a half to three years, when inner genital sensations (Kestenberg, 1968, 1975) rise to the fore and object constancy becomes more secure, that such fantasies will be most in evidence. A little boy (or girl) this age will reveal in his mute activities and doll play more than in words and ideas, which are still so primitive, his "cloacal birth wishes" (Freud, 1905, 1908, 1909b), desires that derive from his identification with what Van der Leeuw (1958) called "the active producing mother."

Gradually, as concerns with different sexual attributes intensify and the semantic ability to articulate these develops, a little boy may come to entertain hermaphroditic ambitions, desires to possess in addition to his penis his mother's powerful breasts and her mysterious if not quite knowable womb. Boys this age may wish to give birth, insisting on their ability to do so. At least, they may aspire to nurse babies in the manner of mothers. In fact, they can be quite unshakable in their conviction that they, too, have "special creases that people come out of," as one of the children in my early research put it, or, in the words of another, a woman's "big pimples" (J. M. Ross, 1974).

In time, a boy learns that being one sex precludes possessing the attributes of the other (Kohlberg, 1967). He witnesses in his father his own manly fate and, with it, the impossibility of willing or choosing a gender identity. He then becomes steadier in the recognition of his masculinity and ever more reluctant to relinquish it. Unable to be a mommy, a boy comes to cherish his penis instead, and as phallic aims and anxieties gain sway, he becomes an aggressive little chauvinist.

But fecundity still eludes him, proud as he is of his burgeoning virility. Only a further sense of himself as a man, and of the future, can fill the void left by a three-year-old boy's unrequited and only half-abandoned maternalism. It is the oedipal drama that intimates the solution to this conflict, making for a crisis in both a boy's sexual and his parental identity. The power of a boy's phallic and sadistic fantasies is such that even a merely absent father offers himself in the guise of an aggressor, distorting his intuitions into the primal scene and providing models of men as alternatively violent and dangerous or weak and insubstantial. But if the father presents himself as a libidinal provider for mother, son, and family, then his son can begin to grasp the man's generous, loving, pleasurable, and, above all, creative role in intercourse. With this, he need not relegate tenderness, care, affection, or productivity to the realm of mothers alone. With such a "good father" and a mother who affirms him, a son may resolve the conflicts between his burgeoning but still brittle masculinity and his maternal strivings by identifying with the father as parent—as a procreator endowed with a concrete and metaphorical "giving penis." Otherwise he may erect a stereotypical he-mannish identity or sink back into a protective identification with mother that comes increasingly to portend effeminacy, homosexuality, and, ironically enough, perhaps the effective sterility of an exclusive, obligatory perversion or inversion.

Such advances have been facilitated by emerging concrete operational thinking. More sexual knowledge has been assimilated, enabling a boy of five or six to glimpse the chain of events linking phallic impulses, intercourse, reproduction, birth, and nurturing. But in the absence of ejaculatory capacity, these are not tied to any physical reality and hence are open to fantastic elaboration and distortion, serving a variety of pregenital wishful and defensive ends.

A boy overcomes his identification with mother (qua mother) only to then find himself unable to possess her as a man and hence to father a child. By virtue of his status as a child, a boy remains physically inadequate and dependent upon the family status quo, despite his protests and ambitions to the contrary. Frustrated in his quest for generational equality, many latency boys embark on an age-specific regression in the service of ego development in other realms. Thus, their creative play will betray not only phallic and intrusive but also "ambisexual" themes and modalities (Erikson, 1963). These children may even give implicit voice to "parthogenetic" promptings by somaticizing these in the physical complaints typical of this age or else by sublimating their urges to enact the roles of mother, father, and child. Ideally, school children become concerned with discovering the facts of life, birth, growth, and death. Children this age, boys and girls, occupy themselves with a variety of endeavors centering on life, its creation and care: raising and feeding animals, caring for younger children, and so on.

Once more the father's presence, this time in the concrete role of a mentor who helps his son become more competent, will serve to assuage residual anxieties over the maternal tendencies underlying activities such as these. In latency, a renewed companionship with the father, his erstwhile oedipal rival, helps a boy feel manly and tender at once. It also militates, in the care-giving model offered by the man, against any rigid division in his mind between work achievement and family involvement and, hence, between the narcissistic and object-related aspects of productivity. In some respects, this reunion parallels on a less dramatic scale the boy's earlier return to mother during the rapprochement subphase.

With prepuberty the pseudodetachment of latency falters, revealing conflicts and ambisexual currents hitherto submerged. As Blos (1962) has underlined, the early adolescent relives the crisis of his early years—the rapprochement struggles that climax the separation-individuation process, the feminine identifications and homosexual object choices that precede the oedipal period, the Oedipus complex itself. Thus beleaguered from within, an adolescent may seek refuge in group stereotypy and conformism, shunning all that does not jibe with a gender identity once more in doubt.

At the same time, however, he discovers altogether new developments in himself: the ejaculatory capacity first manifest perhaps in wet dreams and later in masturbatory activity and, with this, a variety of fantasies about the content and import of the ejaculate; the maturation of his body and its secondary sex characteristics; the perfection of hypotheticodeductive thinking; increasing autonomy and intimacy outside the home. All lend new substance to his gender identity and deepen sexual identity with the foretastes, as it were, of genital love. And these advances are accompanied by the imminence of psychosocial independence. But as far as parental identity is concerned, adolescence indeed constitutes a "moratorium" when paternity, unwanted and irresponsible, is to be avoided. That is, biological parenthood must be delayed until the boy (or girl) can cement his sexuality and his selfhood, ready himself for choices in work and love, and become a man.

(This is not to dismiss the epidemiological problem of teenage parenthood, one pertaining to boys as well as girls. Indeed, fears of sterility may emerge as heirs to an earlier castration anxiety compounded now by concerns about the vitality of the ejaculate and a more general preoccupation with the adolescent's mortality.)

According to Erikson, there is one further way station en route to the generativity—in procreation and work productivity—that is the hallmark of maturity, of generational authority. Again recapitulating his early development, a young man must strive to sustain a capacity for intimacy with a woman, at least if he is to be an effective father. Such intimacy presents a number of paradoxes. Kernberg has noted (1977) that sexual union entails a temporary traversing of boundaries, requiring both flexibility in identification and firmness in essential selfhood. Empathy in sex implies that one integrate cross-sexual identifications with one's actual gender identity, for only then will a male lover flow with the needs and rhythms of the woman with whom he makes love, and vice versa. An ongoing mutuality and working union further intensify a man's needs, along with the demands made of him, and can burden and threaten not only his sense of masculinity but also his independence. Even sexual passions may vie with autonomous strivings and more narcissistic promptings. The interchanges between a man and woman are such, moreover, that an assumption of both active and passive positions, of both initiative and receptivity, must be embraced and tolerated by each partner. More specifically, in intimacy a man will re-experience his own childish dependency as he is mothered by the woman he loves, as well as the maternal and paternal urges held in abeyance until now when he mothers and fathers her. Important in their own right, to be sure, intimacy and love nonetheless thus serve to prepare the way and may be seen to provide a rehearsal for a man's forthcoming parenthood. They build strength and create emotional elasticity, facilitating adult responsibility at the same time as they encourage regression in the service of empathy and insight.

At a certain point, even so seemingly complete an experience as genital love needs fruition, else it ends in stasis. The decision to have children is, ideally, a choice to participate in the generational process, a choice, furthermore, that is an embodiment and outcome of the union itself. This is not to dismiss the narcissistic satisfactions and problems imposed by procreation—the unconscious parthogenetic fantasies, the anticipation of self-extension, the sacrifices of freedom and privacy, the confrontation with the limits of one's one life cycle. I only mean to emphasize the mutual act of love in insemination. No one sex has the unilateral physical ability to make babies. Nor do children conceived in order to fulfill this fantasy on a father's part enter life with receptive, complementary, and differentiated parents. Mothers and fathers need each other, and babies need them both.

The Paternal Identity Crisis

As Therese Benedek once outlined in a critique (Panel, 1975) of her own concept of "parenthood as a developmental phase" (1959), becoming a parent is not really a discrete event but rather the culmination of a long "developmental process." Fatherhood recapitulates its own prestages.

Were I to distill an essence from the successive strivings for paternity during childhood, I would cite a truth derived by Erikson (1969) from his study of Gandhi, namely, that a "sublimated maternalism" is crucial to the "positive identity of a whole man." A fatherly identity in adulthood provides for just such a self-completion, even as actual fatherhood reactivates the various sexual ambitions, ambiguities, and anxieties that have accompanied the quest for it. Fatherhood attests to one's manhood while it allows for a transcendance of the limits inherent in a single gender identity, thereby making for what one gratified and successful father spoke of as a sense of an expansive, irreducible "security." Nonetheless, for these selfsame reasons, becoming a father shakes a man's foundations.

Fatherhood cannot be taken as a particular state tied to one moment in psychological time. I suspect this adult developmental stage divides into substages, with external reference points—for instance, the phases of a woman's pregnancy, the child's birth, and the major stages in the child's development. Such timetables and sequences are subject to a host of individual differences, which make matters various and complex. The idea of a psychological developmental phase in the absence of physiological correlates also poses difficulties. Once more, the gen-

eralizations tendered here have more heuristic value than empirical
validity.

A man's identification with his pregnant wife has received much
attention (Gurwitt, 1976; Trehowan, 1965; Boehm, 1930; Horney,
1926; and others). Authors have underscored the womb envy precipitated by the new-found power of a woman's body as well as the
man's longing to enter as a child into the symbiosis taking shape
before his eyes, a mystery from which he is excluded. Few men
consciously entertain the meanings of the spectacle. Rather, these are
revealed in concrete if symbolic form—in abdominal and other somatic complaints and in rituals like couvade—all of which express
wordlessly a man's wish to be privy to a union which is fundamentally
organic and therefore not quite subject to representation or reflection.
A father-to-be may only identify with his wife's motherhood, an age-
specific adaptation harking back to his beginnings in the "dual unity"
of mother and baby. And thus, apart from gestures at provision, and
some nesting, most first-time expectant fathers find it difficult indeed
clearly to envision themselves in the paternal role.

Boehm (1930) suggested that the expulsion of the child from the
vagina is a far more potent act than a male's erection and ejaculation.
Prepared-childbirth methods have enabled men to witness parturition
in recent years, to be awed by birth, and to achieve, as so many of
the men I have studied in clinical and research settings strove to believe, a semblance of equal power as they assist their wives in over-
coming the pains of labor. Some describe envy of a woman's productive
and nurturing powers. And some suffer castration horror. Many feel
the tension, strain, agony in their own viscera, affectively and em-
pathically initiating themselves into parenthood. Still others report a
sublime, joyous, nearly orgastic response to the birth and the later
sight of the newborn at the breast.

The new status, authority, and attendant obligations implied by
pregnancy and birth further signal the end of childhood. With this,
paternity portends the inner loss of one's own parents as parents, so
many of their functions being adopted now, willingly or not, as one's
own.

Certain men, sound and therefore flexible enough to entertain competing, seemingly incompatible, images of themselves and others, em-

brace the variety and profundity offered by their paternal role. Others, less mature, cannot withstand the contradictions and flee by retreating into childish states, by scotomatizing the child, by avoiding contact or by denying the affective impact of it all.

Becoming a father, especially if the child is a son, renews a man's confrontation with his own father in all its intrapsychic manifestations. Gurwitt (1976) has demonstrated the revivification during pregnancy of a multifacted intergenerational rivalry and of other aspects of the charged relations between fathers and their parents. These strains can become acute with the baby's actual appearance and especially with his increasing demands for handling and emotional responsiveness. A man holds in his hands a tiny being on whom converge conflictual affects and intentions, some of which are not in the infant's best interests.

With the appearance of the baby, what I would call the Laius complex is born, a transfiguration of the childhood Oedipus constellation (see also Rangell, 1970; Anthony, 1970). A man will recall through his child his erstwhile ambivalence toward his own father. Anticipating that a son, or a daughter for that matter, will be similarly moved, a man may be secretly tempted to abandon or to hurt the baby. If he is capable of loving him, he will of course recoil from his darker and more terrible promptings. Perhaps he will perform a reversal and foresee Oedipus' tragic fate as a baby and old man— abandonment—visited upon himself. His horror of such exile may then be betrayed in feelings of being somehow "left out," of being but a vehicle for child support, in images of himself as unneeded and unloved, useless and ineffectual. And a man fears his child *as a child*. Remembering his secret and unwanted ambitions and seeing them realized in his biological fatherhood, a father not only suffers oedipal guilt but, further, glimpses the ironies implicit in the generational cycle. His child is at once his crowning achievement, his legacy, and the harbinger of his mortality.

The struggle to resolve the conflicts rife within him moves a new father to discover another unsettling truth about his origins. Making his way through a maze of competing and incompatible paternal representations, looking into himself, he happens upon the reality of his father as a man, a man who until now he may have idealized, dismissed, or devalued, but in all events has pretty much relegated to his paternal function and little else. With fatherhood, primal fathers—good and bad, oedipal and otherwise—fall away to expose simply men with all their various frailties and virtues.

Exacerbated by this inner loss, a nagging sense of his father's relative absence from his childhood and youth may then supplant the childish complaints and veneration to which the man has hitherto been subjected. Pondering what and how much he himself will do for this child at the same time that he has been bereft of his own inner father, negatively or positively aggrandized, a man may find himself as if suddenly orphaned. He may cast about urgently for memories and fantasies about fathering from which to synthesize a paternal ideal for himself, a partial self-image with which to replace his representation of an all-powerful "good father." He needs such a figure with whom to identify and ally as a guiding force if he is to offset the maternal identifications revived in him, the regressive pulls exerted by the child, and the hostilities excited by the child, which may be associated with images of the "bad father." Oedipal and negative oedipal strivings, now potentially reciprocated, also require modulation. And above all, the child himself appeals to the sustenance and direction provided by a "good father" who has been internalized and transmuted as an aspect of a man's own identity.

Bound up with these struggles, which recapitulate the preoedipal relationship of mother and son and the later competition with the father, are many narcissistic problems. As Freud (1914) and later analysts suggested, children can serve as would-be embodiments of idealized selves or simply as extensions of the self. Moreover, defenses may be mobilized to subdue strivings in this vein. Projectively identified with sons and daughters, many men remember parental intrusions into their life choices, those moments at which their feelings and wishes were misapprehended and overridden because they were not distinguished from those of the parents' inner world. In the face of these recollections, many fathers may conscientiously retreat from articulating any values or expectations for the child (failing to recognize that their wishes and goals will be embraced or not by a child who becomes ever more his or her own person). Many parents seek to disavow the narcissistic pleasures proferred by children, so much so that at times they may overcompensate and deprive their families of ethical guidelines and of spontaneity in an enjoyment of the children's beauty and accomplishments. The irony is that it is the child's self-esteem which is apt to suffer most.

This is not to say that children do not require attention, interest, and, hence, a certain disinvestment in the self. And they present, as intimated earlier, the specter of one's own mortal limits. Under such inevitable circumstances, can a man shift his focus from himself to a concern for the future of another person? Can he give love in the face of the fact that this will never be completely repaid by the child, who by nature is egocentric and consumes generosity (and who later forgets what he once took in)? Only the man who is more or less secure in his individuality, integrity, and worth, and who has not withdrawn into an illusory and self-protective grandiosity—only he will be able to love parentally without either martyring himself to the child or reconstituting in his offspring a reflection of the man's own "grandiose self" (Kohut, 1971).

These, then, figure as some of the leitmotifs from the past revivified by fatherhood. During the course of the child's growth, other issues will come to the fore: "oral" hunger and the incorporative prototypes of both love and destruction—the "Kronos" motif; the ability or not to say "no"; reactions to the child's anality, active from the start in the father's need to adjust to the infant's and toddler's incontinence and disruption of routine schedules; what Nathaniel Ross discovered to be "rivalry with the product" (1960); masturbatory conflicts; tolerance for incestuous and homosexual inclinations and a more general capacity for sensuality without sexual seduction; modulation of aggression—most specifically, the ability to refrain from retaliation (so often moralized) yet to discipline and limit the child; the acceptance of responsibility without omnipotent guilt; and so on. In all instances, the assimilation of the good father as an aspect of the self-representation provides the crucial counterpoint, facilitating an optimal detachment (a decentering) without emotional disengagement.

This recourse to the "good father" of childhood actuality and fantasy makes for a viable paternal identity, which allows a father to contend with the age-specific demands besetting his parenthood. He must accept and, ideally, take pleasure in a radically changed relationship with his wife. He must meet her needs and his own in addition to the child's. At the same time, work and financial security, so often serving the purposes of resistance, are pressing realities; he must provide. As a mentor and model, he must know his limits without interjecting the kind of unwanted confession of impotence tht robs children of fodder for self-invigorating and sustaining idealizations. He must modulate his affects and impulses, without rigidifying restraint.

A father's tasks are many and hard and often paradoxical. Only with a solid foundation will he be free to appreciate the real object that is his son or daughter and, as a "good enough" father, to care for the child. Only then can he enjoy fully the deep parental love that is now his, the absolute pleasures afforded by children—pleasures which cannot in the end be reduced to anything but themselves.

Attunement to the Child

In command of himself, a father can then attune to his child's evolving needs and modes of communication. These are both predictable, in the sense of the unfolding perceptual and object-related capabilities schematized by Spitz (1965), and variable, dependent on the child's constitutional activity level, temperament, and particular inherent proclivities, which lend different meanings to apparently similar significant encounters (Escalona, 1963; Brazelton, 1969). Most important, from the early months babies seem to respond and behave differently with fathers from the ways in which they react to mothers, whatever the representations of these interactions may be (see Lamb, 1975; Brazelton et al., 1976; Abelin, 1971, 1975; Panel, 1978). An affective interchange between father and child is established fairly early on, paralleling and counterpointing the child's communication with mother. Typically, of course, the interchanges within the maternal orbit are more intense and more crucial. Nonetheless, the "paternal dialogue" exists as well and can also become "derailed," in Spitz's words, in fact all the more easily, since a father and child usually have less time to know each other.

That a father and child know each other differently is self-evident. Before six months, in Spitz's (1965) view, or even 25 months, according to Mahler et al. (1975), babies and toddlers lack object constancy (the definitions differ). Thereafter, even with relative object constancy in Mahler's sense, perceptions of and attitudes toward parents change with the volatile winds of fantasy, desire, and fear. A more or less well-adapted father, in contrast, pretty much knows his child for who he or she is.

And yet, up to a point, a father will mirror the wants of his children as well as their peculiar modes of expression and representation. During the first months, for instance, he too must bond to some extent with the child by sharing the baby's successively coenesthetic and proprioceptive, tactile, and only gradually visual object experiences. That is, he must be with and close to his infant if he is to remain affectively impressed with the child's concrete presence, to keep his "feel" for the baby. Thus, it makes sense that even men who later cement profound and tender relationships with an older child should recall the formlessness and physical functions of that child as an infant—forever, it seemed to them, merely crying, eating, and defecating.

Later, when the child begins to differentiate, to single the father out, then to imitate his sounds, to reach, crawl, walk, and finally run toward him, the image and connection become more durable. Indeed, there may be an encapsulated moment affirming paternal competence, akin to that experienced by mothers, perhaps "released," as it were, by the word "Daddy." In any event, the object relationship deepens with a child's greater mobility, increasingly complex and intelligible communications, the recourse made to the father during rapprochement, and those delicious identifications, adventures, and romances that serve to consolidate gender identity between the ages of two and three, ushering in the oedipal era.

As the child develops, the father becomes more of a character in his fantasy life as well as a caretaker in reality. In a sense, a man must play out both roles at once, allowing ambitious desires without requiting them, facilitating psychosocial progress without abetting a precocity that is so frightening that it disrupts internalization and forestalls future growth. In Erikson's (1963) words, father, like mother, helps a child dream the imaginable and expect the possible.

The very fact of the father's receptivity to the child's expressive modalities is thus essential. At the same time, a child is alerted to a host of cues, many of these nonverbal, which express a father's understanding and expectations of him (I would refer here to Kestenberg's pioneer work on movement exchanges between parent and child [1975]); postures, shapes, and rhythmic patterns; unique ways of holding, comforting, or containing the child; characteristic roughhousing and other play; mirroring of the child's movements and bodily state or acts or gestures that are in opposition to these. Words, of course, are significant, as are the implicit paternal fantasies betrayed in telltale games and make-believe. That many a father's messages are emitted emotionally and preconsciously suggests that his "doing the right thing" must emanate from the wellsprings of a deeply paternal sense of himself. Lip service and role-playing only confront a child with real-life contradictions of the kind that encourage and abet splits in self- and object representations.

Developmental Contributions

The father's specific contributions to a son's or daughter's development have tended to be obscured by two successive traditions in analytic thought. First, Freud's (1912a, 1921, 1930) emphasis on the father of the primal horde and the Oedipus complex tended to underplay a man's loving, nurturing, and facilitative impact on children, especially his role as a figure for identification. Subsequently, Spitz's (1965), Jacobson's (1964), and Mahler's (Mahler et al., 1975) exploration of the maternal union tended to relegate the father to a mere ancillary role, at least during the first stages of the epigenesis of identity upon which they concentrated. Here and there, however, these theorists and their colleagues and collaborators began to speak more and more of the vital necessity of good fathering, notably in helping a child disengage from and disidentify with the mother (Loewald, 1951; Greenacre, 1966). Implicitly responding to the current movement for a reorganization and redistribution of sex roles and domestic duties, subsequent authors have watered these seeds, as it were, to produce an efflorescence of articles and books on the importance of the father in his children's emotional development (Abelin, 1975; Biller, 1974; Lamb, 1975; J. M. Ross, in press).

Active, empathic fathering helps a boy or girl to create an integrated identity and object-relatedness; to secure an enjoyment of activity and of the world at large; to build a firm yet rich sexual identity; to become competent in learning and industry; and, of course, to be capable of romantic and parental love. While all these virtues and strengths are challenged repeatedly, they nonetheless come to the fore at critical developmental junctures.

As Greenacre (1966), Loewald (1951), and Abelin (1971) have indicated, the father first figures prominently in the child's experience during differentiation from the mother, beginning at roughly six months. He then becomes a special and exciting figure with the practicing subphase and the rapid spurt in muscular activity which accompanies this, when he comes to stand for "nonmother" space, enhancing a child's "love affair with the world" (Greenacre, 1957).

During a child's problematic rapprochement with the mother, which marks the death throes of the illusion of omnipotent union with her and solidifies object constancy, a father serves many essential functions. He provides an alternative to mother, a target both for ideal love and, later, for rageful defiance as a senior toddler struggles by splitting his increasingly internal objects to come to terms with his inevitable ambivalence toward single whole objects in reality (see Ross and Dunn, in press). Most important, a father now offers to a child an image of another integral object in relation to but not fused with the mother. A toddler can gradually liken himself to this distinct object, whose presence thereby lends its support and constancy to a child's nascent, tenuous, and labile representation of self.

With individuation come the beginnings of triangulation (Panel, 1978). A child becomes cognizant of two parents in addition to himself and of his own increasingly differentiated affects and desires with regard to each of them. The stage is set for the consolidation of gender identity and the assumption of an even more dynamic sexual identity between two and three years (Stoller, 1975a).

During this period a father's presence complements the mother's, crystallizing a child's notions about the male gender and sex differences. Furthermore, a father must appreciate his son's and daughter's

burgeoning efforts to express their sexual identity in relation to him
by being genuinely receptive and admiring in ways that permit them
to enjoy and esteem their own sex, their bodies, and the very selfhood
with which these are associated. For example, at this point and during
her oedipal phase proper, a father may seem indifferent to a daughter's
wooing of him or may make apparent promises of exclusivity, only
to disappoint her later. Many little girls attribute such indifference to
their own deficiencies, suffering a mortification which becomes associated with their femininity and their genitals. Alternatively, a father
may overstimulate a daughter, cast her as a coquette, or move her to
renounce her assertiveness for a caricatured girlishness. Similarly,
fathers may either thwart or abet their sons' increasingly phallic
aggressions. They may also invite or else disparage an object love and
identificatory longing that take on quasi-homosexual overtones (Socarides, 1968b).

In all events, a father must be in possession of his own wishes and
uncertainties if he is to resonate with, as well as help contain, a son's
or daughter's intense yet delicate instinctual stirrings. His relationship
with the mother and her view of him, especially during the oedipal
era, are also vital in counteracting, for instance, the sadistic imagery
surrounding a man's sexual role, fantasies of the kind to which both
boys and girls fall prey and from which they may retreat, substituting
various condensations of pregenital and phallic aims.

During middle childhood the father serves as a mentor to a boy,
of course, but to a girl as well. Indeed, a girl's relationship with the
father is now fraught with pitfalls. She lingers longer in her oedipal
position than a boy does, an attachment to the father continuing to
invite her out of her symbiotic entanglement, whereas a boy's desires
to possess his mother erotically also connote re-engulfment by her. If
a father seduces, rejects, or suppresses a daughter, in all cases somehow betraying her trust, she may well make restitution and reparation
in the sort of penis envy and excessive tomboyishness that now represent secondary defensive reactions to an unacknowledged and frustrated womanhood (as Horney [1926] so rightly stressed). Or she may
abjure independence and success, fearing that these will alienate men.

In order to put symbiotic and incestuous yearnings to rest, adolescent sons and daughters typically repudiate their parents. Both par-

ents will require a basic security in their adult stature if they are to withstand the onslaught of reproach and indifference leveled at them without "taking it personally." It is vital during this protracted transition between childhood and adult authority that the generations remain in communication while each takes a firm stand in declaring its differences. It is vital, that is, if sons or daughters growing toward maturity are to discover their generational continuity as well as their historically innovative potential—collective and individual. The father or mother who gives in or plays the fellow-traveler to a teenager's revolution is a hanger-on, an intruder who deprives the child of a foil, of necessary self-defining opposition, of paradigms for independence of mind and devotion to principle. Attempting to hold the reins is more fettering, of course, but it further constitutes a breach of empathy and an abrogation of those inner freedoms fought for in external battles.

These, then, are but a sampling of the functions served by a father as both a parent and a man during a son's or daughter's development. He is also simply an individual, another person in a growing person's contacts with people—a person to be loved, admired, emulated, learned from, hated at times, disparaged, and simply recollected, a person whose closeness to the developing child in the most formative years makes him of unique importance. My emphasis here has not been on the infinite variety of father-child pairs but only on the significance of the father's paternal identity as felt by him and responded to by the child, an inner consistency that informs and sustains the father's paternal part in his child's development.

A Note on Context

The father does not exist in a vacuum; nor are his actions determined by him exclusively. Rather, he fits one way or another into a role which is partly shaped by a variety of factors outside his absolute influence. A word or two on the impact and the inputs of the family as a whole and of the surrounding cultural context may therefore be in order.

Earlier, I indicated that a boy's image of his father in his sexual and procreative role and his own identification with this are very much functions of what he witnesses in the partnership of father and mother. Of course, the mother is an active participant here. In addition, she is a personal myth-maker who further conveys in word and deed distinct impressions of who the father is and what he should be, as well as a potent family force who does much to determine the amount, quality, and circumstances of a man's parental interaction with the children. Just as objects cannot be fully defined without reference to the self, so, too, they cannot be apprehended independently of one another; mother and father reflect each other for their children.

A mother's womanly relation to men in general, the notions, stereotypes, and fears she gives utterance to, and the use she makes of her husband as a parent will confirm, negate, and/or prejudice a child's unfolding representation of the father. Some women actively disparage spouses, for example; others passively defer to their husbands; still others find mutuality in marriage. Mothers may discourage a child's involvement with a father or welcome the relief he provides. Fathers may be cast by mothers in the specific roles of playmate, authority, or disciplinarian. Children may be made to feel that they should approach worthy and loving fathers or be punished, explicitly or implicitly, for any overtures on either their own or the father's part.

Add to these contributions by the mother a father's different transactions with siblings, no two of whom have phenomenologically equivalent parents, and the various paternal impressions falling within the child's purview become exceedingly intricate. His needs to repress or deny aspects of his own self and its attributes or perhaps to split off elements of certain objects, notably the mother, and to reconstitute these in other persons (the father, for instance) along with a whole gamut of other expectable intrapsychic motives and distortions—these complicate matters still further. Once more, a child's basic vision of his father owes itself primarily to a preconscious communication—to some elemental and emotional declaration of paternity which underlies more elaborate and occasionally obfuscating superstructures.

Finally, the cultural ethos and the mechanics of social organization inform and directly control the hours a father spends with the family. Collective archetypes of masculinity and prescriptions about a father's importance obviously affect a man's attitude toward his children and his freedom to be affectionate and open with them. In our own society, for example, radical notions about androgyny, at one pole, and traditional views about a father's virilized authority, at the other, have been synthesized in the form of a new consciousness about a man's invaluable, irreplaceable role with children. Indeed, pieces like this very chapter are cases in point of this trend (see also Lamb, 1975; Biller and Meredith, 1974; Levine, 1976).

In other, simpler, societies, paternal and filial relations may be regulated by various rituals, such as rites of passage. Many of these may be seen to symbolize simultaneously affirmations of a boy's newfound adult male status, of the castration threat posed and indelibly retained as scars of circumcision suffered in its achievement, and of the collective fatherhood's claims to birth-giving power (see Nunberg, 1947; Freud, 1912a; Bettelheim, 1954). And social realities may influence fatherhood in more straightforward ways. There is the contrast, for example, between the exigencies of urban work, which typically remove a man from his home for many hours, and those rural or village livelihoods—crafts, husbandry, farming—undertaken in collaboration with the whole family, with fathers serving early on as concrete mentors and sons as essential helpmates. Even some of these patterns may be changing—modified as more and more urban—especially middle-class—men and women begin to lobby for the kind of part-time employment that permits a more equitable distribution of domestic responsibilities and satisfactions, while the men of the rural areas continue their migration to the cities.

This last point raises many important class and economic issues of the kind all too readily dismissed or simply ignored by the analytic movement. The facts of sociohistorical life do indeed conspire to shape men's destinies, in coloring and impinging on their sense of self-fulfillment and self-esteem, the opportunities they may offer to their families, their expressions of accomplishment and failure, and the ambitions held out for their offspring. And while all individuals are, within the dictates of biological and social fortune, at least partial masters of their lives, nevertheless, their lives cannot be accounted for on a purely individualistic or intrapsychic basis. At a certain point, the analytic theorist must acknowledge the elucidation offered by disciplines and kens other than his own.

Beyond the Father: A Postscript

In 1919, Franz Kafka sent his studiedly disembittered "Letter to his Father." To read it is to find, all at once, the trials and terrors, the nameless and unwarranted guilt afflicting his fictional protagonists falling into place, in the image of the arbitrary tyrannies of the writer's father.

In much the same way, neurotic and more disturbed individuals continue obliquely, almost deviously, to suffer their fathers' failures, omissions, and impositions. The guilt Kafka expresses is a veritable presence in the lives of many people, bespeaking not only the secret hatred and fantasies of murder leveled unconsciously at a father who is an overlord, real or imaginary. This guilt is also his representative, as it were, in the child's personality, an introjection of his punitive power into the self-representation. Furthermore, self-condemnation of this kind on the part of a conscience rampant in its excesses (what analysts call an archaic, sadistic superego) serves to substitute for a self-love never achieved because the foundations were wanting in love from without. Something, even a bad part-object linked to an equally fragmented self by hatred and remorse (see Kernberg, 1976) is better than nothing; the enraged and fearsome father may be, therefore, more tolerable than the insufficient and absent one, another of his protean manifestations.

Slowly, it seems, Kafka came to a realization of his terrible father's basic weakness. He recalled the man's ultimate abdication: "all one gets from you is: 'Do whatever you like . . . I've no advice to give you,' and all this with that frightful, hoarse undertone of anger and utter condemnation that only makes me tremble less today than in my childhood because the child's exclusive sense of guilt has been partly replaced by insight into your helplessness, yours and mine."

It occurs to Kafka, as it will to the analytic patient, or to the insightful man en route to his own paternity, that his father is limited, fallible, and human. Such knowledge does not discharge the parent of responsibility or absolve him of culpability. Rather, it tempers the effects of his wrongs and his failures by removing the wrongdoer from his elevated position, a sinecure in which a father is ensconced partly by virtue of the child's sense of his immediate world's enormous (to him) proportions, but also because, wanting in self-assuredness, feeling tiny, he finds it safer to have him up there. Laments to a less than perfect father and unjust excruciations before his dark and secret eyes, now within the self, will give way before what Erik Erikson (1963) once called a "paternity of self."

CHAPTER 7

The Soiled Pinafore:
A Sexual Theme
in Psychiatric History

ARNO KARLEN

The editors of this book asked me to take a historic view of sex in psychiatry. As the title shows, I am limiting myself to one major theme. That is because I don't dare pretend to an encompassing knowledge no one possesses. Attempts at the history of sex in psychiatry are few, fragmentary, or inadequate. When a thorough study of sexual attitudes, theories, and therapies in psychiatry finally appears, it will fill a fat volume, draw on a dozen disciplines, and summarize books and journals in many languages over many centuries. And the author will have to offer more than a trek through an intellectual museum; a psychiatrist not only creates knowledge but reflects his culture, class, and personality.

The job, besides being vast and complex, draws fools, frauds, and special pleaders. The subject of sex always does. Many of the fools and frauds leap into public view and fade. Unfortunately, the special pleader with advanced degrees may intrigue both laymen and colleagues. Perhaps driven by a secret kink, he rides his hobbyhorse over distant fields of learning to prove that pedophilia is a vital stage of social and individual development, or that the right to love a marsupial is part of our birthright of joyful pansexuality. I am only half joking when I say that I expect the emergence of Necrophilia Lib, backed by liberal psychiatrists, to protect a ''viable sexual alternative''—or at worst a ''victimless crime.'' The special pleader's ideas may range from *recherché* to outright loony, but few can dispute his historical panorama and baroque theory, because the references he brandishes are so specialized and scattered.

Some scholarly ground has been broken—here with a fine tool, there with a shovel. Information lies scattered in surveys of psychiatry and the biographies and memoires of psychiatrists. There is good general background in Gregory Zilboorg's still unsurpassed *A History of Medical Psychology* (1941), Michel Foucault's provocative *Madness and Civilization* (1961), Steven Marcus's *The Other Victorians* (1964), William Cole's *Sex in Christianity and Psychoanalysis* (1966), Crane Brinton's *A History of Western Morals* (1959), and the two volumes by Alfred Kinsey and his associates (1948, 1953). In the name of honesty, if nothing else, I must recommend my own book *Sexuality and Homosexuality* (1971). There I outlined, in a few hundred pages of a larger work, Western social and scientific ideas about sex in general and homosexuality in particular. I especially recommend the critical bibliography, where I said which sources I thought reliable and which ones bunk. I invite others to do the same, if only to alert readers to our own intellectual prejudices.

Some writers have covered limited areas with care. Ilza Vieth's *Hysteria: The History of a Disease* (1965) shows how a syndrome has bounced from one scientific lap to another for millenia. Medical and psychiatric ideas on masturbation have been surveyed in Alex Comfort's *The Anxiety Makers* (1970) and in excellent monographs by Hare (1962) and Spitz (1952). In their essay on "Sex as Work" (1967), Lewis and Brissett deal with some recent professional attitudes. Specialized survey chapters exist in some books, such as the excellent one on homosexuality in Charles Socarides' *The Overt Homosexual* (1968a).

Many books, though useful, call for critical reading because they are a bit one-sided or idiosyncratic. Among these are G. Rattray Taylor's *The Angel Makers* (1958) and *Sex in History* (1954), Vern Bullough's *Sexual Variance in Society and History* (1976), and the detailed but relentlessly "anti-Victorian" *The Physician and Sexuality in Victorian America* (1974), by Haller and Haller.

By now I have given the reader a springboard for studying theories and values about sex, while excusing myself from giving a systematic history. I have said that our picture of the subject still consists of scattered patches. However, one can detect one powerful motif—or, more properly, a vision of sexuality—that runs through Western history and has infused much psychiatric thinking. It deserves an emblematic name, to dramatize its often unrecognized force. I call it the Principle of the Soiled Pinafore. If my description of it contains satiric notes, especially in passages on some eminent psychiatrists, including Freud, it is with a spirit of skepticism they themselves would probably relish. Solemnity, they knew, doesn't indicate wisdom, nor does slack-jawed reverence.[1]

The theme of the Soiled Pinafore is related to what has variously been called Victorianism, puritanism, and "Judeo-Christian repressiveness." All three terms are misleading. Long before the Victorians and puritans, long before Christianity, the West discouraged or forbade sexual activity other than marital coitus. (The mainstream of Judaism, however, has affirmed sexuality as much as condemned it, and has not made a virtue of chastity for its own sake.) Despite the polemics of early Church Fathers, many or most "pagans" of early Europe had strict sexual codes (Karlen, 1971; May, 1930). True, there have always been countercurrents of sexual permissiveness and healthy coarseness; but the hedonistic and pragmatic views of sex have never prevailed for long over the basic restrictiveness of major social institutions, from church to civil law.

When the Christian church gained moral and legal authority over sex, it equated chastity, virtue, reason, and will. Opposed to these was another cluster of ideas—sex, sin, unreason, and impulsiveness. St. Augustine (1961) typically likened lust to a fit of epilepsy or rage and said that the mindless tempest of orgasm sets man farthest from God. The Christian argument was that reason allows one to distinguish virtue, which is a life above the impulses of sex and rage; the will enables one to control impulse.

In the Renaissance, as science developed, and the authority for controlling sex passed to the secular state, these values were restated: It became obvious that what had once been sin was now sickness.

---

[1] I did draw the line at a friend's suggestion that I call this essay "A Pinafore is Being Soiled," which has echoes bordering on presumption.

Between 1600 and 1800, the Bicêtre and many other hospitals housed not only psychotics but many others charged with "losing control"—homosexuals, political undesirables, beggars, the venereally diseased, people accused of promiscuity or of filial disrespect (Foucault, 1961). Medical and then legal definitions of insanity centered on loss of reason, and doctors argued that orgasmic uncontrol was a bulldozer before the walls of sanity. This Augustinian view hardened into psychiatric dogma. Soon the ideal of "moral" insanity would be invented to describe people who obviously hadn't lost reason but "let go" sexually (Zilboorg, 1941).

Until the early eighteenth century, for instance, masturbation had been the subject of little medical comment. Then around 1717 there appeared anonymously in London the Urtext of masturbation scare literature, *Onania, or the Heinous Sin of Self-Pollution*. The author, probably, a quack doctor and nostrum salesman, said that masturbation caused numberless diseases, epilepsy, madness, "lying, forswearing, perhaps murder." Terror of sexual "excess," especially excessive masturbation, swept over Europe as an advance wave of the extreme repressiveness that would later be called Victorian. A half century after publication, the book was in its 80th edition and had become famous on the continent. Its ideas were then given medical respectability by Samuel Tissot, the eminent Swiss physician to the Pope. In his own book, also called *Onania* (1760), Tissot affirmed that excess, especially in the form of sexual solitaire—"the flagrant crime of masturbation," he called it—opened the door to consumption, blindness, impotence, melancholy, catalepsy, and imbecility. By comparison, the threat of hairy palms was a relief.

The wave of medical warnings against sexual calamity kept mounting. When Benjamin Rush wrote the first American text on mental disorders in 1812, he said that masturbation caused fearsome ills from tuberculosis to "fatuity and death." Esquirol in France (Comfort, 1970) and the Scots physician David Skae (1863) defined a specific psychosis caused by masturbation; the French Lallemand described a type, The Masturbator (Karlen, 1971), who could be recognized by pallor, downcast eyes, lack of love for family and country, and other squalid deficiencies. By the middle of the nineteenth century, it was widely assumed that at least half the people in asylums had arrived there literally by their own hands. Between 1850 and 1950, at least several hundred thousand people in the United States and Europe, very many of them children, were saved from such fates by castration, ovariectomy, clitoridectomy, and cautery of the genitals (Karlen, 1971).

During the nineteenth century, the "guide to marriage" had become a popular genre. Most such books tried to terrify readers away from any sex acts except infrequent and restrained marital coitus. The eminent Victorian Dr. Acton (1871) said that the "ordinary [sic] practice of sleeping with the hands bound behind one's back should not be ignored even by grown men." Boys, men, and, less commonly, females were protected by cold showers, mittens, and straitjackets. There was even an ingenious electrical device with an alarm set off by nighttime erections, warning child and parent of impending "nocturnal pollution," which was thought to weaken the nervous system.

Many societies have feared loss of impulse control, loss of semen, and loss of reason, and felt that any or all of these are somehow linked. The fear reached one of its peaks in our society during the period from the late eighteenth to early twentieth centuries, for reasons we do not fully understand. One result was a firm medical doctrine, fully developed a generation before Freud in the first major psychiatric work on sex, Krafft-Ebing's *Psychopathia Sexualis* (1892), that sexual excess leads to weak nerves, more sex, imbecility, more sex, raving madness, more sex, and finally death.

For males, this evoked a picture of an adolescent idiot or a prematurely senile libertine who stares moon-eyed at the madhouse walls, spittle dribbling from his lips as he whacks away at himself without respite. His female counterpart was a bedraggled hag of seventeen—once she was pretty and wore a blue pinafore—humping all comers in an alley till early death ended her crazed misery. If this seems an exaggeration, reread Victorian scientific and popular literature, and recall the street lore of your youth. If it seems quaint, ask your colleagues for a definition of sexual excess, its causes and effects, and see how many give you a diluted dose of the above.

The images of a decaying boy and of a girl with mud on the back of her dress show little faith in exhaustion as a fact of life. They do not even allow for the normal desire for a variety of hobbies. But they do show the tenacity of the old equation of sex, loss of control, unreason, sickness, and antisocial behavior—an enduring Western view of sex as a destructive beast howling for release. Once loosed, it can never again be chained. If it cannot be totally controlled, it must at least be redeemed by procreation, marriage, love—something "higher." This view of sex I have called The Principle of the Soiled Pinafore.

In 1925, A. Lorand would still write that "Too frequent sexual intercourse may soon sap the vitality of the glands, and, indeed, hasten the symptoms of old age, even in young persons . . . even young girls may acquire some of the attributes of old age . . . become fat and bloated, the features lose their juvenile aspect, and the cheeks become pendant . . . there is a marked difference between the muscles of a young maiden and those of a woman who has been leading a life of debauchery for some time. The latter will invariably, if not always [sic], look older—which ought to be an object lesson. . . ."

Few psychiatrists defend the Pinafore Principle in its pure form today. It just won't do to claim that masturbation, premarital coitus, or any other sex act causes meningitis, chronically downcast eyes, and teenage decrepitude. But the Soiled Pinafore is still with us in many deceptive shapes. Dr. Acton and Dr. Lorand no longer monitor the bedroom, stern negatives tumbling from their lips. Yet from the late nineteenth century until today, many psychiatrists—probably a large majority—have continued to redefine what used to be a sexual sin or crime as neurosis or immaturity. Paradoxically, they have often done so in lectures about sex as a good thing. While one hand has removed the scarlet letter and brushed the dirt off the back of the Soiled Pinafore, the other hand has bestowed gentle, learned admonitions that mean, quite simply, "Don't!"

A new trend of the last decade has seemed to praise sex and orgasm as ends in themselves. Even many proponents of this trend use terms that express a subtle, disguised Pinaforism: All the cultivation of orgasm is ultimately in the service of Higher Aims. Clearly most mental health professionals still don't see sex as an ultimately self-limiting part of life, but as a disruptive tide held by brittle floodgates.

On the positive side, one must admit that such Pinaforism has created unintentional comedy, which is among science's least praised gifts to an ever grimmer world. The reason is the phoenix nature of

Pinaforism. During each sexual revolution, from Freud to Masters and Johnson, it rises from its own ashes in splendid new feathers, trailing a glory of doctorates.

But we have leaped ahead of ourselves. Let us return to the Soiled Pinafore as envisioned by Krafft-Ebing, Freud, and the other early anti-Victorians who helped to move sexuality from the categories of virtue and sin to those of illness and health. If I emphasize not the full grandeur of theories but attitudes and images, it is to dramatize the forces that consciously or unconsciously help shape theory.

The Freud-to-Fifties version of Pinaforism was strongly rooted in eighteenth and nineteenth century concepts of biology and society (energic instincts and a scheme of social evolution). But ultimately it rests on an ancient mental scenario. It locates sex primarily within the male. It says that if men had *their* way, we'd all go at it like mad puppies—on floors and roofs and subway aisles, standing in elevators, sprawled on the city hall steps, without pause or discrimination. Mail and milk deliveries would stop, electric power fail. Only confirmed masturbators would show up for work. This *On the Beach* cataclysm would end with weeds growing up through the pavement, cars frozen and rusting in midintersection, and a slavering humanity reverted to rut on all fours. To keep civilization from thus crumbling into anarchy, brutishness, and chaos, women must control men. To do so, they must first control themselves.

Nature, thank God, has ingeniously provided. Women care more for love than for sex; they are less quickly and easily aroused, their sexual response is more emotional and diffuse than men's. Only the Devil, neuropathy, neurosis, or immaturity (pick your authority) could make them have sex outside marriage or at least a long-term love affair ("stable affectionate relationship"). Therefore, if men are to enjoy sex outside rape, whoring, and a variety of other lonely misbehaviors, they must reduce their sexual voltage to women's diffuse, emotional—let us say, domestic—level. In short, the sexes are naturally Victorian.

Obviously the first great anti-Victorians of psychiatry and sexology carried more Pinaforism in their radical juggernaut than they knew. Freud, the most important of them all, saw sex as the enemy of civilization—today one might rephrase that as "a poor alternative to adaptive socialization'' or some such stuff. Like the Church Fathers, the puritans, the Victorians, he believed that without such forces as latency and sublimation, boys and girls might never learn to read, write, and do research. Instead they'd just muck about in the barn or the basement, and go on dissipating their lives in sex play to the point of mindless exhaustion. They'd end up like those permissive primitives lolling in hammocks and waiting for others to invent the calculus, the rococo, and psychoanalysis. Civilization rises at the price of impulse and sexuality. Oh, the white man's burden! This brutal simplification, like several that follow, is as true as it is open to cavil.[2]

Freud's Pinaforism, of course, contradicts our present cross-cultural knowledge. Modern high technology originated chiefly in only one culture area, and it happens to be sexually rather restrictive. But many restrictive societies quite lack high technological, or artistic culture. And many permissive societies have elaborate (if not highly technological) cultures. In fact, sexual restrictiveness and permissiveness are not known to correlate with any particular kind or degree of culture (Ford and Beach, 1951; Karlen, 1971; Marshall and Suggs, 1971). And here I cannot even begin to review the evidence from social and biological science that the regulation of sex and the existence of the nuclear family are safely inherent in us as biosocial creatures. Yet many psychiatrists, historians, and social scientists continue to evoke later Roman days, wave the Soiled Pinafore, and claim that the West has earned its imminent doom by the sweat of its genitals.

An important shift in the tactics and rhetoric of Pinaforism is apparent when one compares Krafft-Ebing with Havelock Ellis and his heirs. Krafft-Ebing, before Freud, had welded available sexual knowledge into a comprehensive theory. Like Freud, he helped in the revolutionary task of urging pity or treatment for the sexual deviant and nonconformer, rather than punishment. But he did warn (1892) firmly and ominously against what he narrowly defined as sexual excess, and claimed that a normal woman feels ''little sexual desire . . . and the dictates of good breeding come to her aid.'' A few decades later, innovaters seeking to liberate women and men from

---

[2]I deliberately do not dwell here on the related larger themes in such works as *Beyond the Pleasure Principle* and *Civilization and Its Discontents,* where Freud became a great tragic philosopher with affinities to Plato and Bergson. I stick to his Pinaforan aspect.

such "Victorian" antisexuality mistakenly thought they had escaped Pinaforism. Though not all wore the title psychiatrist, they deeply influenced psychiatric thought, and the psychiatric imprimatur on certain ideas in turn affected other sciences.

The most influential of the next reformist wave was Havelock Ellis, the great pioneer sexologist of the English-speaking countries. Like many anti-Victorian reformers, Ellis (1936) found spiritual and political allies in the feminist movement (Calder-Marshall, 1959). Like many feminists of that day and ours, he agreed with the Victorians that man is a brute who crushes love's blossoms in greedy paws while woman weeps to have her finer needs fulfilled. He also agreed on one of the chief reasons: forthright male sexuality is a blight on women. Ellis agreed with Balzac that the average male making love resembled a chimpanzee trying to play the violin. He wrote pitiful descriptions of men who ruined their brides for life on the wedding night by despotic callousness. This doubtless did happen sometimes; but Ellis and his heirs prescribed odd remedies that remain, in essence, sexological dogma today.

Ellis's most reknowned heir was the author of the work that for decades represented advanced learned opinion on sex to laymen and professionals. Dr. Theodoor Van de Velde did not call his book *Ideal Sex:* despite some notorious audacities in his own life, he wasn't sure he approved of coitus for widows and divorcées, let alone the yet-unmarried (Beigel, personal communication). *Ideal Marriage* (1930), in an apparent about-face from Krafft-Ebing, said that every coition without orgasm for the female causes her physical and mental damage. It makes one envision ladies lying awake at three in the morning, gnawing their knuckles and softly weeping while their smug husbands snore. Male sex is abrupt, rough, and unpleasurable. But love and marriage may move a man to become considerate. In fact, he must become a Paganini of the sexual andante. *Ideal Marriage* is a paean to a weird blend of tenderness, lust, overcontrol, and solicitude. Its advice makes one imagine two hysterics trying to keep each other calm through the best of the Marx Brothers. One of Van de Velde's heirs (Street, 1959) wrote: "Foreplay should never last less than fifteen minutes even though a woman may be sufficiently aroused in five." Having laden sex with self-consciousness and guilty apprehension, the author belittles the penis as a way to improve it. "The disillusioning fact remains that the forefinger is a most useful asset in a man's contact with the opposite sex." We shall speak later of those who now go a step further, belittling even the male digit and enshrining the vibrator.

The disciples of Ellis and Van de Velde have continued to write most sex and marriage manuals in the past twenty years. Few seem aware of the evidence that female orgasm is not necessarily slower and more diffuse than male orgasm, and that foreplay may not always aid orgasm. Few of them leave a horny, high-spirited couple feeling in good mental health. Some permit an occasional romp, nip, hard squeeze, or sudden, passionate coupling. Many, however, specifically ban unpremeditated sex. One widely read manual of the past decade (Eichenlaub, 1969) said, "An ardent spur-of-the-moment tumble sounds very romantic. . . . However, ineptly arranged intercourse leaves the clothes you had no chance to shed in a shambles, your plans for the evening shot, your birth control program incomplete, and your future sex play under considerable better-be-careful-or-we'll-wind-up-in-bed-again restraint." One can imagine the poor couple as their panting subsides, ruefully regarding her ripped pantyhose, realizing they're twenty minutes late for the P.T.A. They look into each other's eyes and make a solemn pact: "We'll never, *never* do that again!"

No one in his right mind would knock tenderness, altruism, and cunning eroticism. But when a physician warns that one must always achieve them, the effect can be an aphrodisiac. Who can be simultaneously tender, calculating, and wildly excited? Can the passionate always follow the commandment Help Thy Neighbor Before Thyself? The coitus envisioned in such books, and still by many professionals and laymen, retains many of the controls St. Augustine prayed for. The climax sometimes sounds like a lyrical anticlimax—not a bang but a sweet, sweeping ecstasy, the erotic equivalent of listening to Tannhäuser while lolling in a hot tub and eating loukoums. Experts who recommend that partners take turns giving each other body rubs with fragrant oils may also take some people on a stroll down the line between the sensual and the laborious.

Freud-to-Fifties Pinaforism took sex out of the sin category, but it continued to say that sex is the servant of love, love the servant of marriage. More and more psychiatrists have blessed sex without marriage—in long, loving relationships. The change is surprisingly slight. Consider an example. Not very long ago, I picked from a shelf in a New York paperback store every guide to sexuality written by a psychiatrist. Not untypical was one by Dr. Ellen Birchall (1974). Some of her "liberal" metropolitan colleagues may find her conservative. But as we shall see, this may only show that the more straightforward a middle-class professional's values, the easier it is to know what he really thinks.

Dr. Birchall praises the beauty of sex, but she starts the chapter on premarital coitus with a pathetic case from a mental hospital. She does admit that not all premarital affairs cause psychosis, but she adds, "I can only issue a solemn warning to every young unmarried woman: if you have one or more affairs before you marry, the odds are great that, later in life, you'll have to pay the piper." She says it isn't worth the trouble anyway, since the chances for orgasmic pleasures are nil. A woman needs "prolonged love play . . . tenderness, gentleness, and understanding." She thinks these are inoperative in cars and motels, which she considers the only possible places for premarital degradation.

Some psychiatrists, as I've said, may smile at such advice, thinking it represents the radical-right fringe or the *lumpen* level of their profession. Yet if one substitutes love for marriage in Dr. Birchall's message and eases out the ominous, dogmatic tone, the message could be from many eminent "liberal" psychiatrists. Like Dr. Birchall and the Church Fathers, they call for less *Eros* and more *Agape*—as if each weren't hard enough to find without dismissing the other.

The fear of excess is still common. One recent Pinaforian ploy is to applaud sex and then shroud it in vague quantitative doubts. Dr. Jules Masserman (1973) writes that masturbation is "physiologically harmless in moderation." But like most clinicians and researchers, he doesn't specify the limit of moderation. Nor does he name the ills of the immoderate—though a chafed penis or clitoris is probably nature's own control. Imagine an adolescent reader trying to puzzle it out for himself.

Many psychiatrists now write that the only damage caused by masturbation rises from guilt over it. Of course, few people, especially younger people, are quite free of such guilt, and rare are psychiatrists who suggest the alternative of coitus during youth (Rogow, 1970). Imagine a young reader's vague apprehension as he awaits the un-named damage caused by his masturbatory guilt. Telling a young adolescent that only his guilt is damaging is like telling an obsessive phobic that he has nothing to fear but fear itself.

One of the most instructive examples of Pinaforism's reincarna-tions is the history of writings on premature ejaculation. My perusal of medical and psychiatric literature suggests that prematurity was rarely mentioned as a major, common problem at the turn of this century. Over the next few decades, as women were encouraged and then expected to reach orgasm, it became a standard part of most books about sex for specialists and laymen. As attention grew, so did the amount of time that defined prematurity. Now, there certainly is a problem when a man often ejaculates before or just after entry. But by the Thirties, a man might be labeled premature by some psychia-trists for ejaculating after 30 minutes of coitus, because the woman still hadn't arrived. One must ask, premature for whom?

These definers of prematurity rarely noted that in many animals, fast and energetic mating might be thought a sign of healthy vigor. Nor did they mention societies in which people prefer one or more hard, quick coitions instead of one long one, and female orgasm is apparently common (Ford and Beach, 1951; Suggs, 1966; Maslow, 1942). A woman isn't called premature if she has orgasm before or just after penetration; in fact, she may be thought passionately re-sponsive. Prematurity is by definition a male problem, to which psy-chiatrists have historically responded by telling men to slow down, rather than asking women to hurry up.

There are problems when prematurity is defined in minutes rather than seconds: in fact, only a minority of American males regularly take more than a few minutes to reach orgasm (Kinsey et al., 1948). And the call to prolong coitus for very long periods raises conflicting demands. Many women find a man exciting if he is assertive, pas-sionate, takes initiative, all of this even (or especially) despite some signs of female reluctance. But as soon as coitus starts, the very qualities the woman found exciting become selfishness or neurosis. The man is to increase his control in measure with his exitement, engineering coitus to end in simultaneous orgasm as if playing an adagio with all the repeats. The latest variation of this approach recommends *not* reaching orgasm simultaneously, so that both people aren't lost in excitement at the same time. Woe to the abandoned, fie on the frenzied. Are they capable of love? Can they be healthy?

Kinsey pointed out many years ago (1948, 1953) that male responsibility for female orgasm is a middle-class idea. Masters and Johnson (1966) have confirmed that men from lower socioeducational levels are more likely to think a man should reach orgasm whenever it seems natural. Such men are less likely to think they must rouse female pleasure from its wintry sleep with prolonged foreplay, prolonged coitus, patience, ingenuity, and sympathetic cunning. Yet many researchers (Adams, 1963; Kinsey et al., 1953; Marshall and Suggs, 1971) have believed that female unresponsiveness depends more on a woman's background and development than on her husband's coital technique. In fact, one interesting study[3] has suggested that there is an odd gap between the middle-class husband's efforts and his wife's response. The husbands in a group of married couples said that they tried to prolong and vary coitus for their wives' sakes. Yet the majority of wives thought their husbands didn't care about their pleasure or try to increase it. Apparently the problem was female unresponsiveness, with both parties blaming the men. I suspect this is still common.

The Mangaians, in Polynesia, believe males must teach females to reach orgasm, and their coital ideal is for the woman to reach orgasm once or twice and then for both partners to enjoy orgasm simultaneously. But Mangaian girls learn very fast—through vigorous, straightforward intercourse (Suggs, 1966) and relatively little foreplay. Students of the culture (Marshall and Suggs, 1971) say that female orgasm is achieved "virtually universally and without difficulty . . . in further contrast, the direct Polynesian approach resembles in many respects that in a number of [poor Western cultures], in which female dissatisfaction with sex runs high." Kinsey et al. (1953) even suggested that "the use of extended and varied techniques may, in not a few cases, interfere with the female's attainment of orgasm," be-

---

[3] I regret that I have notes taken from that paper several years ago, but not the paper or its source. I would appreciate being reminded by any reader familiar with it.

cause it may prevent steady, vigorous build-up of excitement. So there remains the question whether male lack of foreplay and restraint is the *cause* of unresponsiveness, or one of several causes, or largely a reflection of the individual woman's development.

This is no argument against long, cunning coitus. I think it one of life's finer pleasures. But I also believe it is impoverished as an exclusive sexual style. I use this word because I recently heard a psychiatrist use it of working-class sexuality, with its rigid orgasmic to-each-his-own. I agree, but I find the middle-class pattern of conscientious control and solicitude equally impoverished. Its spokesmen, in Pinaforian tradition, often imply that women are hurt by male lust rather than liking it, and they prescribe subdued and extrinsically justified sex in the name of health and ethics. I think that missing tenderness and finesse is a shame, but so is missing assertiveness, vigor, and spontaneity.

In fact, I cannot help seeing shades of the Soiled Pinafore in much recent talk about tenderness, nonexploitation, and sharing. The words sometimes manage to take on tones of "virtue" and "health." As an exclusive sexual prescription, they create a cult of control and muted passion. And that takes us to the newest, best disguised form of psychiatric Pinaforism. Its nature is clear in the different responses first to Kinsey and then to Masters and Johnson. Consider the case of "the myth of the multiple orgasm."

Kinsey et al. reported (1953) that 14 percent of their female subjects experienced two, three, or even a dozen or more successive orgasms. They interviewed a woman of 60 who could have dozens of orgasms and end coitus happily whenever her partner did. Now, multiple orgasms were no news to some men; with luck, they'd encountered it several times. But fury and disbelief appeared in learned journals, in essays by doctors who obviously had never had the pleasure. Bergler and Kroger (1954) devoted an entire book to calling multiple orgasm "one of the most fantastic tales the female volunteers told Kinsey (who believed it) . . . The 14 percent of Kinsey's volunteers, all vaginally frigid, belonged obviously to the nymphomaniac type of frigidity where excitement mounts repeatedly *without* reaching a climax. . . ."

Of course, later research confirmed Kinsey's view, not Bergler's and Kroger's (Masters and Johnson, 1966). Masters and Johnson made a good case for multiple orgasm being biologically potential in many women. Critics can argue many points in the works of Kinsey and Masters and Johnson, but multiple orgasm is no longer one of them.[4] Kinsey avoided polemics, but later his associate Wardell Pomeroy (1966) wrote, "Whenever we thought of the Bergler and Kroger attack, we remembered our sixty-year-old subject and smiled." So could have done 14 percent of the women in America, and the men who had known them.

But the Pinafore was unfurled by others. Dr. Natalie Shainess (1966) wrote that what seemed to be multiple orgasms "occur in relatively frigid women who have never experienced orgasm." She also said that the sex flush recorded by Masters and Johnson was probably just prickly heat caused by those fiendish photographic lights. Some other mental health professionals jumped on what *might* be wrong with sex-behavior studies and how else the findings *might* be explained. Now, it had been no surprise when Clare Booth Luce and some religious groups called Kinsey's work "statistical filth," nor when they objected to turning on the bedroom light and "coldly" watching what happened. But why did so many scientists object to even rough baseline data on subjects of ignorance and impassioned muddle?

Kinsey had begun his work precisely because some professionals labeled patients frigid without knowing for sure what an orgasm is, or called them hypersexual or underactive without knowing the actual norm from which they allegedly deviated. In short, mental health professionals often spoke of "immature" and "deviant" acts without knowing *what most adults do*—an obvious contradiction in terms. Kinsey's data, however flawed, were and still are the best wide-scale behavioral data available.[5] And they surprised almost everyone in

[4]Dr. I. Singer's work on female orgasm (1973) and some other studies and reports suggest that the de-emphasis of "vaginal" orgasm by some recent researchers is as dogmatic and perhaps unrealistic as early, orthodox analysts' contrary conviction, but the existence of multiple orgasm is not thereby put in doubt.

[5]About five years ago, I routinely asked every professional I met who specialized in human sexuality whether he had read the Kinsey books through, not merely skimmed, read summaries, or looked himself up in the charts. Perhaps one in twenty had done so. Kinsey did have some biases and methodological soft spots, but many who criticized him in print obviously had not even read the chapters on methodology; they criticized strong points instead of soft spots! These chapters are still important scientific and human documents.

some way. In the volume on males, Kinsey et al. listed three ideas
that any scientist should consider prejudices till proven true, for they
were not supported by reliable evidence: that masturbation leads to
poor adult sex adjustment, that homosexuality is a biological abnormality, and that adultery inevitably breaks up homes. Of 58 psychologists among their subjects, all but one defended at least one of these
ideas. So did 70 of 74 psychiatrists.

But the most significant criticism of Kinsey by many psychiatrists
was that behavioral data are meaningless without their emotional contexts. To the clinician dealing with an individual patient, this is doubtless true. The charge, however, seems almost disingenuous. Kinsey's
professed effort had been to gather massive behavioral data, precisely
because the emotional and cultural contexts had made emotion-laden
assumptions flourish—had, in fact, prevented, the gathering of such
data. Behavior without an emotional context may indeed be limited,
but no more than assumptions about behavior without any base in
data.

It would indeed be disingenuous to criticize a researcher for doing
what he set out to do. But the attacks, one must assume, were rarely
disingenuous. (One might make a few exceptions, if one is to believe
Kinsey's statement [1948] that he invited some psychiatrists to join
his project early on and add their discipline's contribution, but none
accepted.) The motive for the attacks seems rather to have been a
devious and sophisticated sort of Pinaforism. The argument about
meaningless data led easily to the statement that sex itself is meaningless if it is "without emotion"—that is, outside a long, loving
relationship. In fact, it led to the statement that such sex acts are
beneath serious *attention* by professionals.

It is significant that many professional critics feared laymen would
pick up Kinsey's "cold" attitude and get the wrong ideas from behavioral data. The disaster to the public wasn't specified, but it evoked
a previous generation's insistence on putting the "good parts" in Latin
to protect the unwashed from their own stupidity and bad instincts.
Apparently the public would become emotionally crippled sex ma-
chines if science didn't remind them that sex without emotion—without
love—is too base for attention, even dangerous to public hygiene.
Many intellectual essayists joined this hand-wringing. Lionel Trilling
(1954) clucked about the anxiety Kinsey's figures might rouse in read-

ers unrefined in higher math. It is reassuring to know that according to a Gallup poll, five out of six laymen with opinions on the subject considered Kinsey's work and its availability a good thing. They were apparently less Victorian than many experts.

This reaction to Kinsey gave way to an even subtler kind of Pinaforism, which has flourished during the past fifteen years. Kinsey et al. mentioned that they had observed sex acts to understand the physiological mechanisms, but they didn't dwell on the matter; they had enough trouble just presenting the behavioral data. But they did, as a result, suggest ideas about female sexual response that defied most current expert opinion. Certainly it defied the opinion of many women struggling in psychotherapy to rise above their "immature" clitoral orgasms, and those labeled frigid nymphomaniacs because they could enjoy multiple orgasms. It is, in retrospect, extraordinary that people devoted to the study of psychosexual life ignored Kinsey's leads, along with other data that upset them.

Masters and Johnson later picked up those leads, had the benefit of more compact and sophisticated instruments, and began to present their results—what would be chapters of *Human Sexual Response* (1966)—at medical gatherings. The reception was often icy silence, according to some observers. When their first volume appeared, some critics reacted as they had to Kinsey. There was the same rush to keep souls unhardened and to preserve social order by protecting the "intimate" context of sex. However, many critics adopted a new, modified Pinaforism, a subgenre I call The New Earnestness.

Masters and Johnson roused some obviously irrational howls and stubborn demurrals. Again, whatever the limitations of their work, they provided new baseline data. But instead of belaboring them mightily, many critics seemed to raise the backs of their hands to their mouths to cover yawns. In the Sixties, when rhetoric about a sexual revolution had become commonplace, the new posture of Pinaforism was a mildly belittling nod, a sigh of knowledgeable amusement—and then a call to higher moral commitment. The argument ran, in effect, "This sort of research is all right, I suppose, but is it really that important? We know so much about sex, there's so much of it and it's so open, that the real problem is alienation and the banalizing of sex."

Such critics never produced evidence that people are in fact more alienated sexually than they used to be. They did not dwell on the vast ignorance and suffering that underlie so much confident rhetoric in a society still basically cautious and negative about sex. They did not even pay attention to further behavioral studies showing that the "sexual revolution" was far greater in attitudes than in behavior; they even ignored the obvious fact that in our society, on any given night, an awful lot of people don't want to go to bed alone but do so, the final disproof of sex-revolution rhetoric. But they did take an air of fearless familiarity with sex, and set their sights higher, toward love and authenticity and self-actualization, etc.—wonderful aims, but they do sometimes betray the presence of the New Earnestness. The Earnest critics are not really against sex without feeling, but against sex without the feelings they approve.

This kind of Pinaforism claims that sex is good, but ends up calling for less of it. Its motto is the sexual equivalent of Nothing But Champagne—sex only as a perfect fusion of *Eros* and *Agape*. Its classroom method seems to be Learning without Doing. In all, it is false tolerance of sexuality. The blunt vernacular might term it the wisdom of the tight-assed. If the vernacular offends, one could turn to the elegant apothegm of Denis de Rougement that the Devil's best disguise is to deny that he exists. Pinaforism's final ploy is to say it isn't there.

As a classic example—perhaps an exaggerated one, but instructive—consider Dr. Shainess's impassioned case (1966) against Masters and Johnson. She said that our sex lives were becoming more mechanical, hostile, and impersonal. More cold facts might batter us senselessly blasé. After saying that multiple orgasm might be frigidity (orgasm happens once and detours around the clitoris) and the sex flush prickly heat, she concluded, "But perhaps the major false premise is the assumption that studying sexual response genitally will offer meaningful information."

Since sex is, with luck, performed genitally, she may be wrong. But she was worried about things nongenital—a spirit of "libertinage" and the loss of "tenderness, love and dignity." It's difficult to reject a call for love and tenderness, but somehow she made one picture them as delivered from a height, with an almost melancholy air. As for making love to the dignified, it is a fate I cast upon mine enemies.

Actually, Dr. Shainess apparently feared what Augustine and Freud feared, along with much of Western society for millenia: The Beast

Unleashed. She worried that if we read and believe Masters and Johnson, we may trample each other in a rush to writhe in cold, frantic couplings on the floor of their lab. Considering our upbringing, the worry is premature.

A less bristling but similar attack was written by Dr. Leslie Farber (1966) and reprinted many times. It was an essay called "I'm Sorry, Dear," which appeared originally in *Commentary* (Earnestness begets Earnestness). It satirized Masters and Johnson as Strangeloves of sex, degrading and dehumanizing their subjects, putting them "at the beck and call" of the research staff. As one reads on, one sees that his humor has Earnest intent—to protect us from being brainwashed into cynical sexual zombies. Obviously he feared that such would be the result of people reaching orgasm without love. Like Dr. Shainess, he was doubtless impelled by a compassionate wish to save others from what he wouldn't want for himself. He is entitled, but the charity may be misplaced.

Similar Earnest noises have appeared recently in the works of many psychiatrists I deeply admire. They warn that the bed has become a vale of frozen banality and claim that sex without "feeling" threatens civilization. They seem to be talking about real problems, but identifying them poorly. They do not point out that our society still teaches fear, avoidance, and overcontrol of sex from infancy on. They do not ask whether more restrictiveness will help people feel and make emotional commitments, which they seem at times to imply. They rarely consider the possibility that for some people, at least, greater sexual comfort and expressiveness might enhance feeling rather than banish it.

The question inevitably arises: how many researchers and clinicians are Portnoys unredeemed by frankness, humor, and wide personal experience? A medical background is hardly the best training. Dr. Harold Lief, who has led the effort to add human sexuality to the medical curriculum, describes (1976) the typical medical student as seen by his teacher: "He is a hard worker, extremely conscientious, a little shy and retiring, doesn't let go of his feelings, is somewhat hard to draw out." Lief adds, "Often he has had little personal coital experience. He tends to solve his personal sexual problems by methods of 'overcontrol.'" Lief has also alluded to the number of medical colleagues who are secretly or openly censorious of premarital, extramarital, noncoital, "recreational," and many other kinds of sex. Although psychiatrists as a group tend to be more liberal in their attitudes than all physicians as a group (Rogow, 1970), every psychiatrist reader of these pages probably knows a colleague who shares such strictures. It is difficult to believe that their patients don't somehow get the message.

A study of 1,300 psychiatrists about a decade ago (Rogow, 1970) showed that psychiatrists and analysts are more permissive about the social control of sex than the United States population as a whole. Yet 38 percent of psychiatrists and 17 percent of analysts agreed that unmarried college students should avoid sexual affairs "at all costs" or warned against them on the grounds that they might "lead to trouble." More striking was the finding that 55 percent of psychiatrists and 29 percent of analysts believed extramarital affairs should be "avoided at all costs" or would lead to trouble. Only seven and six percent, respectively, called such affairs "useful" or even "all right." And about the same percentages approved or disapproved of sexual affairs in high school—though many high school students engage in sex, can legally marry, and often do so. Of psychiatrists and psychoanalysts together, 55 percent disapproved of premarital sex in high school students, and six percent approved. Many sexually active and healthy sixteen- and eighteen-year-olds would run into trouble in their offices.

One must point out that the great majority of psychiatrists come from middle- and upper-middle-class backgrounds, which are thought to teach impulse control above spontaneity. People from such backgrounds tend not to reach until middle age the degree of sexual experience many blue-collar people achieve in their midteens. In reflecting their background and projecting their own sexual patterns as norms, many psychiatrists are no better or worse than many priests, bricklayers, housewives, hairdressers, busdrivers, and judges. It is quite normal for people to insist that what they do is normal, less is frigid, and more is sick.

An interesting light was thrown on this several decades ago by A.H. Maslow (1942), in a pioneering effort to apply ethological concepts of dominance and social hierarchy to human sex behavior. He defined high dominance as a feeling of assurance and capability, low dominance as timidity and self-devaluation. He rated a group of women individually for dominance; only then did he inquire about their sex lives. It turned out that every low-dominance woman was a virgin, and none had ever masturbated. High-dominance women tended to like sex, to try everything at least once, to speak of sex as fun, and to describe desirable men in terms of their qualities as lovers. Middle-dominance women spoke of sex in terms of romance and sentiment, and they praised attractive men for moral and domestic virtues. That is, they spoke Earnestly.

Maslow's attempt to define levels of ''dominance'' wouldn't hold up under psychiatric or ethological scrutiny today, but he may have had his finger on an emotional-behavioral continuum ranging from confident assertion to guilty inhibition. What he called dominance was probably a combination of individual, social-class, and other factors; and what he described as middle dominant seems typically middle class, the background of most professional people in our society. Maslow's essay does suggest that some of the talk about meaningless sexual data, about banality and dignity and tenderness, are typically middle-class and middle-dominant rhetoric, which moralizes, sentimentalizes, and domesticates sex, and seeks to justify it extrinsically even while seeming to freely praise it.

High-dominance zest may strike the middle-dominance observer as unfeeling, trivializing, even callous. It may seem to lack the seriousness proper to serious matters. Some middle-dominant people may be somewhat threatened by the thought of being in bed with the high-dominant, even of being judged in their eyes. What, after all, would a true Van de Veldian have done with a horny, high-spirited girl who didn't need all that foreplay, let alone the bond of marriage, in order to enjoy sex? He would probably doubt, quite humanly, the reality of something beyond his personal experience—that people unlike himself can healthily have sex without being in love, without deep mutual knowledge and respect, without all that foreplay—all without suffering neurosis, immaturity, even without losing the ability to love. And that, perhaps, is the key: the danger of any clinician or researcher setting up one style of sexuality (invariably his own) as a standard of psychosexual health.

Maslow himself, about a decade after his paper on dominance and sex, wrote Earnestly (1954) that, "We cannot go so far as some who say that any person who is capable of having sexual pleasure where there is no love must be a sick man. But we can go in that direction." He added that "novelty in the sexual partner is very exciting and attractive, especially for definitely neurotic people. . . ." I leave it to the perspicacious reader to separate medical fact, moral conviction, innuendo, and defense of the girls' locker room.

Those who think we have leaped a long way since Maslow's later essay should take a careful look at the recent trend that seems to value sexual pleasure in and for itself, without medical or moral justifications. This trend leans for support on the work of Masters and Johnson and has indeed encouraged a more positive attitude toward sex. Still, it contains some oddly Pinaforian elements, even where it encourages eroticism with a variety of animate and inanimate objects. It emphasizes, as Van de Velde did, the cunningly prolonged sexual encounter devoid of impulsiveness—devoid, in fact, of passion and thus of many opportunities for other kinds of pleasure and for profound feeling. Like many feminist doctrines, it suggests that men should leash their sexual assertiveness while women increase theirs.

This recent Oil-the-Body-and-Tease-It-Out school seems to forget that lust and impulse can be wonderfully infectious. For some people, stroke-it-slowly may be the best way of sex; for others it may be anaphrodisiac, limiting, sometimes boring, or even downright frustrating. We should add that there is apparently an almost universal biosocial law (Tinbergen, in Karlen, 1971) that if the male does not show more aggression than the female, mating does not take place; one wonders how far humans can successfully digress.

As I have briefly charted the route of Pinaforism, some of my own views have probably become clear. I do not believe that more sex will destroy civilization or wither the best in humanity. I do not believe some people's inability to show warmth or commitment results from a sexual revolution, but it may indicate that no such revolution has taken place. I am convinced that there are some inherent biosocial limits on sex behavior in our species, as in all others. And I do not believe that any one style of sexuality can properly be prescribed as a sign of, or path to, mental health. I do believe that sex is potentially a vehicle for the entire personality and thus for every emotion. It can be tender, playful, vengeful, ecstatic, banal, a power play, a performance, a sedative, with elements of female aggression or male passivity, all without guilt or apology. In fact, even guilt has its place. One could hope that in sex, as in other aspects of life, a flexible and versatile personality will express all its qualities at various times. Doubtless, different styles and emotions will predominate in various people. But to say that one is right and healthful and should drown out the others seems to me unrealistic and tyrannical.

The history of Pinaforism shows how the ''shoulds'' of one tradition, one social class, one lifestyle, one personality type, can be justified and rejustified as scientific truth. If psychiatry claims special knowledge and authority about sex in clinical situations and in matters of public policy, it endangers its credibility when it speaks from inherited conviction rather than evidence.

But perhaps that worry is exaggerated. In fact, perhaps the apparently indestructible Soiled Pinafore helps psychiatry as well as hinders it. Even as psychiatry has taken the lead in nudging society a short way from the depths of its ancient terror of sexual impulse and excess, it has unconsciously retained enough of that fear to keep the organic social connections without which it couldn't survive. It may even succeed in walking that ambivalent path for some time to come. Come to think of it, I'd be delighted not to be a psychiatrist on the day the field loses all Pinaforism, if there are crowds of citizens nearby, and stones small enough to throw.

CHAPTER 8

Sex in the Elderly

STUART A. WALTZMAN
and TOKSOZ B. KARASU

Introduction

The circulation of humor about sex in old age is commonly associated with themes such as the decline of sexual ability, the peculiarity of continued interest in sexual issues, and humiliation for ''excessive'' lustiness. The suspicion of sexuality in the elderly has ample historical and literary support, including early sexologists such as Krafft-Ebing. Although he indicates that ''the manifestation of sexual instinct in old age is not in itself pathological,'' he also implies that when the elderly, especially one whose sexual needs were in his early life perhaps not very marked, experiences reawakening of sexual urges, a ''presumption of pathological conditions suggests itself at once'' (Krafft-Ebing, 1892, p. 37). He goes on to warn against the dire consequences of these sexual urges by stating that the ''first objects for the attempts of these senile subjects of brain atrophy and psychical degeneration are children'' and further mentions sexual acts with geese, chickens, etc. as well as ''horrible perverse sexual acts with adults'' (p. 38). While it is true that on occasion people with organic brain disease may manifest unusual (for the individual) sexual behavior, Krafft-Ebing chose to emphasize the perversely dramatic rather than the normal, especially in association with sexuality of the aged.

Unfortunately, fallacies about sexual expression in the aging did not stop with Krafft-Ebing and persist even at the present time. The traditional notion of sex for procreation rather than recreation has been reinforced even by the young who would reject it for themselves. Guilt and fears of punishment concerning sexuality are frequently projected onto an aging parent, who may be treated as he/she treated the child decades before. For many people, the childhood rejection of parental sexuality in order to cope with their own emerging sexual feelings persists or even becomes aggravated later in life. Misconceptions such as the cessation of sexual desire for men and women after middle age, the inability of older men to avoid behavior such as exhibitionism and child molesting, the debilitating or dangerous effect of coitus, and the psychopathology of masturbation affect the elderly, especially those who have lived according to rigidly held standards. It will be interesting to see whether the present generation of youth, who have been exposed to more permissive sexual mores, will manifest different sexual behavior patterns in their later years.

There are approximately 30 million people in the United States above the age of 60, and their aging and sexuality occur within the context of a cultural milieu that has changed markedly from previous generations and continues to change at a rapid rate. It has become increasingly difficult for the elderly to satisfy their basic needs in our present cultural milieu. The traditional elevated status that the elderly enjoyed in agricultural societies has declined in an industrial society that has become increasingly youth-centered. Modern living arrangements have changed drastically from the past when family members lived with or geographically close to one another. At present, society fosters the notion of the independence of children, resulting in a concomitant loss of status for the elderly. They no longer are endowed with the responsibility for dispensing wisdom and assigning economic and social roles, because knowledge in these areas can be concentrated and stored in books and disseminated through the media.

Partially owing to geographic mobility and the decline of the extended family structure, the aged are frequently concentrated in relatively segregated living situations that further isolate them from the mainstream of modern society, thereby depriving them of the opportunity to perform useful services. Early retirement to make room for the young further contributes to this loss. Loss of status and retirement also mean loss of purpose and concomitant decline in income, further restricting activity and involvements. New roles must be learned, even though previous commitments to lifestyles become increasingly difficult to alter. In order to minimize the guilt associated with the extrusion of the elderly, they are frequently and prematurely relegated to areas of low visibility—retirement communities or old-age or nursing homes. The decrease in social contact and process of disengagement is further aggravated by the physical decline of the elderly, which makes them more threatening to the young and allows the rationalization that residential institutional facilities are a necessity. The sense of isolation and rejection tends to produce feelings of sadness and resentment in the aged, thereby making them less pleasant to deal with and easier to withdraw from. In fact, this increasing isolation of the old from the young reinforces the negative stereotypes of the old and ignores their strengths.

Although stereotypes abound concerning the elderly, they are by no means a homogeneous group. Health, social class, educational level, all do make for differences. Certain experiences can, however, be expected at this stage of life, experiences that place great stress on those who suffer them. Significant losses of family and friends occur through death, disability, or relocation. The most significant loss is that of a spouse of longstanding, no matter how ambivalent the relationship has been. The spouse is usually the person with whom one has shared most of the gratifications and sorrows of living. For some, it means the loss of one of the major reasons for survival or the loss of an object upon whom one has been extremely dependent. This applies especially to women, since the male life expectancy is shorter and most women tend to marry men older than themselves. The result is a ratio of approximately 135 women for every 100 men in the older population (Butler and Lewis, 1973).

Whatever the cause, aging represents a process in which there is a decline in physiological function at the cellular level, resulting in increasing vulnerability to diseases combined with the loss of the capacity for repair of damaged tissues. This is most apparent in the decline of physical vigor. The aging individual is usually keenly aware of the major aspects of the decline and certainly reacts in lesser but definite ways to the more subtle signs. Physical decline produces direct effects on cognitive functions and symbolically represents deterioration and disability, which are frightening.

Cardiac and cerebrovascular disease represent the major chronic contributions to failing health. Cardiac output and central nervous system perfusion volume decrease with age, and minor changes in their status can produce major shifts in acute cognitive function. Cardiac arrythmia, infarction, and congestive failure can all produce discomfort, fear, and acute and chronic changes in cognitive status. Loss of visual acuity brought on by cataracts, presbyopia or more specific diseases is extremely common. Loss of hearing may create isolation or distrust. In most aged individuals, there is considerable loss of taste and smell and this, combined with defective teeth and gums, tends to deprive them of the pleasure and security of certain familiar foods. Muscle mass and strength decrease, thus diminishing tolerance to exercise. Arthritis can limit movement and produce discomfort and pain. Medical or surgical intervention may increase pain, disability, and a sense of helplessness, thus aggravating any other difficulties present. It has been estimated that a total of 86 percent of the elderly have chronic health problems of some kind (Butler and Lewis, 1973).

In spite of all that can go wrong, approximately 81 percent of the elderly are able to move about on their own. Although chronic disease is common, limitation of function is usually mild. In addition, most older people have some support of others. Only about 5 percent are confined to institutions, and this group appears to differ from the majority: a much higher proportion of them have never married or are widowed (Butler and Lewis, 1973). Unfortunately, the older the person the more likely he is to live alone (Shanas, 1969). Nevertheless, it seems that in spite of the stresses, the elderly employ a variety of coping mechanisms which allow a significant percentage of them to continue to achieve gratification from living.

General Anatomic Considerations and the Changes Occurring During the Sexual Response Cycle

Aging produces physiological changes in the sexual area as well as the other psychobiological systems mentioned above, but knowledge of these was limited until the revolutionary studies of Masters and Johnson (1966). Their findings, in addition to delineating the physiologic changes occurring during sexual activity for younger adults, also provided initial data on the elderly. While they cautioned (p. 223) that ''it will require at least another decade to obtain the cooperation of the aging men and women in numbers sufficient to provide biological data of statistical significance,'' their results are sufficiently important to review in some detail.

The Female

A significant degree of elasticity is lost from breast tissue with aging, causing sagging, flattening, and reduced vasocongestive response. The lining of the vagina becomes thin and atrophic, with a concomitant decrease in lubrication. This increases mechanical irritation of the bladder and urethra during intercourse and may produce urinary burning and frequency for as long as two or three days after coitus. The wall of the aging vagina becomes thin, loses its rough, corrugated look, and changes from reddish purple to light pink. There is also shortening of the vaginal length and width as well as some loss of its expansive ability.

Clitoral size may be reduced, but this does not usually occur until the age of 60. Generally, clitoral response continues in patterns similar to the premenopausal female as long as the stimulation is gentle. The labia majora lose fatty tissue as well as some elastic tissue, depending upon the extent of sex steroid hormone reduction. This results in the loss of the flattening, separation, and elevation of the labia that occur in younger women when they are sexually stimulated. The cervix and uterus also shrink in size.

While nipple erection during the excitement phase is unchanged from younger age groups, the vasocongestive increase in breast size in response to sexual tension is reduced as aging occurs. The intensity of the engorgement of the areolae which occurs during the plateau phase is diminished.

As women age, there is a delay in development of vaginal lubrication and a decrease in the amount, in spite of the feeling of being sexually stimulated. The development of the sex flush occurs less often than in younger women and is restricted to the epigastrium, interior chest, neck, face, and forehead. Generalized muscle-tension elevation in response to sexual stimulation decreases as the woman ages. In contrast to the younger female who responds almost equally to manipulative and mounting activity with expansion of the inner two-thirds of the vagina, the older female responds less to manipulative activity. The development of an orgasmic platform in the outer third of the vagina during the plateau phase is reduced. There is also a reduction of the involuntary uterine elevation, which is another major factor in the reduction of the expansion potential of the vaginal barrel.

The orgasmic phase of the older woman is significantly shortened, especially in those who are estrogen deprived. The number of contractions of the orgasmic platform in the outer third of the vagina is reduced, although there are exceptions to this in women who have a higher than average history of sexual activity. Rhythmic uterine contractility during orgasm usually remains, but there may be spastic contractions felt as pain in the lower abdomen and radiating to the vagina, labia, and legs. This also occurs particularly in women who are estrogen deprived and may produce reluctance to participate in sexual activity because of the intense cramping pain. Rectal contractions, which are seen in younger women during orgasm, are observed much less frequently. The return of the pelvic organs to their unstimulated state after orgasm is rapid compared to younger women.

The most important conclusion that Masters and Johnson derived from their data of older women is that significant sexual capacity, effective performance, and orgasmic responsivity are retained by the aging female, especially if she is exposed to regular sexual stimulation.

The Male

The response of a young man to effective sexual stimulation is the development of an erection within a matter of seconds. Most older men, however, do not develop an erection for several minutes. The older the male, the longer it takes to achieve full penile erection. Once achieved, penile erection may be and frequently is maintained for extended periods of time without ejaculation. Full penile erection frequently is not attained by the male over 60 until just before ejaculation.

The testicular elevation that occurs in younger males during the late excitement phase or early in the plateau phase is reduced by at least half, and there is little of the vasocongestive increase in testicular size that occurs in the younger male. Scrotal skin thins, and there is loss of elasticity as well as a reduction in the scrotal vasocongestive response to sexual tensions. The degree of nipple turgidity during the plateau phase is reduced. There is loss of the vasocongestive maculopapular flush of sexual tension, and total absence or marked reduction of the pre-ejaculatory fluid emission secreted by Cowper's gland.

The plateau phase usually lasts longer for an older man, and he frequently may wish to maintain this kind of pleasure for an indefinite period of time without a drive for ejaculatory release.

The force of the expulsion of the semen during ejaculation is about half of the younger male, and at times only seminal fluid seepage may occur. The older the male, the fewer the number of expulsive contractions, and the intercontractile interval rapidly lengthens after the second expulsive contraction. There may be orgasm without the stage of ejaculatory inevitability. Instead of a two-stage well-differentiated ejaculatory process, there may be a single-stage expulsion of the seminal fluid, with the prostate, seminal vesicles, and vas deferens contracting simultaneously with the penile expulsive contractions rather than preceding them by two or three seconds. Occasionally, the prostate may develop spastic contractions, thus lengthening the first stage of the orgasmic experience to as much as seven seconds. The volume of seminal fluid produced by ejaculation is decreased. After ejaculation there is rapid loss of erection. As aging occurs, the refractory period may extend for a considerable period of time.

While these changes are normal for the aging male, they may produce considerable anxiety if their significance is misunderstood. If the male or his partner interprets them as meaning a loss of sexuality, considerable anxiety may accumulate and secondary loss of potency may result. If there is awareness of the physiological nature of the changes occurring, sexual activity and techniques can be carried out to coincide with the level of performance. It is also important to note that performance levels vary even in the same individual, and at no time do physiological changes mean the end of sexuality. If elevated levels of sexual activity are maintained from earlier years and neither acute nor chronic physical disability intervenes, aging males are able to enjoy an active sexuality. Indeed, the factor of reduced ejaculatory demand can be a basis for effectively prolonging the satisfaction of the female partner, thus providing the male with considerable pleasure without the necessity of an accompanying orgasm. Even though sexual activity has been avoided for long periods of time, elderly men can be returned to effective sexual functioning if adequate stimulation is accomplished by an interested partner.

Review of Surveys of Sexual Behavior

While Masters and Johnson's work on the physiology of sex has established a beginning data base, there has been a relative paucity of studies to determine the manifest sexual behavior of older people. Moreover, it is difficult to compare these studies because the nature of population samples differ, methods of data collection are not uniform, and the nature and detail of data obtained varies.

The first series of studies of any real importance were the ones organized by Kinsey et al. (1948, 1953), which involved a survey of the sexual behavior of 14,084 males and 5,940 females. Of those, only 106 men and 56 women were over 60 years old, but some tentative conclusions were drawn. They found that at age 60 only one out of five men was no longer capable of intercourse, but by age 80 this proportion rose to three out of four. Kinsey's findings suggested that the rate of decrease in the frequency of sexual outlets did not decline any more rapidly in old age than the relative decline in the years between 30 and 60. He also reported that single men and those who had been married had frequency of sexual outlets only slightly below their married counterparts.

Kinsey's observations on women were also a portent of future studies. He reported a gradual decline in frequency of intercourse between age twenty and 60, but attributed this to the aging process in the male. He also noted that in contrast to men, single women and those who had been married had frequency of sexual outlets considerably below married counterparts.

The next behavioral studies were done by Masters and Johnson (1966). In addition to their extensive physiological studies, they obtained careful and detailed sociosexual histories of a highly selected group of 212 men and 152 women over the age of 50. Of these, 133 males and 54 females were over 60. They reported that the human male's sexual responsiveness diminishes as he ages and that, in comparison to males aged 41-60, those over 60 have diminished levels of sexual tension, reduced intensity during sexual expression, and decreased coital activity, masturbation, and nocturnal emissions. They state that among the "most important factors in the maintenance of effective sexuality for the aging male is consistency of active sexual expression." High levels of sexual activity during formative and middle-aged years meant continued sexuality in old age.

As far as women were concerned, they concluded that regular sexual expression either by coitus or masturbation was necessary for the maintenance of sexual capacity. They reported that many women became more interested in sex after menopause because of the diminution of the fear of pregnancy. The major factors related to continued good sexual adjustment were earlier satisfactory sexual relationships and social and economic security. For those women who had a previous history of unsatisfactory sexual experiences, withdrawal from sex was the norm. For the females who had never married and who had employed masturbation for relief of sexual tensions during their twenties and thirties, the same patterns persisted through the forties and into the sixties. For women who had heterosexual contact but no longer found it available, masturbatory practices increased. They state, however, that "there is a reduction in the frequency with which manipulative relief is deemed necessary beyond 60 years of age."

The most extensively reported investigation of the aging process thus far has been the Duke Longitudinal Studies (Busse, 1966). The first study was started in 1954 and involved 260 community male and female volunteers aged 60 or over. The subjects were initially studied with the goal of obtaining a wide variety of economic, social, physical and psychological data, among which was information about their sexual activity and feelings. However, the sexual information obtained, although relatively specific, was limited in detail and scope. Studies were carried out on these subjects approximately every three years over a ten-year period. A second longitudinal study of 502 men and women aged 45-49 was conducted in 1969. In the initial studies, six of the original group of 260 subjects did not complete the study and were therefore eliminated from the sample, thus leaving a total of 254 subjects.

Newman and Nichols (1960) reported the data of the first evaluation of the initial longitudinal study. They delineated four married groups on the basis of age—60-64, 65-69, 70-74, and above 75. The first three groups had about the same percentage of people reporting sexual activity, about 60 percent. However, in the group above 75, this dropped to 30 percent. This group also contained more people affected with systemic disease. They found that while 7 percent of the single subjects were still sexually active, 54 percent of the married group continued to be. This tended to confirm the findings of Finkle et al. (1959) who had studied a group of 101 men between 55 and 86 years of age in an attempt to construct a baseline of sexual activity in older males. These were ambulatory patients with medical complaints, but whose complaints were judged by the investigators not to interfere with sexual activity. They found that age and marital status were the primary influencing factors in sexual potency, defining the latter as having had sexual intercourse at least once during the previous year. About twice the percentage of men were sexually potent under 70 (65 percent) as over 70. Of the sexually inactive men, about two-thirds were either never married or were widowed or divorced at the time of the study. Among the sexually potent men, marital status was more influential than occupation or age in contributing to continued sexual activity.

In a series of analyses of the data from the first longitudinal studies, there is a clear indication that sexual interest, and to some extent activity, continued to play a strong role in the lives of many elderly people. Pfeiffer and his co-workers (1968) report that while analysis of cross-sectional data revealed a gradual decline of activity and interest with advancing age, longitudinal data revealed three different and distinct patterns. One was the gradual decline but there were also patterns of a steady level of interest in activity over a ten-year period as well as a group who demonstrated rising patterns of interest in activity (Verwoerdt et al., 1969). In addition, Verwoerdt et al. reported that age and degree of sexual activity are not related in a strictly linear fashion, but that such intervening variables as age-related illness or physical disability exist. Their studies indicated that the incidence of sexual activity declined from a level of more than 50 percent during the early sixties to 10 to 20 percent after 80 and that there was a sharp drop during the mid-seventies. They concluded that sexual interest was probably more directly related to aging per se than activity, with a significant decline in strong interest occurring beyond the age of 75, but a persistence of mild to moderate sexual desire in half of the subjects surviving into the eighties and nineties.

The factor of gender was significant in the report of interest and activity. At every age, men reported greater sexual interest and activity than did the women of similar age. This was especially so among an elite subgroup whose health, intellectual status, and social functioning were not significantly impaired during the course of the study. In this group, 33 percent of the women as compared to 80 percent of the men acknowledged sexual interest, and twenty percent of the women as compared to 70 percent of the men reported sexual activity.

One factor that may make the above data more comprehensible is marital status. In the aged, the combination of life expectancy and the tendency of women to marry men somewhat older than themselves produces a significant percentage of women without men. Data from the longitudinal studies indicated that the level of sexual activity and interest was almost identical for married men and nonmarried men, but there were major differences in the level of sexual interest and activity between married and unmarried women, with the percentage of nonmarried women reporting sexual interest and activity that was considerably lower (Verwoerdt et al., 1969).

This is further borne out by the fact that, among men and women asked to give reasons for having stopped sexual relations in later life, men generally tended to place responsibility on themselves and women also tended to place responsibility on their husbands (Pfeiffer et al., 1972; Pfeiffer et al., 1968). This is especially true with men in their seventies who appear at this time to undergo a consistent decline in sexual abilities (Verwoerdt et al., 1969). The implication is clear in that a woman may continue to maintain high levels of interest and activity if she has available to her a socially sanctioned and sexually capable male.

Additional analysis of the data of the Duke studies confirms the previous impression of Masters and Johnson that a high level of sexual interest and activity in youth was highly correlated with continued sexual activity in later years and was true for men and women (Pfeiffer and Davis, 1972).

Christenson and Gagnon (1965) compiled data from a group of 241 females age 50 or over who had been married and were interviewed for the Kinsey studies. For married women at age 50, marital coitus was the predominant sexual activity with seven-eighths of them still reporting coitus at a rate of over once a week. By age 60, participation had dropped to 70 percent and at age 65 to 50 percent. Masturbation did not drop as much in this particular group of women, varying from 30 percent at age 50 to 25 percent at age 65. For women no longer married, the percentage changed from 37 percent having coitus at age 50 to 12 percent at age 60 and to none at age 65 and 70. The incidence of masturbation for these women, however, was nearly double those who were still married at comparable ages. Educational attainment on the part of the women did not appear to have any effect on any of the sexual activities, although religious devoutness did. The more frequent the Church attendance, the lower the rate of coitus and masturbation for both married and unmarried.

Women who had a more active sexual life before age 30 had a greater incidence of postmarital coitus.

Their data also underline the role of the available male. The females with younger spouses had higher rates than those with older ones. However, the orgasmic capacity of females tended to be higher with husbands of the same age than with husbands younger or older.

Christenson and Johnson (1973) further reported some of the Kinsey data on sexual patterns in a group of 71 older women who had never married. These women had an age range of 50-69 with only one-fifth over the age of 60. Of the 71, ten stated that they never wanted to marry and twenty had "some desire" for marriage. The remainder reported that they had wanted "very much" to be married. They indicated a wide range of reasons why they never married, attributing it most often to parents, family, career, or lack of sexual desire.

About a third of the subjects (23 cases) reported that they had never experienced any overt sexual activity beyond simple petting, and even during the petting episodes erotic arousal had been minimal. These women said they had never experienced orgasm from any source, including masturbation. They also reported a higher degree of religious devoutness than the remainder of the sample. The remaining two-thirds reported an active sex life at varying levels, including 79 percent masturbation to orgasm, 62 percent intercourse, 52 percent orgasmic sex dreams, and eight subjects described extensive homosexual contact.

While some of these women continued their sexual activities and interests into their postmenopausal years, the majority did not. As would be expected, there were some differences between various subgroups. Most women with no sexual experience in their younger years were free of sexual feelings later, although some women who started to have sex at the age of 30 continued to have sexual outlets in later years. The early sexually active part of the sample nearly matched in their patterns of sexual aging a group of sexually active women in the separated, widowed, and divorced group who were also studied.

Apart from coitus, the most significant form of sexual outlet for both sexes over 60 is masturbation. According to Kinsey, for people over 60, about 25 percent of men and 30 percent of women continue masturbation even if they are having intercourse. For the never-married women reported above, the incidence of masturbation decreased from 49 percent at age 45 to 35 percent at age 55 to 23 percent at age 60 (Kinsey et al., 1948; Kinsey et al., 1953). But those rated as having high early sexual experience had masturbatory activity of 80 percent at age 45 and 70 percent at age 55. Christenson and Gagnon (1965) reported that in a group of widowed, separated, and divorced women, 44 percent were still masturbating at age 60.

In summary, while it is difficult to draw valid generalizations from the data available, some trends may be significant. In most people, sexual activity decreases with age, but the relative decrease may be no more than in younger years. There is, however, a sharp drop in the mid-seventies in activity and interest. Major factors in the decrease seem to be physical illness or disability and the unavailability of partners. Factors which appear to have a strong correlation with continued sexuality are high levels of sexual activity in the formative and middle years as well as a history of satisfactory sexual relationships. Many additional factors that play a role in delineating and defining subgroups remain to be clarified.

Homosexuality

Homosexuality presents even greater problems for some aging men than heterosexuality. A homosexual frequently does not have children to spend time with or to provide a focus for an ongoing relationship with another adult. In addition, the aging homosexual living in a world that especially worships youth and physical attractiveness is subject to derision.

Weinberg (1969) gathered questionnaire data from 1,117 male homosexuals and stressed that his findings were supported by data obtained at the Institute for Sex Research from another 458 male homosexuals. He found that there was a decrease in involvement in the homosexual world on the part of the older homosexual (those over 45) and a decrease in the frequency of homosexual sex. Nevertheless, according to self reports the older group did not appear more lonely or depressed than younger homosexuals and were ranked higher on a psychological adjustment scale. It appears from this data that older homosexuals, like older people in general, develop acceptance of their overall situation even though it may demand a lowering of expectations.

Calleja (1967) studied 1,700 men whose average age was 64 and found that over 6 percent had engaged in homosexual acts after they reached the age of 60. The vast majority of these men were either married or widowed and for most of their adult lives had been heterosexual. These men placed a great deal of emphasis on the warmth and sensitivity they found in their homosexual partners and appeared to stress affection as their primary need. It is unclear from the data why they found more warmth and sensitivity in males rather than females at this point in their lives.

The Geriatric Sex Offender

The geriatric sex offender is a grossly overrated phenomenon in our society (Whiskin, 1970). Aggressive assaults such as rape are primarily carried out by the younger sex offenders. Older persons are more likely to be involved in exhibitionistic behavior or pedophilia involving caressing and fondling without causing physical injury. Kozol et al. (1966) reported that between 7 and 8 percent of 141 patients committed as ''sexually dangerous offenders'' were over the age of 60, but even of these only some were involved in violent acts. Some older sexual offenders may be merely trying to gain physical affection, while others have been able to resist their impulses until the stresses of old age combined with diminishing controls produce expression of impulses that had previously been repressed.

The role of organic brain damage in the elderly sex offender is still unknown. In one study of fifteen men over the age of 60 who had committed a sexual offense, nine had an organic brain syndrome (Whiskin, 1970). However, there have been no reported systematic studies of the subject. Nor are systematic data concerning the relationship between sexually perverse behavior and increasing age yet available.

Nature and Etiology of Sexual Dysfunctions

The disorders most commonly occurring in the aged are loss of interest or desire for sex, pain during sexual relations or upon climax, premature ejaculation, erectile dysfunction, retarded ejaculation, and orgasmic dysfunction.

Pathogenesis of Sexual Dysfunction

Any view of the etiology of sexual or other dysfunction must encompass the concept of multiple causality, with contributions in varying degrees from biopsychosocial factors. Sexuality, and particularly sexuality in the elderly, is prone to the intervention of these multiple factors. Successful sexual relations depend upon the integrity of the physical apparatus and a sense of physical well-being as well as psychological and social factors. The integrity of the physical apparatus includes the sexual organs as well as their supporting neurological, endocrine, and vascular systems. These systems are for the most part dependent on the individual's general health, the presence or absence of specific diseases, and the use of prescribed or nonprescribed chemicals. These factors are especially important in the elderly because of the decline of physical vigor and the increased incidence of sustained and sometimes debilitating physical illness. Nevertheless, the connection between physical disorders and ultimate sexual behavior is complex, and rarely is there a one-to-one relationship. The same physical disability may have varying effects on different people whose coping styles in response to the real and symbolic meanings of the impairment are different. Factors such as self-esteem, frustration tolerance, previous level of sexual adjustment, and the nature of the relationship with the partner all combine to produce the final level of sexual function. Most illnesses do not destroy the sexual response completely, but may produce a chain of events of emotional reactions which culminate in complete dysfunction. If a person reacts with severe anxiety to a physical incapacity, a temporary sexual disability may be compounded by performance fears and concerns about retaliation or rejection by the partner. Because of this, the treatment of any person with an illness affecting sexual function must include both specific modalities for the illness and psychological intervention, which can help prevent further disability secondary to anxiety.

Biological Factors

In any initial work-up of a patient complaining of sexual dysfunction there must be an inquiry about the present stress factors, fatigue, or the presence of depressive symptomatology. It is unknown at the present time how the presence of depression may influence the level of sexual interest and performance, but clinical experience leaves little question that the influence is significant. Aging may even combine with specific or nonspecific effects of illness on the central neurohormonal system, which may act through the peripheral effects of sex steroidal hormones. The confluence of aging, sexuality, and depression may reside in the central nervous system concentration of such monoamine neurotransmitters as serotonin, dopamine, and norepinephrine. In fact, Segall et al. (1975) have reported that the growth in sexual maturation of rats can be delayed or prevented by restricting their intake of tryptophan which is an amino acid involved in serotonin synthesis. In addition, there is suggestive evidence for the involvement of central monoamines in sexuality. This was demonstrated in studies using p-chlorophenylalanine which inhibits serotonin synthesis combined with pargyline, an MAO inhibitor. This combination was used to increase the ratio of dopamine to serotonin and produced intensified sexual behavior in male rats (Gessa and Tagliamonte, 1975; Tagliamonte et al., 1969). Some additional evidence, although questionable in its significance, has been derived from clinical observations of Parkinsonian patients placed on L-Dopa. Some patients develop increased sexual activity in conjunction with a general increase in physical improvement, but it has also been reported that other patients note the return of spontaneous penile erections after L-Dopa therapy (Goodwin, 1971; O'Brien et al., 1971). While there may be no definitive connection to sexuality at this time, the biogenic-amine hypothesis in mood disorders has been receiving widespread interest and investigation for at least two decades (Baldessarini, 1975).

Some systemic illnesses depress sexual interest in their very early stages. Hepatic, renal, pulmonary, endocrine, malignant, and infectious disorders may present with vague generalized complaints which affect sexual drive. The lowering of androgen levels either metabolically or surgically may lower sexual interest in both males and females and possibly impair the erectile response of males.

Diseases specifically affecting the brain sex centers are unusual, and such conditions as brain tumors affecting the limbic lobes and producing changes in sexual behavior of the elderly are rare. However, global brain disease producing dementia may induce cognitive, affective, and perceptual dysfunctions resulting in poor judgment as well as the inability to modulate behavioral responses, including sexual ones. Any disorder affecting somatic or autonomic sensory or motor nerve supply to and from the genital area, as well as spinal-cord reflex centers which control vasocongestion and orgasm, may impair the sexual response. The damage may be vascular, infectious, degenerative, traumatic, or surgical. Most patients with these lesions continue to desire sex and are aware of the diminution of function. In males, spinal-cord lesions result in some degree of reflex or spontaneous erections which may last from a few seconds to many hours or days, as well as impairment in the capacity to attain and maintain an erection willfully. With low or incomplete lesions the patient retains some

perineal muscle control and sensation and often experiences psychogenic erections. About half the patients with complete lumbar lesions
experience both psychogenic erection and orgasm. Events in women
parallel those in men in the sense that clitoral erection and lubrication
of the labia and vagina are affected. Some patients with cauda-equina
lesions are capable of erection and orgasm although they may be even
further reduced in intensity than in the normal elderly male when
associated with systemic disease (Horenstein, 1976). Ordinarily,
chronic, symmetrical peripheral neuropathies do not usually affect
male potency unless the illness is severe, but diabetes may well be an
exception to this.

It has been estimated that 50 percent of all diabetic males will
develop impotence, although when impotence precedes the systemic
manifestations of the disease it is usually temporary (Campbell and
Clarke, 1975). Impotency may be transient in those diabetics whose
disease is not properly controlled or be unremitting in patients who
have been ill for many years. The probable cause is autonomic nervous
system neuropathy, although other mechanisms such as metabolic abnormalities have been suggested. Impotence in diabetics is usually
chronic, of insidious onset, persistent, and progressively worsening.
Other than irregular menses and fetal abnormalities, the impact of
diabetes on women has been inadequately studied and is therefore
unclear.

Severe vascular occlusive disease involving the distal aorta and
the internal iliac branches (The Leriche Syndrome) may result in impotence. Usually Gluteal claudication as well as intermittent claudication are accompanying symptoms. During the surgery for this
difficulty, the sympathetic nerve fibers which pass over the internal
iliac vessels may be cut, thus resulting in loss of ejaculatory ability.
Abdominal aortic aneurisms also present a significant threat because
of the difficulty they pose to blood supply, possibility of rupture, and
surgical threat to the sympathetic nerve fibers (Lord, 1973). Correction
of aneurisms of the common iliac arteries may result in decreased
arterial flow to the genital organs through the internal iliac arteries.
In women, there is no obvious effect on sexual function of a bilateral
lumbar sympathectomy.

Although a significant increase in systolic and diastolic bloodpressure occurs during intercourse, thereby elevating the already increased blood pressure of the hypertensive, there is little evidence that the rise is immediately dangerous to the patient. Oaks and Moyer (1972) found that the patient whose hypertension is in its early stage and has not yet become associated with any illness such as diabetes or Leriche syndrome will not have any specific sexual problems associated with it. In view of the fact that the present inclination of most physicians is to treat blood pressure elevations early, most of the sexual problems of people with hypertension occur because of the drugs used to treat the illness. This is difficult to evaluate at times because, although women report no changes in sexual adjustment with blood pressure management, some men report that when blood pressure is carefully controlled they do not feel as well.

The drugs available to treat hypertension include peripheral sympathetic blocking agents such as guanethidine, methyldopa, and propanolol and peripheral vasodilators, such as hydralazine, and diuretics. Some types of sexual dysfunction occur consistently with certain drugs through their known pharmacological actions, but other medication interferes with sexual desire and potency via unknown mechanisms. Most of the studies done to investigate these areas have relied on retrospective data, so it is difficult to assess how many patients had these symptoms before the drugs were begun. Loss of sexual desire occurs in both male and female patients taking methyldopa, and males occasionally develop the inability to sustain an erection. Some patients report impotence on Guanethidine as well, but its main problems are failure of ejaculation or retrograde ejaculation which occurs in over 50 percent of people on adequate dosage (Carver and Oaks, 1976). Decreased desire for sex may be associated with propanolol and clonidine, as well as with reserpine if a significant depression develops. Spironolactone and methyldopa produce gynecomastia in males and dose-related loss of desire in males and females (Page, 1975). In fact, failure to comply with antihypertensive therapy is frequenty associated with the onset of side effects related to the compromise of sexual functioning, and patients may not report this without specific questioning.

Stroke is one of the high-risk complications of hypertension and one of the most common disabling illnesses of the aged. Changes in many areas, including vision, mobility, and speech, may severely hamper self-esteem and force the individual to alter characteristic coping styles. While many patients have the same sexual desire post-stroke, there may be embarrassment to try sexual relations with a disability or fear of not satisfying the partner.

Sex is a primary concern of the postcoronary patient. Fear of impotence and fantasies of dying during sexual intercourse may inhibit sexual activity or surround the act with enough doubt and anxiety so that it is no longer enjoyable. Physiologically, the cardiac patient generally responds to sex in the same way as the noncardiac person. The maximum responses of heart rate and cardiac output for both occur during the orgasmic phase in which elevation of blood pressure and increase in respiratory rate are greatest. Hellerstein and Friedman (1969) have demonstrated that intercourse between middle-aged, long-married couples does not appear to produce significant danger for postcoronary patients. While people report different subjective responses at different times, physiologically, the response is fairly constant. Patient reports tend to demonstrate that there is a decrease in the amount of sexual activity after the recovery from a coronary as compared to levels of sexual activity prior to the insult. This is probably due, however, to psychological and interpersonal rather than physical factors. The fantasy of a coronary death will play an important role in the reluctance of many coronary patients to involve them-selves in sexual intercourse; yet most of the data pointing to it as a significant factor is anecdotal. In fact, in a study by Ueno (1963), death during coitus accounted for .6 percent of 5,559 sudden deaths, and of the 34 coital deaths, 27 occurred during or after extramarital intercourse. Perhaps the most important factor is the total setting in the sense that a comfortable, familiar, relatively tension-free atmosphere will protect even the coronary-prone patient.

Surgical conditions which damage the genitals or their nerve supply may produce sexual dysfunction. Sexual difficulties often follow radical surgery for cancer of the rectum and colon or any surgery that results in retroperitoneal node dissection (Bernstein, 1972). The nerves of erection are particularly vulnerable in the dissection between the rectum and prostate. For benign disease, however, it should be possible to preserve the ability to ejaculate by preserving the sympathetic nerve fibers covering the aorta and the major vessels below the bifurcation and sexual potency by carrying dissection of the pelvis as close to the rectal walls as possible. Surgery resulting in ileostomy or colostomy may result in sexual difficulty even if no structures directly involving the sexual response are affected. The reasons are a combination of fears about the illness necessitating the surgery, grief for the lost organ or natural body orifice, concern for appearance and cleanliness, fear of rejection, and symbolic reawakening of early psychosexual conflict. Nevertheless, with an accepting partner, most ostomy patients adjust well sexually (Olin and Pearlman, 1972).

Urologic disease is a common cause of sexual dysfunction. Congestive prostatitis does not affect potency, but may decrease the sexual drive, due to physical discomfort. Infectious prostatitis resulting from gonorrhea or other nonspecific bacterial organisms may lead to impotence and decreased desire for sex because of dysuria, frequency, and discharge, as well as the attendant anxiety, and sometimes guilt, about the basic condition. Benign prostatic hypertrophy is an extremely common condition of elderly men. Although there is no theoretical reason for men who have a transurethral resection, retropubic, or suprapubic prostatectomy to lose potency, it has been reported in anywhere from 10 to 66 percent of cases (Gonick, 1976). The reasons for this, however, are probably due to such factors as a welcome opportunity to stop intercourse for a variety of reasons, the attitude of the physician who conveys impotency as a frequent sequel to prostatectomy, and a concern that intercourse will impair health. In spite of the fact that potency should be maintained, an inevitable sequelae of all types of prostatectomy is retrograde ejaculation because of trauma to the internal urethral sphincter. Radical perineal prostatectomy for carcinoma of the prostate usually results in impotence because of block dissection that includes the autonomic nerves to the penis, and also because there may be vascular damage to the penile veins and disturbance of mechanical support to erection. With radiation for early cancer of the prostate, approximately 30 percent of patients become impotent, and the remainder note some decreased sexual activity (Ray, 1975). Even after orchiectomy and estrogen therapy, impotency is not an inevitable complication, particularly over the short haul (Dubin and Amelar, 1971).

Peyronie's disease is a deformity of the penis due to the formation of a fibrous plaque in a hyaluronic acid-rich sheath lying between the tunica albuginea and the corpus cavernosum (Smith, 1976). When severe, it may be associated with a painful deformity causing bending of the penis on erection and interfering with vaginal penetration in coitus. Various treatment techniques have been used, including symptom relief with potassium p aminobenzoate, injection of a steroid preparation into the plaque, use of parathyroid hormone extract injected into the plaque, excision of the plaque with skin graft of the corpora, and, if necessary, a penile prosthetic implant.

Priapism is a pathological erection not associated with sexual desire or ability to have intercourse. It may become annoying and disabling and can occur in association with certain illnesses like leukemia or conditions producing anoxia of the central and peripheral nervous system. Unfortunately, when surgical correction by incision or drainage of the corpora cavernosa is required to reduce the erection, the patient is usually impotent thereafter.

In the menopausal woman, complaints of dyspareunia and pelvic pain are very common and may be related to estrogen depletion, with accompanying physical changes or vaginal pathology such as infections or post-irradiation vaginitis. Some women with uterine prolapse experience dyspareunia, bleeding, or leukorrhea, which may lead to alterations in sexual behavior. Occasionally, surgical treatment of uterine prolapse leads to dyspareunia because the scarred area may be pulled into the depth of the vaginal barrel and the penis comes in contact with this area on deep penetration (Mueller-Heubach, 1972). Care to construct a vagina which admits two fingers, can, in most instances, prevent this complication.

Alterations in sexual reactions are relatively infrequent after gynecological surgery if patients have supportive relationships with the physician and family members and are adequately prepared preoperatively and given the reassurance that sexual behavior will follow the same patterns after surgery as before. If adverse reactions occur, they are usually due to inadequate sex education or misinformation, estrogen depletion, marked pre-existing ambivalence about the feminine sexual role and sexual dysfunction, depression due to real or symbolic loss of the part removed (Lindenmann, 1941), or concerns about a change in physical appearance, such as with surgery of the vulva.

Another surgical procedure that may result in decreased desire for sex is mastectomy, but the postoperative dysphoria is related to loss of self-esteem and concerns about loss of attractiveness and femininity.

The use of exogenous substances can have marked effects on sexual desire and performance. The most common substance used is probably alcohol. A small amount decreases inhibitions, a moderate amount may delay ejaculation, and a large amount may prevent erection. Habitual heavy alcoholic intake tends to impair the sexual response of both males and females, but it especially has effect on the potency of the male. Many other drugs, such as phenothiazines, tricyclics, monoamine oxidase inhibitors, barbituates, narcotics, estrogens, cortisone, ACTH, and anticholinergic or antiadrenergic drugs, all produce sexual dysfunction.

Psychosocial Factors

While there are many psychosocial causes of sexual dysfunction in the elderly and the problem is almost always multifactorial, the most common basis is inadequate education, including constricted upbringing and reinforcement of negative attitudes by the social and cultural milieu. Most of the present generation of elderly grew up in an era in which they were trained to view sex as, at best, occasionally pleasurable, and, at worst, depraved. While the portrayal of sex in the media has changed considerably, it is far more difficult for the elderly to discard learned and continually reinforced familial and cultural patterns. In addition, the self-esteem of many elderly people throughout most of their lives may have rested on their being relatively asexual. When social conditioning has produced someone who lacks interest in sex and at the same has the need for marriage, conflict tends to arise if one partner is more interested in sex than the other. Under these circumstances, sex may be experienced as an onerous burden and something to be dispensed with as soon as possible. Those who feel this way about sex will use the end of procreation, illness, disability, or age itself as legitimate reasons for the cessation of all sexual activity. In these circumstances, the forbidden or dangerous conscious and unconscious meanings of sex become predominant, and abstinence is viewed with considerable relief.

Knowledge of the effects of aging on sexuality is still clouded in extreme ignorance for most of the elderly. Since menopausal changes in women sometimes lead to pain on intercourse or urinary-tract difficulties unless adequately treated, many assume that these changes mean the end of all sexuality. The positive sexual aspects of the menopause for women are rarely stressed, even in relatively sophisticated circles. Many people are still ignorant of the physiological aspects of sex as well as erotic areas and methods of pleasurable stimulation. They have frequently spent their lives being too frightened and guilty to explore themselves and others or to experiment with different sexual variations and techniques. Men in their late middle age, aware of losing their accustomed quick erective potential and unaware that it is normal, become anxious and are unable to accommodate to their changing needs. Sexual myths abound, but two of the most common are that the male should ejaculate at every sexual encounter and the female must ''achieve'' orgasm or experience the episode as a failure.

In conjunction with the prevalence of ignorance, some people have spent their lives denying their own sexual needs consciously or unconsciously. Whether this has been expressed in the avoidance of excitement with the same partner or the avoidance of potentially exciting partners, high levels of sexual tension are seen as dangerous. Usually, other activities serve as an outlet for the release of tension and the maintenance of self-esteem. Problems arise only when a partner, old or new, makes sexual demands that promote intense anxiety.

The anticipation of being unable to perform in a sexually adequate way is extremely common in both men and women and plays a significant role in many sexual difficulties. Whether this is brought about in conjunction with an episode of performance difficulty, the onset of illness, surgery, the use of exogenous substances, concerns about aging and failure, or transactional difficulties, the results are the same. Fear of failure leads to failure, and failure produces anticipatory anxiety related to sexual performance. Not uncommonly, the atmosphere of failure is also related to the desire to please the partner and the projection of a performance demand that may or may not be real.

Lifelong patterns resulting from inadequate education, conflicts over sexual pleasure, and fear of failure usually lead to behavior during sex that reinforces distance. Such behavior has been described as spectatoring: instead of allowing sex to unfold naturally, the participants maintain a tight rein over their emotions and observe their own sexual reactions. This is especially prevalent in those that are anxious about their performance and are concerned about rejection. The fear of rejection also may lead to the failure to communicate one's sexual needs or desires. Failure to communicate often perpetuates existing sexual difficulties and leaves no room for the development of new sexual patterns.

Boredom frequently leads to sexual difficulties in later life, although many people are acknowledging these feelings at much younger ages than previously. With age, people may become less physically attractive, and factors such as poor hygiene, excess weight, bad breath, and flabbiness may diminish physical arousal in a partner. At the same time, the level of intimacy may diminish as time passes. In addition, the initial novelty and excitement of mutual exploration wears off, and sexual encounters become routinized. This tends to increase disappointment and reinforces withdrawal. Boredom may especially occur in people who take rather rigid sexual positions and in those whose view of others tends to be stereotyped. Unconscious conflicts concerning sexuality may become major factors at this time. If a wife is increasingly viewed as matronly, latent unconscious oedipal conflicts of her husband may become manifest, thus producing even more withdrawal. The reawakening of oedipal conflicts may also occur in the female.

Mutual withdrawal as well as specific sexual difficulties may also be produced by changes in self-esteem of one or both participants, which can begin independently. This may occur as a result of the process of aging, the onset of illness and disability, or situational problems, such as job loss or dissatisfaction and financial reverses. Many people assume that they are vulnerable to sexual failure as soon as other failures have occurred. The concern, anxiety, and withdrawal that occurs will reinforce the negative atmosphere in which adequate sexual functioning cannot take place.

Dyadic discord is a significant factor in the production of sexual difficulties in the elderly as well as in younger people. Marital maladjustment has always been widespread, and overt dissatisfaction seems to be increasing. The divorce rate in the elderly is less than in the general population because of previously held mores as well as a decrease in options. Many marriages appear to be stable, but consist of chronic exchanges of anger and resentment. In some relationships the increase of contact which occurs after retirement aggravates previous difficulties which had been submerged because of relative lack of time spent together. Couples who have maintained covert resentment may become frankly hostile to one another.

Resentment over the unrealization of mutual expectations may become aggravated in the elderly should they become less capable of obtaining gratification from a variety of other sources. Fear of abandonment may increase demanding behavior, which only results in further withdrawal. Power struggles in which both partners attempt to control one another result in sustained rage and a need to frustrate and defeat the partner at all cost. This does not necessarily occur in an overt way and therefore may not be open to mutual exploration. Such difficulty may only reinforce the communication problems which already exist in many couples.

In a retrospective study of 175 couples who presented with a variety of problems at their marital counseling clinic, Berman and Lief (1976) reported that the most common complaints were sexual problems and long-standing communication difficulties. The most prevalent characteristic of the couples they saw was difficulty within the relationship, including active hatred of long-standing duration. Their impression was that many couples they saw were unresponsive to any therapeutic intervention including sex therapy because of the difficulties in the relationship. For those with a relatively good prognosis, the most important factors were a friendly marital relationship and a relatively short-term period of sexual dysfunction—less than six to eight years—after a prolonged period of good sexual functioning. Their findings were similar to those of Masters and Johnson (1970), who also reported that a frequent cause of treatment failure was marital units traumatized in such depth that there was no chance for reconstitution of an effective marital relationship. Kaplan (1974) also agrees with this point of view, stating that ''couples who are clearly physically or mentally incompatible or frankly hostile to each other are not good candidates for sexual therapy.''

Diagnosis and Treatment

The attempt to make a diagnosis of specific sexual difficulty should not focus on whether an abnormality is either organic or psychologically produced, but on the relevant contributing physical and psychosocial factors in each situation. It is vital for the physician or health professional who sees any elderly person, no matter what the presenting complaint, to take a complete sexual history along with the standard medical history. Direct, empathic, nonjudgmental questioning will usually elicit honest responses. A careful medical history is important because it might be possible to detect evidence of the early onset of medical illnesses. A detailed description of the sexual difficulty and the exact circumstances under which it occurs is necessary, as well as an attempt to elicit the patient's understanding of what is happening and why. Standard laboratory studies, including steroidal hormone levels, should be done, as well as any additional studies suggested by the history and physical examination. Nevertheless, unnecessary extensive studies should be avoided unless there is a specific reason for pursuing them. A psychosocial history focusing on family or dyadic transactions should be taken as well.

If the presenting complaint is impotency, questions concerning nocturnal erections and emissions, morning erections, or erection with other partners should be asked. If there is a remaining question about the presence or absence of erections, the phenomena of the occurrence of erections during REM sleep should be pursued. Karacan et al. (1972) have reported that nocturnal penile tumescence (NPT) occurs consistently in healthy males of all ages, although the percent of REM periods accompanied by tumescence decreases with age. The presence of full erections during REM sleep tends to rule out significant organic pathology, just as abnormal NPT implies the presence of organic factors.

Treatment of any difficulty, including sexual problems, should always proceed from the relatively simple procedures to the more complicated ones, if that is at all possible. Nevertheless, in most situations, several types of interventions will probably be necessary. After the removal of any potentially offending exogenous substances, the treatment of any medical or surgical illness, and basic educational counseling, other techniques may still be indicated.

The use of hormones or other exogenous substances such as vitamins or drugs has long been advocated by some in the treatment of sexual difficulties, especially in the elderly. There are, however, few well-controlled double-blind studies validating the use of these substances and specifying their precise indications. For example, some of the claims for the use of systemic procaine have been improvement in sexual interest and capacity, stimulation of pelvic hair growth, improved testicular function, and, in women, slowing of genital atrophy, return of the normal appearance of the vulvo-vaginal mucosa, and repigmentation of the labia minora. In a recent review, Ostfeld et al. (1977) surveyed the use of systemic procaine in sexual dysfunctions in men and women and concluded that the work in the field consists of "preliminary observations which did not reach the point of controlled clinical trials." They further stated that procaine may or may not have beneficial effects on endocrine and sexual functions, but "that data are inadequate to support any conclusions."

Although there is wide agreement that androgens are important in the initiation and maintenance of puberty in males, their precise role in adult male sexuality is controversial. There seems to be a gradual reduction in testosterone levels, although this is not uniform (Stearns et al., 1974). Attempts to stimulate sexual interest and potency using testosterone formulations have not, however, met with uniform improvements, although there is some anecdotal evidence of efficacy. Improvement may be related to a sense of well-being associated with anabolic androgenic substances and the placebo effect, unless there are demonstrable low testosterone and abnormal gonadotropin levels. A problem with the use of testosterone in men over 50 is that carcinoma of the prostate may be testosterone dependent, thereby stimulating development of latent cancer.

The efficacy of replacement estrogens is more clear-cut. Estrogen-replacement therapy can improve the physiological problems of postmenopausal women during intercourse, and maintenance estrogen reverses many of the degenerative changes occurring in the organs of the genital tract (Easley, 1974). Complaints of dyspareunia, spasms of the uterus during orgasm, lack of feeling of well-being, fatigue, and hot flushes may respond to estrogen therapy. While many women have welcomed the symptoms as a way to justify cessation of sexual activity, others are very disturbed by their presence and welcome estrogen therapy as a way to renew sexual interest and activity. Estrogen may also be helpful in combating arteriosclerotic changes, osteoperosis, loss of skin elasticity, and atrophy of fatty tissues, which may occur after menopause. The suspected relationship of estrogen to thromboembolic phenomena as well as to certain kinds of cancers, such as breast and endometrium, makes it difficult to recommend estrogens without reservations. In addition, many women do not develop estrogen deficiency, and careful clinical evaluation is necessary before estrogens are prescribed on a maintenance basis.

In addition to the precise determination and treatment of the organic factors present in any sexual problem, the psychological factors must be carefully delineated and treated as well. The use of psychotherapeutic methods should proceed from the simple to the complex with nonspecific, inexpensive treatment modalities attempted initially and more demanding and time-consuming treatments attempted only if necessary. Finkle, in a series of papers, has reported the efficacy of urologic counseling for males who are impotent (Finkle and Thompson, 1972; Finkle, 1973; Finkle and Finkle, 1975). The principal treatment method consists of "sympathetic listening to the patient's problems and reinforcing his self-esteem by emphasizing the positive features of the self-expressed history" (Finkle and Finkle, 1975). The patient is complimented on his courage for having sought help, and, while he is told that the physician has no specific medication or techniques to restore potency, help is given by explaining that most potency problems are produced by "psychological" factors and are amenable to treatment. It is further suggested to him that "congestive prostatitis" may play a role in sexual difficulties, and that this is treated actively by fluid intake and sulfonamide. The patient is then given permission to attempt intercourse when he has had adequate rest and has enlisted the "active interest of his partner." The success or failure of this attempt is discussed with the patient, and additional suggestions may be made concerning sexual techniques or discussion of the types of distress precipitating sexual dysfunction.

Similar attempts may be made with women who have concerns

about their sexuality as well as ongoing life stress. Empathic history-taking, treatment of physical conditions, hygienic advice, permission to expand sexual expressiveness, and instruction in sexual techniques may be very helpful in ameliorating relatively acute problems.

Frequently, however, the techniques just mentioned are inadequate to the task at hand. This will prove especially true in certain dyadic transactional difficulties where couple-therapy must be undertaken. The presence of significant communication problems, intense power struggles, and ongoing mutual hostility prevent any meaningful sexual relationship. Only when these conflicts are to at least some degree resolved will an attempt to help the specific sexual problem be fruitful. The theoretical orientation of the marital therapist or therapists is probably less important than the agreement among all the participants to resolve the prevailing difficulties and foster understanding, acceptance, and compromise.

Individual and group psychotherapy, as well as adjunctive pharmacotherapy may also be pursued, although their specific indications in the aged with sexual problems is still unclear. Here, the presenting symptoms are presumed to be only one manifestation of many other significant problems or a manifestation of unconscious conflicts. Attempts to understand and correct symptoms, relieve dysphoric states, improve capacity for intimacy, and enhance the meaning of existence may be explored. In addition, the presence of feelings about sexual variations or perversions may be explored and placed in the perspective of a total life situation.

Sex therapy may be a valid treatment alternative for many elderly people, provided the dyadic unit is functioning adequately. Disorders which are responsive to sex therapy are: erectile dysfunction, premature ejaculation, retarded ejaculation, vaginismus, and orgasmic dysfunction. Masters and Johnson (1970) have reported their treatment of 56 elderly couples or a total of 89 individual cases of sexual dysfunction. The success rate in women with secondary orgasmic dysfunction was 60 percent and their success rate in men with secondary impotence and premature ejaculation was 75 percent. Their techniques with the elderly were the same as the techniques used with other age groups. Unfortunately, their sample of patients is probably not representative of the general population, since all their couples were in good health, Caucasian, middle-class, intelligent, and motivated with short-term dysfunctions (six to eight years or less).

Treatment involves the assumption that both partners must participate in the therapy program and that the marital unit is the focus. Treatment is behaviorally oriented, stressing communication and correcting those situational factors that reinforce sexual dysfunction. The couple is prohibited from any sexual play other than that prescribed by the therapist or therapists if it is a dual therapy team. Specific exercises are prescribed which initially focus on heightening sensual awareness to touch, sight, sound and smell and permit couples to learn to give and receive pleasure without the presence of performance demands. Types of genital stimulation as well as other treatment techniques are gradually introduced, depending on the dysfunction being treated and the needs of the particular couple. Many modifications of the original techniques or new treatment approaches are being added as more therapists incorporate sex therapy in their treatment repertoires.

For those who cannot have significant restoration of function from the usual biological or psychosocial therapies and who are willing to experiment with mechanical aids for sexual pleasure, the use of mechanotherapy may be indicated (Dengrove, 1973). This includes the use of such devices as an artificial phallus, vibrator, and the Kegel Perineometer to promote sexual activity and increase the chances of sexual gratification. It also includes the use of a device called a rubber donut which is slipped over a partially erect penis and fits tightly at the base, thus retaining the blood necessary for erection. Presentation of these possibilities must be done tactfully, since some patients will respond with a decrease of self-esteem and others may view their use as morally repugnant.

Some surgeons are turning to penile prostheses for the treatment of erectile dysfunction which is unresponsive to other modes of therapy. Pearman (1972) has reported the use of a Silastic penile prosthesis which is surgically inserted into the penis and provides sufficient rigidity for vaginal penetration. Although other devices giving the patient a permanent erection have been used, the most promising development may be the inflatable prosthesis (Small et al., 1975; Scott et al., 1973). It consists of a totally implantable device using paired inflatable sili-

cone cylinders within the corpora cavernosa connected to a hydraulic
pumping device in the patient's scrotum. The fluid reservoir for pumping pressure is placed behind the rectus muscle. This device allows
the patient voluntary control of erection. There undoubtedly will be
further refinements of these prostheses and other surgical techniques,
and only careful evaluation of the data of future studies will clarify
for whom they are indicated.

Prevention of Sexual Dysfunction

With adequate education in the formative years within the family
and in the sociocultural milieu, sexuality could be a pleasurable and
fulfilling experience for most people throughout the life cycle. In many
areas of society, sex has carried certain negative connotations which
have become unconscious, self-reinforcing, and will shape attitudes
and behavior for a lifetime. Notions of sex being unladylike, indecent,
physically harmful, or even immoral haunt many people and produce
numerous situations of premature withdrawal from sexual activities as
well as interpersonal hostility and mutual recriminations. Mythology
especially abounds concerning sex in the aging and, combined with
disapproval of healthy curiosity about the body, confines many people
to permanent ignorance and fear.

Basic information concerning normal physical changes must be
disseminated to as many people as possible combined with the basic
facts of sexuality with increasing age. Normal changes in general
physical status, hormonal levels, physical capacity for sex, and the
expected effects of emotional life stresses and physical illness should
be standard information given to the entire population (see also chap.
23, this volume). This does not necessarily mean that the message
should be that everyone must include sexuality as a central part of
their lives for this might produce guilt and feelings of inadequacy in
those who choose not to do so. However, it would help those people
whose withdrawal from sex is not one of choice but of misinformation.
It would mean that for those people who might want to continue sexual
activity, the opportunity for the expression of excitement, affection,
admiration, and commitment would still be open to them.

New information about how to deal with the physical changes occurring with age should be available to all. The importance of men's being aware of the physiological changes which occur in erection and ejaculation cannot be overestimated. Knowledge of these facts helps remove the fear that ultimate impotence, loss of sexual pleasure, and inability to gratify a partner are inevitable, and would in all likelihood diminish the level of sexual impairment as well as the degree of loss of self-esteem which now occurs in many men. The level of discomfort in the urogenital system which many women experience and which acts as a trigger for sexual withdrawal can be dealt with by a combination of hygiene, medication, regulation of fluid intake, and change in sexual techniques.

Information about the importance of general health care and the specifics of how to preserve adequate physical functioning should be available. Instruction concerning exercise programs, adequate nutrition and vitamin intake, and the importance of individually appropriate amounts of rest should be disseminated on a large-scale basis. Attention to personal hygiene and physical appearance and the preservation and maintenance of the functions of the organs of special senses, all contribute to self-esteem, communication, optimism, and retention of physical attractiveness and sexual functioning.

The willingness to experiment with new ways of relating to others socially as well as sexually within the limitations of physical capabilities can enhance the quality of living as aging occurs. Some people may have to learn new ways of communicating about sex, as well as different techniques and a slower pace for mutual sexual gratification. Some of these techniques may involve sexual activities that are relatively new to the individual, and emphasis on communication is therefore extremely important. Different positions of intercourse, especially those which may accommodate to various physical changes, can be learned, as well as coital techniques which are helpful to men who are able to achieve partial erection or to women able to accept partial penetration. Sexual alternatives or additions to intercourse such as manual or oral stimulation can be introduced as techniques which others have found satisfying. Masturbation should be openly explored as an outlet, in addition to sexual contact with another person or as a substitute, if unavailability or disability prevents mutual sex (see chap. 3, this volume). Vibrators should be offered as acceptable en-hancers if a woman has been unable to achieve gratification by manual stimulation or if a desire for more intensive stimulation is present. Caution must be taken in presenting these techniques because many elderly people have felt personally uncomfortable with these ideas before, nor must they be made to feel inadequate if they reject newer approaches.

Health care personnel and physicians are in a unique position to help others adjust to their changing sexuality. It is only in recent years that medical schools have begun to teach students about the behavioral issues involved in human sexuality, although they had always been educated in reproductive physiology (see chap. 12, this volume). Fre-quently, physicians are uncomfortable and embarrassed in dealing with the elderly about their sexual lives, and it may be necessary for many physicians to attend ongoing seminars in which they have access to the didactic material as well as open discussion of feelings concerning their role as sexual counselors.

Most physicians should be included in this education process be-cause the education about sexuality must occur in conjunction with the treatment of many illnesses and disabilities of the elderly. The physician can be instrumental in preventing needless sexual disability, guilt, and feelings of inadequacy. Re-education in these areas involves anticipation of questions and concerns, as well as clarifying issues, providing realistic information, and counseling about sexual tech-niques. The physician may have to broach the subject before the pa-tient does, for many people are too shy or frightened to open the discussion. The patient should be told the nature of his or her diffi-culty, the likelihood of resuming sexual activity, which sexual activ-ities are possible, and which techniques may enhance those sexual activities.

Counseling in Specific Illnesses

For spinal-cord injuries, couples should be taught techniques of reflex stimulation of erection, various coital positions, techniques of adequate lubrication, and how to introduce a turgid, but not fully erect penis into the vagina (Horenstein, 1976). Uses of foreplay and the development of new techniques of erogenous stimulation based upon retained sensory ability can also be encouraged. Surgical restorative techniques designed to compensate for erectile insufficiency can also be tried. With patients who have had cerebrovascular accidents, evaluation must be made of the residual, motor, sensory, or visual changes which have occurred and which would impair some aspect of the sexual response. Suggestions, such as approaching the patient from the area of the intact visual field, touching the parts of the body which have intact sensation, and respecting muscle weakness, are practical but frequently neglected. Embarrassing loss of bladder or bowel control may be avoided by suggesting that emptying be done before sex. Changes in the physical aspects of the bed that allow for greater stability or maneuverability may be helpful (Renshaw, 1975a).

Patients with cardiovascular disease need a great deal of education and guidance as well as reassurance about their sexuality. Hypertensives should be counseled that regular sexual intercourse is ordinarily not dangerous, but that sex in unusual or stressful situations may be. In addition, when patients are given drugs to lower their blood pressure they must be carefully advised about the potential side effects affecting sexuality. If they are not advised, poor compliance with the therapeutic regimen should be expected. Another area where the physician must take the initiative is in counseling the postcoronary patient. Many patients are frightened of having another coronary or dying, and this may lead to anxiety about the sexual situation, producing withdrawal or impotence. These patients can be encouraged to resume sexual activity when they can perform exercise which expends up to eight calories per minute without chest pain, shortness of breath, or the production of abnormalities in pulse rate, blood pressure, or the electrocardiagram. In addition to the clinical determination, the use of portable EKG tape recorders, which can be used during sex in the privacy of the home, will provide sufficient data to make the decision. Those patients who have symptoms during sexual intercourse can usually be permitted to continue sexual activity on a restricted basis, as long as attention is paid to when symptoms actually develop and adequate precautions are taken. If necessary, supplementary oxygen can be given to chronic cardiac or pulmonary patients. Postcoronary patients should also be wary of engaging in sex with partners about whom they are ambivalent or in places that might engender stressful emotions.

Urinary-tract infections must be treated vigorously in men and women, since recurrent infections may lead to painful ejaculation and dyspareunia. It has been postulated that a significant decrease of sexual activity may lead to noninfectious prostatitis by causing congestion of the prostate, thus producing a vicious cycle, culminating in further withdrawal.

Males must be counseled carefully prior to any surgery involving the urogenital tract, because many people believe that such surgery automatically results in impotency. Unless the patient and his sexual partner are reassured, postoperative psychogenic impotency may ensue.

Radical surgery of the lower gastrointestinal tract may result in sexual difficulty if the patient has not undergone adequate psychological preparation, even if there is no damage to the nerve supply. This is especially true if surgery results in an ileostomy or colostomy. Patients should be reassured that sexual play will not injure the stoma, and advice can be given about emptying the stoma before sex, and about the use of deodorants. Counseling can also be given concerning the use of different sexual positions; this can alleviate anxiety about direct contact with the stoma or the production of pain.

The physician and health professional must also be alert to changes in sexual functioning as a result of various depressive syndromes. The usual presenting sexual complaint is reduction in desire for sex in someone who is having sex regularly, but other sexual difficulties may occur as well. The extent of the difficulty may vary from a transitory one when the depression is relatively minor and short-lived to total cessation of sexual activity in severe depressive episodes. When other symptoms and signs of depression are present and there is a close association of the sexual dysfunction with the clinical onset of the depression, the primary treatment should be directed toward the depression and the patient reassured that adequate sexual function will return when the depression clears. If it does not, further evaluation and specific treatment for the sexual dysfunction should be pursued.

Implications for Future Research and Planning

The needs for further research in the area of sexuality and aging are multiple and varied. Perhaps the most significant need is for definitive data on the prevalent patterns of sexual behavior, which encompass sociocultural, economic, biological, and characterological factors. This would serve as a broad base against which data acquired in future studies could be measured. It would then be possible to begin to conceptualize the factors that contribute to normal and abnormal sexual behavior as well as temporary and long-term sexual attractiveness. Further hypotheses about etiology and pathophysiology would occur after neuroendocrinologic, neuroanatomic, neurophysiological, autonomic, hormonal, and sexual physiological studies are pursued and evaluated. The role of intrapsychic conflicts, cognitive factors, child development, family dynamics, and sociocultural factors must be studied, using the theoretical background of a systems approach.

While the basic data are collected, empirical treatment of sexual dysfunctions cannot be ignored. There is a significant need for carefully controlled prospective studies of different treatment techniques and their correlation with the biopsychosocial factors of aging in general and the individual in particular. Studies could begin with comparisons of groups of patients with the same sexual response patterns and proceed to patients with similar characterological and coping styles but whose sexual responses are significantly different. Far more than exists at present, there is a need for studies with precise definition of terms, use of standardized instruments for evaluation, and rigorous criteria for treatment efficacy.

There must also be considerable political, economic, and social planning concerning the aged, including organized attempts at education in the basic facts of sexuality and human behavior. Their economic and social needs cannot be ignored within this context, as evidenced by the fact that many elderly people must endure feelings of guilt in order to cohabit with others of the opposite sex, to prevent the loss of significant amounts of their social security allotment. Education must begin with younger age groups in order to prepare them for old age and to prevent their disapproval of the behavior of their elders.

Above all, there must be continued attempts to provide the elderly with opportunities for physically and emotionally expressing their passion, affection, and commitment to one another, as well as for reinforcing and enhancing their self-esteem.

CHAPTER 9

A Unitary Theory of Sexual Perversions

CHARLES W. SOCARIDES

The delineation of perverse practices and fantasies remains a milestone in the evolution of psychoanalytic thought. Freud's (1905) earliest discoveries of infantile sexuality led him to assert that in perversion sexuality is replaced by one component of infantile sexuality, that perverse tendencies or occasional perverse acts or fantasies are present in the life of every individual, whether normal or neurotic, and that, in the latter case, during analysis, symptoms are often revealed to be disguised as perverse acts. Perverse sexuality was deemed to be identical with infantile sexuality, and therefore we were all capable of manifesting perverse acts or experiencing perverse fantasies by the very fact that once we all were children.

Perversions could result from arrested (sexual) development or, 'secondary to repression,' sexual disappointment. Fenichel's (1945) "simple formula" that "persons who react to sexual frustrations with a regression to infantile sexuality are perverts; [while] persons who react with other defenses or employ other defenses after the regression are neurotics" reflected psychoanalysts' thinking on this issue during the first five decades of psychoanalytic history. This formulation placed the perversions firmly in a position of singular importance alongside the neuroses and affirmed that, in understanding the secret of the cause of perversions, one would be casting light on the etiology, dynamics, and course of the neuroses. My focus in this paper is therefore on phenomena of central importance in psychoanalytic theory and clinical practice, with direct and indirect implications for all psychopathology. My efforts will have been justified, whether or not the new unitary theory proposed in these pages is further validated, if they succeed in recapitulating previous developments in psychoanalytic theory; in describing the current status of our knowledge, while expressing divergences of opinion and attempting to integrate new clinical and theoretical material into a whole; and finally, if they point to experimental findings that suggest a direction for future research.

Clinical observations during psychoanalytic treatment of perverse patients have led me to prepare a unifying system in which sexual perversions may be placed and understood. I am suggesting that all perversions have a common core disturbance. This theory has been especially stimulated and reinforced by new theoretical and clinical knowledge of the earliest years of life, secured by the technique of direct psychoanalytic observation of infants and children, as well as by further refinements in our knowledge of ego psychology.

This unifying system initially grew out of my intensive work with homosexual patients in which a preoedipal nuclear conflict emerged dramatically and repetitively in individuals showing no evidence of overt psychosis; and who, except for their perversion and its attendant difficulties in their external lives, were apparently functioning relatively well. I have observed the same phenomena in cases of fetishism, transvestitism, pedophilia, exhibitionism, sexual masochism, sexual sadism, voyeurism, and transsexualism.

My provisional theory arises from the extensive psychoanalytic clinical research of individual patients with perversions over the past twenty years. It is restricted to perversions of the obligatory type, where nonengagement in perverse practices would induce severe anxiety. In brief, my theory is distinguished by two central areas of emphasis: the stress on preoedipal causation, and my view that object relations pathology is more important for the development of perversions than the vicissitudes of the drives. In other words, the central conflict of the pervert is an object relations one rather than a structural one involving the three agencies of the mind. What I have to say, therefore, applies to relatively pronounced cases in which perverse development is clear and definite. Because the perverse acts are usually the only avenue for the attainment of sexual gratification, and are

obligatory for the alleviation of intense anxieties, and because the
intensity of the need for such gratification is relatively pronounced,
I refer to such cases as "well-structured perversions." It may be that
there are other cases of sexual perversion that do not originate within
the etiological framework described. And it goes without saying that
preoedipal conflict may also be responsible for clinical states other
than perversion.

Previous Theoretical Contributions

In 1955 Gillespie presented a paper on "The General Theory of
Sexual Perversions," a landmark in our understanding of these conditions (Gillespie, 1956a). He remarked that the subject of perversion,
although not neglected by psychoanalysts, had received surprisingly
little attention, especially since it occupied a place of such central
importance in Freud's theories, both of sexuality and neurosis. The
explanation was simple: Freud (1905) had written a masterpriece on
the subject in the pioneer years of psychoanalysis. The "Three Essays
on the Theory of Sexuality" was an outstanding example of his genius,
and in this work he clearly perceived that the manifestations of earlier
sexuality were of profound relevance for, and had intimate connections
with, the later development of adult sexual perversion and of neuroses
and psychoses.

Gillespie's formulation represented the psychoanalytic theory and
understanding of sexual perversions of 22 years ago. His paper is
remarkably comprehensive, taking infantile sexuality into account and
affirming that the problem of perversion lies in the defense against
oedipal difficulties. He underscores the concept that in perversion
there is a regression of libido and aggression to preoedipal levels rather
than a primary fixation at those levels. While I am in major agreement
with Gillespie's formulations and have found them to be immensely
valuable theoretically and therapeutically in dealing with all cases of
perversion, my hypothesis proposes an alternative theory of causation,
placing causation earlier.

Three years before Gillespie's comprehensive paper, a panel was
held by the American Psychoanalytic Association on the "Psycho-

dynamics and Treatment of Perversions.'' The opening statement by
Lorand highlighted the consideration that the perversions constitute a
''wide and varied set of clinical phenomena for which no clear-cut
specific concept of classification, etiology or psychodynamics has
been established. An organized summing-up of our knowledge in this
field is therefore in order,'' he added. ''Is fixation,'' he asked, ''at
a pregenital sexual level of primary significance in the etiology of perversions, and if so, how does it influence the psychodynamic understanding of therapeutic achievement? On the other hand, if frustration
and regression to previous levels of fixation are more significant
causally, is it possible in the course of therapeutic technique to by-
pass the systematic sexual development in infancy and concentrate
mainly on the cause and effects of such frustrations?'' (Panel, 1952,
pp. 316-317). While the panel members noted that an increasing number of clinical studies had begun to emphasize the role of separation
anxiety in the formation of perversion, most of the participants maintained that the derivation of perversions was still to be found in oedipal-phase conflict and that castration anxiety was of central importance.
Supporting the view of an earlier causative process, Bak, illustrating
from the analyses of two fetishists, suggested that the ''utilization of
fetishism as a defense against castration anxiety . . . must be determined by early experiences, experiences from the prephallic
stage. . . . the untoward results of disturbed early mother-child relationships'' (Panel, 1952, p. 317). It was Bak's opinion that in the
potential fetishist, ''. . . the threat of separation from the mother is
experienced as an equal if not greater danger than the loss of the
penis'' (p. 318).

My clinical research during the ensuing decade gave further substance to my growing conviction in both a preoedipal theory of causation and a common origin for all the perversions. In 1968 Greenacre
(1968a) conveyed to me her feeling that there may well be a ''unifying
structural relationship between the perversions . . .'' and ''. . . that
all the perversions were derived from a similar base of disturbance in
the early ego (especially in the sense of identity) . . .'' The type of
perversion itself was in all likelihood dependent on: the degree or
increase in early aggression, both primary and secondary; the degree
and nature of involvement of the body ego (in contributing to the

defective ego development); specific traumata at particular vulnerable times in the libidinal progression (the organizing trauma); the special nature of the superego development and ego ideal, which is dependent on the extent of invasion of the Oedipus complex by the narcissism and the actual character of the parents (Greenacre, 1968b).

Preoedipal Theory of Causation

My preoedipal theory of causation was first introduced in my volume *The Overt Homosexual* (1968a). It has undergone considerable elaboration during the second decade of this research, espeially with regard to the inclusion of new and valuable information derived from our advances in object-relations theory, differentiating criteria that exist between perversions and perversions in psychotics, and an increased understanding of the differences that exist between preoedipal and oedipal forms of the same perversion. A considerable number of these findings arrived at from the analysis of adults have been in many instances confirmed by infant and child observational studies, especially those in the area of the development of sexual identity. The proposition set forth here, that the genesis of perversions may well be the result of disturbances that occur earlier than has been generally assumed and accepted, namely, in the preoedipal phase of development, is grounded in the following tenets:

(1) The nuclear conflicts of all sexual deviants derive from the preoedipal period of development, forcing these individuals into sexual behavior that not only affords orgastic release but also ensures ego survival.

(2) The preoedipal period, especially the years between one and a half and three, is crucial to the genesis of a sexual perversion. In this period a preoedipal fixation occurs and is primary; a regression may occur to this early fixation point under conditions of stress.

(3) The sexual deviant has been unable to pass successfully through the symbiotic and separation-individuation phase of early childhood, and this failure creates the original anxiety from which sexual perversions arise. This developmental failure results in severe ego deficits and faulty gender identity.

(4) Sexual perversion serves the repression of a pivotal nuclear conflict: the urge to regress to a preoedipal fixation in which there is a desire for, and dread of, merging with the mother in order to reinstate the primitive mother-child unity.

The preoedipal theory of origin of the perversions rests on three pillars: the first is the presence of a fixation in the first three years of life during the separation-individuation phase; the second is the early disturbance in gender-role formation (sexual identity) found in all these patients; and the third is the Spitz (1959) theory of synchronicity.

The Separation-Individuation Phase and Preoedipal Nuclear Conflict

The formulation of my unitary theory relies heavily on the separation-individuation theory of Mahler and her co-workers (Mahler, 1968; Mahler and Furer, 1966; Mahler et al., 1975). The term separation-individuation refers to an intrapsychic, developmental, gradual process of separation of the self from the mother and the beginnings of the establishment of individual identity. This process is an intrapsychic event, independent of the physical separation, and infers an intrapsychic conflict existing around both a wish for and a fear of ''re-engulfment by the object'' (Mahler, 1966a). Mahler uses the term symbiotic to define an archaic state serving a restitutive function by insuring survival through the infant's delusion of oneness with the mother. Opposite needs in the infant lead him to separateness and differentiation and to regaining the primitive state of his original unity with the mother. These needs leave their imprint on the developing modes of drive manifestations and ego formation. They exercise a determining influence on the structuring of the introjects and their subsequent projective dramatization in the external world.

In previous writings (Socarides, 1968a, 1968b, 1969b) I noted that the fixation to the mother so prominent in homosexual patients, and their characteristically narcissistic object choice (Freud, 1905) may be traced back to the separation-individuation phase of development. Although it was my original impression that the fixation was to the earlier subphases of the separation-individuation process—even to the symbiotic period, because of the revival of intense archaic ego states in which there was a threat to ego cohesion and a threat of loss of object-relations during analytic therapy—it is now my belief that the fixation has occurred at a later period, i.e., at the rapprochement subphase. I was led to this conclusion by the observation that although some patients re-enact and relive fears and wishes derived from the earliest months of life (even of the oral phase), these patients do not suffer a complete loss of object relations and other ego functions. Furthermore, even in the depths of regression, they maintain the transference relationship to the analyst and, despite florid transference reactions of even a transitory psychoticlike character and the vivid re-enactment of oral fantasies, they do not become psychotic. In agreement with Arlow (1963), I think it important to realize that we are not dealing with an actual regression to an oral fantasy that originated during the oral phase, but to one that originated during the phallic-oedipal period, but derived from preoedipal-phase difficulties.

To the sexual deviant, the mother has, in his infancy, been dangerous and frightening, threatening the infant with loss of love and care. On the other hand, the mother's conscious and unconscious impulses were felt as working against separation. The infant's anxiety and frustration press for withdrawal of libidinal cathexis from the mother and result in a shift of libido toward increased aggression. This image of the introjected mother leads to a rupture (split) of the ego. In his narcissistic object choice, the homosexual, for example, not only loves his partner as he himself wished to be loved by the mother, but reacts to him with sadistic aggression as once experienced toward the hostile mother for forcing separation.

The inability to make the progression from the symbiotic phase of earliest infancy to separation-individuation results in a fixation, with the concomitant tendency to regression to the symbiotic phase. This is manifested in the threat of personal annihilation, loss of ego boundaries, and sense of fragmentation.

The homosexual, for instance, and other types of sexual deviant repeatedly demonstrate that they were unable to make these advances. In a child so unsuccessful, ". . . the fear of re-engulfment threatens a recently and barely started individual differentiation. . . . Beyond the fifteen- to eighteenth-month mark, the primary stage of unity and identity with mother ceases to be constructive for the evolution of an ego and an object world.'' By this age, the father has become an important object. This relationship ordinarily has the advantage that the inner image of the father has never drawn to itself so much of the unneutralized drive cathexis as has the mother's, and therefore there is less discrepancy between the image of the father and the real father. . . . From the very beginning, the infant creates a world in his own image, wherein the symbiotic partner is the indispensable catalyst and beacon of orientation'' (Mahler and Gosliner, 1955, p. 200).

During the separation-individuation phase (18 to 36 months) the infant is attempting to evolve and jealously guard his developing self-image ''from infringement by mother and other important figures . . . . a quasi-normal negativistic phase . . .'' can be observed along with ''the process of disengagement from the mother-child symbiosis.'' The more parasitic the symbiotic phase, ''. . .the more prominent and exaggerated will be this negativistic reaction.'' If there is severe negativism there is severe fear of re-engulfment. ''Inasmuch as all happenings in the symbiotic phase are dominated by orality, the infant furthermore loses the necessary and normal delusional experience of incorporating and thus having the good mother in himself, restoring the blissful state of omnipotent fusion with the mother. Instead, he struggles in impotent rage and panic, with the catastrophic fear of annihilation, by introjected bad objects, without being able successfully to invoke the good part object, the soothing breast or the ministering mother'' (Mahler and Gosliner, 1955, pp. 200-201).

Sometimes the ''. . . symbiotic parasitic mother cannot endure the loss of her hitherto vegetative appendage . . .'' (Mahler and Gosliner, 1955, p. 201). This is the type of mother-child relationship I have found in the study of homosexuals and other sexually deviant patients. The father could constitute an important support against the threat of maternal engulfment, but this resource is totally absent. In actuality there is a complete lack of the necessary support from either parent. Under such conditions, ''. . . a re-engulfment of the ego into the whirlpool of the primary undifferentiated symbiotic stage becomes a true threat'' (Mahler and Gosliner, 1955, p. 210).

Several clinical indicators may be cited as pathognomonic of preoedipal fixation. Foremost among these is the observation that in all sexual deviants there exists a primary identification with the mother, with concomitant sexual (gender) confusion. This identification with the all-powerful, the almighty preoedipal mother permeates every aspect of the patient's life; he feels he cannot survive without her. Efforts to separate from the mother result in his experiencing intense anxiety, anxiety well evident before the age of three and persisting unabatedly throughout life. In this connection it is important to recall that, following the birth of the child, the biological oneness with the mother is replaced by a primitive identification with her. The male child must proceed from the security of identification and oneness with the mother to active competent separateness and male (phallic) striving. If this task proves too difficult, pathological defenses, especially an increase in primary identification and archaic aggressiveness, may result. These developments are of the greatest importance for the solution of conflicts appearing in the oedipal phase and in later life. In the oedipal phase, under the pressure of castration fear, an additional type of identification with the mother in the form of passive feminine wishes for the father is likely to take place. However, beneath this feminine position in relation to the father, one may often uncover the original passive relation with the mother, i.e., an active feminine preoedipal identification.

Secondly, I have noted that the general behavior of these patients is markedly pregenital, characterized by acting out, poor affect control with occasional aggressive outbursts, and a predeliction for fantasy over reality. Preoedipal material is, furthermore, closely linked with particular traits characteristic of the psychosexual phases of that period of development, e.g., oral and anal fantasies and practices predominate.

Third, there is a severe disturbance in the sense of ego boundaries and body image.

Finally, oral-aggressive and incorporative tendencies, along with tendencies toward paranoidal anxiety, largely dominate the patient's life and may result in oral (transitory) delusional formations, dreams of internal persecuting objects, fears of poisoning, and fears of being swallowed.

The pervert therefore struggles with preoedipal fantasies, but these may serve as a defense against the emergence of oedipal material and vice versa. Hoffer (1954) has aptly described these phenomena under the heading of defense organization. Thus, castration anxiety, the direct result of the superimposed oedipal conflict, may also be utilized as a defense against anxieties of the preoedipal phase. Similarly, preoedipal drives may have a defensive importance in warding off oedipal wishes and fears. There is always an interplay between the two.

Sexual perversions, therefore, constitute early developmental fixations or developmental arrests. In some the fixation is less than in others. Upon meeting vicissitudes of later development, patients regress to those conflicts which have left a weak point or scar formation. The greater the oedipal weakness, the stronger the tendency to regression to the preoedipal period with the danger of severe psychoticlike manifestations threatening loss of ego functions and other regressive symptomatology, together with re-enactment of the earliest traumata. The tendency toward regression is dependent not only upon the preoedipal fixation, but also on the strength of the ego and on superego formation. Some sexual deviants may therefore vacillate in the enactment of their perversions and not vividly portray the merging phenomenon, the threat of dissolution, and the striking elaborations of anxiety. However, the merging phenomena may be seen in its derivative forms, e.g., the fears, dreams, and fantasies of being surrounded by snakes, being swept into whirlpools, being enclosed in a cage, being propelled in an elevator whose walls are disintegrating, etc. Some patients may never approach the merging phenomena with its danger of regression to the earlier phases of development, especially if they do not seriously attempt to interrupt their perverse practices. Others, deeply afraid of facing this overwhelming anxiety, may prematurely terminate psychoanalytic therapy in a period of resistance, and with many rationalizations for a premature interruption. Some of these will return to therapy for shorter or longer periods of time to relieve their suffering, only again to escape facing the deepest conflicts. The failure to successfully understand and resolve these conflicts and overcome these fixations is largely responsible for the inevitable later continuance of perverse practices.

Disturbances of Gender-Role Formation (Sexual Identity)

Central to the concept of etiology in the preoedipal perversion is the disturbance of gender-role identity in all of these patients. This observation, while more apparent in some individuals than in others, emerged as a central finding in all my psychoanalyzed cases of sexual perversion, despite structures and personality traits which attempt to compensate for this inadequacy. Even a masculine-appearing homosexual, for example, reveals deep feminine unconscious identification during analysis. I use the terms gender-role identity or sexual identity to indicate an individual's awareness of being masculine or feminine in accordance with anatomy. Although its foundation is laid by the ages of three to four, gender-role identity is not a fixed entity, but is subject to fluctuations and variations even into adulthood.

In their most recent publication, Mahler and her co-workers (1975) note that in the course of understanding the attainment of enduring individuality they discovered that this consists of the attainment of two levels of the sense of identity: the first being the awareness of being a separate and individual entity, and the second a beginning awareness of a *gender-defined self-identity*. They noted that gender identity in the male develops with less conflict if the mother ". . . respects and enjoys the boy's phallicity . . . especially in the second half of the third year." The early beginning of the male's gender identity is facilitated by an identification with the father or possibly with an older brother. The mother must be able to relinquish her son's body and ". . . ownership of his penis to him." Crushing activity or forcing passivity is extremely damaging to the development of gender identity. The rapprochement struggle unfortunately may take on the character of a more or less desperate biphasic struggle on the part of the boy to ward off the dangerous mother after separation. Mahler et al. contend that ". . . fear of engulfment by the dangerous mother after the separation, fear of merging that we sometimes see as a central resistance in our adult male patients, has its inception at this very early period of life" (p. 215).

While Mahler and her associates' major interest was to achieve an understanding of the development of the human infant and child in the course of normal separation and individuation processes, leading to the establishment of object constancy, self constancy, and enduring individuality (the attainment of a separate and individual self), Galenson and Roiphe, in their psychoanalytic observational study of infants and young children over a ten-year period, directed their attention to illuminating the factors in the preoedipal phase that lead to the awareness of a *gender-defined self-identity* (sexual identity). An account of their findings and conclusions is reported elsewhere in this volume (see chap. 1).

I would like to briefly highlight their results, for they provide further theoretical validation to my clinical findings which were made in advance of their hypothesis. In 1968 Roiphe made a definitive connection between the fear of object loss and early castration anxiety, noting that the major thrust of development during the period between eighteen and 24 months of age was a concern with the differentiation of the self from the object and the internalization and solidification of the object representation. This early period of genital interest and activity takes place entirely during the preoedipal period and is concomitant with the consolidation of object representation and self representation. During these early phases of genital arousal, a primary genital schematization is taking place which gives shape to an emerging sexual current and a later primary genital schematization. Roiphe concluded that early experiences that tend to challenge the child unduly with a threat of object loss or body dissolution result in a faulty and vacillating genital outline of the body at the time when a genital schematization normally undergoes a primary consolidation (1968).

Galenson and her associates concluded from their work with healthy and disturbed children that there exists an early castration anxiety (a "nursery castration," if you will) which is later compounded by the castration anxiety of the phallic phase. In such children not only are there faulty, blurred, or vacillating body-ego outlines, but in addition one can clearly discern the beginnings of perversion formation (Galenson et al., 1975). Somewhat earlier, in 1972, Roiphe and Galenson had firmly established that there is a normal period of genital interest occurring somewhere between fifteen and nineteen months of age, involved with the consolidation of object representations in the body-self schematization, and free from oedipal resonance.

Roiphe and Galenson's findings suggest an additional explanation for a common clinical finding in patients with perversions, usually attributed to oedipal-phase conflict and castration fear, namely, the presence of the "ubiquitous fantasy" (Bak, 1968) of the phallic woman. This fantasy helps deny that castration of the oedipal period can take place, and, even more importantly, it lessens body dissolution anxieties of the preoedipal period. For example, the belief in ''completeness,'' absence of differences between the sexes, would tend to reaffirm and reinforce in those patients so traumatized a vacillating body-genital outline and early genital schematization which has been imperiled by experiences constituting object loss and threats to body integrity.

Important as the role of the mother is in allowing the child to separate and individuate, the father also serves a vital function. Abelin (1971) notes that it ''. . . might be *impossible for either* [the mother or child] *to master* [intrapsychic separation] *without their having the father to turn to*'' (p. 248). The absent, domineering, hostile, detached father will not allow the male child to make an identification with him and thus become a bridge in achieving both an individual sense of self and a gender-identity sense of self. This is later dramatized in the continuation of a lifelong poor relationship between father and son. Similar clinical phenomena are observed in the adult analysis of female patients, although perversions of the female are not as common, except in those with a strong masculinity complex. In this connection, Greenson (1964) noted the importance of substituting a normal identification with the father in place of the mother—in his phrase, ''dis-identifying with the mother.'' Stoller's (1968b) important work during the past decade underscores the crucial importance of a father with whom a boy can identify in order to successfully traverse the separation-individuation phase.

Lastly, Edgecumbe and Burgner (1975) of the Hampstead Child Therapy Clinic have examined the development of object-relatedness and drive development in the ''preoedipal phallic phases'' (a precursor of the oedipal phase) and the oedipal phase proper, tracing the development of the body representation as an integral part of the developing self-representation and the processes of identification affecting these representations. They state: ''This development of self and body representations and of identifications makes a crucial contribution to the establishment of differentiated sexual identity . . .'' (p. 163). They concluded: ''The process of acquiring a differentiated sexual identity rests largely on the child's capacity to identify with the parent of the same sex'' (p. 165). They verify that the acquiring of a sense of sexual identity begins during the child's second year, continues through the anal phase, and reaches its peak during the phallic phase. Although in agreement with Mahler's concept, they differ from Mahler with respect to timing (she holds that the sense of sexual identity is formed somewhat later, beginning in the earliest period of the phallic phase) and "attach great importance to the phallic-narcissistic (preoedipal) phase as the time in which the child may be expected to acquire and to shape his own sexual identity; having done this, the child is then better able to enter the oedipal phase of development" (p. 166).

I have cited the work of these investigators in some detail because it constitutes considerable verification of the second pillar of my theory; namely, that in all perverts there is a pronounced disturbance in sexual identity which began in the separation-individuation phase and was not a secondary development resulting from a negative oedipal reaction. My clinical findings in this regard are to be found in my several writings on various perversions (Socarides, 1959, 1960, 1968a, b, 1969a, b, 1970, 1973, 1974) and, most recently, in my book *Homosexuality* (1978).

Synchronicity of Maturation and Psychological Development (Spitz)

Spitz (1959) has shown that ". . . when a psychological development, which is age-adequate for a given critical period, cannot take place, it will be difficult, if not impossible, for the individual to acquire it at a later stage [because] at the appropriate critical period a given item of psychological development will find all the maturational conditions favorable for its establishment." He called this *maturational compliance* and its counterpart *developmental* (psychological) *compliance:* "synchronicity of maturation and development is an absolutely essential feature of normal development" (pp. 76-77). Spitz showed that, if a child does not have the wish to walk when the maturation of the innervation of the lower part of the body enables it to walk, the child may later be unable to stand or walk without support. Later ". . . as a consequence of a traumatic affect deprivation, he regress[es] to the stage when he could neither walk nor stand nor sit. . . . If, during the critical period, the appropriate (psychological) developmental item is not forthcoming, then the maturational factors will seize on other (psychological) developmental items available. These developmental items will be modified and distorted until they comply with the maturational needs. An integration will be established which deviates from the norm. . . . As a result, when the bypassed (psychological) developmental item finally does become available at a later stage, it will find the maturational positions occupied by a *compensating, though deviant, structure and unavailable for normal integration*'' (pp. 77-78, emphasis added).

Spitz's observations can be applied to the problem of the early development of the sexual deviant. He has failed to make the separation from mother at the proper stage of development, and as a result a chronic intrapsychic stimulation, a fixation point, remains to which he stays fixed, despite other developmental-maturational phases that he may have in part successfully passed. In these maturational positions, compensating and deviant structures have been formed because of the infantile deficiency. These structures are intimately concerned with identity, disturbance in object relationships, faulty ego boundaries, introjective and projective anxieties, and fears of invasion and of engulfment.

More specifically, the patients with sexual perversions were unable to pass through the developmental phase in which they would have established a separate identity. This deficit in development led to profound difficulties, e.g., faulty identification, disturbances in both the sense of self and in the development of an appropriate sexual identity, a fluidity of ego boundaries, impairment of body ego, introjective and projective anxieties, fluctuating states of object relationships. Out of the inability to separate and the wish for continuing the primary identification with the mother, which have continued in the unconscious through the years, emerge a threat of identifying and a threat of merging, a threat of being annihilated and a threat of the consequences should the patient retreat inside the mother's body. The fear that crystallizes is then compounded by castration fears of the oedipal period.

These patients enter late childhood with an inhibition of self-assertion and profound conscious and/or unconscious female identification. The strong inhibition of male sexuality insures the avoidance of the female and of the merging phenomenon. These patients attempt to attain masculinity or forefeit it or try to cling to the illusion of femininity. For example, the homosexual transiently obtains masculinity through incorporation of the partner's body and penis and thereby avoids the dangers connected with the mother, all the while remaining close to her. He substitutes the male for the female, the penis for the dreaded breast and the genitalia of the maternal body. The mechanism by which this occurs was first described by Sachs (1923), and I have suggested (1968b) that these intricate intrapsychic events be called the Sachs mechanism of perversion formation. The Sachs mechanism, which can be observed in the formation of all perversions, giving to each perversion its surface manifestations, all the while excludes from consciousness the deeper, more destructive anxieties. It is a solution by division, whereby one piece of infantile sexuality enters the service of repression (that is, is helpful in promoting repression through displacement, substitution, reaction formation, and other defense mechanisms) and so carries over pregenital pleasure into the ego, while the rest undergoes repression. This repressive compromise mechanism allows a conscious suitable portion to be supported and endowed with a high pleasure reward so that it competes successfully with genital pleasure. It is acceptable to both the ego and to the superego: a split-off part of the superego derived from the parents may sanction the perversion, and the manifest perversion gives expression to preoedipal drives in a masked form. On the other hand, a repressed portion may still remain strong enough so that in the course of life it may threaten a breakthrough, and the pervert may at any time develop neurotic symptoms. Thus, the instinctual gratification takes place in a disguised form while its real content remains unconscious. Viewed in this light, the manifest perversion can be likened to the relationship which exists between the manifest dream and latent dream content, and the true meaning of the perversion can be ascertained only through the analysis of the unconscious meaning of the perverse action.

In perversions, the patient attempts to rid himself of the damaging, destructive union with the mother, ward off incorporative-introjective needs, and seeks to maintain an optimal distance and/or closeness to her. When the pressures of adaptation to the masculine role become too intense, regression to the earliest phases of ego development occurs. The great dangers inherent in this regression promote further perverse behavior in a frantic attempt to seek relief.

Perversions and Schizophrenia

Elaboration and refinement of my theory has required an explanation for those perversions which exist in schizophrenic individuals. While psychotics may also suffer from perversion, most individuals with a perversion are not psychotic and, in my experience, do not become so during psychoanalytic therapy, or indeed during long follow-up periods. The frequent coexistence of schizophrenic symptoms with perversions has been explained in various ways. Gillespie suggested that this affinity existed because strong castration anxiety leads these patients to a partial regression to pregenital levels. ''A successful perversion evades psychosis by means of a split in the ego, which leaves a relatively normal part capable of coping with external reality while allowing the regressed part to behave in a limited sexual sphere in a psychotic manner'' (Gillespie, 1956b, pp. 36-37). In Gillespie's view, therefore, the pervert is saved from psychosis largely by the mechanism of splitting. While splitting mechanisms of both ego and object are ubiquitous in perversions, they cannot, in my opinion, be assigned a prophylactic function as their major achievement. A more modest function can be directly observed through the analysis of the patient's unconscious fantasy system (the unconscious significance of the perverse act) and the multiple substitutions, displacements, and splitting mechanisms inherent in it. Through these mechanisms of disguise, the perverse act becomes possible, yielding pleasure and simultaneously avoiding more serious intrapsychic dangers, those related to both drives and object relations. A second objection, that which arises from Gillespie's belief in ''regression from oedipal conflict'' theory, is diametrically opposed to my own and has been discussed in earlier parts of this paper. My disagreement with Gillespie and others as to the etiology of well-structured perversions lying in the oedipal period does not in any way detract from my appreciation of the accuracy of his conceptualizations (including those of others) with regard to many of the mechanisms involved in the formation of perversions. I would reserve much of the etiological explanation provided by Gillespie for a different form of perversion, the oedipal form of these disorders.

Before turning to the differentiation of the oedipal from preoedipal

forms of perversion, it is important to discuss what I consider to be
essential differences between well-structured perversions and those
which appear in the psychoses, and to explain why I think that these
schizo-perversions should not be included in the unitary system I have
described. For example, schizohomosexuality (the coexistence of
homosexuality with schizophrenia), a term coined by this author (1978),
is due neither to a fixation to the preoedipal phase of development nor
to a failure of resolution of the Oedipus complex and a flight from
castration fears leading to a regression in part to anal and oral conflicts.
One may postulate a similar designation for the other perversions
which coexist with schizophrenia, e.g., schizopedophilia, schizotrans-
vestitism, schizoexhibitionism, etc. Although unconsciously motivated and arising from anxiety, the perverse act in the schizophrenic
does not serve the magical restorative function of the preoedipal form
of perversion. Severe gender-identity disturbances, when present, are
part and parcel of an underlying schizophrenic process which has led
to profound identity disturbances and a confusion with the object. The
schizopervert shows a failure to invest the object successfully, and
thus the object cannot be retained or cathected, even though there are
fused body images and fused genital representations. This is in direct
contrast to the nonpsychotic preoedipal perversion in which objects
are retained, protected, and invested successfully despite some degree
of fused body image or fused genital representation.

Bak's (1956) contributions on this topic are close to my own. He
suggested that "the frequent coexistence of schizophrenic symptoms
with perversions indicates a common fixation point in the undifferentiated phase and in defenses against unneutralized aggression; the
perverse symptoms represent an attempt at restitution of the narcissistic object relationship . . ." (p. 240). Indeed, the severity of the regressive experiences of my patients, the pronounced use of primitive
and archaic psychical mechanisms, and the transference reactions bordering on psychotic-like manifestations initially led me to believe that
perversions may be explained by their relationship to autistic and symbiotic modes of adaptation (this was strongly suggested in my book
[1968]). This assumption would connote a fixation of the autistic phase
in order to ward off the fear of a dissolution of the self representation.
The absence of true psychotic reactions, despite intense regressive

experiences and the capacity of these patients to recover from them, indicated, however, both a capacity to synthesize new structures from these experiences and a capacity to maintain object relations and analyzable transferences. I later concluded that most well-structured perversions, despite somewhat alarming manifestations, were in all likelihood due to fixations during the later phase of the separation-individuation process, most likely during the rapprochement subphase, and thus preoedipal in nature.

When homosexuality or other perversions coexist or alternate with overt psychosis it may be due to "alterations of the ego" (Bak, 1971, p. 242). For example, the ". . . ego may resort to temporary *abandonment* of object-representations [during the psychotic phase] . . . but *not* to the abolition of representations as in schizophrenia." I am in agreement with Bak's opinion that ". . . there is *a basic qualitative difference between the schizophrenic process* and the neuroses and other incidental psychoses, and there can be no possibility of a continuum between them."

Although the schizohomosexual has a preponderance of insistent and intractable anxieties and an abundance of incorporative and projective anxieties similar to the preoedipal type, together with fears of engulfment, ego dissolution, and loss of self, the homosexual act in the schizohomosexual does not insure ego survival but only fleetingly decreases anxiety over the impending loss of self. The perverse symptom in these cases is ego-syntonic as in the preoedipal type, but the aim of the perverse act is not the reconstitution of a sense of sexual identity; it is a frantic attempt to *create* object relations.

Bak (1971) brilliantly defined the differences between homosexuality in the nonpsychotic individual and the schizophrenic. His conclusions can be listed as follows: Homosexual impulses as well as other sexual impulses of a perverse nature are a frantic attempt to maintain object relations. These impulses, so often seen in paranoid schizophrenia, are not "etiological," but represent conflicts and their delusional elaborations, which are "consequences of a schizophrenic process rather than its cause" (p. 239). Bak warned against concluding that there is a neurotic structure in those individuals with paranoid delusions operating within a "relatively benign schizophrenic process" (p. 239), even though a homosexual conflict may be discovered behind these delusions. Perverse acts in schizophrenics with self-object-dedifferentiation difficulties show significant differences from the well-organized perversion. The latter show better object relations and considerably more intact ego functions. There is a basic qualitative difference between perversions in schizophrenics and those in non-psychotic individuals. In the true well-structured preoedipal perversion, object relations are maintained despite a diffuse body image and confusion in genital representation, in contrast to perverse activities in the schizophrenic. In some instances, paranoid delusions with perverse content do occur. In those cases the object relationship may still be highly pathological but is nevertheless preserved. Perverse symptoms in the psychotic are an attempt to create object relations in the face of severe regression, threatened or actual destruction of object relations in an individual severely damaged by a primary defect or deficiency in the autonomous functions of the ego, and an inability to maintain a protective stimulus barrier.

Preoedipal and Oedipal Forms of Perversion:
Differentiating Criteria

To distinguish preoedipal perversion from oedipal forms of these disorders is of equal importance to differentiating them from perversions coexisting with schizophrenia. It is clinically verifiable that perverse symptoms can also arise from the oedipal phase of development. In those instances the pathological behavior is usually slightly deviant, transitory, and not well structured. Failure to engage in the perverse act does not induce severe or intolerable anxiety. These forms must be differentiated from preoedipal perversions, which arise from preoedipal levels of development with which we associate narcissistic neuroses and impulse disorders. We may find pedophiliac, voyeuristic, transvestite, homosexual, fetishistic, etc. behavior in which the clinical picture is largely one of oedipal-phase conflicts, and regression does not involve severe impairment in object relations or other ego functions.

Several differentiating criteria are briefly noted here:

(1) In oedipal forms, object relations are unimpaired and consist of a relation of self to object, in contrast to preoedipal forms in which

object relations are mildly to moderately impaired and consist of object to self.

(2) In the oedipal forms, the prognosis for the removal of the perverse symptom and the attainment of object love is often more favorable than in the preoedipal forms.

(3) In the oedipal forms, the perverse symptom is due to the failure of the resolution of the Oedipus complex and castration fears which lead to a negative oedipal position. In preoedipal forms, oedipal conflicts may be present or apparently absent, but preoedipal conflicts predominate.

(4) In the oedipal forms, there is no fixation at preoedipal levels but often a partial regression to the preoedipal phase. In preoedipal forms, fixations may be mild to moderate and are located in the later phases of the separation-individuation process, probably in the rapprochement subphase. In the more severe perversions, such as sexual sadism and pedophilia, the severity of fixation may be considerably more intense and may lie in very early phases of separation-individuation, bordering on the symbiotic phase.

(5) In the oedipal forms, the conflict is *structural*—between ego, id, and superego. A regression to preoedipal levels may produce an object relations conflict existing alongside those of the oedipal period. In the preoedipal forms, an *object relations conflict* predominates. This consists of anxiety and guilt associated with the failure of development of self-object differentiation.

(6) Clinical observations reveal that the Sachs mechanism may play a minor role in the oedipal forms in which regression takes place and is partially effective. Therefore, the symptom remains ego-alien. In preoedipal forms, the intense attachment, fear, and guilt in the boy's relationship with his mother brings about certain major psychic transformations, which are effective through the mechanism of the repressive compromise.

(7) In the oedipal forms, the tendency to regressive states is mild, and when it occurs it is similar to that which appears in neurotics. The threats of the oedipal period have disrupted the already formed identity; a regression occurs to an earlier period in an escape from the dangers of the oedipal period. This is a partial preoedipal regression to anal and even oral conflicts. In the preoedipal forms, the tendency to regressive states is moderate to severe, although there is an adequate

capacity in most instances to circumscribe these regressions and to recover from them.

(8) In the oedipal forms, transference manifestations are similar to those which appear in the transference neuroses, and therefore the degree of potential analyzable transferences is ideal. In the preoedipal forms, a transference neurosis may also take place because there is sufficient self-object differentiation and internalization of object representations (Panel, 1977).

(9) In the oedipal forms of perversions, reality testing and impulse control are intact. Thinking is unimpaired, and self concept and ego boundaries are essentially unimpaired. Conflict is internalized, affect is appropriate, and aggression is essentially well defended against. In the preoedipal forms, reality testing is often intact but unconsciously or consciously ignored. The boundary between fantasy and reality can be indistinct. Impulse control may be incomplete, or only partial control may be present, which leads to acting out of impulses and pursuit of instantaneous gratification. Preoedipal patients frequently reveal an elevated sense of self-esteem bordering on omnipotence, which alternates with feelings of extreme self-depreciation. Ego boundaries may be fluctuating. There may be a disturbance in affect and affect control in the preoedipal type.

As I have suggested elsewhere (Panel, 1977), further refinement in our understanding of the types of perversions may well lead us to conclude that indeed the true perversions are preoedipal disorders and do not arise from oedipal conflict with a regression to earlier phases. Oedipal perverse symptoms constitute a different form of perversion, which may be treated similarly to the neuroses and may be called *perverse behavior*. Perverse behavior occurs secondarily to a temporary regression and does not represent a primary fixation and developmental failure with gender-identity disturbance; nor are the manifestations by which we know these disorders a result of the repressive compromise, as in the true perversions.

Common Psychical Origins and Distinguishing Features of Nine Perversions

A schematic representation follows of nine major sexual perversions as they apply to the male. This schema (p. 184) summarizes the origin, function, motivation, and sexual object choice or aim of the perversions. It depicts the stratification, from a root preoedipal nuclear conflict, of subsequent superimposed oedipal conflict and the resultant perversion. This schema depicts the common psychical events and differences in the production of the various perversions and the crucial differences in their formation and meaning. It should be noted that the oedipal conflicts are superimposed on the preoedipal and that a continuum exists between the two. Were preoedipal conflict not present (the root of our schematic design), no well-structured perversion would be formed. It can be seen that the various forms of perversion all reflect different compromises between the simultaneous identifications with the mother who is seen as possessing a penis and, at the same time, castrated (Bak, 1968).

In all nine perversions the individuals have failed to successfully pass through the separation-individuation phase of childhood development. Common to all of them is a fear of fusion and merging with the mother, a tendency to lose ego boundaries, and a fear of loss of self or ego dissolution.

They all suffer from a primary identification with the mother, conscious/unconscious faulty sexual identity, and disturbances in object relations. Faulty gender-role identity plays an important role in propelling them in various directions in search of psychic equilibrium, e.g., the homosexual toward men; the transvestite toward accepting his feminine identification contrary to anatomy; the fetishist toward alternately being man and woman (consciously not accepting his feminine identity but unconsciously desiring it); the heterosexual pedophile to becoming a child and/or mother alternating with an attempt to maintain his masculinity; the exhibitionist toward visual reassurance of masculinity; the sexual masochist toward a passive, submissive re-enactment of the dreaded destruction and re-engulfment at the hands of the "cruel" mother, with a built-in assurance of survival; the sexual sadist toward an angry, defiant re-enactment of the dreaded destructive re-engulfment at the hands of the "cruel" mother, with a built-in guarantee of victory; the transsexual toward the "achievement" of femininity through radical surgical procedures; and the voyeur to reinforcing masculinity through visual reassurance.

The choice of a specific perversion is a multifactorial one, depending on variables still to be adduced. For reasons not yet established, one person finds it much easier to accept one particular aspect of infantile polymorphous sexuality than another. This may be due to specific organizing traumata occurring at vulnerable periods of libidinal-phase progression in the context of a defective early ego development. The ego's acceptance of this aspect of infantile sexuality into consciousness serves to keep in repression and also alleviate the deeper anxieties.

There may be fluctuations in the balance of psychic economy that force the individual to manifest now one, then the other, perverse

A Unitary Theory of Sexual Perversion in the Male
(A Schematic Representation)

Basic Preoedipal Nuclear Conflict
    (6 months—3 years)

Failure in Traversing the Separation-Individuation Phase of Development
    (Failure to make intrapsychic separation from mother)
    (1) merging and fusion phenomena
    (2) predominance of primitive and archaic mental mechanisms
    (3) defective early ego development
    (4) increase in early aggression, both primary and secondary
    (5) disturbance in body-self schematization, particularly of the genital area

Persistence of Primary Feminine Identification

Faulty Gender Identity

Specific Organizing Trauma Leading to Choice of the Later Perversion

Passage Through the Oedipal Phase
    (3–5 years)
    (increased castration anxiety, negative oedipal position; specific ego and super-ego problems superimposed on preoedipal fixation)

Perversion
    All perversions reflect:
    (1) different compromises between simultaneous identifications with the "phallic and penisless" mother
    (2) wish to maintain optimal distance and/or closeness to the mother without fear of engulfment
    (3) faulty development of object representations
    (4) lack of adequate separation of self and object
    (5) a reassuring and reaffirming function

practice. On these occasions the defensive value of one type of perversion appears insufficient to maintain the mental equilibrium, and multiple perversions may appear. The alternation or combination of perversions may in some instances indicate that we may be dealing with an underlying schizophrenic process.

Upon entering the oedipal phase, patients with perversions often experience a negative oedipal complex superimposed on earlier development. A split in the ego and/or object is more evident in fetishism, and a split in both ego and object is commonly found in pedophilia. Common to all forms of perversion is a varying degree of body-disintegration anxiety and a fluctuation of body-ego boundaries, most pronouncedly seen in pedophilia and fetishism. At the center of all of these conditions lies the basic nuclear fear, that is, the fear of merging with, and the inability to separate from, the mother.

THE PERVERSIONS

1. Transvestitism

Function: achieves "femininity" through cross-dressing while retaining penis; reassures against and lessens castration fear.

Psychosexual Motivation: orgastic desire; yearns for femininity; (a) envies mother and sisters, (b) wants to be powerful like mother, (c) wants to have babies, (d) in wearing feminine apparel, experiences a heightening of the pleasure of vicarious feminine identification while retaining the phallus.

Sexual Object Choice or Aim: person of same or opposite sex. Occasionally no sex object, but sexual aim important (blissful reunion with mother).

2. Transsexualism

Function: achieves "femininity" through radical surgical and plastic procedures designed to remove all traces of true anatomical gender and to promote enactment of synthetic and assumed feminine role in the environment and in the sexual act; escapes from homosexuality; undergoes the dreaded castration ("riddance phenomenon"); vicariously identifies with the powerful mother, neutralizes fear of her and consciously enjoys infantile wish for intercourse with the father (the negative Oedipus complex realized); escapes paranoid-like fear of aggression from hostile, stronger men who could damage him in homosexual relations; neutralizes aggression.

Psychosexual Motivation: orgastic desire; consciously yearns for femininity and enacts it with full anatomical reassurance; wishes to displace mother with father.

Sexual Object Choice or Aim: person of sex prior to elective recasting.

3. *Homosexuality*

Function: achieves "masculinity" through identification with the male sexual partner; reassures against and lessens castration fear.

Psychosexual Motivation: orgastic desire; yearns and searches for masculinity; narcissistic object choice; tie to mother through breast-penis equation.

Sexual Object Choice or Aim: person of the same sex.

4. *Pedophilia*

Function: achieves the status of being the "loved" child and also of being the "loving" mother without giving up his penis; discharges and relieves disintegrative aggression; reassures against and lessens castration fear.

Psychosexual Motivation: orgastic desire; yearns and desires to become the loved object, the loved child, through incorporation of the "good" love object (the child a substitute for the mother) within the self (splitting of the object), thereby maintaining relationship to objects and preserving the self through a fused relationship. Also wants to be the child, envies other children.

Sexual Object Choice or Aim: prepubertal child, usually a boy, the ideal representation of the self; if a girl, the fear and dread of engulfment by the genitalia of the mother is still present, although alleviated by the lack of pubic hair.

5. *Exhibitionism*

Function: achieves "masculinity" through the visual reassurance to himself and the emotional reaction of others; "If I show myself to a woman and she reacts, then I am a man and I do not need men (avoids homosexuality) and I am not a female" (defense against feminine identification); reassures against and lessens castration fear.

Psychosexual Motivation: orgastic desire; yearns for masculinity and dramatizes it, simultaneously denies his strong feminine identification.

Sexual Object Choice or Aim: mode of sexual release (sexual aim) rather than sexual object choice of importance.

6. *Sexual Masochism*

Function: achieves masculine sexual functioning through the play-acting of the dreaded event and achieves a "victory" over the hating but seemingly loving mother; reassures against engulfment and destruction and provokes love responses from the object; vicariously identifies with the cruel, aggressive mother; controls aggression through projective identification; reassures against and lessens castration fear.

Sexual Object Choice or Aim: person of same or opposite sex.

7. *Sexual Sadism*

Function: forces and extracts love; destroys the threatening body of the mother rather than be destroyed by her; discharges aggressive impulses which threaten annihilation of the self even to the point of sexual murder; achieves temporary freedom from fear of the engulfing mother until next episode of resurgence of fear of the female body; reassures against and lessens castration fear.

Psychosexual Motivation: orgastic desire; to force love from the depriving mother; to overcome body-disintegration anxiety by inflicting rather than by passively enduring pain and destruction (sexual-lust murders often include disembowelment, ripping out of external genitalia and internal generative organs in order to overcome anxiety over engulfment).

Sexual Object Choice or Aim: person of same or opposite sex, more often adult woman; less commonly a female child or old woman.

8. *Voyeurism*

Function: reinforces masculinity through visual reassurance in viewing the female body and/or heterosexual intercourse (sexual intercourse taking place outside of himself); is reassured that he is not being swallowed up through the female's orifices; frequently accompanied by masturbation (exhibitionistic component); avoids homosexuality and is relieved of castration fear.

Psychosexual Motivation: orgastic desire; dramatizes masculine strength and ''control.'' In some instances voyeurism can proceed from looking to touching to seizing to assaulting and destroying (sexual sadism).

Sexual Object Choice or Aim: person of the opposite sex.

9. *Fetishism*

Function: achieves ''femininity'' with the capacity ''to have babies''; can be alternately male and female and often does not seek homosexual or heterosexual orgastic release because he can use his fetish; reassures against body-ego dissolution and lessens castration fear.

Psychosexual Motivation: orgastic desire; unconsciously yearns for and searches for femininity: (a) wishes to be like mother, (b) wishes to have babies, with resultant body-disintegration anxiety arising from wish for and dread of pregnancy, (c) remains masculine in appearance and attempts to enact the role of the male.

Sexual Object Choice or Aim: the fetish as a durable, inanimate, immobile object which (a) defends against body-disintegration anxiety and merging phenomena, (b) substitutes for the penis, (c) is a split representation, e.g., can serve either male or female identity (female covering over the body); splitting of the object, hence sexual release (sexual aim) rather than sexual object choice of importance.

Concluding Remarks

Future research should now be directed toward defining why one perversion is chosen over another. The solution to this problem may well lie in the careful observation of the early development of perverse acts in children and the careful clinical description of perversions occurring in adult patients. Long-range studies of the same individual from infancy to adulthood are likely to prove especially valuable.

Our therapeutic aim in cases of perversion is to discover the location of the fixation point and to make it possible for the patient to retrace his steps. This requires the lessening of compensatory, reparative moves in his adaptive processes to the point where they no longer distort and inhibit his functioning, and ultimately lose their tendency to be self-perpetuating (analysis of defenses). As in all psychoanalytic therapy, we help the patient to trace the part of his development that has been distorted by his infantile and childhood deficiencies. His personality is liberated through the transference situation, and a process of developmental unfolding can take place independent of the anachronistic anxieties and perils of childhood.

CHAPTER 10

Transsexualism:
As Examined from the Viewpoint
of Internalized Object Relations

VAMIK D. VOLKAN

What Is Transsexualism and Who Are Transsexuals?

Many men and women claim that they belong to the sex other than the one indicated by their physical structure, and that their imprisonment in an inappropriate body is a cruel trick of nature. They seek to correct this by demanding surgery and endocrinological help to change their bodies. Some men's desire for such alteration is sometimes so compelling that they take matters into their own hands and cut off unwanted genitals themselves. They are generally referred to as "transsexuals" and, indeed, typically diagnose their problem in terms of transsexualism, for which they claim surgical alteration offers a cure. To define the term would not be inappropriate insofar as it first appeared in the literature only three decades ago (Caldwell, 1949). The public became aware of transsexuals with the publication of the Christine Jorgensen story. Hamburger and his colleagues (1953) operated on an American soldier, removing his penis, testicles, and scrotum, and putting him on estrogenic hormones. On a descriptive level, Benjamin (1953, 1966) and Hoenig and Torr (1964) are among those who distinguished transsexualism from homosexuality and transvestitism.

Benjamin and Ihlenfeld (1970) offer an "educated guess" that such individuals number about 10,000 in the United States. The ex-

perience of these investigators with more than 700 such patients who
fell within the normal physiological and biochemical range established
by our present knowledge for individuals of their anatomical sex indicated that there were eight times more men (male transsexuals) seeking sex reassignment than there were women (female transsexuals).
Of some 465 letters Hamburger received from persons seeking sex
change after reading about Christine Jorgensen, three times as many
came from men as from women. The Johns Hopkins Gender Identity
Clinic received 1034 inquiries from self-declared transsexuals within
the three years beginning in 1966 (Meyer et al., 1971), but in spite
of the always strong and often passionate statements of need these
people expressed in the letters that brought them into initial contact
with the Clinic, 42 percent did not pursue the matter or respond to the
investigators' poll of prospects. Fifty transsexual candidates applied,
between 1970 and 1974, to the University of Virginia Clinic, although
this is no doubt a misleading number since investigators in Virginia,
wanting to work intensively with a small number of these patients, did
nothing to encourage referral.

It is clear that the demands of these patients are being met everywhere with increasing frequency. The notion of transforming into a
"woman" an individual who is biologically a man—and vice
versa—seems less bizarre now than in the past, in view of the successful transplantation of body organs, the introduction of such prosthetic devices as artificial heart valves, and the continuing refinement
of surgical techniques. Also, social change in sexual matters in general
has influenced public attitudes toward sex change by means of surgery
and has made surgeons in many countries willing to undertake it.
Pauly (1965, 1968), in his cumulative surveys of the world literature
on the number of surgical sex-change operations performed, indicated
that in 1965, for example, the literature had reported 603 biologically
male individuals desiring surgical transformation into women, and 162
biological females wanting to become men. Ninety-four of these men
and nineteen of the women had secured some form of "demasculin-
izing" or "defeminizing" surgery. In 1968 he summarized the surgical outcomes for an additional 121 patients. It is generally believed
that Pauly's figures are conservative and that, since 1968, the number
of persons seeking surgical sex change has increased rapidly. Pauly
tentatively suggested that satisfactory results from the surgery are

usual, but he did not deal with the complicated emotional states of these patients.

These early reports of satisfaction with the surgery performed notwithstanding, some investigators began to feel uneasy about the steps being taken to transform men and women into beings of the opposite sex by endocrinological and surgical means, causing Stoller (1973a) to refer to the activity as a runaway practice. A call for a more searching study of transsexualism has been sounded, and warnings have been issued about the dangers of a bandwagon effect in the acceptance of transsexualism as a condition for which surgery holds out the promise of cure (Socarides, 1969a, 1970; Stoller, 1973a; Volkan, 1974, 1975, 1976; Volkan and Berent, 1976; Volkan and Bhatti, 1972). As long ago as 1968 Kubie and Mackie stated that the term is "loosely used and has received premature acceptance in the literature." Meyer clearly demonstrates what some other workers in the field have already noted, that patients requesting sex change fall into separate categories. He states that it is "incumbent on physicians to specify whom they are calling 'transsexual.' . . . Greater specificity in patient categorization can be achieved by using the general term 'gender dysphoric syndrome,' with secondary modifying terms deciding the primary features of the clinical presentation" (1974, p. 556). Socarides (1969a, 1970, 1977b) states that an individual's desire for sexual transformation does not constitute in a strict sense an independent category, and that transsexualism may be defined as a psychiatric syndrome found in association with several different clinical conditions, i.e., neurosis, in which there is fear of the anatomical (biological) sex role; homosexuality, in which the individual is unable to deal with his or her anatomically determined biological role; and transvestitism, in which there is an unconscious wish to play-act through anatomical change. Socarides points out four characteristics of those suffering from this syndrome: an intense, insistent, and overriding desire to be transformed bodily into a person of the opposite sex; a conviction of being trapped in the body of the wrong sex; concomitant imitation of the behavior of the opposite sex; and an insistent search for sexual transformation by means of surgery and endocrinological supplements. Socarides believes that the soil from which transsexualism emerges is either homosexuality or transvestitism.

Person and Ovesey (1974a, 1974b) consider homosexual and transvestitic transsexualism secondary transsexualism, but they believe in the reality of *primary* transsexualism. Patients having this syndrome, they say, are ". . . schizoid-obsessive, socially withdrawn, asexual, unassertive, and out of touch with anger. Underlying this personality, they have a typical borderline syndrome characterized by separation anxiety, empty depression, sense of void, oral dependency, defective self-identity, and impaired object relations with absence of trust and fear of intimacy" (1974a, p. 19).

Stoller (1973a, 1973b), also aware that many different kinds of men demand sex change, sees male transsexualism as a clear-cut entity with a fairly precise clinical picture and typical dynamics and etiology. He is, however, quick to add that among the many who seek sex-reassignment surgery only a very few—and those the most feminine—fit his criteria for transsexualism. He differentiates transsexualism from perversion; his views, as well as those of Socarides, will be discussed in further detail and critically evaluated later.

The sex-change candidates in our studies ranged from psychotic to neurotic (Volkan, 1974, 1975, 1976; Volkan and Berent, 1976; Volkan and Bhatti, 1972; Volkan and Kavanaugh, 1977). The neurotic was a man with a primarily structural conflict who masochistically sought castration in compliance with superego demands. I diagnose as "true" transsexuals those who possess the four characteristics Socarides described, and who have felt trapped in the wrong kind of body from early childhood—around three years of age—and when I sense that their main symptom is a preoccupation with the appearance of their genitalia and a search for perfection. The man who is preoccupied with his penis before surgery, wanting to be rid of it, is no less preoccupied later with the "vagina" his surgeon has constructed. "She" wants it to be perfect, and is likewise concerned with having perfect secondary sexual characteristics of a feminine type, or achieving perfect womanhood. I have concluded that the true transsexual has a variation of borderline personality organization (Kernberg, 1967).

In spite of the absence of any clear consensus about what real transsexualism is—beyond some descriptive studies that fail to deal with the complex issues involved—irreversible surgery unfortunately continues to be performed on *almost anyone* who seeks such mutilation. Some investigators (Benjamin, 1966; Green and Money, 1969)

stress constitutional factors, but I agree with Socarides (1977b) that
the defense of this causation in the literature is not conclusive. Money
(1974) himself, a leading advocate of the surgery, says that the transsexual "has no identifiable genetic, anatomic, or physiologic defect
or abnormality that can be measured by today's technique. The same
is true both for female and male transsexuals. The most likely site
where some etiologic defect *might be uncovered in the future* is the
brain, possibly in connection with a fetal hormone effect" (p. 341;
italics added). Stoller (1975a) holds that "So far, no method has
revealed biological abnormality in those people whom I call transsexuals" (p. 258). As we have stated (Volkan and Berent, 1976), considerably more than a superficial study of the issue must be undertaken,
since the psychodynamic patterns of the person who presents as a
transsexual have their roots in early childhood. Psychoanalytic treatment of patients fitting the description of the typical transsexual would
no doubt reveal extremely valuable clues to the genesis of this condition within the transference-countertransference axis; the early fantasy life of these patients and the nature of their defensive resolution
of early conflicts should tell us much, especially those concerning the
internalization of object relations. The only such case in the literature,
a twenty-year-old biologically male individual who "agreed to undergo
psychoanalysis, with the provision that his parents would reconsider
their opposition to surgery" (Socarides, 1970, p. 342), unfortunately
remained in analysis only six months. Stoller is the other psychoanalyst who spent a great deal of time with transsexuals, but his material,
like that of Person and Ovesey (1974a, b), comes largely from relatively brief therapeutic case histories and long patient-assessment interviews.

I attempted the analysis of a male transsexual who, like Socarides'
patient, remained on the couch for only six months. After this time
his resistance against experiencing anxiety led him back to the surgeon
who had referred him to me, and this physician actively encouraged
him to abandon his analysis and performed the surgery the patient
wanted. I have also seen in psychotherapy 24 other transsexuals, nineteen male and five female, all of whom stayed in treatment for many
months, but who demonstrated no structural change as a result.

It is a handicap, I feel, not to have the transsexual patient in psychoanalysis proper or in psychoanalytic therapy for at least three weekly sessions for many years, inasmuch as all analytic investigation points to the likelihood that the seeds of this clinical phenomenon are present in very early childhood. Nevertheless, enough data have been collected to encourage the application of psychoanalytic theoretical insight to the transsexual phenomenon.

The Transsexual "Experiment"

Stoller (1973b, 1975b), who uses the term "experiment" to describe two of his studies on transsexualism, clearly believed that work with those most unusual patients would enrich our theories about the earliest stages of infantile development, in which he stressed the role of parental influence. He chose the term gender identity to designate "part of oneself, a set of convictions concerned with masculinity and femininity" (1964). "Sex and gender identity are not necessarily directly related. For instance, a biologically normal male (sex) may be as feminine (gender identity) from earliest childhood throughout life as a feminine woman and will live his life, undetected, as a woman; this is the transsexual" (Stoller, 1973b, p. 216).

As indicated, Stoller considers male transsexualism a clear-cut entity and points to the birth of an individual manifesting it as having occurred in a certain type of family constellation, one in which the mother is chronically depressed and bisexual and the father is distant and passive. The boy child is seen as the cure to the mother's lifelong hopelessness—"the transsexuals' mothers discourage masculinity and encourage femininity. All this occurs unimpeded, without trauma or conflict in its earlier stages" (Stoller, 1975a, p. 238). In this relationship she wants the child to serve as her phallus and also to provide her with a satisfying mother. This type of relationship produces a profound disturbance in the infant's body ego; he has no impetus toward separation and differentiation from the mother's female body, and since there is in the environment no psychologically available male, there is no one to counteract the "excessively blissful" mother/infant symbiosis.

Wrapped in the mother's "endless embrace," the child never comes to yearn for a relationship with a male figure and rejects his father as an object with which to identify. Since he experiences no oedipal conflict and no castration anxiety (Newman and Stoller, 1971; Stoller, 1973b), his developmental solution is quite unlike that worked out by either the normal individual or those who turn to perversion.

While it is easy to agree with Stoller that parental views of children play a role in determining their gender identity, his assumption that the core gender identity of the male transsexual is nonconflictual and that the mothers of transsexuals imprint femininity on their infants deserves serious debate. Although he uses the term "imprinting" rather reluctantly, he states that when he does so he is not talking about identification.

In reading Stoller one gains the impression that he sees the imprinting-learning of gender taking place within the child/mother unit as a separate process, uncontaminated with other affective or conflictual processes, as if he does not consider gender identity as part of a gradually developing ego identity, something intertwined in the development with other early self-images.

Mahler (1975) differs with Stoller, saying, "From my own rather limited experience, it is difficult for me to believe that transsexuality ever takes place in the baby's earliest stages without severe trauma or conflict, and particularly without some contribution in that direction being made by the baby's constitutional predisposition" (p. 245). She reminds us that what Stoller called a prolonged "excessively blissful mother-infant symbiosis" does not persist beyond the fifth month of life "whether or not the mother or the father wants it to remain so!" (p. 246).

We know—Mahler's (1968) methods of careful observation are persuasive—that the mother's unconscious attitude toward her own self, her belief in her femininity, and her own motherliness, as well as her penis envy, etc., affect her attitude toward her young male child. Stoller emphasizes the mother's role is "imprinting" attitudes upon her child, but he indicates that the mothers of male transsexuals are characterized by psychopathology, i.e., bisexual conflicts and depression. How, then, can a symbiotic relationship in which there is an affective flow between the partners be "blissful" with such a mother? Symbiosis as a phase of development is, in effect, dynamic, since the child experiences a maturational push to go beyond it to achieve further differentiation of self- and object representation and to become capable of individuation. Any interference with this forward movement creates conflicts. Whenever one speaks of "prolonged symbiosis" or "endless embrace," severe pathology rather than a blissful state is suggested. This is why "The child who later becomes transsexual shows the greatest degree of conflict of all the sexual deviants. He is overwhelmed with anxiety, paranoidal fears, incorporation fears, body ego deficiencies, overwhelming fear of engulfment, and paranoidal fear of attack" (Socarides, 1975, p. 243).

Stoller's idea of imprinting also needs careful review. Ovesey and Person (1973) hold that there is no evidence for imprinting in man in the ethological sense, as there is in animals. Stoller states that the term "imprinting" refers to a "non-mental" process in which something "is impressed upon the malleable infant's unresisting proto-psyche and unfinished CNS" (Stoller, 1975b, p. 55). Mitchell (1976) finds that Stoller's explanation fails to make it clear whether the imprinting is nonmental for the infant only or for the mother as well. The model is the human being who succeeds in imprinting a gosling in such a way that when the goose is mature it will seek to mate only with humans. Mitchell holds that if Stoller is suggesting that the process is a nonmental one for the mother as well as for her child, further difficulties can be expected. She asks: "Does the human being imprint a *gender* identity on the goose? If not, then why should the non-mental human mother imprint femininity as opposed to 'human-ness'? . . . [and] If it is the mother's unconscious with which we are dealing, then why should this be 'genderized'—the unconscious of men and women is neither masculine or feminine but bisexual" (p. 358). Stoller is, of course, making an attempt to replace Freud's notion of a biological bedrock on which femininity and masculinity are based; in doing this, he changes a biologically oriented formulation to one that is ethologically oriented. Mitchell says: "If Stoller is right in his argument that the transsexual's gender assumption, which ignores biological sex and the difference between the sexes, is non-psychotic and is formed on the basis of non-mental gender imprinting, then this 'femininity' is a rose that should go by another name" (p. 360).

I have earlier suggested (Volkan, 1974, 1975; Volkan and Berent,

1976) that in his theoretical thinking Stoller offers, wittingly or unwittingly, justification for transsexual surgery. He says in effect that if the core gender identity of these patients is nonconflictual and the patients are not neurotic or suffering from perversion or psychosis, why not change the body to fit the core? Holding also that transsexualism is not helped by psychoanalytic psychotherapy, he says, "In each of us, the psychic elements first created (core gender identity) are untouched by life experience or intensive treatment like analysis" (1973b, p. 217). I believe that Stoller's ideas play into the hands of transsexual organizations, the members of which may or may not have a theoretical understanding of them. In their prolific publications, these organizations promote the concept of transsexualism as "normal," and deny that psychiatry has anything to offer the transsexual. On this account I am happy to see that, although Stoller (1973a) does not suggest that the "medical" mutilations sought by the transsexual come to a full stop, he does issue some thoughtful warnings and concludes that surgical "cure" should be restricted to only a few of the many candidates for sex change. It is because his novel notion of imprinting gender identity provides theoretical support for sex-change surgery, and in order to compare it with formulations that I will be putting forth, that I have dealt with it at such length.

In respect to the family background of male transsexuals, Weitzman et al. (1971) found in their study of a male transsexual that although his mother conformed to Stoller's expectations, his father departed strikingly from them, being bisexual and far from distant in dealing with the child—indeed, an extension of the mother in overwhelming physical closeness and overstimulation. The experience of Person and Ovesey (1974a, b) with a sample of twenty *male* transsexuals differed from that of Stoller; among those the investigators designated as *primary* transsexuals, excessive closeness with the mother was not found, the relationship between son and mother being "rather excessively distant." I regard "excessive closeness" and "excessive distance" as two sides of the same coin of a disturbed child/mother relationship in early childhood.

Socarides (1970) sees in the so-called transsexual no nonconflictual core, holding that the sexual pervert, including the transsexual, has been unable to pass successfully through the symbiotic and separation-individuation phases (Mahler, 1965; Mahler and Furer, 1966) and this creates the original anxiety from which perversions arise. He adds: "Sexual perversion serves the repression of a pivotal nuclear complex: the urge to regress to a pre-oedipal fixation in which there is a desire for and dread of merging with the mother in order to reinstate the primitive mother-child unity. There is in Victor-Valerie [his transsexual patient] an unrelenting wish to merge with the mother, to die, and to be rejoined with her" (p. 347).

Also, by adopting transsexualism, an individual can avoid visible homosexuality; he undergoes the dreaded castration and vicariously identifies with the powerful mother. Socarides believes that this maneuver neutralizes his fear of his mother; he unconsciously enjoys the wish for intercourse with the father and escapes the dangerous aggression of strange men who might bring harm to him in a homosexual relationship. Stoller (1973b) replies to Socarides by indicating that although those who exhibit the kind of motivation Socarides describes may seek sex change through surgery, they are not "true" transsexuals. Nevertheless, as will be clear, our studies of those patients at the University of Virginia who qualified for inclusion in Stoller's category of "true" transsexuals support the views of Socarides; their family background resembled that of Stoller's true transsexuals, and their conviction of having been given a wrong-sexed body had come at a very early age.

We found Stoller's description of the family of the true male transsexual to be generally applicable. In interviews with the mothers of our male transsexual patients we could detect, even many years after the transsexual's infancy, how they had unconsciously seen their sons as belonging to their own sex. Occasionally, such mothers made slips of the tongue and referred to their sons as female (Volkan and Berent, 1976). But total conformity to Stoller's descriptions in all particulars was not invariable. The mother may have had an unconscious wish to hold onto her child in a symbiotic relatedness, but also have had defenses against this wish. Further, one may expect that she has designated this child as a "special being." We found that his interaction with his mother perpetuated the child's inability to integrate early self- and object images built up under the libidinal drive ("all good" self- and object images) with most of those built up under the aggressive drive (the "all bad" self- and object images). This inability requires a defensive splitting of representations within the early self-representation, which includes, among other concepts, the core gender identity of the future transsexual (Volkan, 1976). The feminine core of the male transsexual is, then, "primitively" split (Volkan, 1976), with accompanying pathological internalization of object relations.

Thus far I have dealt only with Stoller's consideration of the *male* transsexual and compared the views of others on this subject with his. Nevertheless he does describe the prototypal family in which one finds the *female* transsexual, and his observations are much like ours (Volkan, 1976; Volkan and Berent, 1976; Volkan and Bhatti, 1972). In this family, the biologically female child wants to become a man in order to substitute for a father unable to relate helpfully as a husband to the mother's depressed state. At the outset of our work with female transsexuals (Volkan and Bhatti, 1972) we found that as a child the girl who was to become a transsexual had a depressed and sexually hungry mother whom the daughter regarded as a martyr in need of rescue. One girl child became aware of her mother's sexual hunger when she observed her mother taking pictures of herself, naked, and sending them to her husband, a military man stationed in a foreign land.

The purpose of rescuing the mother is not altruistic but selfish—to make the mother "good" enough to mother her child. The girl fantasies that only a man can save her mother from her depression and sexual hunger in a household where the father is usually much away from home, and she wants to be this man herself. In this kind of family setting, the child cannot integrate the images of the caring and needy mother and the corresponding self-images. The illusion that girls have penises is never surrendered; the girl keeps searching for one. The "bad" mother is seen as being without one, and hence the girl dreads fusion with her; if the girl acquires a penis, this will differentiate her from the "bad" mother but permit her to fuse with the "good" one. We found that the female patient's artificial penis or surgically constructed approximation of one is related on a broad spectrum to the fetish. At the lower level of the spectrum such artificial organs are "childhood fetishes" (Mahler, 1968; Speers and Lansing, 1965; Sperling, 1963), or reactivated (Volkan, 1976) transitional ob-

jects (Winnicott, 1953) used for coping with separation anxiety; on a
higher level they are the classical fetish that deals with castration
anxiety.

With our later work (Volkan, 1975, 1976; Volkan and Berent,
1976) we concluded that the true female transsexual, like her male
counterpart, has a personality organization that is a variation of the
borderline type. Like the boy child, the typical female in this situation
exhibits a defensive splitting of positive and negative representations.

The Search for Perfection

An object relations conflict exists within both the male and female
transsexual. One can begin to identify this conflict when one realizes
that the transsexual is actually searching for something that can be
conceptualized as perfection—perfection in respect to the body parts
the patient wants corrected and in respect also to a more generalized
self-concept. For example, the patient in humble circumstances regards with longing the splendid lifestyle of the rich and is convinced
that he or she would be ''perfect'' if a substantial income became
available. Transsexuals use a variety of phrases and behavior patterns
to express this aspiration to be altogether perfect. One male transsexual
said he expected to be ''virgin white'' after his surgery; another, a
man of slender means, employed an artist at considerable expense to
paint an idealized and feminized portrait of himself, which he then
took to the surgeon as a blueprint for his work. Knorr et al. (1968)
have encountered this same phenomenon, and suggest that the conflicts the transsexual may have with his surgeon arise from his inordinate demands to be made truly and completely of the opposite sex.
Person and Ovesey (1974a) also note ''the endless striving for perfection in the feminine role'' among male transsexuals.

Our observations indicate that the patient may behave for a while
after surgery as if he (now she) has indeed found what he has been
searching for, an identity as the perfect idealized woman, but the old
preoccupation with the appearance of the genitalia soon returns. One
patient, not unlike the one with the portrait, drew a picture for his
surgeon to show him what areas of the vagina needed modification.

One of our patients had had genital surgery eighteen years before we saw "her," but at the time of our first encounter was planning the *seventh* surgical step to become a more perfect woman. The male transsexual wants changes not only for his face, chest, and genital area, but for other body areas as well. Surgery to modify the adam's apple or to make the legs more feminine is common. One male transsexual, looking to all intents and purposes like a woman, confided the day before his scheduled leg surgery his belief that one day the plastic surgeon would tell him that nothing more could be done, and that on that day there might be nothing left but suicide. After undergoing six surgical procedures over a period of several years in an effort to complete his transformation into a woman, he is now, four years after his last operation, a tragic sight due to complications of leg surgery, and is killing himself with drug addiction.

Female transsexuals also embark on the search for perfection. Indeed, having a penis constructed "from the flesh" offers hope that perfection may at last be obtained and a replacement provided for a series of inadequate substitute "penises." We describe elsewhere (Volkan and Bhatti, 1972) one such patient's presurgical use of everything from Q-tips to prosthetic gadgets in her effort to approximate a penis. Another female transsexual confided that if, after having a penis constructed surgically, she were to hear of another surgeon who could provide a better one, she would go on and on with surgery for more and more improvement.

A closer look at this clinical phenomenon, the search for perfection, suggests that it can easily be translated as "a search to be uncontaminated by aggression." When Person and Ovesey (1974a) describe the "primary" transsexual as being "out of touch with anger," they are, I believe, describing the defensive surface picture. My clinical observations have led me to conclude that the transsexual seeking to have all traces of his or her true anatomical gender obliterated unconsciously withholds information about something else he (or she) feels compelled to get rid of—untamed aggression, which contaminates him (or her) and interferes with the sense of feeling "perfect." What is called "sex-reassignment surgery" might as well be called "aggression-reassignment surgery."

Rorschach results reported by Berent (Volkan and Berent, 1976) indicate that the male transsexual sees the penis, on one level, as a symbol of evil. It is bad and aggressive; he therefore devalues it and wants surgery to rid him of it, not only in order to be a woman, but to be without aggression. He sees the idealized mother as pure and all good and wants to fuse with her only. Berent's Rorschach results also show that the female transsexual feels that her lack of a penis makes her incomplete. It appears that she sees the acquisition of a penis as not only completing her but giving her so much power that she need never again exhibit aggression.

Clinical observations support the idea that what lies behind the search for perfection in either case is a search to be free from contamination with aggression. A male transsexual came to his psychiatrist's office dressed sometimes as a man, sometimes as a woman. As the former, he was loud, complaining, and aggressive. Dressed as a woman, he was quite the opposite. I videotaped two interviews with him on the same day; in one he was dressed as a man and in the second as a woman, and outside observers viewing the tapes agreed that when he "identified" himself as a woman he stopped using his obscene vocabulary and became extremely gentle. His search was not only to become a woman but to rid himself of aggression. He found it difficult, during a childhood made traumatic by separations from his mother—a prostitute—to individuate himself fully from the representation of this mother. He had perceived the men coming to enjoy his mother's favors as bees coming to a hive. As an adult, he became a beekeeper and learned that the male bees perished after mating with the queen. At the hive, he separated his bees into "good" and "bad" ones and killed the latter with ceremony. The division of the bees represented the split of his mother images. The proposed construction of a vagina in his body promised many benefits—his transformation into a "virgin white" being, fusion with his "good" mother, and a life altogether moral, pure, and without aggression.

During one hour he attended in feminine dress he exhibited his mother's photograph. His therapist was struck by the resemblance between the patient in his woman's dress and the prostitute mother in the picture, and the patient himself suddenly saw the likeness, going into an anxiety attack at the discovery. His search had always been for perfection, and he was unable to accept a resemblance that hinted at "badness."

The following vignette provides another illustration of the male transsexual's desire to be rid of aggression by being rid of his penis. On the night before he had genital surgery, a male transsexual had a dream (Volkan and Berent, 1976; Volkan and Bhatti, 1972) in which he carried a stick in his hand and acted aggressively. When he turned a corner—which we both believed to be the irreversible surgery undergone during the day—the stick fell to the ground in what we considered a representation of his losing his penis. He had once fantasied that his amputated penis might fall into a mud puddle. After turning the corner, the dreamer, now without a stick, felt relieved to find himself gentle, loving, and loved, with his aggression gone. However, the dream, like the surgery, expressed only a wish to achieve a position without aggression rather than its realization. In a dream months later, he saw himself with a penis—thus with aggression—and awakened in anxiety. The surgical procedure had not removed the mental representation of the penis or what it meant to him. This patient continued the quest for the ultimate perfection with more surgery in the genital area, and surgical feminization of the adam's apple and legs.

Observation of such behavior led me to conclude (Volkan, 1975) that the continuous search for perfection (to be uncontaminated by aggression) *is itself a defense against anxiety*. The surgery itself does not put a stop to such conflict. This finding led us to question Stoller's idea that the male transsexual has an ego-syntonic core gender identity. The patient wants to include in his feminine core only "good" and idealized self-images, and wants to believe that the core will be uncontaminated by aggression. When Stoller (1973b) wrote that the mother "holds her *perfect child* [italics added] in an endless embrace" (p. 215) one gets the impression that he, too, noted the idealized aspect of the mother-child unity that the transsexual later seeks to attain. He failed, however, to take into account the corresponding "all bad" mother-child images to be found in such an "endless embrace," which threaten the blissful state of affairs even when they are externalized.

The Internalized Object Relations of the Transsexual

In 1956, Gillespie summarized the general theory of sexual perversions as it could be formulated at that time. The main point was that a perversion represents a defense against the Oedipus complex and castration anxiety. While it was acknowledged that this defense involves regression of libido and aggression to pregenital levels, Sachs's (1923) well-known formulation was not replaced, but additions were made to it, such as the part played by the superego, the central importance of castration anxiety, the role of aggression, and the relation of perversion to reality sense and to psychosis. Gillespie also summarized psychoanalytic knowledge about the splitting of the ego as well as the splitting of the object, using the theoretical insights available at that time. Bak (1956) was among the first to emphasize the framework of the theory of dual drives in perversion, pointing to the role of the aggressive drive. He also referred to splitting, although not precisely in the way we use this term in the theory of internalized object relations. He stated that in perversions the ego undergoes a split rather than using repression or other supporting defenses against the representations of fixated drives. Part of the ego allies itself with one of the basic drives, while the other basic drive is felt to be ego-alien and is projected upon the object.

Socarides, influenced by the work of Mahler, has produced a unitary theory of perversions (see chap. 9, this volume), suggesting that the preoedipal period, especially between eighteen months and three years, is crucial to the genesis of sexual perversion. In this period a preoedipal fixation occurs and is *primary*. This fixation includes the desire to merge with the mother to reinstate the primitive mother-child unit, and an equally strong dread of such merging. The sexual perversion serves to repress these wishes. I believe that the application of object relations theory (Kernberg, 1972) further illuminates the clinical phenomena exhibited by both the male and female transsexual. Both Mahler (1968) and Jacobson (1964) refer to the way in which the infant develops memory islands in *bipolar* fashion, creating them respectively out of pleasurable and unpleasurable instinctual, emotional, ideational, and functional experiences and the perceptions that have become associated with them. Images of the love object as well as the bodily and psychic self emerge from these memory islands. "Libido and aggression," says Jacobson (1964, p. 44), "are continuously turned from the love object to the self and vice versa, or also from one object to the other, while self and object images as well as images of different objects undergo temporary fusions and separate and join again." Jacobson, as well as Kernberg (1967) and myself (Volkan, 1976), describes the tendency to cathect one such composite image unit with libido only while the aggression is directed to another one, until ambivalence can be tolerated. These cathectic processes are reflected in introjective and projective processes. Kernberg (1966, 1967) describes how the inability of the early ego to integrate opposing representational units may become a major defense ("primitive split-ting") and be continued into adult life in the so-called borderline personality organization, although in normal development the images of the object (the mother, for example) are not only differentiated from the images of the self, but are more and more integrated until it becomes possible for the one unit to contain both "all good" and "all bad" elements at the same time and the child's view of himself and others becomes more consistent with reality. If the "all bad" units are early loaded with aggressive drive derivatives, the primitive splitting will not mend, and, as long as representations are primitively split, the corresponding drive derivatives cannot interpenetrate and thus cannot be tamed; this is the situation in which the individual with borderline personality organization finds himself.

In applying the theory of internalized object relations to both male and female transsexuals (Volkan, 1976), I have been able to show how their defensive organization resembles that of people with bor-derline personality organization. The male transsexual seeks to unite his "all good" self-representations with his "all good" mother rep-resentations to become himself a "perfect" woman; at the same time he dreads merging with the "all bad" mother representation, and keeps that representation as well as his own "all bad" self-represen-tation primitively split. This takes place at a level at which self- and object images or representations are differentiated except in regard to genital body parts. As Bak (1971, p. 242) stated, in perversions (as in transsexualism), unlike the situation in schizophrenia, "objects are retained and protected and remain invested in spite of fused body image or fused genital representations."

The following vignette will illustrate the latter point. The male transsexual patient whom I treated on the couch was preoccupied with Hawaii, especially with its *volcanic* landscape. This had a transference reference due to my last name, although I learned that his fixation with Hawaii predated our association, for he had spent some time on the island. As the analytic process unfolded I came to understand that his fascination was related to his inability to differentiate the image of his genitalia from that of his mother's, in spite of his intellectual awareness that they were not alike. The volcanic terrain that changed as eruptions took place and lava-flow hardened attracted him by its plasticity and constant alteration, wherein he saw a way of dealing with the "uncertainty" (Bak, 1968) of genital outline.

This patient was in his early twenties and still living with his mother and sister. He was a true transsexual with the typical family background Stoller describes. He had decided at an early age that he was a girl. He was not psychotic, having the capacity to know as he talked to me where he ended and his mother began, as it were.

As he lay on the couch I noticed a bulge between his legs, and I discovered that he had had his trousers pocket extended so that a wallet placed in it lodged between his legs as a bulge. On one level, this bulge represented his mother's genitalia; was there a vagina or a penis there? What is interesting here is the clinical observation that although this patient had no difficulty separating himself from the mother representation, once the analysis focused on the bulge he began to make frequent slips of the tongue in which he referred to himself and his mother interchangeably. He could separate himself from his mother in most areas, but in the genital area differentiation was not possible for him.

With the use of primitive splitting of self- and object representations, the transsexual of either sex externalizes the "all bad" units to other people, and this inevitably causes him to see the world as full of dangerous and frustrating forces and to remain always on guard against the creations of his own introjective-projective mechanism. The transsexual sees a threat in anything that blocks his search for perfection through surgery and his regressive hope of merging with the "all good" mother. Since psychotherapy is often perceived as such a threat, it is vigorously resisted. The psychiatrist who withholds permission for the sex-change surgery so eagerly sought may be seen as dangerous, or may be toppled from his position of power and special competence; the transsexual sees him as contemptible and tries to break off the association, perhaps seeking another therapist who will be more compliant. Indeed, the patient may not be content to break away from the noncompliant psychotherapist and may feel required to display great hostility toward him or others involved with him. The patient's failure to synthesize contradictory self- and object images and their accompanying aggressive and libidinal drive derivatives may lead to an eruption of primitive affect in aggressive behavior. When one female transsexual was told that surgery would not be permitted until psychiatric approval was given, she attempted to obviate all this by bribing the therapist. When this failed, she went to the plastic surgeon's office, knife in hand, and threatened to amputate the breasts of the secretary there—and her own as well—if the desired surgery was not made available to her.

We observed at the gender identity clinic that the transsexual may see the surgeon as "all good" and the psychiatrist as "all bad," shifting such qualities from one to the other according to which one appears to be at any moment the source of frustration. This proclivity of the transsexual can make ongoing consultation between the psychiatrist and the surgeon extremely difficult. When the surgeon, unaware of the unconscious psychological processes at work, allies himself with the patient's determination to have surgical sex change and thus basks in his regard as an "all good" champion, the results can be tragic.

Because he or she lives in a world regarded as dangerous, and lacks the wisdom to see that what is feared is actually an externalized part of himself or herself, the transsexual needs allies for protection. During the course of one study my colleagues and I interviewed the sexual partners of the sex-change candidate whenever possible. The relationship maintained by a transsexual with a sex partner is characteristically so ardent that one may mistakenly see it as representing the emotional investment of a mature person, but this is far from the truth. The transsexual uses his or her partner to re-enforce the "all good" constellation that he or she is trying to keep within. The relationship with the partner is a "part-object" relationship (Klein, 1946) inasmuch as the partner is seen only as an "all good" object, thus only partially. Anything "bad" about him or her is denied. Such relationships are intense but, unfortunately, extremely labile. While in treatment, the transsexual tries to force the therapist to become a witness to the glory of the idealized relationship that he or she has achieved with the partner; such a validating witness is needed for any claim made on such shaky grounds. Since the true transsexual is unable to tolerate ambiguity in an intimate relationship, a partner seen as "all good" is likely to be rejected suddenly as "all bad" whenever he or she disappoints the patient.

I believe that some transsexuals channelize their hostile behavior in some social situations in order to deal with their dangerous world, and they tend toward overzealous crusading for this or that cause, chief among them the claim that transsexualism is not an illness. Having something to fight keeps alive the hope that the externalized "all bad" representational units can be kept at bay, primitive splitting maintained, and felt anxiety prevented.

The Family of a Nine-Year-Old Transsexual Boy

Our psychotherapeutic experience with a nine-year-old boy and his parents provides clinical evidence for the theoretical formulation of transsexualism that I have described here. Our access to the boy's family gave us the opportunity to see that his syndrome of entrapment in a wrong-sexed body was but one aspect of a complicated conflictual involvement of libidinally and aggressively loaded self-and-object constellations. The work done by Zinner and R. Shapiro (1974) on the families of borderline youngsters is relevant here, as is that done by E. Shapiro et al. (1975). They proposed a need for the *family group* to provide a "holding environment" (Winnicott, 1963) to facilitate the child's integration of positive and negative constellations pertaining to the self and to others. They further concluded that the parents of borderline youngsters typically have themselves failed to loosen altogether their symbiotic ties to their families of origin, and that they lack the ability to integrate positive and negative ego states adequately. By means of projective identification they select their borderline child to participate with them in a relationship that embodies the aggressively contaminated self- and object representations they would deny.

In such families the child's autonomous wishes are designated as "bad."

When the boy was eight his teachers suggested to his parents that they seek psychiatric help for him because he seemed to be emotionally disturbed, but when I saw the parents they evidenced little distress about him. He had announced to them that he was a girl rather than a boy and, after seeing a television program on sex change, asked that he have such surgery himself. They were fully aware that he had for years claimed the identity of a girl and had behaved like one, playing with dolls, wearing his mother's shoes and dresses, and walking with a feminine twist of the hips. When he complained to his mother about his inappropriate sex, she would say: "God made you a boy, so you are a boy." But when he insisted, she equivocated: "Wait until you are 21 and leave home. Then you can decide to have surgery." During my early interviews with the parents they were interested chiefly in their son's "two personalities," as they described his abrupt switch from being "an angel" to being "very bad," screaming, and expressing hatred of his parents.

The mother was 46 when I first saw her, and her husband was five years older. The couple had a 21-year-old son, and the mother had had a series of miscarriages until she conceived the patient. Since both parents worked, the infant had been cared for by his mother for only six months before being turned over very largely to the care of his maternal grandmother. He nearly died of pneumonia when he was three, and as he convalesced his mother took care of him for a while before engaging a babysitter, who cared for him in the family home. He was then no longer taken to his grandmother's as he had been before he fell ill.

It was initially suggested that after his bout with pneumonia his mother became overprotective; certainly a sticky relationship between mother and child developed. I learned about a number of unusual household routines; for example, the father goes to bed at about 8:30 in the evening and leaves the mother and son sitting up late together. Then, she explained, "we" go to bed. She slept all night with the child or left the child's bed for her husband's during the small hours. A role reversal between the boy and his father seemed apparent in these sleeping arrangements. The family's eating habits were also unusual. The child seldom ate with both parents, although occasionally with his mother. He had no breakfast, but ate at noon, in the late afternoon before his parents returned from work, and again around eleven at night as he watched television with his mother. His parents were vaguely aware that the household routine was strange, but felt ''controlled'' by their son and unable to alter the arrangements, although occasionally they quarreled about them and the father would demand in effect that she ''divorce your son and marry your husband!'' The couple always took the boy with them when they went out, and discouraged any autonomous behavior on his part. He had no playmates, but stayed home by himself or with his parents.

His mother said that when she was young she was a tomboy. In one of her dreams she saw herself turning into a boy. Remembering, she told of having played only boys' games, and compared her play as a child with her son's absorption in girls' activities. She said she had never learned to dress, to be a lady, to walk in a feminine way, and these were the areas of ''womanhood'' with which her child was concerned. There were indications that she saw her son as her penis; for example, she described a fantasy she had had while pregnant that there was ''something special'' in her body. She ''waited for it to come out of me,'' but thought ruefully that ''it wouldn't grow up'' after all. In describing her son's aggressivity she made gestures with her hand to indicate his ''building up'' and his ''heightening,'' putting her hand between her legs and moving it upward as though pointing to an erection. In spite of this apparent closeness, she had only a meager relationship with her son. Once, in my office, she heard thunder and suddenly began speaking of her son's fear of thunder as though he were speaking through her. When he played with dolls, the boy identified himself with the female doll and announced, ''I am mamma.'' There was certainly nothing ''blissful'' in this mother/child relationship. The ''closeness'' between them was accompanied by a dread of being close to one another, and the image each had of the other was contaminated with fearful aggression. The mother's first impression of her son at birth was that he was an angel, but this thought was followed by the conviction that he would die. The child's fearful image of his mother was apparent in his refusal to drink milk. The two quarreled until the father threatened to whip him, and the mother's overvigilant attitude was accompanied by a wish to reject him.

As my investigation of this case continued over a period of months, I learned that the childhood experience of each of the parents was reflected in their handling of their child. The father came from a poor family, and when his mother died (when he was two) he slept with his grandmother. His grandfather and uncle shared a bed, and his stepmother and father slept together in an upstairs room. He was ten before he slept alone. He perceived himself as coming between his grandparents and accepted the idea that a small boy could separate a couple in their bedroom.

There were similar elements in the mother's background. Her parents had been party-goers and social drinkers. Her father, a salesman, took his wife with him on business trips. Although she had her own bed at home, whenever her parents were away she stayed at her grandmother's, where she slept in her grandmother's bed while her grandfather slept elsewhere. When she was ten, her parents moved away and she stayed with her grandparents on a regular basis.

As the boy's therapy progressed and he made some attempts toward individuation, he began to say to his mother, "Lady! Blame you!" Her response was to have an "angina" attack; for a while it seemed that the child's therapy had been sabotaged, but the parents were persuaded to continue treatment for all three. What the mother now revealed began to shed light on her son's problems. Five years before his birth she had embarked on an odd affair with a man twenty years her senior who worked where she did. Although they had sexual relations occasionally, the affair centered chiefly around their daily contact at work, her getting his tea, their talking together, and the like. The man was now 65, scheduled for retirement, and she was determined to keep on working until he retired. She claimed to have a "split personality," to be one person working beside her lover and quite another and more serious individual when five o'clock came and it was time to go home. At the outset of this thirteen-year-long affair, she and her lover had been surprised by his wife while they were kissing in the park, so both spouses knew of the attachment but were unaware that it had ever involved sexual relations; all four were "friends."

Her lover urged the patient's mother to become pregnant, and when she did conceive she was uncertain whether the father was the lover or her husband. She fantasied that her son was the product of both men, and believed it physiologically possible that semen from each had fertilized her. When the child was born she wanted to name him for her lover but feared that this would tell too much about their relationship, so she gave him a name different from her husband's in only one letter. She insisted *"My son was born two people.* I know this sounds like a fairytale, but it is the truth."

I observed that the mother routinely put her child between her husband and herself; the child was her aggressive penis, and he clashed with her husband. Almost every day she maneuvered a fight between the two at which she took the role of a bystander. When her husband was not around, however, she saw her son as the representation of her lover-mother, and, on occasion, actually thought of him as a girl.

While some elements in the story of their daily routine had an oedipal ring—e.g., the child's sleeping with his mother and dethroning his father as the mother's possessor—what seemed to be more dominant was the reactivation of preoedipal object relations in the family setting. It is clear that the mother's experience with "multiple mothers" was transferred to her having "multiple husbands," and, accordingly, "multiple children" in her son. The father's experience with "multiple parents" furthered this split. The mother related alternately with libido and with aggression to the two images of her son. He, in turn, could not integrate corresponding self-images, but had an image of himself as "two persons."

Issues of Psychosexual Development and the Oedipus Complex

I have indicated that the "true" transsexual, male or female, is an individual with a variation of borderline personality organization. He or she habitually searches for perfection, evidencing a wish to be uncontaminated with aggression and, hence, perfect. As a defense, this search helps maintain primitive splitting and the illusion that as long as there is hope of being "pure" there is hope that one need not face the primitive anxiety that attends the possibility that positive and negative self- and object representational units will come together.

Pathology in the internalization of object relations results in the deficiency of some functions of the ego. I have suggested, for example (Volkan, 1976), that persons who utilize primitive splitting as their major mode of defense have a deficiency in their repressive ability. If a child reaches the oedipal level with the habitual use of primitive splitting, superego integration will not take a normal course. ''All good'' self- and object representations which eventually accumulate into an ego ideal—and thus fuse with the superego proper in the normal course of events to form an integrated, benign, depersonified superego—will fail to do so. Sadistic superego elements may be projected, and the idealized elements included in the self-concept. Because of the deficiency in the ego's repressive ability and also because of the depersonified nature of the superego, the individual will be keenly aware of wishes that stem from different psychosexual levels of development and will experience severe castration anxiety as well. Patients with borderline personality organization try to escape from oral-level aggression and fear, so ''premature development of genital strivings'' takes place. Such development, in the case of a boy, fails ''because oedipal fears and prohibitions against sexual impulses toward mother are powerfully reinforced by pregenital fears of the mother, and a typical image of a dangerous, castrating mother develops. Also, the projection of pregenital aggression reinforces oedipal fears of the father and castration anxiety in particular, further reinforcing, in turn, pregenital aggression and fear. The positive oedipus complex is seriously interfered with under these circumstances . . . a frequent solution is the reinforcement of the negative oedipus complex'' (Kernberg, 1967, pp. 679-680).

Kernberg finds the above formulation applicable to the male homosexual who is predominantly oral, and I suggest that it applies also to the male transsexual. Girls with the same type of oral pathology tend to develop prematurely positive oedipal strivings to get away from frustrations connected with the early dangerous mother, and this stirs up penis envy.

We found in our work with male transsexuals that the wish to merge with the early mother, accompanied by the dread of doing so, existed alongside severe castration anxiety. My earlier papers (Volkan, 1974; Volkan and Berent, 1976) give examples, although Newman and Stoller (1971; see also Stoller, 1973b) hold a contrary view, reporting the absence of castration anxiety among male transsexuals. We also give clinical examples of intense penis envy among female transsexuals (Volkan and Berent, 1976; Volkan and Bhatti, 1972). On the clinical level, then, what is observed generally is that oedipal elements are superimposed on the pathology of early internalized object relations. Self- and object identities become confused with male and female identities.

It is clear to me that the establishment of a borderline personality organization, although evidence of developmental arrest, does not of itself refer to a specific clinical picture; the possession of a borderline personality organization is not predictive of transsexualism, homosexuality, or any like manifestation. The specificity of the clinical picture will require further research. Our work (Volkan and Berent, 1976), however, suggests that, when the child becomes preoccupied with the genitalia at the oedipal level, the effects of some trauma that directly or symbolically heightens this interest are superimposed on a pathological early child-mother relationship to crystallize transsexualism. In some cases the physical injury to the genitalia occurred before the oedipal age; for example, one of our patients had had a surgical operation on the penis while very young, the psychological scar of which was rekindled when he arrived at the oedipal stage of development. The clinical example that follows illustrates the main points of my theoretical discussion.

A woman in her mid-twenties had considered herself male since her early childhood. At the time she came to our attention she anticipated undergoing surgery for sex reassignment and marrying her ("his") fiancée. This patient had been working as a truckdriver and looked, to all intents and purposes, a man; the hormones with which she had been supplied had given her a faint beard, and she walked with an exaggerated masculine swagger. In therapy she voiced the usual complaint of the transsexual, saying that she had been trapped in a body of the wrong sex. What interests us here is her revelation of two symptoms which had become evident around puberty and had lasted for several years until she learned from a newspaper article about the possibility of sex change through surgery, when they disappeared. Although she had thought of having a penis constructed, she had had had no idea of the real surgical possibility before reading about it in the paper; the news led her to seek surgery for herself with great determination.

The first of the two symptoms was her belief in two coexistent worlds, one of which was ''bad.'' She lived in the country then, and whenever she left home on an errand, perhaps to the country store a mile from where she lived, she was afraid that on the way back she might slip into the ''bad'' world; to avoid doing so, she compulsively marked her path on the outgoing trip in order to be sure she would find her way back again. The second of her symptoms was that, whenever she looked at the corner of an object, such as a table, she thought that her eyeballs were caught on its sharp point; before she could stop looking at it she had to gesture with her hands as though she were replacing her eyeballs in their sockets.

As I came to know this patient I was able to make a formulation about her symptoms. The notion of a ''bad'' world, one separated from the ''good,'' had a precursor in her childhood when she had had a perception of her mother as poisonous. As a small child she had had another symptom, which she vaguely remembered herself and about which she had been told as an adult by others in the family; this was her belief that the food her mother prepared for her was poisoned. The child had either totally refused to eat this food or had accepted it only after going through certain rituals designed to purge it of harm. Her mother had been cold, but preoccupied with her child's health. The patient had suffered from many childhood illnesses, including painful earaches, and it would appear that the mother's limited mothering ability was further reduced by her inability to relieve the pain. As will become clear, the child fantasied an idealized, giving mother incompatible with the image of the ''bad'' mother. I felt that she translated this discrepancy into the belief that there are two worlds, and that she attempted to stay with the idealized mother.

When I first saw her she had a lover, a woman twelve years her senior and a prototype of motherhood, with eight children. Neither felt that their love relationship was homosexual since both accepted my patient as a man. My patient never undressed completely in front of her lover, the better to deny her femininity; both eagerly awaited the day when surgical intervention would make my patient sufficiently male in body to make its disclosure gratifying. The two had met at a church gathering, and after a brief acquaintance had idealized one another and come to feel that their relationship was the best in the world. The older woman left her husband and followed her new friend to another state in search of a surgeon who would provide the latter with a penis. An interview with the older woman by one of our researchers disclosed that she was an orphan whose search for a savior had turned her into the savior of other people who needed mothering. In this sense she had become a "supermother." Her involvement with my patient was selfish rather than altruistic, since, to her, my patient represented herself, and her effort to be an "all good" provider to her odd friend was an effort to provide well for herself.

During her hours with me my patient tried to enroll me as a "witness" of the glory of this "all good" relationship while she was at the same time feeling threatened by "bad" objects peripheral to their union, projecting them onto me even as she projected her "witness" expectations, either simultaneously or alternately.

Thus her first symptom can be understood by looking at her pathologically internalized object relations, but the second is best understood when seen in the light of trauma experienced in her psychosexual development, and of what we know about symptom formation concerned with penis envy and castration anxiety. When the patient had been at the oedipal age she had once seen her father castrating raccoons, hearing the animals' horrifying outcry. It seems that her father had taken sadistic pleasure in his behavior, and after witnessing it, his daughter developed a fantasy that she herself had once had a penis that her father had removed in the same brutal and gloating way. During her frequent childhood bouts with illness she associated her discomfort with the condition of the mutilated raccoons, although this fantasy faded and was to some degree repressed in latency. During the second rendition of the oedipal situation at puberty (Blos, 1967) her fantasy reappeared in the form of detachable body parts (eyes-penis) that could be removed and replaced at will. When she read about transsexualism, her notion that she had once had a penis and that she was actually a boy was validated, in her view, and it is understandable that her symptom vanished when she came to believe that a surgeon could restore her missing penis to her. Beneath this formulation, however, lies the formulation that the construction of a penis for her would resolve the pathology of internalized object relations and would not only differentiate her from the ''bad'' and devalued mother who was without such an organ, but would make intercourse feasible and thus allow fusion with the partner who represented her ''all good'' mother. Like other ''true'' female transsexuals this patient had an ego defect in the area of object relations; this came from a pathologically incomplete separation from the mother representation and the consequent loss of body integrity. As I have indicated, transitional and fetishistic phenomena tend to merge in cases like this, in which there is an attempt to fuse with the ''good'' mother while avoiding the ''bad.'' The artificial penis helps the illusion of a connection between the good subject and object representations, first of all, and denies separation between them; it also helps maintain the illusion of a female phallus that is a denial of castration.

The case of a male transsexual patient demonstrated how oedipal elements are superimposed on the wish to unite with the ''good'' mother. The patient in question here has already been mentioned as the one who was preoccupied with the volcanic landscape of Hawaii and who had a special pocket made in his trousers. During one of his hours with me, he experienced something like the Isakower (1938) phenomenon—he felt his mouth filling with colored balloons. His associations indicated that this represented his wish to be united with the breast of his ''good'' mother. After five or ten minutes of enjoying the experience, he felt that the balloons moved away from him and turned into rays of light coming in through the window. The window itself became the Eiffel Tower, and then the Tower of Babel, which reminded him of a strong man standing facing him with legs apart. His pleasurable sensations gave way to anxiety. He connected the Tower of Babel with heaven, where he hoped his dead father, now brought to mind, had gone when he died during his son's pubertal age. He had been a distant man and had left his son in the care of the depressed woman, his wife. The patient, born eight years after his next sibling, had been unwanted in a home already left behind by the older children. However, his mother saw him as a ''beautiful baby'' and held him tightly in what Stoller calls ''an endless embrace,'' which I saw as evidence of a pathological child-mother relationship.

He still lived with his mother when he became my patient in his early twenties, and his relationship with her even then reflected clearly the situation of his earlier years.

During his treatment he began dreaming about his father, although he insisted that he had never really known him or cared for him. I sensed that within the developing transference he not only wanted to relate to me as the "good" mother and to merge with me, but to do this alternately with the "bad" mother who frightened him; and I also clearly detected his surrender to me as a male child surrenders to the oedipal father in a negative solution of the oedipal conflict. As a child he had identified himself with a cat (pussy), which on one occasion he threw at his father (who, as usual, was paying little attention to him) in an effort to engage his concern. He repeated this on the couch, as his dreams evidenced.

His father had been employed in the artificial insemination of cattle, and when I first came to know the patient I realized that he regarded his parent as a "pregnancy effector." He had actually watched his father inserting the semen-filled tubes in the vaginas of cows. As he longed to have his body made to match the sense he had of female gender identity, he also longed to become pregnant; his concept of perfect femininity was the female gestating.

He had made his selection of a feminine name to use after his surgical transformation, and this he legally adopted. The name he chose was a variation of the name of his elder brother's bride; after their father's death this brother had become a father figure to the patient, who now wanted to surrender to him symbolically, talking about his brother's strong, muscular figure. His castration anxiety was further evidenced by his declaration that he greatly feared the sight of blood. This disclosure was made in his last hour with me when he talked about his fear of surgery. In spite of my active effort to help him postpone the surgery and to give him more time to understand himself, he felt compelled to go on with it, terminated his relationship with me, and made an appointment with the surgeon. It was during this hour that he talked about his soap phobia; he claimed that he feared that every bar of soap he used contained a razor blade and that while bathing he felt anxiety lest the concealed blade lop off some extremity or protrusion of body tissue. Unfortunately, we had no time in which to work out the meaning of this phobia, but it referred, at least descriptively, to castration anxiety.

The Disclosures of Follow-Up

Not one of the twenty transsexuals I saw after they had undergone partial or total surgical sex alteration stated openly that he or she regretted having done so, and I believe that this has been the finding of other investigators as well. The apparent satisfaction of these patients seems to some observers to validate surgery as an appropriate "remedy" for their disturbance, but what seems superficially to be success needs further examination, in view of the propensity of such borderline personalities to employ a search for perfection through surgery as their major defense in life.

Any statistically oriented follow-up of transsexual patients who had surgery falls far short of telling the whole story. A long-awaited report from the Johns Hopkins Clinic recently became available, and in it Meyer (1977) gave follow-up information about the 50 candidates for sex change seen in 1971 he was able to locate out of the entire caseload of 100. About half had undergone surgery and half had not, but Meyer found the social circumstances of all slightly improved over what they had been at the time of first contact. It is significant, however, that those who had *not* had surgery had improved to the same degree as those who did have surgical alteration. If one is to acknowledge that the operation itself brought only modest benefit to the transsexual's social life, one is obliged to consider, in view of a smilar modest improvement in the lives of intact patients, that the passage of time alone had improved matters for each group, although none of the surgical patients sought reversal of their bodily changes.

We were unable to accomplish a systematic follow-up of our transsexual patients at the University of Virginia. I believe that their primitive splitting had succeeded in producing a split, as it were, between the surgical and psychiatric staff involved, and that patients returning for surgical follow-up were, in effect, "protected" from the scrutiny of the psychiatrist. Nevertheless, whenever psychiatric follow-up was facilitated, we renewed our efforts to understand the patient's psychodynamic state. The tragic outcome within four years of surgery of one postsurgical case has been described elsewhere in some detail (Volkan and Berent, 1976).

Even when the patient declares himself or herself greatly improved following the surgery, one must seek an understanding of his or her psychodynamics in order to grasp the nature of the adaptation he or she has made. An illustration of this is the case of the patient whose preoccupation with the terrain of Hawaii came to light during his six months of treatment on the couch. Three years after treatment terminated, this patient came to my office as a young woman. "She" had no appointment and said that she had just "happened" to be passing and wanted to say hello. When I displayed an interest in what had happened to her during the last three years, she agreed to diagnostic interviews with me if there were no charge. I agreed and we met twice. She spent most of the first hour telling me how grateful she was that she was now a woman. She had gone to college, was on the point of graduating, and was looking for work. She had scores of boyfriends who knew her story, and one wanted to marry her. Her happiness would be complete if only she were able to become pregnant. She still had her soap phobia, no more or less compelling than it had been before. She expressed satisfaction with her physical being, although the reconstructed "vagina" was so angled that a partner's penis was apt to slip out of it. She had, however, learned how to position her body during intercourse to overcome this difficulty. Her surgeon considered her case a great success, and she knew that he presented it to professional meetings as an example of surgical cure.

Although she was very convincing, I could not escape feeling that her appearance in my doorway was no accident. I surmised that she felt some need of me, and that on the basis of our six months of therapeutic association she felt that perhaps I was the only person who would understand something that was troubling her. When I asked about her dream life, the other side of the coin became evident—one that was never shown to those who thought of her as "cured." She had terrifying experiences at night, and during the last six or seven months these terrors increased to from three to four appearances a week. She was actually living two lives, one by day as a successfully "cured and happy woman," another between midnight and two in the morning, when she was in a different world, waking up, feeling cold, to be faced by a midget three or four feet long. On occasion it seemed to her to resemble her father, and she would say, "Dad, go away! I don't want to talk to you now." Later, she called the midget "the spirit," describing it in a way that indicated to me that it was a symbolic representation of her amputated penis. The midget sought union with her through her ribs. The talk of entry through the ribs suggested an identification with the story of Adam and Eve, but she gave me no direct associations to this. Most of her associations concerned the resemblance the midget bore to her dead father. She reported that sometimes the midget, as a spirit, succeeded in entering her body, whereupon she would break out in a cold sweat and feel half dead.

These terrifying experiences, split away from the rest of her life, became so frequent that she made arrangements with friends to call on them in the middle of the night when the terror came. She also felt that if she were not alone in her bedroom the midget might not appear, but this attempted reassurance failed when her boyfriend joined her; *both* of them had recently seen the midget, and both were terrorized by it.

She had become interested in lives she might have led in a previous reincarnation, and she and her boyfriend often visited a hypnotist who regressed them into lives they were said to have lived before this one. I asked if she were ever a boy in the glimpses of herself in the past that this experience provided her. She asserted that she was always a woman, and that, in fact, in her more recent regression under hypnosis she had been an Indian maiden who had been given a "golden stallion" which she grasped with her thighs as she rode.

It would appear that when the penis is externalized as a weapon of aggression, and when its amputation supports such externalization, the rejected "badness" continues to display itself. It is thus that the midget haunts this "woman" by night. The golden stallion might also be viewed as a "good penis," a defense against castration anxiety. However incomplete this follow-up may be, it does indicate a need to go beyond the simple statements of statistical summary to understand the kind of "adaptation" transsexuals achieve after they have undergone surgical alteration.

CHAPTER 11

Transvestitism:
With Special Reference to
Preoedipal Factors

MILTON E. JUCOVY

General agreement prevails on at least one aspect of transvestitism—that the term describes those who are erotically stimulated by wearing, or wishing to wear, the clothes of the opposite sex. Still at issue are its cause, what it defends against, and how it differs dynamically from other perversions. The literature on the subject deals exclusively with male transvestitism—little seems to be known of its occurrence in women—and I shall be following in this tradition, for my own experience has been confined to treating the male transvestite.

Transvestitism was first described as a specific perversion by Hirschfeld (1910), who found transvestites attracted to women of a masculine type and, thus, unlike passive homosexuals. He said, and Ellis (1936) agreed with him, that the transvestite shows one characteristic not seen in purely fetishistic perversions: For him, the fetish becomes erotically important only when it is brought into contact with his own body; when not worn, its capacity for erotic arousal appeared to be considerably reduced. This observation, while essentially valid, requires some qualification. Considerable variation exists among transvestites; some may be sexually stimulated simply by the sight of the fetish and others only when it is worn either by themselves, other transvestites, or by women.

Transvestites have been compared with homosexuals because transvestites frequently express the wish not only to wear women's clothes but also to live like women. A large group of transvestites whose object choice is a homosexual one fall into this category, but grouping them all with effeminate homosexuals would be incorrect. The transvestite I am considering here is one who wishes to wear women's clothes while retaining both a heterosexual object choice and the preservation of a male gender identity.

The early psychoanalytic literature dealing with transvestitism emphasized the role played by castration anxiety and the reluctance to relinquish the belief that women possess a phallus. Both Freud (1927), writing on fetishism, and Fenichel (1930), writing on transvestitism, stressed the regression from castration conflicts in the oedipal phase as a determining element in producing perverse sexual symptoms. Fenichel, one of the first to deal with this challenging and enigmatic subject, saw the transvestite as someone who has not been able to give up his belief in the phallic nature of women, and, in addition, identifies himself with the woman who possesses a penis. The identification is represented through the ritual of dressing up and by the clothes themselves, which are exhibitionistically displayed. Addressing himself to the question of the transvestite's object choice, Fenichel noted two tendencies. On a superficial level he is asking his mother to love him like a sister or like a little girl, without having to sacrifice his penis by being loved in this fashion. On a deeper level, he is asking his father to love him the way father loves mother, again with the reassurance that castration will not result. Fenichel proposed a general hypothesis for all perversions, including transvestitism. This may be summarized as a wish to retain infantile sexual desires and impulses, even though they may provoke intense castration anxiety, by indulging in infantile sexual practices that deny the possibility or reality of castration.

Recent increasing interest in how gender identity is formed has helped to differentiate the primarily heterosexual cross-dresser from the homosexual "drag queen," on the one hand, and the transsexual with severe core gender identity problems, on the other. Stoller (1965, 1966, 1968b), Socarides (1960, 1970, chap. 9, this volume), Ovesey and Person (1973, 1974, 1976), and Volkan (chap. 10, this volume) have contributed extensively in this area and have attempted to delineate phenomenological, genetic, and dynamic issues in homosexuals, transsexuals, and those heterosexual men whose interest is confined to fetishistic and transvestite behavior. One result of the significant advances in our understanding of ego function and maturation, the studies of separation and individuation, the importance of the aggressive drive, and the increased interest in the questions of self- and object representations and problems of identity has been to increase our awareness of the operation of more complex defense mechanisms and the role of pregenital fixations and weaknesses in ego structure in various sexual deviations.

Bak (1953) and Greenacre (1953, 1955, 1958, 1960b, 1968b) were among the first to apply this newer knowledge to the theory of perversions. While preserving a link with Freud's earlier work in emphasizing the importance of the castration threat, the necessity of denying castration, and the mechanism of ego splitting observed in perverse psychosexual development, Bak stressed a number of other important issues. These include a weakness of ego structure, either constitutional or as a result of illness or other physiological dysfunction that increases separation anxiety, the importance of pregenital fixations, and the concept of simultaneous and alternating identification with the mother who is imagined as possessing a phallus and, at the same time, as being castrated. Bak also stressed the significance of an intense need, arising before the onset of the phallic phase, to identify with a woman, thus increasing the castration threat from within, not simply as a result of exposure to the anatomical difference between the sexes. It might be noted how Bak's concept of "simultaneous and alternating identification" is predicated on Freud's concept (1940b), of the mechanism of ego splitting as a defensive process. A striking clinical example to illustrate Freud's early concept and Bak's elaboration can be cited from the analysis of a patient who had both fetishistic and transvestitic interests. My patient (Jucovy, 1976) constantly needed to blur the distinction between the sexes. He would speculate whether a transvestite could fool a normal man into thinking he was a woman. He regularly wore his tie in an idiosyncratic fashion, tucking the end of it under his shirt, so that part of it remained hidden. He reported a dream in which he appeared with a friend, both stark naked. His penis was detached from his body. He said: "My friend is showing me how to replace some tubes in the penis. He went to get new tubes, and I was apprehensive until he came back. We were greasing up the tubes and working them back in, and my friend told me this was easy to do.'' In another dream the patient was watching a show and a man came on the stage who was naked, with an artificial penis, shaped like a box, strapped to his pelvis. The patient realized he too was naked and that everyone could see his erection.

Greenacre has also written extensively on the pathogenesis of perverse sexuality, particularly fetishism, which she sees as arising from disturbances in the pregenital phase. She suggests that there are two main eras of disturbance, those of the first eighteen months, and those occurring at three to four years of age. The earlier disrupting influences may include physical disturbances causing marked sudden fluctuations in body image or subjective feelings produced by febrile illness or massive overstimulation. Disturbances of the mother-child relationship, which might be produced by mothers who hold their child as if it were a contaminating object, or mothers who are severely phobic and reach out with their eyes instead of providing sufficient cuddling, may affect the infant's sense of his own body outlines and his emerging ego. Greenacre stressed the role of trauma, either chronic or recurring from an earlier time, as a disruptive influence in the second era, or the occurrence of an overwhelming and castrating trauma which intensifies and patterns the child's emerging castration complex. The result of these disturbances is an unstable body-image formation, with uncertain outlines and a clouded sense of size. Later, there may be complementary disturbances in the phallic phase, with an exaggeration of the castration complex. Greenacre suggests that, of all parts of the body, the infant's concept of the genital area and face are the least certain. When the pregenital phase is disrupted, body-disintegration anxiety derived from the early phase reinforces strong castration anxiety and depletes the genital outlines. This contributes to further intense bisexuality and to a corresponding split in the ego.

The emphasis that Bak and Greenacre place on preoedipal factors receives unwitting corroboration from Fenichel (1930). The transvestite Fenichel describes in considerable detail also had an intense dread of death, which, Fenichel tells us, was connected with the ''early'' death of the patient's mother. From what Fenichel says about the influence the patient's stepmother had on the patient, I think it safe to infer that "early" definitely lay in the preoedipal period. Hence, while Fenichel attributes the transvestitism to castration anxiety, he offers evidence of a preoedipal trauma of formidable proportions.

My own clinical experience appears to confirm the formulations expressed by Bak and Greenacre. The patient I referred to earlier suffered no discernible sudden preoedipal trauma, but he had been subjected to a mother who was both extremely seductive and intrusively denigrating (see Jucovy, 1976). Following the birth of his younger sister, shortly before he was four, he developed colitis. He had severe bouts of bloody diarrhea and was subsequently told that his life was considered to have been endangered. Later, there was considerable evidence to support the idea that, for him, the potential loss of his phallus was only the prelude to total disintegration of a precariously held body image. During his early adolescent years he had numerous fantasies and fears of mutilation. After reading a book about a woodsman, he had a recurrent thought that he might step on an axe. He felt that parts of his body were held together in a precarious way and that, if a tendon in his foot were cut, the entire foot would collapse. When he was fourteen he developed an infection of the thumb which required incision. He believed his finger had been shortened and was greatly relieved to find his thumb intact when the dressing was removed. He subsequently placed inordinate emphasis on the idea of finding something intact beneath layers and was fascinated during adult life with the experience of looking and finding women's high-heeled shoes discarded in trash cans under layers of garbage. Greenacre calls particular attention to a persistent tendency to primary identification, reinforced through visual stimuli, in the individuals she discusses, which makes the sight of a castrated sexual partner particularly terrifying because of the wish for, and fear of, the underlying feminine identification. Support attained through the employment of a fetish or by a transvestite solution reinstates the phallus of the object and preserves the phallus of the subject.

Clinical experience with transvestite patients, either analytic or psychotherapeutic, has not been easily attained. Many individuals regard their fetishistic interests and requirements and their cross-dressing activities as ego-syntonic, do not suffer because of them, and are therefore not urgently motivated to seek treatment. Although more continues to be written about perversions, each article devoted to trans-vestitism contains, at most, only one or two extensive case reports. Nevertheless, each contribution has some interesting and significant points to make, many of which are strikingly parallel to and underscore the themes and formulations which had been noted by earlier writers previously mentioned.

Lewis (1963) reported a case of transvestitism with multiple body-phallus identification. He indicated that an early disturbance of the body-image formation, brought about through excessive contact with the mother, bathing with girls, and a probable constitutional predis-position to clinging, led to a primary identification with the mother, who was a powerful and active figure. The disturbance was reinforced during the phallic phase and led to a bisexual, clouded, and insecure body-image, featured by the equation of body and phallus. The patient had also been exploited by his sister in sex play, when she would dress him as a girl and beat his erection painfully. By later dressing himself up as a girl, he became his sister's appendage and was united with her and through her to his mother in an intimate symbiotic re-lationship. However, the threat aroused by being used as a woman's phallus undermined his already insecure self-representation, which then had to be warded off by becoming his own "beautiful girl." In his daily life, this man behaved in an apparently opposite fashion, differentiating himself from women by appearing excessively mas-culine, as if he were a tall and erect phallus. Lewis concludes that transvestitism, which began originally as a need to fuse symbiotically with the woman, now served as concealment in the service of pre-serving a degree of phallic function. In a discussion of perversion (Panel, 1954), reference is also made to a series of dual identifications seen in the transvestite. He can alternately dramatize complementary roles of active-passive, mother-child, male-female, and can simulta-neously both affirm and negate separation from the mother.

Segal (1965) confirms and amplifies the relation between separa-tion anxiety and multiple identifications in transvestitism He focuses on the role played by the symbiotic process in its evolution. He earlier proposed (1963) that an underlying aim in acts of perversion is to establish a necessary symbiosis with a maternal image in order to allay tension and maintain ego integration. He regards the neutralization of separateness and the alleviation of separation anxiety as crucial in the development of this perversion. Segal sees transvestitism as a compromise formation between homosexuality and fetishism, like the former in its passive feminine appearance, like the latter in the re-creation of the symbiotic mother-child relationship. The themes of symbiosis and separation anxiety are also stressed by Yazmajian (1966) in his description of a boy who was bilaterally cryptorchid from birth and developed transvestite practices as a man. For this patient, castration or separation threats could be calmed only by dressing as a woman and becoming the phallic mother whose breasts he associated with the testes. M. Sperling (1964) described her analytic work with a boy who showed transvestite tendencies. She concluded that they resulted from an intense oral fixation and a desire to be both sexes. This desire appeared to stem from a reaction to primal-scene trauma which provoked separation and castration anxiety, leading to bisexual confusion. The boy had fantasies of being half male and half female, which derived from preoedipal fantasies of a father with breasts and a phallic mother. The transvestitism thus expressed the wish to be both a man and a woman. Friedemann (1966) described two cases of male transvestitism. His observations of a ''mirror ritual'' practiced by his patients are worth noting. Both patients felt compelled to watch themselves in the mirror when dressed as women, which appeared to enhance and sustain their sense of identification with a woman. Friedemann considered the mirror ritual a keynote for understanding transvestitism. He based this on the fact that under ordinary circumstances, one has only a partial visual perception of one's own body, whereas, gazing into a mirror allows for a fusion of subjectivity and objectivity and thus a fusion of oneself as both a man and a woman. The blissful experience described by his patients of a union with a woman during the mirror ritual confers a feeling of protection and is reminiscent of the calming effects described by several other investigators.

An overview of the contributions to the literature on transvestitism would be incomplete without reference to the recent work of Ovesey and Person (1973, 1976). Their point of view falls within the framework of classical conceptualizations, and their sample is undoubtedly the largest to be found in the literature on this subject. In their earlier papers referring to the transsexual syndrome in males, they differen-

tiate the so-called primary transsexuals from transvestites and effeminate homosexuals, but believe that all three conditions originate in
disturbances in core gender and gender role identity arising from separation problems in the first three years, corresponding to three discrete yet overlapping phases. Some differences exist between their
findings and formulations and those of Stoller (1965, 1966, 1968b),
Roiphe (1968), and Roiphe and Galenson (1972, 1973a, b, 1975),
who suggest that the sense of core gender identity is firmly established
by the early age of approximately eighteen months.

Ovesey and Person (1976) studied a group of transvestites who
participated in transvestite or "network" society. Most were seen for
a brief number of sessions, while several underwent psychoanalytically oriented psychotherapy. The study was augmented by observations made during visits to transvestite sorority meetings and "drag
balls" and further supplemented by reading the transvestite literature,
both pornographic and nonpornographic. The focus was on a group
that would rarely be seen in an analyst's office.

The authors accept the conventional definition of transvestitism as
heterosexual cross-dressing in which the clothing and adornments of
the opposite sex are used fetishistically for sexual arousal. Believing
that the sexual component is outweighed by various nonsexual phenomena, they feel that transvestitism may be more aptly described as
a disorder of the sense of self, manifested by distortions of both gender
identity and sexuality, rather than broadly considered as a sexual disorder alone. In support of their point of view, they call attention to
the fact that most of the psychoanalytic literature deals with the transvestites who struggle with the wish to wear female clothes, but do it
in privacy. They remind us that transvestitism appears to exist on a
gradient, ranging from the evocation of fantasies to florid dramatizations with extensive involvement in transvestitic society, where some
members may live as women for periods of time. Some of this number
seek a transsexual solution through surgical procedures and sex reassignment. Ovesey and Person acknowledge that, because many transvestites engage in widespread symptomatic behavior, they are rarely
seen in the offices of psychoanalysts, and a skewed picture may emerge.
Their methodology raises certain questions. While certainly more
comprehensive in numbers and range, there is a certain sacrifice of

the in-depth study available through the application of the classical psychoanalytic method; further, the lumping together of all individuals who are cross-dressers may blur the very distinctions we would prefer to delineate.

On the basis of their observations, Ovesey and Person state that the characteristic adult transvestite has been appropriately masculine in boyhood and not effeminate. They may fantasize about being girls, but, unlike transsexuals and effeminate homosexuals, assert their maleness in overt behavior. Cross-dressing usually begins, spontaneously, in late childhood or early adolescence; it may start nonsexually to promote a sense of well-being or it may be sexualized from the onset. The initial experience may involve a partial or complete cross-dressing, and a favored article can become erotized and used fetishistically, at first during masturbation, later in sexual intercourse. Although some transvestites have occasional homosexual encounters, they prefer heterosexual activity where the fetishistic arousal may be intense, but the interpersonal sexuality attenuated. Ovesey and Person offer a personality profile of a typical transvestite. He is described as aggressive and competitive, with proclivities for power struggles with other men. He seeks self-employment to avoid conflicts with authority, and there is often a history of job rotation. Tender affects are invested in marital partners, but relations with children, while dutiful, are rarely warm and affectionate. Success in a marriage is frequently dependent on the personality of the wife and her capacity to tolerate the cross-dressing, if known to her, and the relatively minimal frequency of sexual advances by the transvestite husband, whose sexual arousal depends so greatly on the anticipation of a wife's awareness of his fetishistic conditions and wishes. The incidence of divorce is therefore high among transvestites. The affective life of a transvestite is characterized by irritability and depression, which occur under stress when dependency needs or feelings of masculinity are threatened. The use of cross-dressing and alcohol may assuage depressive symptoms, but Ovesey and Person gathered that suicidal attempts are common in a group so prone to depression.

The family histories of the group of transvestites studied by Ovesey and Person reveal the mothers as more frequently being recalled as warm and affectionate and less often as domineering and overbearing.

Maternal care often appears to have been erratic, either through ineptitude or some realistic misfortune. Constant deprivation was not reported, but there seem to have been repeated interruptions of maternal gratification.

These findings are not consistent with Stoller's observations (1966). He believes that the transvestite is partly a creation of the mother's unconscious wish and her need to feminize her little son. Ovesey and Person found only two histories of maternal induction into cross-dressing. They stress that the transvestite defense is essentially one's own invention, related to a process of self-object differentiation, only occasionally primed by some explicit parental directive, but not created by it. They nevertheless acknowledge that they were dealing with retrospective data and that other sources in the literature suggest evidence of conspiratorial factors. Their conclusion lends some support to the ambiguity; it does not seem to be possible to say how widespread such complicity appears in the histories of transvestites and to what extent it plays an etiological role in the development of transvestitism.

The fathers of transvestites, as described by Ovesey and Person, are frequently perceived as being verbally or physically violent. In a minority of cases the father was either absent or aloof and self-contained. On the basis of my own psychoanalytic experience with a transvestite patient, the personalities of the parents resembled those in the minority described. His mother was an intensely domineering matriarch who ruled the family harshly. She was cold, arbitrary, rigid, and moralistic in her personal relations and social attitudes. She was also highly prejudiced in her political opinions and on racial matters. She was preoccupied with cleanliness, and her preoccupation with her son's genitals could only have provided a high degree of overstimulation. In contrast, the father, who lived in his wife's shadow, was a mild and passive man who was largely absent from home because of his work. The mother's punitive weapon was a ''switch,'' the father's a bedroom slipper, a fitting enough metaphor for the difference in their personalities. As for the element of complicity, it appeared to be important for this patient, who used to play dress-up games with both his older and younger sisters during childhood. In addition, between the ages of six and ten he shared a bedroom with a feisty maiden aunt whose dressing routine he watched with fascination every morning.

These observations, however limited, led me to share the views of Lewis (1963) and Stoller (1966) that unconscious wishes on the part of mothers and mother surrogates may play a more important role in the final choice of a transvestite symptom than Ovesey and Person found in their cases.

Considering further their major thesis that transvestitism is a disorder involving the sense of self, Ovesey and Person note that several observers have viewed transvestitism in a number of disparate but related ways. Some stress dual or multiple identifications, while others view it as a defense, with the perversion representing a reparative condensation of the self and the maternal object, for purposes of security or to alleviate castration anxiety through identification with the phallic woman. While the formulations vary in their main thrust, they do not seem to be mutually incompatible. Freud's concept (1940b) of a split in the ego in the service of defense can be invoked in the alignment. It was formulated to account for the existence, side by side in the ego, of two contradictory attitudes, one consonant with reality, the other with the wish to deny reality. Such splits seem to occur when the infantile ego is faced with the necessity of erecting a defense against a trauma. In transvestitism, the dual self-representation seems to reflect a split in the ego where two mutually incompatible gender identities exist. Transvestites frequently express feelings of having two personalities, male and female, at war with each other. One may also note the presence of different ego states, depending on whether or not the individual is cross-dressed. The reporting of a greater sense of ease coincides with my patient's remark that he felt that women who dressed in glamorous clothes appeared "invulnerable." However, there was a curious and contradictory quality in his feelings: He also said that the same women looked somehow weak and vulnerable as they teetered along in their high-heeled shoes. Ovesey and Person conclude that the essential dilemma of the transvestite is the need to validate two incompatible realities, which are in turn predicated on the split in the ego and the conflicted sense of self. While aware that the ultimate etiological explanation has not been definitively formulated, they nevertheless suggest that it may lie in a better understanding of the defenses against unresolved separation anxiety during the separation-individuation phase of early development.

One aspect of Ovesey and Person's findings concerning transvestite fantasies and their enactment might be singled out for particular
attention. In the group of transvestites they studied, the key fantasy
seemed so simple and devoid of structure that they hesitated to call
it a fantasy. In this group, the act of dressing, accompanied by erection, masturbation, or even sexual intercourse, seemed the central
point of the fantasy. While some reported consciously elaborated fantasies, most seemed to have a stereotypic fantasy life and a rather
impoverished dream life. Underlying fantasies could only be surmised
from modes of enactment of the transvestitism, or the themes involved
in transvestite pornography. The need to objectify seemed paramount.

In contrast to the rather meager conscious fantasy life and the more
florid acting out of these network transvestites, my analysand revealed
a series of striking and dramatic fantasies which played a most significant role in his mental and emotional life and suggested some
important themes in the dynamic issues involved in the psychology of
the essentially heterosexual transvestite who is neither a transsexual
nor an effeminate homosexual. I had already been marginally alerted
to the central core of this patient's fantasies some years before, when
I saw another young man briefly, who came into treatment because
of urgent desires to dress in women's clothes. The first patient spoke
with intense feeling of a wish to meet a girl who would tutor him in
the art of cross-dressing, and he spontaneously used the term "initiation" in speaking of his fantasies. Because of a concern about a
possible thought disorder and other circumstances, this patient was
seen for exploratory psychotherapy for only a short time before he left
treatment. While noting the presence of his "initiation" fantasies, I
was not forcibly struck by them until some years later when I saw the
man referred to above for an extended period in a classical psychoanalysis. This patient, whose ego functions appeared intact, sought
treatment because of a desperate desire to be relieved of his wish to
dress in women's clothes; feelings of shame and humiliation played
an important role in his motivation. This patient reported a prominent
and persistent fantasy of meeting a glamorous woman who would tutor
him in the art of cross-dressing and the use of feminine make-up.
Ideas of being protected and shielded by the woman were an important
feature of his fantasy. Culmination would be reached by having sexual

intercourse with his tutor while both wore their stylish clothing and adornments. Fetishistic requirements played a large role in sexual relations with his wife. He felt gratified only when she fulfilled conditions of being seductive, dressed in sexually provocative undergarments, and initiated advances. He wished he could confess his problem to her and implore her to help him act out his fantasies, but his better judgment dictated against such action, for fear that she would turn from him in pity and revulsion. With some sense of conviction, the patient told me that if only his wife would assume the role of the seductress, would tutor and "initiate" him, and if only they could have sexual intercourse after such conditions were met, he would rid himself of his fetishistic interests and transvestitic urges and thus achieve a "cure."

During the course of the analysis, wishes for initiation appeared in connection with the transference when he confessed with some embarrassment a wish that the analyst and his wife would act as his tutors. The patient also described another version of the initiation fantasy which had appeared during adolescence, at a time when he rebuffed his own father's fumbling advances to form a closer relationship with him. The fantasy involved a dashing and virile man, someone like one of his favorite film stars, who flew a plane near the patient's home and crashed. He found the burning aircraft, rescued the pilot and nursed him back to health. In gratitude, the pilot adopted the patient as his protégé and taught him how to develop his muscles. As a result the patient became a model of masculinity and overcame the shyness he felt with girls. The first version of the fantasy contains some significant elements, although it is similar to the popular and rather conventional fantasies of many adolescent boys. The nursing back to health of an injured hero who then teaches him how to develop his muscles contained reverberations of ambivalent oedipal fantasies of hostility and aggression toward the father, but also featured tender and solicitous feelings. The patient, feeling injured and castrated himself, identifies here with the protecting nurse-mother. As a reward for his caring, and through contact with the powerful and idealized man, he becomes transformed into a powerful and virile youth. The later and adult version of the fantasy required elaboration at least partly because the patient considered his father such a poor model for identification, as well as for other reasons connected with his earlier relationship with his mother. Now the required initiator was a seductive, glamorously dressed, charismatic, and obviously phallic woman. The patient's thought that this initiation experience would cure him of his perversion is worthy of note. The ultimate expectation of liberation from the phallic mother after merging with her in sexual intercourse appears to be a central and vital feature of the initiation fantasy.

In a published discussion of my previous communication, Person (1976) agreed, on the basis of a study of transvestite pornography and personal observations, that such initiation fantasies seem to permeate the collective fantasy life of transvestites. There are prominent references in the personal columns of newspapers and magazines inviting acquaintanceships for the purpose of being instructed in the art of cross-dressing and the use of make-up. Masochistic themes are occasionally interwoven, as are ideas of protection and rescue. In many of the stories appearing in transvestite publications, the culmination is not sexual arousal. The aim of the cross-dressing appears to be to afford the transvestite the opportunity to live in a kind of easy intimacy with women in a dormitorylike situation, while his real sex remains unknown. In the course of her investigations, Person attended meetings of sororities of transvestites, some of which have existed on a national scale in this country for at least fifteen years. A regular activity of these sororities is to sponsor monthly meetings attended by members dressed as women. During the course of such meetings, members eat, talk, and drink. Sexual contact is frowned upon, for these transvestites maintain a militant antihomosexual stance. The transvestite members of the sororities are thus afforded the milieu of a ''make-believe'' world inhabited only by women, in which men are excluded. Meetings are devoted to a re-enactment of the central initiation fantasy. The members offer each other advice, help, and instruction about clothes and make-up. A transvestite becomes both the initiate and the initiator into the more subtle points of cross-dressing. An important aspect of a meeting is the encouragement of the attendance of wives of members. A gratifying experience for the group was provided at one meeting by the host's wife. She greeted each new arrival at the door and offered to comb out hair and wig, thus enacting the core of the initiation fantasy in which an authentic woman acts as the tutor of the transvestite. Material relating to initiation is prominently featured in the newsletters of each sorority. Subscribers are advised on how to tell their wives of their interests and how to enlist support and sympathy. Some wives contribute to the newsletters and encourage other wives to help their husbands express their transvestitic yearnings.

Person's observations appear to confirm the centrality of initiation fantasies in many transvestites. She believes that interpretation of the meaning of such fantasies may provide further clues to the structure of this still obscure perversion. She also stresses the significance of one aspect of the fantasy, the act of intercourse with a woman while both are dressed in feminine clothes. Her own speculation concerning this detail stresses the purpose of gratification of incestuous wishes while protecting the transvestite from retaliation by a male competitor. Masculinity is disguised, and rivals may thus be disarmed. This point of view stresses phallic-oedipal conflicts, but does not necessarily conflict with simultaneous emphasis on pregenital conflicts.

An inquiry into the meaning and importance of initiation fantasies led me to study anthropological observations which demonstrate the important role played by dressing in clothes of the opposite sex during boys' initiation rites among a number of primitive and preliterate peoples. I was struck by the frequency of transvestite elements in such ceremonies. Admittedly, caution must be exercised in extrapolating meanings of behavior from one culture to another, and it is possible that deviant psychopathology existing in one culture may be different in its underlying structure from institutionalized and ceremonial behavior in another. However, the similarities and overlapping are so striking and dramatic that I thought it worthwhile to draw attention to the parallels that suggest the possibility that one aspect of a transvestite's behavior may serve a similar adaptive function to that found in initiation rites, where the young boy is being prepared for a transition into the status of manhood. Further evidence to support this attempt may be found in the fact that forms of cross-dressing find a certain sanction in our own society. I am speaking here of the examples found in the frequency of transvestite features in children dressing at Halloween and the cross-dressing during fraternity initiations.

Bettelheim (1954), Frazer (1959), and Bateson (1958) have all written extensively on how common it is for a novice or initiate to wear the clothes and adornments of girls during initiation ceremonies before they are inducted into the community of men. The Naven ceremony described by Bateson is a central rite of a New Guinea tribe, called the Iatmul, where the practice of transvestitism is especially stressed. The ceremony is carried out during initiation rites, and at other times as well, to celebrate achievements such as a boy's first killing of certain animals or an enemy, or even during a marriage ceremony. The result of an initiation rite is for the boy to become a man and enter the masculine world of his peers. Evidence seems to suggest that in the Iatmul tribe the adult masculine state does not become stabilized. Perhaps because of the excessive sharing in the life of women during the early childhood of an Iatmul boy, initiation does not succeed completely, and the Naven ceremonies, carried out over and over throughout life, provide institutionalized opportunities for repeated cathexes and decathexes, thus warding off the regressive pull toward passivity and bolstering any faltering sense of masculine identity. Although not socially ritualized and institutionalized, except in the ''make-believe'' netherworld of the transvestite sorority, the act of transvestitism in our own culture may provide the same opportunity for a man with a similarly shaky and unstable sense of masculine identity.

The special significance which initiation fantasies have for certain transvestites may be further clarified by reference to Greenson's emphasis on the importance for a boy in ''dis-identifying'' from the maternal object (1968). This work utilized material from the treatment of a transvestite boy, Lance, which had been described earlier (1966), forming an interesting tandem with Stoller's (1966) description of the analysis of the boy's mother. Stoller's data revealed that this mother wished for and had shaped the feminization of her son. The wish expressed her desire to possess a feminized phallus, comparable to a transitional object, which would fulfill her need to counteract her own upbringing by an empty mother and an aggressive father. The mother had in the past dealt with her aggressive younger brother, bearing the same name as her son, in the same way. This overly intimate mother with bisexual conflicts and intense penis envy had solidified the symbiotic tie with Lance, which led him to develop a body image that included both the body and the bisexuality of his mother. Stoller's clinical material suggested to him that the boy's problems were not primarily the result of defenses against anxiety in the phallic-oedipal stage. Lance became a patient of Greenson's, who suggested on the basis of his observations that the overgratification Lance experienced produced poorly individuated gender identity. Loving was equated with becoming the love object, which represented a primitive form of identification. Lance seemed to show some of the features of an "as-if" (Deutsch, 1942) personality, and, for him, transvestitism grew out of this failure of individuation and represented a defense against separation anxiety. The clothes, as transitional objects, represented the mother's skin, to which he would at times retreat during periods of instinctual excitement or anxiety, as if they were a kangaroo pouch.

Greenson later (1968) called attention to the difficulties inherent in the development of male children who must replace the primary object of identification (the mother) and identify with the father. He used the term dis-identify to delineate the complex processes that occur in the child's struggle to free himself from the early symbiotic fusion with the mother. Greenson emphasizes that the fact that transvestitism is so common in males, and more prevalent than commonly believed, seems impressive testimony of the strength of the early attachment to the mother and underlying wishes of males to identify with a woman. He notes that many male patients reveal that they frequently may wear women's undergarments while masturbating. My own clinical experience confirms this observation; I have heard from many patients, particularly during accounts of adolescent memories, that the wearing of a mother's or a sister's lingerie provided considerable erotic gratification. In most instances this was transitory, but in many the experience evolved into certain fetishistic preferences of a mild to moderate nature, usually ego-syntonic, and served to enhance potency during sexual relations with the heterosexual partner.

Greenson (1968) summarized the difficult path boys must pursue to disidentify from their mothers and identify with a male figure. These steps proceed from primitive symbiotic identification with the mothering person to differentiation of self-representation from object representation, processes which have been described by Freud (1914, 1921, 1923a, 1925a), Fenichel (1945), and Jacobson (1964). Mahler

(Panel, 1957), Greenacre (1958), and Jacobson (1964) have also illuminated how different forms of identification play a central role as maturation makes it possible to progress from total incorporation to various selective identifications. The renunciation of the pleasure and security a male child obtains with mothering for the potentially uncertain identification with a less accessible father can be markedly influenced by the personality and behavior of both parents. Mahler and La Perriere (1965) pointed out the crucial role played by both parents in the ultimate outcome. Anna Freud (1965) also indicated that the mother must be willing to allow her son to identify with the father and may facilitate it by enjoying and admiring the boy's talents and skills.

Greenson (1968) suggests that mothers of the past who dressed their sons as girls for brief periods in childhood recognized the necessity for gratifying the boy's need to identify with the mother and thus eased the path toward his later identification with the father. The custom may have been a salutary one in instances of relatively stable and even development, but in others it may verge on complicity and seduction and enhance the development of later pathology, intensifying conditions for a driven need to return again and again to a state of temporary fusion with the mother before a reassertion of masculine identity can be even partially realized.

Attempts to understand transvestitism, both its regressive and adaptive aspects, its connections with oedipal and pregenital phases, and the significance of the prevalence of initiation fantasies among a group of cross-dressers are condensed in a particularly perceptive and poetic comment on the Naven ceremony offered by Muensterberger (1962), who spoke of it as an example of complementary identification and identification with the body image of the omnipotent phallic mother. He thought that transvestitism is utilized in initiation rites as imitative magic in the service of denial to prove the existence of a female phallus. He also spoke of the resurgent need to restore the sense of body completeness by a re-creation of the traumatizing condition of a feeling of abandonment before a restorative process can take place. He says: "We cannot escape the fact that here, detached more or less forcibly from the world of reality, in fantasy and dramatizations we witness a spectacle, the thematic content of which relates to the strug-

gle against the early passive attachment of the infant to the disap-
pointing mother'' (p. 181).

CHAPTER 12

The New Sexuality: Impact On Psychiatric Education

ROBERT DICKES

There is now little doubt that considerable change has occurred in the sexual attitudes and behavior of the young people of today as compared with that of their parents' generation. Whether these changes constitute a revolution or a process of evolution is a matter of semantics, and, in order to see the so-called revolution in better perspective, I shall, instead of debating the issue, place the changing sexual mores in the context of the history of sexual behavior over the centuries. I shall then consider the significance of the present-day sexual attitudes in relation to what is taught in medical schools and comment on the place of courses in sexuality in the medical school curriculum.

In view of the inhibitive approaches of Western society as noted over the centuries, we should remember that in pre-Christian times sexuality was accepted as a biological necessity, overtly practiced, and in a manner quite different from our own. (The following historical remarks are based upon the work of Hunt [1959], Licht [1932] and Vanggaard [1972].) The Greeks, for example, had several classes of women, all of whom sold their sexual favors openly and without interference from the state. The lowest class, the *pornae*, were ordinary prostitutes in brothels, which were designated by a sign—a painted or wooden phallus. Next in rank were the *auletrides* who not only offered their bodies, but could sing, dance, and play instruments, thus offering amusement as well as physical gratification. The most elevated type of courtesans were the *hetaerae*, who were intelligent, highly educated, and able to function as intellectual companions as well as mistresses. Many of these women had their own homes and enjoyed considerable status as individuals. Hunt tell us that many had a social status considerably higher than that of the legitimate wife. Citizenship and inheritance of property in Athens depended, however, on legitimate birth. A considerable number of *hetaerae* became famous and the companions of such people as Socrates and Pericles; the latter actually divorced his wife and then lived with Aspasia, a courtesan of uncommon beauty and brains.

The open acceptance of sexuality in Greece also included the acceptance of homosexuality as well as heterosexuality. The homosexuality, however, was of a special type. Vanggaard (1972) quotes a well-known tablet found at a temple site which states, ''Invoking the Delphic Appollo, I, Cremon, here copulated with a boy, son of Bathycles.'' This inscription of the seventh century B.C. was similar to many others found chiseled in rock in various parts of Greece. Such inscriptions should be understood in the context of the time (750 B.C. to 350 B.C.), when pederasty was an accepted practice and was regulated by law. Solon, who established the decrees that governed much of Greek society, took note of pederasty and expressly forbade slaves to have sexual intercourse with freeborn boys. This activity was reserved for the wellborn. Typically, the relationship was between an older man and a boy. We ordinarily think of such relationships as purely erotic. The Greeks, however, regarded them as an important factor in the development and education of their wellborn youths. They were conducted in a formal manner, requiring the consent and approval of the boy's father. Following this approval, a public announcement was made of the intention to have the boy live with an older man as his lover, a mock capture of the boy then being enacted. The parents were no longer held responsible for the boy, who went to live with his lover, who became his guardian and teacher. Anal penetration was part of the relationship, the Greeks believing that the boy would absorb the good qualities of his guardian. (Analytically, we could say that the anus functioned as the incorporating organ.) The youngster was expected to develop into a cultivated man and citizen, as well as a brave soldier. In fact, the famous ''Sacred Band of Thebes,'' the mainstay of the army of Thebes, was composed of paired

lovers who fought together. They remained unconquered until Philip
of Macedonia defeated them at the battle of Cheironica. All died
together on the battlefield, pair by pair (Vanggaard, 1972). The homosexual relationship continued until the boy developed a beard and
exhibited the usual changes characteristic of adolescence. The young
man then was expected to function heterosexually, marry, and father
children—a resolution one would not expect today.

Bisexuality was also characteristic of the Romans. Julius Caesar,
when young, perfumed himself and denuded his body of hair. He
openly practiced homosexuality, and was at one period in his life
called the "Queen of Bythynia" because he slept with the King. The
term Queen is still used today to denote the feminine male homosexual. Caesar was mocked as Queen, not because he slept with the King
of Bythynia, but because he was the passive partner in the act, this
being considered a sign of submission, and therefore of weakness.
Caesar was competent with women as well and remained bisexual.
The Romans called him the lover of any and all women as well as a
mistress to many men. Bisexual behavior was not considered especially unusual in Rome, and the respect for Caesar the general was
not affected by his sexual behavior. Pederasty was also accepted in
Rome. Hadrian the Great's love affair with a young man was widely
known, and Hadrian made no secret of his grief when the young man
was drowned; indeed, he had statues raised in honor of the youth.

We know little about the sexual behavior of Grecian wives but
more about Roman women. Early Rome was far from licentious and
enforced a strict inhibitory sexual code on women, according to which
a woman was held accountable even if raped, as is illustrated by the
story of the rape of Lucretia by Tarquinius. Lucretia killed herself in
order to remove the stain upon her husband's honor, his honor being
considered more important than her life. Alive, she was only a symbol
of his dishonor. The Tarquins were eventually punished, but not to
avenge Lucretia—it was her husband who had to be avenged!

During the course of the years a considerable liberalization of the
sexual customs developed. By 100 B.C. Roman wives took lovers
freely and went about as they pleased. Their lovers entered their
homes, and any gentlemen could and did pursue a wife, provided she
was not his own. Catullus the poet, for example, openly conducted

a love affair with one Clodia, the wife of a provincial governor, and no one seemed to mind. In time, Imperial Rome became more and more licentious, its excesses having become history.

Perhaps the real sexual revolution began with the emerging Judeo-Christian prohibitions and pronouncements about sexuality that affect us to this day. Masturbation was condemned and the pleasures of sex were denounced, while the value of continence was extolled. Thus our biological inheritance and sexual nature, the means of species preservation, were denigrated. It was St. Paul himself who said that it was good not to touch a woman. This applied to married as well as single men. The celibate marriage was considered holy, and the normal carnal elements of marriage were viewed with disfavor. These ideas dominated church thinking for centuries, the avoidance of sexual gratification having been considered more desirable than its healthy expression.

The celibate marriage of Amon and his unnamed wife exemplifies this type of thinking. The couple, deciding to live without physical contact of any sort and devote themselves to asceticism, moved out into a hut on the desert and practiced self-mortification. The church extolled this type of marriage, and many people emulated it. Variants of this type of unconsummated marriage also existed. So-called "spiritual marriages" for the clergy abounded. Virgins, termed *agapetae*, were taken into the homes of clergymen, who were then supposed to live in harmony and celibacy with them. You may well imagine that this approach was more often honored in the breach. Eventually, the church forbade these relationships. The church's general attack on sexual activity even in marriage is further exemplified by St. Jerome's statement that a man who loved his wife too much was an adulterer. The preoccupation with the interdictions against sexuality continued and eventually led to the establishment of a celibate clergy. Asceticism and mortification of the flesh were practiced, and sexual interest and fantasies were regarded as visions sent by the Devil. The infamous Malleus Maleficarum (Kramer and Sprenger, 1486) constantly attacked women as seducers and destroyers of men. The Council of Trent, in 1563, declared that celibacy was better than marriage and the virginal state was ideal for women.

Many other vagaries of the sexual drive could be described. I shall do no more, however, than mention one phenomenon, that of courtly love, which was related to an idealization of women in direct opposition to the concept of women as rapacious and the sexually insatiable perpetrators of evil. In courtly love, women were revered and men were required to abstain from intercourse with the ladies of their choice. Nakedness and petting were acceptable—echoes of this approach can be observed in the premarital conduct of the twentieth century—but full sexual expression with ladies was considered improper, although this did not apply to low-born women. No basic changes in attitudes ensued until the Reformation, when Martin Luther approved of marriage for the priesthood and condemned celibacy, stating that the best way to deal with temptation was to indulge in moderate enjoyment. He declared that the sexual impulse was natural and not due to demonic forces. John Calvin, however, held to the old traditions of asceticism. He meted out punishment while attempting to expunge evidences of pleasure. John Knox and others also adhered to this doctrine, later known as Puritanism, which was espoused primarily by the middle classes. The aristocracy remained more hedonistic. These two opposing trends have continued, thus expressing society's ambivalence to the gratification of the senses.

The contradictions in our culture's attitudes toward sex and women persisted throughout the nineteenth century and became fairly extreme. Marital sexual activity received approval, but the mention of sex in the presence of ladies was unacceptable. Sex could not be referred to even by innuendo; even the leg of a chicken was considered too suggestive, and a lady was not offered one at dinner, though offering the chicken breast was presumably quite acceptable. Some librarians, in their efforts to avoid anything suggestive of sexual contact, separated books by male authors from those by females. We may be inclined to laugh at these foibles, but we behave in a similar manner. People ''sleep together'' and go to powder rooms, smoking rooms, or to the ''john.'' We do not mention the natural functions involved.

The changes in the twentieth century have been considerable; some even regard the emerging sexual behavior of this century as revolutionary (Crist, 1971; Robinson et al., 1972). Taking the long view, however, what we are witnessing seems only another variant of human activity. What is truly revolutionary about the recent approaches to sexuality are the discoveries of Freud and his colleagues about the psychological aspects of the sexual drive in both men and women. Freud not only introduced the first scientific approach to the study of sexual behavior and its motivations, he also correctly predicted that much about neurotic phenomena would be learned from biology and organic chemistry (1926).

The physiological studies of Masters and Johnson (1970) enlightened us about the body changes during intercourse. In addition, the fundamental discoveries in endocrinology and in the biology of reproduction have further changed our understanding of the human being as a sexual creature. The present methodologies of scientific investigation have led to continuing increases in our knowledge about reproduction and sexual physiology. We have learned about many other factors pertaining to the psychology of sex. Derivative of these findings is the increasing ability to aid people who experience sexual difficulties. Thus, it seems to me that the real revolution is related to the scientific approach to sexuality and to human conduct.

Additional changes in sexual attitudes have occurred during the twentieth century, centering for the most part on changes in attitudes toward women. The Industrial Revolution, the production of labor-saving devices, and the changing economy have freed women from their domestic roles and put them into the marketplace both as competitors and helpmates to men. Two World Wars have also contributed to the developing economic independence of women. These and other factors have done much to change the old equilibrium between the sexes and, therefore, their sexual relationships. The Second World War accelerated the process of change.

The last several decades have produced a wealth of material that lays stress on a scientific rather than religious or moral approach. The first of these was the Kinsey report on males (Kinsey et al., 1948) followed by the report on females (Kinsey et al., 1953). Since then, numerous surveys have been published, including those of Reiss (1960, 1967), Simon et al. (1972), Offer (1971), and, most recently, Zelnik and Kantner (1977). This latest study, compared with their 1971 study, clearly indicates a considerable increase in the prevalence of intercourse among fifteen- to nineteen-year-old unmarried women. Zelnik and Kantner's (1971) study revealed that 27 percent of teenagers had intercourse at least once. The 1977 report indicates that 35 percent had intercourse, with the actual increase in numbers from 2,187,000 to 3,225,000. What is of interest in terms of education is that, in the 1971 sample, only 45 percent used any type of contraceptive and those who did relied essentially on the condom, douche, or withdrawal. Only 16 percent used either an IUD or the pill. In the latest sample, 63 percent used some form of contraception, of which about 33 percent used either the pill or the IUD. This shows a considerable increase in women's knowledge of the more sophisticated methods of birth control and a greater knowledge of their own responsibility to avoid a pregnancy. It is this increasing knowledge that accentuates the real revolution in terms of human sexuality and behavior.

All these matters are pertinent to medical schools and their selected curricula and should have a major impact upon teaching plans. Before turning to what medical schools are actually doing about an appropriate program of education, let us briefly examine what kinds of problems are noted in the general practice of medicine and assess the physicians' attitudes and knowledge of human sexuality.

Burnap and Golden (1967) questioned 87 randomly selected physicians about the types of sexual problems presented by their patients. They utilized a questionnaire dealing with four general areas, which included the frequency with which such problems occurred, the types of problems, and the characteristics of the physicians that might affect the answers in the first two areas. They also asked how the physicians managed the sexual problems presented by the patients. The survey produced a list of at least twenty separate types of sexual problems, only the five most frequent of which will be mentioned. These include lack of orgasm during intercourse, lack of desire, concern over the frequency of intercourse, lack of information about sexuality, and male impotence. The statistics on the first four types of problems reported did not include the sex of the patients, although one may assume that the first two categories included a preponderance of women.

Burnap and Golden reported that 29 out of 60 physicians routinely inquired about sexual problems, while 31 asked only if they felt such questions were indicated. Those physicians who asked about sex routinely reported that the average proportion of sexual problems seen was 14 percent. The remainder stated that the proportion was 7.9 percent. Burnap and Golden also reported on the behavior of the physicians during the interviews. Many showed unusual responses, such as blushing, fidgeting, joking, undue suspiciousness, and open resentment. These findings applied particularly to eighteen physicians. The mean proportion of sexual problems reported by this group was only 2.7 percent as compared with 15 percent for the remainder of the physicians. The doctor's attitudes toward sexual matters clearly affected the number of problems presented to them by their patients.

The authors also pointed out that the majority of patients were treated by their own physicians, who were then asked to state what sort of therapy they used for the common problems they observed. The largest number of physicians, 40, stated that they talked without any specific goals in mind or that they allayed misconceptions or gave reassurance. The types of reassurance offered were not noted. The next largest group, thirteen, simply told their patients that they could offer no help. The remainder gave hormone injections, advised vacations or a drink to relax, etc. All in all, the treatment offered can be described only as quite inadequate. It also should be noted that 83.3 percent reported that they had had no training in dealing with sexual matters at either the undergraduate or graduate level.

Later reports generally confirm Burnap and Golden's findings. At the time of Burnap and Golden's report, medical schools almost never taught about the management of the problems associated with intercourse, which are the types most commonly encountered. At present, this is no longer true, but the reported variability in the incidence of sexual problems remains and is related more to the physician's attitudes than to the patient's problems. It is still too soon for the newer programs to affect the overall picture concerning physician's sensitivity to sexual problems.

The question of adequacy was also considered by Pauly and Goldstein (1970), who reported on the results of a questionnaire answered by 937 physicians. They stated that their respondents felt more adequate than other physicians in their understanding of human sexuality. Self-assessments of adequacy are not always accurate, however, and we should not equate competence with comfort without more evidence. The high degree of comfort and feelings of competence reported by the respondent physicians may nevertheless be related to the fact that the highest response rate came from psychiatrists and obstetrician/gynecologists, who often deal with sex problems, thus skewing the results.

Levenson and Croft (1977) reported on a questionnaire answered by 65 doctors. Obstetrician/gynecologists showed the highest response rate and general surgeons the lowest. More than 90 percent of the respondents reported that they had had no formal course in sex education in medical school, 90 percent believed that more training was needed, yet, 86 percent of the respondents stated that they almost always felt competent in counseling patients on sexual matters. Many of the physicians participating in the study treated sexual problems themselves. There is no record concerning the type of treatment offered or the type of result obtained. Therefore, it is not possible to judge the accuracy of their stated feeling of competency.

Levenson and Croft reported that the five problems most frequently treated were impotence, dyspareunia, premature ejaculation, frigidity, and lack of orgasm during intercourse. The list of difficulties is similar to that of Burnap and Golden, and the reported lack of formal education related to sexual behavior is stressed by Levenson and Croft as well as many other investigators.

Medical schools have steadily resisted the introduction of courses in sexuality. Lief (1969), who had long stressed the need for adequate training for physicians and adequate teachers, was most instrumental in diminishing this resistance. Vincent (1968) pointed out that whether physicians wish it or not, patients expect them to know about sex and counseling. Therefore, the pressure of the patient's needs requires that physicians become familiar with many aspects of sexuality. An editorial in the *Journal of the American Medical Association* (1969) advocated that formal training in sexuality be continuous throughout the medical school years. It has also been shown that symptoms can exist which mask sexual problems. This phenomenon is well known to psychiatrists as well as many other specialists. Stressing this has made more people aware that knowledge of sexual difficulties is even more imperative for physicians.

In March, 1965, a joint committee of the American Medical Association and the National Education Association passed a resolution expressing the need to incorporate ''appropriate learning experience for physicians in the area of counseling relating to sexual attitudes and behavior,'' a resolution important enough to be included here:

> Whereas, the American Medical Association, through its House of Delegates, has expressed concern with respect to the need for medical counseling of patients on sexual attitudes and behavior, and
>
> Whereas, the AMA Committee on Maternal and Child Care and the AMA Committee on Human Reproduction have made recommendations urging increased emphasis on orientation of physicians concerning patient education relating to sexual attitudes and behavior, and
>
> Whereas, physicians frequently serve as resource persons in this area of health education in schools, colleges, and other youth agencies, therefore be it
>
> Resolved that the Joint Committee on Health Problems in Education commend these committees and all others concerned on their action in recommending increased emphasis on orientation of physicians in the area of sexual attitudes and behavior in the curricula of medical schools, and be it further
>
> Resolved that all medical schools and programs of continuing medical education give consideration to incorporating appropriate learning experiences for physicians in the area of counseling relating to sexual attitudes and behavior [Lief, 1969, p. 8].

The pronouncements and evidence concerning the importance of sexual education for the physician notwithstanding, marked resistance to this important approach remains. This was made strikingly clear in an article by Alper (1977) who, in my view, attempted to make a virtue out of ignorance. He indicated and justified the fact that he often skipped the sexual history, and he downgraded the importance of sexuality in human life. He wrote: ''But it could also be that, while there probably isn't anything people *think* about more than sex, its place in life and in relationships between human beings has been vastly exaggerated'' (p. 80). He adds: ''Aside from disinclination, I have as yet to figure out what other people *ought* to be doing about sex.'' He also pokes fun at attempts to educate physicians: ''The different approaches that are being publicized these days only add to my confusion'' (p. 82). Nor is Dr. Alper alone in this attitude.

Some years ago, when I was attempting to persuade the Curriculum Committee of the Downstate Medical Center to include specific hours for sex education, one departmental chairman became somewhat upset by the idea. He believed that teaching about sex would make the students too knowledgeable, and therefore more contemptuous, about sex. He also felt that they would become less interested and less able to perform. He objected to the inclusion of any course at all saying that people have managed by themselves for generations and ''we should not meddle.'' I politely refrained from adding that large numbers had mismanaged for generations.

It is true that many obstacles impede the acceptance of more extensive educational programs on sex in medical schools. Psychological problems play an important inhibiting role and influence many decision-making processes. Other factors exist as well. The medical school curriculum is necessarily limited by time, and most emphasis is placed on the biological and clinical sciences related to life-saving procedures. Those related to happiness and to the human psyche take second place, at best. And, of course, resistances to any innovation exist. Martin and Lief's remarks (1973) regarding the introduction of teaching about marital therapy into psychiatric programs apply to the teaching about sexuality and the briefer methods of sex therapy. Further, there is resistance to change because faculty members either fail to understand the suggested changes or are unimpressed with their value. Skills may be lacking and status may be threatened. We should not, as psychiatrists, be surprised that ''protective prejudice'' hides the basic fears of opponents of change. People who have such needs will resist the obvious. In spite of this, the wide number of sex movies and the increasing tide of pornographic literature point to people's pressing interest in sex and need for knowledge. The divorce rate has increased enormously. Demand for sexual performance is also a characteristic of the changing sexual scene. Thus, a continuing pressure is now exerted upon medical schools to teach more about sex. During the past twenty years, programs have developed and spread from school to school.

As late as 1950, there was no organized course in human sexuality available in the United States. Students were taught about anatomy and about the physiology of reproduction, but little was taught about human sexual conduct other than material concerning perversions and other spectacular or unusual types of sexual behavior. The norms of conduct and the latitude ''permitted'' for healthy sexual behavior was rarely, if ever, discussed. Faculties in general did not consider these subjects worthy of their attention, although occasional teachers did discuss sexual behavior.

In my own experience as a medical student, one teacher saw fit to discuss impotence with us when we were senior students. One day, our instructor, a dermatologist, incidentally, entered the classroom, looked around, and asked if everyone was present. When told that everyone was indeed present, he locked the classroom door and said: ''I'm not supposed to do this, but I'm going to teach you about sex because patients will ask you about it. It's all right for me to do this because I'm 60 now and no longer interested in sex.'' He then explained how to treat impotence. He told us that it was the easiest thing in the world to cure and that all one had to do was tell the couple to sleep in separate rooms for two weeks. He said that nobody could last out the two weeks and all the patients who came back told him they couldn't wait that long and apologized for not having followed instructions. He never did tell us what percentage of the couples came back. Having delivered his little speech, he said: ''That's that, and let's get back to our real business.'' The good will of this instructor was evident; I will say nothing about his lack of knowledge.

The situation began to change when the University of Pennsylvania offered the first course in sexual behavior. This was an elective for senior medical students and was initiated in 1952. By 1960, Bowman-Gray School of Medicine and Washington University in St. Louis were offering courses in sex behavior. The course at Washington University consisted of six lectures given by William H. Masters to second-year medical students. Thus, by 1960, there were only three medical schools with a planned course in human sexuality (Lief and Karlen, 1976).

The decade from 1960 to 1970 saw considerable change in the situation. I earlier pointed to the increasingly outspoken comments of such organizations as the American Medical Association, and I can add that, by this time, numerous deans and faculty members of many schools were supporting the need for sex education. To the best of my knowledge, however, neither the American Psychiatric Association nor the American Psychoanalytic Association has offered any official support to those who stressed the importance of sex education. By 1968, the Center for the Study of Sex Education in Medicine was inaugurated at the University of Pennsylvania and supported by the Commonwealth Fund. Its president, Quigg Newton, stated: ''Identification and management of sexual problems in medical practice concerns one of the most subtle and difficult facets of patient care. The problems are among the most sensitive and anguishing patients bring to their physicians, and at the same time represent an area in which medical counseling impinges deeply on individual and family behavior and values. Thus, medical intervention is often critical to the patient's entire well-being and to that of the patient's family'' (Lief, 1970, p. 1864).

It is clear from the above that the earlier indifference no longer existed; about 30 medical schools were offering courses by the end of 1968. The next five years saw a further burgeoning of this trend, and by the end of 1973 practically all medical schools offered instruction in sexuality. Lief and Karlen (1976) summarized a survey conducted by Lief of the radically changed situation. I shall extract some pertinent data from their report.

At the time of Lief and Karlen's survey, there were 114 medical schools, 110 of which were contacted. One hundred five of these schools had programs devoted to human sexuality. Seventy-two percent presented separate courses on the subject, while the remainder taught the material in the context of other courses. The number of faculty members primarily responsible for these courses varied, and the faculty ranking of the teachers was equally variable. Some schools had as many as sixteen teachers for the course and others had no more than one person responsible for planning and teaching. The two disciplines most often involved were psychiatry and obstetrics/gynecology, with psychiatry represented in 95 percent of the schools' courses and obstetrics/gynecology in 87 percent of the schools' courses.

The importance a given faculty attaches to a course is often demonstrated by whether or not the course is elective or required. Required courses are considered core courses, and 68 percent of the schools made sexual behavior part of the core curriculum. Another measure of a course's importance is attested to by the number of hours allocated to it. Thirty-five percent of the medical schools allotted ten to nineteen hours per semester for sex education and 28 percent offered twenty to 29 hours as a total. Twenty-one hours, however, is the median.

I instituted a new survey in the latter part of 1976 and sent a brief form to 50 medical schools scattered over the entire country. Thirty-one completed the forms. My intent was to choose a random sample and to compare the results with those obtained by Lief and Karlen three years earlier. I chose the smaller sample based upon the knowledge that, by 1973, almost all schools offered either a core course or an elective. The great increase in the number of schools offering courses about sexual behavior occurred between 1968 and 1973. By this time, almost all schools were teaching undergraduates material related to human sexuality. I did not anticipate marked changes. The results of the survey verified the anticipation.

In addition to the questionnaire about undergraduate medical students, I also asked about the teaching of human sexuality and brief sex therapy to residents. Some questions were asked pertinent to post-residency programs. Many of the respondents not only filled out the questionnaires, but also included descriptions of their courses and indicated the history of the courses' development. Almost always, the addition of courses on sexuality was due to the dedicated drive of one or two people who finally overcame the opposition.

The results of my survey do not tally exactly with those of Lief and Karlen, but this is to be expected, since their sample included over 100 medical schools whereas my sample included only 31 respondent schools. Lief and Karlen reported that 60 percent of the schools presented courses as part of the core curriculum. In my sample, only 52 percent indicated that teaching about sexuality was required. Most schools (over 80 percent) also offered elective courses. All but two offered either elective or required courses. Thus, about 6 percent did not identify a required or elective course. These schools may, however, as at Downstate, include appropriate material in the curriculum in departments such as psychiatry.

At Downstate, teaching medical students about human sexual development occupies 25 hours. We also teach about animal sexuality for two hours. In addition to this, ten hours are devoted to lectures and films of an explicit nature on adult sexual behavior, followed by two hours of small-group discussion. Thus, 57 hours are devoted to education about adult sexual practices. This teaching is part of our regular second-year course on understanding human behavior. The course content has just been published (Simons and Pardes, 1977). Included are several chapters on sexual expression and its deviations as taught to medical students (Dickes, 1977). Further teaching is given in another second-year course on history-taking. Included is information on how to take a sexual history and its place in general medicine. During the third year, students serve a clinical clerkship and are taught more about sexuality. The number of hours, being quite variable, cannot be ascertained. Thus, although the answers to the questionnaire would require a negative reply from Downstate, a considerable teaching program exists in human sexuality. The same may well apply to the other negative respondents. It was my intention, however, to deal with identifiable catalogued courses, since this is indicative of administrative and curriculum committee interest and commitment. The general results of this survey indicate that there has been no significant increase in the number of hours of teaching since 1973. There has also been no change in the estimation of the importance attached to sexuality as a factor in a physician's general education for the practice of medicine. The changing sexual mores have therefore had little further impact on undergraduate teaching.

An examination of the survey's results in terms of psychiatric residency training indicates that, in general, the newer knowledge about sexuality has not had any major impact upon the formalized aspects of training either in didactic or case-work application. Not one of the 31 schools prepares even selected residents for certification as brief sex therapists either by the Eastern Association of Sex Therapy (EAST) or by the American Association of Sex Educators, Counselors, and Therapists (AASECT). EAST was organized by a group of eastern medical school therapists who have attempted to establish standards for training and competence in this field. It is composed of people from several disciplines, including psychiatry, obstetrics/ gynecology, urology, psychology, social work, and nursing. A Masters Degree is the minimal requirement for acceptance for training. AASECT encompasses the entire country and does not require the M.D. degree. This organization has its own set of standards. The field of brief sex therapy has, in short, been pre-empted by people from disciplines other than psychiatry.

Only 7 percent of the residency programs at the respondent medical schools offer required courses in sexuality. Only one program includes more than 50 hours of required work. The remaining sex programs offer from three to fifteen hours during the entire three years of training. Many of the residencies offer electives, but the reporters often failed to list the number of hours devoted to the electives. Four did indicate the hours, which were 18, 30+, 42, and 60. Both elective and required programs used lectures, films, and other aids in training.

Some residency programs have no formalized teaching about sex therapy, but interspersed throughout the training program is material on sexuality. The respondents indicated that clinical case assignments by their very nature led to sexual material and, therefore, to teaching about the management of sexual difficulties. This is no doubt true, but it does not often lead to teaching about brief sex therapy, an approach utilizing sensate-focus exercises, which has become more and more widely used since the Masters and Johnson reports. In light of the wealth of new information about sexual dysfunction and its treatment, it seems startling to me that so few psychiatric residencies offer much in the way of a coordinated program that will make psychiatrists experts in this field. The lay public and most professionals expect psychiatrists to be extremely knowledgeable about the various treatments for sexual dysfunction. Such is not the case. I know many psychiatrists who need the special training that makes a person competent in the field of sex therapy. These findings seem in keeping with the failure of the American Psychiatric Association and the various analytic associations to take an official stand in favor of the inclusion of specific training in human sexuality in student and graduate training.

I am fully aware that in all probability every residency does teach much about biological and psychological sexual development and their relation to sexual dysfunction. The general treatment of a patient with psychological problems does not focus directly upon the sexual problem even when present, however, and the results, in terms of sexual function, may be slow in developing. The general dynamic approach is often in contradiction to the approach of brief sex therapy, which focuses directly on the sexual difficulty and utilizes sensate focus as a means of improving sexual function. Obviously, it is not a cure for deep-seated problems and is not suitable for all cases, but this type of therapy should, in my opinion, be one of the tools available to all well-trained therapists. Coupling the brief-therapy approach with the dynamic approach can be very helpful to a great variety of patients.

The methods of undergraduate teaching and course content remain for consideration. As is usual, the lecture format is most widely used and is employed by 90 percent of the survey respondents. It is not, however, the most popular approach. The lecture approach is used because it is most economical in terms of the investment of faculty members and their time. Most people I have talked to favor small discussion groups, but not enough trained staff people are available. Lief and Karlen, in their study of undergraduates, state that 87 percent of the schools use the small-discussion method and 54 percent use seminars. The distinction between discussion groups and seminars at the undergraduate level, however, is blurred. Actual work with patients is minimal in all courses and only 8 percent to 9 percent of the schools use supervised treatment or a community field experience as part of the training. The situation today shows little change.

Many types of teaching aids are in use. These consist of films, slides, reading lists, guest lectures, and audiovisual tapes. Films are by far the favorite teaching aid, and many types of erotic and informational films are utilized.

Although the course content from school to school may seem similar, the variations in method render the courses very dissimilar. I know of one course that lasts a single weekend, which is devoted to the watching of pornographic films interspersed with discussion and lectures. The stated objective of the course is to desensitize the students and to make them more comfortable when faced with patients' sexual problems. The weekend is called a "Fuckarama." This approach is more common than is realized. The instructors are convinced of the lasting value of this brief exposure to sexual material.

The opinion that the approach exemplified by the method just described is of great value is buttressed by the work of Tyler (1970) and Money (1971), who overwhelmed the students by the massive presentation of sexual stimulation, termed implosion, and used such tests as the Sex Knowledge and Attitude Test (SKAT) and others to demonstrate statistically valid changes in attitudes in *all* students after two days of intensive exposure and sexual stimulation. (It is not incidental that students are invited to bring their spouses to the experience.) The majority of educators who use the implosion technique believe that it is the group process work that induces the changes in the students. They consider the films focal points for discussion and acquiring insights.

Tyler, who pioneered this method, stated that the first required course at Indiana University Medical Center, instituted in 1969, was planned as a "straightforward" course and was preceded by an evening elective lecture series in 1968. By 1970, the goal of desensitization to hasty or overreactive responses to sexually stimulating material grew in importance. Time for the course was assigned in the second semester of the second year. This choice was, as is often the case, based upon expediency. The process of film selection for the 1968 course led to the study of erotic films, which then led to the consideration of desensitization. In preparation for the selection of films, the viewer scheduled a whole day of film viewing. By the end of the day he felt, not dehumanized, but desensitized and no longer shocked, angry, or aroused. This personal experience was the basis of the decision to use an implosion technique for the first day. The second day continued with an illustrated lecture of the extensive range of human sexual activity. The "Fuckarama," a term *not* used by Tyler, is a derivative of this approach.

Student attitudes to sexuality and their knowledge and experience in sexual matters greatly influence their behavior in relation to a faculty teaching such material. Lief and Reed (1967) developed the aforementioned SKAT to ascertain the state of a student's knowledge about sex. The test was given before and after courses on sexuality to discover what effect the teaching has had on the student. Lief has reported greater knowledge and comfort in matters related to sexuality. The test is now in use in about 40 medical schools. Lief and Karlen, through the use of the test, point out some of the errors students bring with them into medical school. About 25 percent of the male students and 35 percent of the female students, for example, are convinced that few married couples practice mouth to genital contact. Approximately one-third of all students do not believe that 25 percent of men and presumably women have an active sex life after the age of 70. Also about one-third do not accept the idea that the cause of impotence is almost always psychogenic. Women, by the way, are more apt to dismiss sexual myths and misconceptions than are men.

Chez (1971), an obstetrician, has also used movies of sexual activity as a teaching aid. He taught junior medical students during their clerkship in obstetrics and gynecology. His format differed from that previously described. The movies, without sound, were shown to small groups, and each short film segment was preceded and followed by discussion. Included were brief episodes depicting masturbation, heterosexual intercourse, and homosexual anal penetration. Almost all the students had previously seen films of masturbation, and most had seen heterosexual cunnilingus, fellatio, and intercourse. Twenty percent had seen films of male homosexuality and 45 percent had seen films of female homosexuality. In spite of this previous exposure, approximately one-third of the group reported boredom, repulsion, or surprise by Chez's films. Eighty-one percent were sexually aroused and 60 percent suppressed laughter, a known substitute for arousal if inhibition is present. Other emotional reactions were also noted. I think it important that 82 percent of the total class felt the session was worthwhile as a professional experience and that it would help them in treating patients with sexual problems. This overestimation of the effects of one exposure on the ability to treat is reminiscent of Pauly and Goldstein's report quoted earlier.

Chez indicated that his decision to use films was based on Tyler's report that movies were an aid in teaching students about human sexuality. His teaching time lasted less than three hours and must be compared with Tyler's, who presented the movies within the structure of a twenty-hour, one-week course. The use of movies by both teachers was, hence, in a different context, and course variability, therefore, was marked, although the content was similar. Chez makes the point that repetitive viewing of pornography will diminish sexual responsiveness in the student, but is not an aid in the prevention of arousal while caring for patients. He believes, however, that arousal with a patient is rarely a problem. Chez stresses the need to deal with the student's anxieties in taking a sexual history, rather than in desensitizing him or her to sexual arousal during the viewing of films of human sexual activity.

Confrontation is another device used to develop more tolerant attitudes in students. They may be asked to face patients, talk with homosexuals, and face their own sexual attitudes and prejudices. All this is classified under an affective learning approach. This type of experience can indeed be valuable for the development of tolerance and in preparation for learning much basic material. It does not, however, prepare one to be an adequate therapist for the sexually dysfunctional patient. This requires an adequate clinical experience under expert supervision and time enough to mature as a therapist. Distinctions between the teaching of medical students and residents, therefore, are important.

All physicians need to develop tolerance for other people's sexual behavior as long as this behavior harms no one. One must even understand the child molester if one wishes to provide aid. Loathing and punitive behavior on the part of physicians are not assets in the treatment of the sexually disturbed individual. Physicians must therefore develop a sufficient degree of understanding of these conditions, must know what approach to use for people who express their sexual problems, confident that the doctor's attitude will be helpful. Preparation for this approach must be one of the aims of undergraduate teaching. Certain skills must also be developed in students—the ability to elicit a proper sexual history and to be able to estimate one's own ability to treat so as to know when to refer the patient elsewhere or to treat the patient oneself. Basic knowledge includes not only information about anatomy, reproduction, and body chemistry, but also knowledge about human sexual development and some understanding of psychological growth and its relation to sexual behavior. All this needs to be taught.

Many types of sexual malfunctioning can be treated by a properly trained practitioner. Often, the physician need only give information about physiologic response or reassure a patient about misconceptions concerning sex. Myths may have to be debunked, etc. Other problems, such as occasional failures in performance, can also be managed successfully. The truly dysfunctional patient, however, requires a well-trained therapist skilled in the techniques of sex therapy. I do not believe such training is within the province of undergraduate teaching. It is, however, within the province of the residency training programs in psychiatry. Nevertheless, not one residency program prepares the future psychiatrist for certification as a sex therapist.

The startling fact is that the greater sexual freedom and demands for knowledge and help on the part of the public has had its greatest impact on undergraduate education and on nonpsychiatrically trained personnel. Psychiatrists seem to have been the least influenced by the newer approaches to sexual difficulties. The training programs reflect this attitude. Formalized teaching about sensate focus and its role in brief therapy should be a part of residency training. Clinical case work and supervision by trained and experienced psychotherapists are also necessary. Obviously, every therapeutic approach cannot be taught, but certain skills are more essential than others. Sexual difficulties are commonplace and cut across the spectrum of all emotional disorders. Therefore, residents should be taught the essential skills needed for various types of sex therapy.

Crisis intervention and other types of brief therapy are demandd by more and more people as well as by third-party payers. If psychiatrists who understand dynamic approaches avoid any type of brief therapy, others will fill the breach—and not as successfully. This will be a disservice to the public. One hopes that the present paucity of training in sex therapy will diminish and that more programs will develop. Trained personnel is in short supply, however, and this difficulty also must be overcome before an adequate number of programs can be mounted.

Resistance to the teaching about human sexual needs remains. The number of present undergraduate courses seemed to have reached a plateau in 1973, with no significant increase in course development since then. The enthusiasm of the five-year period of 1968 to 1973 would seem to have diminished. It is known that schools have allowed courses in sexuality to lapse, despite student enthusiasm. In some cases, courses have been re-established. This important type of education requires continuous support from more than a dedicated few. The public's expectation that their physicians be knowledgeable about sexual matters is reasonable. The expectation that psychiatrists be expert in the treatment of sexual dysfunction is equally reasonable. Yet, appropriate programs for residents hardly exist. Let us hope for improvement in this area.

CHAPTER 13

Sex Education and
Its Psychological Implications

JULES GLENN,
HARVEY B. BEZAHLER,
and SYLVIA GLENN

Recent years have seen sharp swings of the pendulum with regard to what sort of sex education is best for children. We here attempt to sort out the different sources and methods of sex education and evaluate their effects. In doing so, we emphasize the child's personality development, because we recognize that no single educational approach is optimal for all ages or groups.

With the publication of his "Three Essays on the Theory of Sexuality," Freud (1905) set out the theoretical background for a rational approach to the problems of sex education. Earlier, psychoanalysis had revolutionized thinking about mental functioning, revealing the importance of the unconscious. With Freud's delineation of the unfolding of the sexual life of normal and neurotic individuals, the concept of infantile sexuality became a central controversial issue, both with Freud's adherents and with others. The innocence of childhood was a cherished ideal that people were unwilling to part with—a testament to the power of the adult's wishful thinking and repressive forces. The early analysts who broke with Freud argued that infantile sexuality, if it existed at all, played only a minor role in human development. One of the major considerations in publishing the case of the Wolf Man (Freud, 1918) was to answer Jung's dismissal of infantile sexuality as unimportant in the genesis of neuroses. Nor could Adler admit to sexuality's prominent part in the etiology of mental illness. Freud recognized that many of the objections to his radical insights represented resistances of deep personal significance to the individuals raising them and held firmly that any truly valid psychoanalytic psychology or treatment must take into account the infantile sexual life. As his insights deepened and broadened, he emphasized the role of aggression and in his final theory—the structural point of view—ego and superego, as well as drives, played crucial parts.

From the start, the thorny question of sexual enlightenment has been plagued by confusion, uncertainty, and controversy over what should be taught, when it should be taught, and who should do the teaching. In December, 1907, at a meeting of the Vienna Psychoanalytic Society addressing itself to the topic ''Sexual Traumata and Sexual Enlightenment,'' Hitschmann stated: ''The need for sexual enlightenment is generally acknowledged. Actually, enlightenment should be given in three stages of life:

''1. When children begin to ask about their origin—between eight and ten years of age. [Nunberg adds a footnote calling attention to the error in placing this event so late.]

''2. Somewhat later in a more specific way.

''3. In puberty (at about sixteen to seventeen years) on the dangers of and the protective measures during sexual intercourse.

''Such enlightenment, however, cannot provide protection against the childhood traumata,'' he cautioned (Nunberg and Federn, 1962, pp. 270-271).

At the same meeting, Sadger spoke of parental ignorance and how lies from parents undermine their authority and a child's love. He also spoke of the dangers of ''excessive demonstration of affection'' (p. 271). Disagreement over the value of enlightenment continued, with some stressing its danger, others its value. Freud noted, ''Children should see the facts of sexual life treated in the same way as all other matters. Precocity is so harmful because the child is so helpless in the face of strong sexual excitement; he does not possess the intellectual means of mastering this feeling. Education deflects the intellectual capacities entirely away from the sexual theme. . . . It is very likely that enlightenment could countermand the effect of such traumata. . . . In spite of all precautions, however, one will succeed only in limiting the severity of neurosis, not in avoiding it altogether'' (Nunberg and Federn, 1962, pp. 273-274).

In 1909, at another meeting of the Vienna Psychoanalytic Society, Freud went on to recommend that sexual enlightenment should contradict the common if not universal childhood theory that sexual activity is sadistic in nature. "Enlightenment should above all make it clear to them that this is a matter of acts of tenderness that . . . their parents love each other very much" (Nunberg and Federn, 1967, p. 230). He added, "As to the process of coition the older children should find out about it in school in their science lessons" (pp. 230-231).

Sexual enlightenment became an important practical issue in Freud's supervision of the treatment of little Hans (Freud, 1909a), the first child to be analyzed. This five-year-old's neurotic symptoms rested heavily on misinformation concerning basic sexual matters: the difference between boys and girls, conception, pregnancy, and birth. Before he was three, Hans's curiosity was rewarded by his mother with the disclosure that she too had a penis—or *wiwimacher,* as he called it. He also faced many perplexing events: his mother's pregnancy—the enlargement of her abdomen—the perceptions of her labor and delivery—cries of pain, the appearance of the doctor, a blood-filled basin, and a new sister. These external events and the confusing sensations he was aware of in his own *wiwimacher* strained his capacity to organize the data. His parents' stories of the stork evaded the issue he was attempting to understand and led to further confusion. Symptoms arose in the compromise between the various internal and external forces; these expressed his antagonism toward his father, whom he saw as keeping him ignorant, and the fantasies he formulated to explain the facts of life. In contemporary terms, Hans's neurosis would require far more extensive understanding, but it cannot be denied that, as Freud insisted, this little boy's sexual education played an important role in his illness.

Historically, it was a short step from the insights of psychoanalysis to a desire to implement such awareness in childrearing practices and educational processes for the general population. If misunderstanding and guilt about sexuality caused neurosis, preventive psychiatry, with proper education, would be easy. This idea unleashed upon the public a multitude of sex-education programs, well intended but all too often inadequately grounded in a thorough understanding of the problems involved. It was the lot of psychoanalysts who initiated the sexual revolution, brandishing the sword against sexual repression, that they now had to expound the need for caution in sex education (Ekstein, 1970; Josselyn, 1970; Winnicott, 1957; Ralske et al., 1971). A desire for simplification, an availability of a specific curriculum could easily miss the complexity involved in the mode of presentation, proper timing, and the nature of the material. The question has never been whether sex education was valuable, but rather what its value, limitations, and dangers were. To isolate the cognitive aspects of the subject from its social and psychological meanings, to see it in stagnant terms outside of the framework of developmental psychology, to be closed to the feelings aroused in teachers dealing with this material—all this would lead to a lifeless exposition of facts or a disruptive stimulation, neither of which would be salutary for the recipients of the information.

It has been repeatedly stated that the primary responsibility for sex education rests in the family, but we would be naïve to think that this responsibility is recognized with any degree of universality, or that it meets with unqualified success. As with religious matters, the family interactions set the tone, provide the ground in which the material furnished elsewhere will grow. Uncomfortable self-conscious discussions between parent and child, source material for many a situation comedy, are of no avail; adult analysands make it abundantly clear that the child intuitively understands his or her parents' true attitude toward sex. The parent who is conflicted, confused, suffering symptomatically will convey his or her difficulties and will have problems responding to the child's questions and, even more significantly, to the expression of the child's preoccupations that come out in derivative form. The appearance of a bedtime problem in a youngster struggling with masturbation conflicts could evoke many responses in a parent. How the parent responds could be of crucial importance in the direction the conflict takes. The question of masturbation, the associated aggressive components, would probably never come up. The child's thoughts and questions, when shared with his parents, often evoke numerous unconscious associations in the parents as they try to respond. The parent's ability to support the struggling ego, to help the child tolerate the impulses, diminish the guilt to optimal levels, find acceptable outlets, and overcome the regressive nature of the symptom will be largely determined by the parent's own success in maturing. Here is a situation where formal sex education as such is meaningless, and knowledge of a child's development, of the unfolding of sexual impulses and of their manifestations would assist the parent. Ideally, this knowledge would be preconscious, and the parent's response cued to the child's needs.

There are unquestionably times when specific information is essential and the parent should give it. Preparation for the menarche is one of these, and it is a commonplace that a girl's lifetime attitude toward menstruation is often given form through her mother's intervention. Similarly, an understanding of genital sensations, erections, nocturnal emissions is a natural arena for the father to engage his son. The dominant principle rests in timing the information to the appropriate stage of the child's growth.

Analysts are often asked about the contemporary openness in sexual matters. Here again, the caution urged by analysts has been seen as running counter to the freedom sometimes urged in present society. The widespread hope that releasing sexual inhibitions would allow a guilt-free attitude to develop has not materialized, nor would that be an adaptive development. The presence of conscious or unconscious guilt is an indication of the existence of a superego. The child who is allowed too much freedom will develop a weak superego that fails to regulate behavior in the sexual arena and in nonsexual areas. (On the other hand, an excessively punitive superego can cause difficulties.) Overwhelmed by his urges, he will have difficulty relinquishing his attachments to his parents and will find his ego weakened by the traumatic effects of overstimulation. The degree of exposure to sexual information should be such that the child can master it without being overwhelmed by it.

These principles apply to parental nudity. Some parents have thought that if the child is allowed to see them naked in a natural setting, he will become free of guilt and, hence, well adjusted. This conclusion appeared to follow from the theoretical premise that neurosis was due to guilt or repression, an oversimplification of the facts. Children whose parents undress freely before them, rather than developing without neurosis, have been found to suffer from marked anxiety. These children are frightened by what they see. Pathological defense mechanisms often have to be instituted to control the fear. Sometimes the children are upset by the sexual excitement that develops. Or comparison of their own genitals with their parents' leads to envy and anxiety. Of course, occasional exposure may occur in a natural and relaxed setting without serious consequences; accidental and occasional exposure is quite different from planned and repeated exposure.

The parents of a ten-year-old-girl came to an analyst for consultation because their daughter was terrified while riding in their automobile. She was afraid that she would jump out of the car. During the consultation, the parents mentioned that the grownups walked around the house naked in order to maintain a natural atmosphere. Although the child had not appeared frightened by this exposure, she in fact, was. When her parents decided to put a halt to the nudity, the child noticed the change in their behavior with relief. "I always wanted to tell you not to do that," she said. Within a few weeks, her car phobia disappeared.

It is from peers that the child obtains most of his or her sex information or misinformation. This is the most unstructured, unsupervised, and prevalent method of sexual education. Set in the framework of a reasonably well-adjusted family capable of correcting blatant distortions when they appear, this route remains of central importance. Hardly more structured is the information derived from films, television, and books, especially those not created for educational purposes. For the people who produce these are not interested in the child's ability to deal with what they contain. There is little question that the impact of visual material vastly exceeds that which is conveyed in writing, and therefore the stimulation experienced from the screen will be greater. Explicit depiction of sexual activity will serve to stimulate and confuse the child who is striving to make sense out of a mass of inner sensations and external events. The child facing overwhelming stimuli will, to his detriment, often resort to denial in order to master or avoid the trauma. A puritanical denial of sexuality, of course, serves the opposite purpose and strengthens guilt-provoking mechanisms.

Most of the responsibility for formal sex education in our society has in the last two decades fallen to the schools, and, with admirable professional concern, educators have worked hard to deal with their charge. Theirs is, however, a most difficult task. They must find general principles, but they must tailor the teaching to different age groups with markedly different developmental needs and capacities. They must convey information that is factual and, simultaneously, deeply charged with emotional intensity, and do it in such a way as to avoid overstimulation. They must be engaging, forthright, and personally assured and secure so as to convey a sense of stability to their students. Teachers often have to overcome personal inhibitions in order to acquire the necessary knowledge and to transmit it to the pupils in a satisfactory manner. Most taxing, they know they are subjected to considerable criticism because of the emotions generated by the subject, and they also know that they can hope only for a limited success where too much is expected of them. Like the Greek runners, they can give all they have and yet be destroyed at the completion of the mission.

There are important values to properly conducted sex education. Ego functions involved in intellectual work have a crucial organizing ability. In the face of confusing, at times even frightening, stimuli received from within and without, the ability to put these stimuli in an understandable framework has a most stabilizing effect. A cognitive exercise reduces the chaos inherent in the fear of being overwhelmed and allows for a focus that permits mastery of emotions and bodily sensations. It reduces the strangeness that might be experienced as isolating and makes clear to the child what is universal, and that he or she is like others. The secrecy attendant upon sexuality and its associated fantasies is diminished, and sexuality is made more ordinary and less threatening. Properly conveyed, sex education also can help to reduce the severity of superego restrictions. Because the sexual sensations are allied to a rich fantasy life—fantasies derivative of conflictual wishes—the psychic reaction of superego restriction leads to intense guilt and struggles to maintain control over the threatening impulses. To learn about sex, focusing on normative processes, identifying physiological and psychological phenomena, naming, identifying—in essence, bringing the intellect to work—mitigates the guilt otherwise inherent in the situation.

We cannot, however, complacently assume that learning about sex in a classroom or in an ''intellectual'' atmosphere is without its dangers. The discussion can become erotized and serve to further stimulate and overwhelm the child, thereby creating a negative effect. In addition, the superego struggles can be so intense that they break through the defense offered by the intellectual activity. Furthermore, dissolution of the superego or production of superego lacunae can eventuate from overzealous attempts to reduce guilt. It is well known that parents may encourage their child to carry out maladaptive acts that violate the parents' conscious standards for behavior (Johnson, 1949). In so doing, they weaken aspects of their child's superego. Teachers may also engage in this process by urging their pupils to sexual activity prematurely.

As we have said, a major concern in sexual education centers on the possible stimulation the child experiences. The setting, the attitude of the teacher or parent, the child's level of psychic development, the peer interaction, and the substantive content, all contribute to the impact on the child. All children will have had previous experiences, fantasies, conflicts, even symptoms suggestive of problems in their sexual development. Depending upon the degree of disruption, the intensity of the fantasies, and the depth of commitment to personal solutions to the mysteries of sexuality, the information offered may or may not be accurately absorbed. We know the power of a fantasy to persist despite any correction from educators. A youngster struggling with unresolved problems, fighting to maintain control over pregenital or genital impulses, limited by castration fears, will easily dismiss what he is told. This is true even of normal children. A boy of four or even eight may insist that babies are born from the anus even when he is told about the vagina.

Children who have been subjected to traumatic early experiences will find little of corrective or reparative value in an intellectual presentation of sexual data and, in fact, will probably distort and select what suits their unconscious needs.

The Significance of Developmental Stages

While the body of knowledge to be imparted may be seen as a totality, recipients of nursery-school age are very different from high school adolescents. Issues facing the nursery school teacher, such as the value of formal discussion, the use of the toilet, open sexual play between children, are quite different from the pressures felt with high school juniors who want to know about contraception, abortion, and homosexuality. Analytic understanding of developmental stages and their pertinent tasks are helpful—even essential—if one is to know what to say at any particular time.

The parents communicate to the small infant their recognition of its gender, leading to the establishment of core gender identity by eighteen months (Stoller, 1968b; Money and Ehrhardt, 1972). Roiphe and Galenson (1972) have noted that children observe differences between sexes by the time they are a year and a half old and may develop castration anxiety. Small children are able to perceive bodily changes and react to them, but only in unusual circumstances do they understand formal explanations offered to them by parents or educators, although Bell (1964) has described the value of reassurances regarding testicular movements in small boys who believe that the elevation of testicles in the scrotal sac signifies their loss. For the most part, the child's cognitive capacity is such that verbal explanations are inadequate before the age of three.

During the oedipal period, from approximately three to six years of age, there is an increase of drive activity and genital awareness, one of the effects of which is to spur imagination and curiosity (J. Glenn, 1978). Children of this age ask questions, but easily form illogical conclusions, which can be frightening to them. Generally, they imagine that sexual interests can lead to castration. For children of this age, formal group approaches are virtually worthless. The sense of group is barely formed, the individuality of their preoccupations is most dominant, and even though issues are, at base, similar, the readiness to take in information varies. In terms of specific data, it is best that the child be addressed in private, in terms of his or her own questions. Answers should be simple and direct, geared to the specific issue under consideration. The educator is limited in what he can convey, but can reassure the child and refrain from reinforcing distorted ideas. At this stage, the variation in preparedness and concern between children of like age can be very marked so that maintaining privacy in an inconspicuous way is important. Whereas the need and right to privacy are important, there is some concern from teachers and parents that children will experience this as inhibiting or guilt-provoking. Similarly, in tune with the recent social movement to reduce artificial differentiation of male and female, a blurring of necessary gender identity processes can develop. It would be throwing the baby out with the bath water to disregard the need to encourage the sense of maleness and femaleness in small children.

Many—perhaps most—nursery schools provide a single toilet for both boys and girls, based on the idea that exposure to sexual differences between children has a positive value. We know, however, that children's fantasies of castration are illogically confirmed and perceived as actuality when they see that some children have penises and testicles and others do not. Repeated exposure frequently frightens the child or results in excessive use of mechanisms of defense to avoid anxiety. Paradoxically, the defenses may include denial of reality rather than lead to a realistic understanding, as some would hope. Many children insist all the more vigorously that girls have penises after seeing that they do not. We believe, therefore, that the free sharing of toilets in nursery school should be avoided. The occasional adventitious exposures that are inevitable in such a setting provide sufficient experiences on which to develop a realistic understanding of sexual differences between children without the repeated exposure inherent in a shared toilet. In some nursery schools where facilities are limited to a single toilet, the teachers attempt to make sure that only children of the same sex use the facilities at any one time, a procedure that often results merely in excessive and ineffective policing.

The teacher in present-day society may feel guilty about restricting children. One teacher, for instance, felt that her preventing a boy from attempting mock intercourse in the nursery was wrong. She tended to overlook the traumatic effect on the little girl he was molesting and on the children observing them. She thought that prohibiting this activity would lead to inhibitions in the children. Her good judgment nevertheless prevailed, and she stopped the activity. Such prohibitive intervention is sensible in that it enables the child to institute adaptive restrictions in his behavior. The child who is unable to inhibit his behavior will undergo difficulties in future development.

At about four or five, the child's superego becomes more organized. Prior to that, superego precursors enabled the child to maintain a degree of impulse restraint. Now, with the ending of the oedipal period, this aspect of mental activity takes a more important role and leads into the latency period of development.

Although some educators are skeptical about the existence of the latency period (Calderone, 1970), the analytic observer can have no doubt about its presence from the age of five or six to the appearance of adolescence (Sarnoff, 1975). During this phase the child's interests turn from the more or less direct sexual preoccupation of the oedipal period to sublimated activities. Freud (1905) observed that the latency period comprises two alternating aspects. The "ideal" latency child enjoys learning, develops hobbies, and engages in organized activities. He makes good use of his increased cognitive capacities. During "interruptions" of latency, instinctual drives break through and afford the child more primitive pleasures. Optimally, there is a proper balance between these two states; the child is neither so civilized that he or she has no instinctual drive satisfaction nor so untamed that he or she cannot be socialized. In pathological circumstances, either of these two extremes will dominate the clinical picture. Sometimes, latency fails to appear, due to organic disturbances, overstimulation, poor superego formation, or other causes.

In our society, the latency period is used for educative functions. The child attends school and masters the basic skills. The school can best serve the latency child by providing models for identification and means for gaining knowledge, but the educational process can be disrupted by inept presentation of charged sexual material at the very time that the child is trying to exert control over his impulses. Presentation of material relating to family life and sexual roles may introduce the child to questions of gender identity of interest to him, without disruptive stimulation. Once again, the teacher must be prepared for the individual who presents a particular question and need—the tact and sensitivity shown in responding to this child can be significant. Some school systems insist that teachers provide formal sex education in latency and, if done with caution, this may succeed in helping the child clarify his confused ideas about sexuality. However, the teacher must be prepared for signs of anxiety and regression in the pupils. For instance, in one such program during which the teacher showed the class a picture of a foetus in the womb, some children became distressed when they learned that the umbilical cord was cut after birth. One child raised questions about nevi on his body, probably as a result of displaced castration anxiety. (The teacher wisely reassured the child about his bodily intactness.)

Preadolescence (Blos, 1962) begins around ten when the child starts to react psychologically to the increase in sexual hormones and subsequent prepubertal bodily changes. We may arbitrarily set the end of preadolescence and the beginning of adolescence proper at the time of the boy's first ejaculation or the girl's menarche. During preadolescence the child is confused by strange new bodily feelings and impulses. He may find himself reacting to increased attraction to his parents by regressive behavior. Many children of this age become sloppy, disorganized, restless, and rebellious. Their school work may falter as concentration becomes difficult. Others, however, are able to make use of increased cognitive development and achieve an academic spurt.

At this time, the intellectual processes, the value of thinking as an organizing force, is quite important, and explanations can be very helpful. Information pertinent to physiological phenomena and recognition of psychological changes should be made available, if possible, in a group setting. Preadolescent youngsters, experiencing the pressure of developmental thrusts, are also subjected to intense regressive pulls as a means of coping with their difficult feelings. The educator's capacity to capitalize on the developed aptitude for thinking must take into account this regressive pull, and stress must be placed on making the new experiences understandable. This leads to a sense of inner control, mitigates against the use of a demanding overrestrictive superego to control actions, and encourages developing higher level ego functions. While emphasis is on the more neutral physiological information, some attention should be given to the psychological as well.

Properly presented material can aid in preparing youngsters for oncoming puberty. Girls can be encouraged to anticipate menstruation, and boys can gain knowledge of their anticipated sexual function. The educator must be prepared for students to become frightened when they hear that genital bleeding occurs. This in particular reawakens castration anxiety in vulnerable youngsters. Some boys, not being fully aware of the variation in onset of ejaculatory activity, see themselves as strange if they are "late." The facts should be presented in a reassuring way.

Adolescence, as we have indicated, has its onset with psychological reactions to the physiological changes of puberty which start with menarche or the first ejaculation. As adolescence fully establishes itself, the youngster, still struggling deeply with rapid changes and shifts, by now usually more emotional than physical, will be in a better position to deal with more complex sexual information and particularly the interpersonal aspects of the subject. Simultaneously there is a maturing of social awareness and an intense and idealistic concern with frankness and honesty. Attempts to elude questions and uncomfortable subjects or to give watered-down answers will be seen as hypocritical. Paradoxically, brutal frankness can also be traumatic. The alternative is not to try to be one of the group and lose sight of the essential importance of being a forthright *adult* offering honest information.

Optimally, the teacher becomes a mentor who is differentiated from the parents, from whom the youngster is trying to break away. The teacher-student relation is heavily charged with particular problems of the age group; the child's wish to identify with the teacher as a step toward establishing his or her own identity may be interfered with if sexual information is presented too provocatively. The students, feeling urged to enact their sexual impulses, may either do so or rebel against the teacher and education as they do against their parents. This requires great caution from the teacher in presenting facts without overstimulating his audience.

One of the problems that students at this age face is uncertainty about sexual identity. During adolescence the increase in drives leads teenagers to turn away defensively from heterosexual objects. They often find themselves preoccupied with conscious and unconscious homosexual as well as heterosexual fantasies. Some engage briefly in homosexual experiences at this time and then resume heterosexual development.

The manner of presentation of sexual information in the classroom may have a powerful influence. Frightening presentations of hetero-sexuality can push a child defensively toward homosexuality. Further, suggesting that homosexuality is a satisfactory means of resolving the conflicts of adolescence may discourage heterosexuality. Bald state-ments indicating that anyone who experiences homosexual urges is "a homosexual" may erroneously give the conflicted adolescent the idea that he is predestined to that object choice.

We would hope that an analytic appreciation of the developmental stages of childhood, a recognition of complexities of dealing with highly emotional material, and an awareness of potential values and dangers will be of assistance to those charged with the difficult task of sexual enlightenment—in the school and out.

CHAPTER 14

Feminism and the
New Psychology of Women

VIRGINIA L. CLOWER

The current pressure from women's groups for a reconsideration and revision of ideas about the nature of women and their place in society is not a new force, but the latest manifestation of a need which has never been satisfactorily met in the known history of mankind.

Anthropologists believe that in the dawn of history when homo sapiens was still nomadic, the relationship between male and female was random, probably determined by male sexual need. The males, who were physically larger, stronger, and—some would say— instinctively more aggressive, roamed about foraging and killing for food. The females, continually burdened with pregnancy and the nursing and care of helpless small children, moved about less freely and performed whatever could be done while remaining more or less sedentary and watching over offspring. To them fell the chore of preparing food and carrying about the infants and whatever indispensable belongings might be accumulated—animal skins for clothing and primitive tools, most likely, at first. The males were thus left unencumbered to hunt and to fight off marauders. Somewhat later, when animals were domesticated, the herds were moved in search of water and pasture. The males moved more swiftly with the animals, shepherding them to grass and water sources, protecting them from beasts of prey. The females undertook the feeding of the group members, and the spinning and crude weaving which supplied fabrics for clothing and primitive shelter.

It seems that, in the beginning, biology was destiny and the necessary division of labor was the basis for the places of male and female in the earliest social structure. In any event, there cannot have been a great deal of time or energy for philosophizing about it. Life was a constant fight for survival, many of the infants died very early, and no one lived long.

With the development of agriculture, the nomadic way of life was abandoned and men stayed in one place to stake out land for themselves, to raise crops, and to cluster in villages built to take advantage of favorable geography—the availability of permanent springs or the protection of rocks or hills. Apparently by that time, which coincides roughly with the Old Testament (about 3000 B.C.), the status of women was institutionalized. When men claimed land and domestic animals, they also claimed women as their exclusive property. It has been suggested that women may have been one of the earliest examples of private property (Komisar, 1971, p. 69). This state of affairs obtained for centuries. Marriage was a business deal in which fathers sold daughters, with other valuable goods thrown in. Adultery was punished severely because it was trespass on someone's territory. Brownmiller (1975) has suggested that women depended on this male regard for property to enlist the protection of one male against unlimited rape by all others.

Pagan religions originally worshipped women, who had the mysterious capacity to give birth. Females were equated with the fertility of nature on whose productiveness everyone's survival depended. Some anthropologists and sociologists (e.g., Hayes, 1965) have suggested that the myth of Adam as progenitor of mankind was a primitive maneuver to restore the confidence of males who did not understand their own role in procreation and feared the powerful childbearing female who could bring forth new life. If this be true, male chauvinism goes far back in human history and is deep-rooted. We need not wonder that fundamental attitudes toward women have changed so slowly when we consider how painfully slowly human beings learn and change in any way. Once any institution is internalized and is handed down from one generation to the next by identification, its origins are lost to memory and the well-understood human investment in keeping the status quo takes over. The original hypothesis is reified and supported by references to history, emphasis on aspects of reality—which may or may not be relevant—and various rationalizations. Alterations in real circumstances, new knowledge, and the opportunity to reassess a hypothesis in the light of better information seem remarkably ineffective in changing well-defended convictions. And so it has been in the case of women. It appears that, once they were identified as uniquely equipped for childbearing, they were defined by men, and by themselves, as fit only for this and whatever menial tasks might be delegated them as sufficiently undemanding or unworthy of the more imaginative, venturesome male of the species. In retrospect, it is truly astonishing that the sincere conviction of the inherent inferiority of women because they are female should have prevailed for 5,000 years. In saying this I am quite aware that the fact it has been held so long has often been used to support the contention it must be true!

A definitive analysis of the development and history of misogyny needs to be written, but is beyond the scope of this paper. However, even a cursory review is striking. Komisar (1971, pp. 59-67) notes some highlights. The Greek myth of Pandora's box makes women responsible for all misery and hardships in the world. Plato wondered whether women could be considered reasonable beings or if they ought to be categorized with animals. Aristotle suggested females might be produced because of a mishap during pregnancy. The men who wrote the Old Testament condemned Eve and in the Book of Genesis pronounced ''. . . in sorrow shalt thou bring forth children and thy desire shall be to thou husband, and he shall rule over thee.'' Also in Genesis someone exclaimed, ''What else is woman but a foe to friendship, an unescapable punishment, a necessary evil, a natural temptation, a desirable calamity, a domestic danger, a delectable detriment, an evil of nature, painted with fair colors!'' The Muslim teacher Muhammad said, ''When Eve was created, Satan rejoiced.'' The Persian prophet Zoroaster said that sex made women diabolical. St. Jerome thought, ''Woman is the true Satan, the foe of peace, the subject of dissension.'' The Hindu Code of Manu declared, ''In childhood, a woman must be subject to her father; in youth to her husband; when her husband is dead, to her sons. A woman must never be free of subjugation.''

Although in the New Testament Christ said nothing specifically about woman and her place, the accounts of his dealings with women at least reflect compassion. He was forgiving of Mary Magdalene, accepted the wish of Mary of Bethany to talk with him rather than wait on him, and, while dying, commended his mother to the care of the disciple John. Christ's followers were not so kind. St. Paul said, "Let the women learn in silence with all subjection" and "Wives, submit yourselves to your husbands." St. Augustine described woman as a temple built over a sewer and believed virginity better than marriage. St. Jerome believed marriage should be only for producing children, not pleasure.

Although in the early Christian church women took an active role, by the Middle Ages, there were debates about whether women had souls. In the 1480's the book *Malleus Maleficarum* (Kramer and Sprenger, 1486) used religious doctrine for a brutal attack on women. They were said to be liars, to have inferior intelligence, and to be sexually lustful. Furthermore, they were the source of witchcraft, which is rooted in carnal lust. Martin Luther believed it was natural for women to be secondary to men. John Calvin thought them useful only to bear children and declaimed that political equality for women would be a deviation from the "original and proper order of nature," although he did make an exception of Elizabeth I, who was "raised by Divine Authority."

And so it has gone. Neither the enlightenment of the eighteenth century, the scientific discoveries of the nineteenth century, nor the democratic philosophy of the twentieth have completely eradicated belief in the basic inferiority of women. Through all of this time has run the thread of fascination and fear of female sexuality. No doubt this timeless anxiety is an enduring element in misogyny, which has been a major force in the debased view of women. Another factor has been the collusion of women in their own subjugation. I believe this is a question deserving of careful investigation and clear understanding. Perhaps only now, as the shifting sociological climate of our time gives a different context to women's liberation, are we in a position to learn why the great mass of women have for centuries accepted and even promoted the various theories about their natural inferiority in intelligence, moral character, physical stamina, and emotional stability.

Of course, there have always been some dissenting voices from men as well as women, and the position of women in society has varied in the course of history. The Greek city-states at different times allowed women to inherit property equally; some women were highly regarded for their intellectual and social skills; and the authority of the mother in the household was respected in certain matters—although the father had the last word. Roman women had rights to their own property and eventually became influential in politics, in religious movements, and in freedom to pursue higher education. In medieval Europe, however, women lost most of their property rights, and the tradition that they had no identity except through men was codified by jurists and became part of English common law, later formalized by Blackstone, who said that the very being or legal existence of the woman is suspended during the marriage. Joan of Arc has been portrayed as divinely inspired, bewitched, and psychotic; she was burned at the stake not because she lost a war but because she was impudent—a presumptuous girl. When Elizabeth I reigned (1558-1603) English women enjoyed greater respect and freedom. The Queen herself, always fending off questions about the fitness of a woman to reign, and constant pressure to marry and produce an heir, said, "I know I have the body of a weak feeble woman but I have the heart and stomach of a King, and a King of England, too . . ." (Jenkins, 1958, p. 285). But in the next century a fresh wave of brutality toward women swept Europe and encompassed the colonies in America when the Salem witch trials dealt with women who did not conform.

Early Feminists

The beginning of organized feminist protest against male domination was evident as early as the seventeenth century. With the advent of the printing press, tracts and letters could be duplicated and passed around, enabling women to learn that others might hold views similar to their own. However, it was not until the atmosphere of enlightened intellectual inquiry and humanism of the eighteenth century that the early movement for women's liberation gained momentum. This took form in England and in the United States. With few exceptions, intelligent and spirited women on the continent of Europe were wont to

take refuge in—or be banished to—nunneries as an alternative to bon-
dage in unacceptable marriages. Some achieved distinction in royal
courts or, later, in sophisticated intellectual and artistic salons, but
they were regarded as unusual, not representative in any way of the
potential for intellectual achievement of women as a group. These few
exceptions were women of the nobility or upper classes, with money
of their own or wealthy patrons. An account of the limited expectations
and alternatives of a bourgeois French girl growing up as late as the
early twentieth century is de Beauvoir's autobiographical *The Second
Sex* (1953). Peasant and working-class women had no choice. The
traditions of society, heavily reinforced by the patriarchal attitudes of
both the Christian church and Orthodox Judaism, offered "Kinder,
Kirche, Kuche" as the only areas for female activity. In Moslem
countries and in Africa, women were chattel, bought and sold with
other slaves.

   I have not as yet discovered any thorough study of the reasons
why women's liberation was finally consolidated as a movement in
the two English-speaking nations. Revolution was in the air; intellectual freedom was prized. English women published work that was
taken seriously: Jane Austen, the Brontë sisters, Mary Ann Evans
(George Eliot), and, in France, Amantine Lucile Aurore Dupin, Bar-
onne Dudevant, as George Sand, wrote great novels. Perhaps because
the first demands of such women were relatively modest—they started
as repudiation of the belief in women's intellectual inferiority and
insistence on rights to equal education—they were not absolutely rejected, although they were stubbornly contested. Perhaps the American women took seriously the promise that all men are created equal
and interpreted it to include female members of the human race. For
whatever concatenation of reasons, English and American women began to speak up. In 1792 Mary Wollstonecraft published *A Vindication
of the Rights of Women*. This was not the first such challenge to
traditional attitudes toward women's intelligence and their place in
society, but it still stands as one of the most thoughtful and coherent.

   In the United States, Abigail Adams wrote to her husband, John,
then engaged in drafting the Declaration of Independence and the
Constitution for the new nation, "In the new code of laws which I
suppose it will be necessary for you to make, I desire you would
remember the ladies and be more generous and favorable to them than

your ancestors. Do not put such unlimited power into the hands of the husband. Remember, all men would be tyrants if they could." And she added, "If particular care and attention is not paid to the ladies, we are determined to foment a rebellion and will not hold ourselves bound by any laws in which we have no voice or representation." John made a reply which feminists denounce as sexist and beside the point. He asserted that women really run the world by running their husbands, and he said, "In practice, you know we have only the name of masters and rather than give this up, which would completely subject us to the despotism of the petticoat, I hope General Washington and all our brave heroes would fight" (Rossi, 1974, pp. 10-11).

By the middle of the nineteenth century feminism, that is, the attempt of women to redefine their role in society, gained the dimension of a concerted movement. In the United States the feminist movement was strengthened by organizations devoted to abolition of slavery. Many women took part in antislavery work, but when the Anti-Slavery Society was formed in Philadelphia in 1833, women attended meetings only to discover that they were denied membership! When Sarah and Angelina Grimké traveled about in New England in 1836 speaking against slavery, they were attacked by the Council of Congregational Ministers of Massachusetts, who declaimed, "The power of a woman is her dependency flowing from the consciousness of that weakness which God has given her for her protection—when she assumes the place and tone of man as a public reformer, she yields the power which God has given her for her protection and her character becomes unnatural." Sarah Grimké replied sharply that such an attitude could "justly be placed on a par with the policy of slaveholder who says that men will be better slaves if they are not permitted to learn to read" (Rossi, 1974, p. 309).

During the nineteenth century, a number of women who later became active workers for women's rights started out in the movement for abolition of slavery. Their experiences confronted them dramatically with the prevailing attitude toward the place of women—at least of "ladies!"—in society. If they circulated petitions, wrote tracts, or attempted to speak at meetings, they were ridiculed as unwomanly. Elizabeth Cady Stanton and Lucretia Mott of the United States were denied seats at the 1840 World Anti-Slavery Convention in London, even though they represented thousands of women who had worked hard for abolition. Shortly after this episode, Susan B. Anthony encountered massive antifemale prejudice in efforts to organize women in temperance societies. During the Civil War women worked in fundraising, nursing, and distributing supplies. Men were always in charge of these affairs, however, and growing numbers of women protested their oppression by both law and custom. A series of Women's Rights conventions between 1848 and 1860 petitioned government reform of the legal rights of women. They urged that married women retain title to their own property and wages earned after marriage.

The feminist battles for the right to vote were grounded in the protest that women were treated as property. Susan B. Anthony declared, ''Women must be educated out of their unthinking acceptance of financial dependence on man into mental and economic independence.'' And she protested the fact that all laws governing women most intimately were made and administered by men only: ''. . . the statutes for marriage and divorce, for adultery, for breach of promise, seduction, rape, bigamy, abortion, infanticide—all were made by men. They alone decide who are guilty—and what shall be their punishment, with judge, jury, and advocate all men, with no woman's voice heard . . .'' (Komisar, 1971, p. 87).

The early feminists apparently were not motivated by hatred of men or their own sexuality. Angelina Grimké was an acknowledged beauty with devoted suitors; many of the women most passionately dedicated to the fight for women's rights to higher education, careers, and the vote were married and with children. A few, like Susan Anthony and Elizabeth Blackwell, never married. Elizabeth Blackwell became the first woman to graduate from medical school in the United States. One of her brothers married feminist Antoinette Brown. The other brother, Henry, finally won Lucy Stone, who had attended Oberlin College and was infuriated that, even there, girls were being prepared only for intelligent motherhood and subservient wifehood. Lucy and Henry were married by a minister who denounced the ''inequity of a system by which man and wife are one, and that one is the husband.'' Lucy Stone kept her own name and joined Henry in a pact which publicly declared their married estate but repudiated the laws of marriage which ''conferred upon the husband an injurious and unnatural superiority.'' After her death in 1893, her husband and her daughter, Alice Stone Blackwell, continued the unfinished battle for woman's suffrage. Few of these women rejected men as friends, lovers, or husbands, although they outspokenly wanted opportunities traditionally open only to men.

Not all men opposed their goals. Thomas Paine in 1775 condemned the position of women who were "constrained in their desires in the disposal of their goods, robbed of freedom and will by law, the slave of opinion . . ." (Friedan, 1963, p. 84). Friedan cites Ditzion, who documented the relationship between man's movement for greater self-realization and sexual fulfillment and the woman's rights movement. Both men and women viewed the equitable balance of power between sexes as leading to more satisfying relationships between the sexes. Robert Dale Owen predicted that the sexual revolution would end unjust monopolies and that women would not be restricted to one virtue, one passion, or one occupation. Mary Wollstonecraft was highly educated by her association with the English school of philosophy. Elizabeth Cady Stanton's father was a judge who allowed her to audit his law classes. Ernestine Rose was a rabbi's daughter who got her education from Robert Owen, then defied her religious background to marry a Gentile. She declared, "We do not fight with man himself, but only with bad principles." John Stuart Mill in 1869 wrote the still-quoted passionate denunciation of the subjugation of women. He was the companion and lover of English feminist Harriet Taylor, who later married him, and he extolled her intelligence as refutation of belief in female inferiority.

Early feminism ended as a movement in America with the winning of the right to vote, the last declared goal of these first advocates of equality for the sexes. Women continued to work as champions for various causes: for victims of exploitation and oppression among the American Negroes, against Franco's Spain and Nazi Germany. But for a time they behaved as if all women's rights had been won.

The New Feminism

In the 1960's a new feminist movement emerged in America. It was a time when one protest movement after another was appearing: civil rights, peace, and antipoverty had many advocates. In 1963 Betty Friedan published her book *The Feminine Mystique*, deploring the

misery of educated women who became suburban housewives, aban-
doning careers and personal development to care for husbands and
children. It attracted world-wide attention and provided the movement
with many battle cries. The first response of the press and other mass
media was scornful. The early voices of New Feminism were often
bitter and shrill, pouring forth tremendous anger at consignment of
women to outmoded stereotyped roles and discrimination on the basis
of sex. Some of the most vehement assertions that women have always
been oppressed and exploited by men came from radicals, dubbed
man-haters who rejected marriage and motherhood and wanted to take
over and run the world. No doubt there were such elements present;
revolutions are not fomented by stable, contented people. But it did
not take long for the movement to gain supporters from many sides.
In 1963 President Kennedy's Commission on the Status of Women
submitted its report on woman's role in private and federal employment, then, further, on her status in politics, education, law, and the
need for adequate child-care facilities. By 1967 each of the 50 states
had its own commission to study the rights and needs of women.

Continuing systematic examination gave substance to feminist protest. By 1965 almost half the adult women in this country, including
35 percent of all mothers with minor children, were in the work force.
Most of these were in relatively low-paid jobs, and there was a wide
gap in pay for men and women in the same jobs—women averaging
40 percent less.

In 1965 there were two women Senators out of a total of 100, but
only ten women in a House of Representatives of 435 members, and
in the state legislatures women held only 370 of the more than 7,800
seats. Hiring practices in industry were frankly discriminatory; women
were kept out of executive positions because it was said men would
not accept their authority, or they were too emotional, or they had
biologically determined physical and mental instability. Maternity leave
with the right to return to a job was unusual. A woman who was the
head of a household and supported a husband could not claim him a
dependent in company life and medical insurance. The proponents of
women's liberation disclosed evidence of discrimination against women
in every area of American life.

In October 1963, the National Organization of Women (NOW)
was founded with Betty Friedan as the first president. The group

adopted a statement of purpose committing itself to working for "true equality for all women in America and toward a fully equal partnership of the sexes as part of the world-wide revolution of human rights now taking place within and beyond our national borders." The statement declared, "We do not accept the traditional assumption that a woman has to choose between marriage and motherhood on the one hand and serious participation in industry or the professions on the other." The new feminism was thus defined as belief in individual right to develop personally as fully as possible. It went beyond the early feminist movements in attempting to transcend achievement of equal opportunity or elimination of differences between the sexes.

There are two major types of feminist groups active currently. Women's Liberation is made up of widespread groups scattered over the country. Their primary function has been to carry on discussion in small groups, so-called consciousness-raising. Through the group process of sharing experiences and feelings, the members explore the traditional feminine role and evaluate other styles of life. In some cases they have moved from discussion to social action.

Like Women's Liberation, Women's Rights groups have taken the issue of women's role-definition as central. These are, however, larger, more structured, and more active groups, including several organized at the national level with subdivisions into local chapters. They have worked actively for changes in women's status by applying legal, social, and economic pressures upon major business and political institutions.

In addition, there are many women's interest groups within professional societies, trade unions, student populations, and religious organizations. The Women's liberation movement was considered revolutionary with its emphasis on "change now." It was responsible for the formulation of feminist ideology and the earliest public awareness of the feminist position. The Women's Rights groups, in contrast, were originally more conservative, dedicated to action through established channels. Since 1970, the commonly heard characterization of Women's Rights groups as reformist and Women's Liberation groups as revolutionary does not hold. Both have attracted members who reflect a wide range of ideological positions and the contrast between the two segments of the movement has become blurred (Carden, 1974).

Most of what is publicized about the new feminism concerns the various efforts to bring about social change. All forms of economic, work, and educational discrimination are under attack through legal, legislative, and social channels. Feminists have worked for passage of the Equal Rights Amendment to the Constitution, demonstrated against and sued companies that pay women less than men for the same work, or hire only men for some jobs. They have insisted that, inside and outside marriage, women should not be treated as sex objects but recognized as complete human beings for whom sex is only one part of the life experience. They have supported repeal and reform of abortion laws and distribution of information and devices for birth control. They have been consistently and increasingly vocal on the crucial question of child care, advocating and establishing a variety of facilities to assist mothers who cannot or do not wish to devote all their time to rearing children. Many feminists have supported the choices of women who reject heterosexual relationships for lesbian relationships. They have written many books and have urged courses in women's studies for schools and colleges.

Sex-Role Stereotyping of Women

Participants in the contemporary feminist movements and the nineteenth-century movement have in common their emphasis on equality for women. But there is a significant difference in ideology. Earlier feminists by and large did not argue the distinction between male and female nature. They accepted the idea of a uniquely feminine biology, which included natural instincts for homemaking and child care. Their contention was that sexual difference did not justify the traditional derogation and subjugation of women by society. Their battle was for the human right to be freed from the restrictions on property ownership, access to higher education, and the vote. While some early feminists elected to remain unmarried and childless to pursue careers, the majority were moved by the conviction that their special feminine attributes were needed, not only in the home, but by all of society. They proposed to work as women to better the lot of humanity. In retrospect it seems that these limited goals of the early feminist movement were attained, at least in principle: women secured the right to vote; college education for girls became acceptable, even expected of bright middle- and upper-class girls; some professional schooling was opened, on a limited scale, to women; in some states the laws regarding property ownership were equalized. Also in retrospect, however, it is clear that the fundamental attitudes of most men—and women—toward the differences between the sexes did not change, nor did sex-role stereotyping change. Women who were acknowledged as intelligent and who achieved good educations and general competence became more usual and acceptable. But those who were not satisfied to invest their skills in running households and rearing children were considered atypical. Very competent women who were successful in fields considered male territory—government, law, the higher echelons of business, most specialties in medicine—were likely to be categorized as "masculine" because they had the energy, confidence, self-discipline, and assertiveness needed to perform well in these callings. Many jobs and professions were considered out of the question even for capable women. Engineering, top-level executive positions, the judiciary, running certain machinery, and surgery are examples of work thought out of the sphere of female competence, presumably on the basis of a lack of certain qualities found inherently in human males and not in human females. On the other hand, work related to nurturing, requiring tolerance and passivity rather than assertiveness, was considered "natural" for women and difficult or impossible for men. The implicit basis for such role differentiation was the continuing belief in biologically grounded characteristic sex differences.

Today's feminists assert that biology plays only a minor part in the observed differences between male and female. They believe the traditional inequitable system for dealing with men and women in our society was derived from the uncontested assumption that biological differences are major, unchangeable, and that they have far-reaching consequences in the psychology of women. Differing from their nineteenth-century predecessors, modern feminists believe that cultural values and sex-role expectations rather than biology determine women's views of themselves and their place in society. They point out that, consciously or unconsciously, every social institution contributes to stereotyping of men and women. Men are expected to be aggressive, outgoing, influencing the environment, competing with each other, doing important things, making money, winning recognition. Women are expected to be absorbed in making a home, bearing children, nurturing a family, providing a backup for the more active male. The successful woman is expected to be long-suffering, selfless, in the service of her husband and her children as her first priority, although she may pursue an intellectual or creative enterprise of her own as long as it does not compromise her primary responsibility. She is not expected to be bold, venturesome, intellectually innovative, creative in abstract ways, competitive, authoritative, or independent; these are attributes valued in men. Above all, women are not expected to *prefer* a way of life which is an alternative to the traditional pick-a-mate, build-a-nest, raise-a-brood pattern considered "natural" for females since time immemorial. The new feminists say that this is not substantially different from the primitive sex-role casting of early human history. They question the validity of perpetuating this pattern in the face of entirely different realities in life today.

Crucial differences in the way people in our society live today have come about with comparative rapidity. Before the industrial revolution of the nineteenth century the great majority of men were workers on the land, and women shared this work, as men shared certain tasks in building and maintaining homes and rearing children. With the coming of machine production the close association between home and labor was lost for both sexes. Progressive industrialization took much of the traditional work of housewives away; clothing, food, household implements, medicines, and laundry could be provided outside the home entirely or greatly expedited by labor-saving devices. At the same time, need for cheap labor made it possible for many women (and children) to go to work in factories. Machine production widened enormously the range to which women could work, once physical strength was no longer a barrier. As business enterprises grew, new opportunities for women opened up in offices: telephone operators, typists, and clerical workers joined mill workers, seamstresses, and teachers in the work force. World War I produced another expansion of women's employment, and more social equality. Working women instigated changes in dress and hairstyle. Corsets, trailing skirts, and elaborately dressed masses of hair gave way to light underwear, short skirts, and bobbed hair. The twenties brought a publicly acknowledged interest in sex and the discoveries of Freud, who was associated with increased sexual freedom for women and erosion of the Victorian double standard. More economic opportunity and a new conception of marriage as between equals was reflected in the beginning of a sharp increase in the divorce rate, a continuing trend. World War II facilitated the further demolition of barriers to sexual equality. Women served in the armed forces in every capacity short of actual combat; they stepped into jobs vacated by men off to war, and subsequently they gained admission to numbers of professional schools, business jobs, and clubs hitherto considered masculine sanctuaries. The mythical "feminine" woman who could not function on equal terms in a masculine world was fast disappearing in the United States by 1950. Nevertheless, there was a curious lull in feminist activity for more than another decade. One sociologist said:

> There is no overt antifeminism in our society in 1964, not because sex equality has been achieved, but because there is practically no feminist spark left among American women. When I ask the brightest of my women college students about their future study and work plans, they either have none because they are getting married in a few months, or they show clearly that they have lowered their aspirations from professional and research fields that excited them as freshmen, to concentrate as juniors on more practical fields far below their abilities. Young women seem increasingly uncommitted to anything beyond early marriage, motherhood, and a suburban house. There are few Noras in contemporary American society, because women have deluded themselves that the doll's house is large enough to find complete personal fulfillment within it [Rossi, 1964, p. 610].

Other sociologists noted that, after the achievement of suffrage in 1920 and the increasing participation of married women in the work force, there was no organized feminist movement, no feminist ideology, and many women did not even exercise the rights they had—such as the right to vote (Degler, 1964).

At about the same time social scientists were making these observations, popular literature was extolling the unique feminine opportunity—and, implicitly, obligation—for fulfillment in full-time motherhood. One widely read and influential book cast doubt on the feminist goals of sexual equality in professions and politics. The authors argued that such aspirations destroyed homes and set women adrift. They considered ambitious feminists sufferers from penis envy and advised women to interest themselves in motherhood and the family (Lundberg and Farnham, 1947).

So-respected an authority on childrearing as Dr. Benjamin Spock encouraged mothers to believe their children required continuous maternal presence and supervision (1963). Women who felt irritable and nervous on this regime were advised to have counseling. Maternal deprivation was held responsible for many serious developmental difficulties and mental illnesses in children, and deprivation was often equated simply with absence. Larger families were stylish in the affluent middle class after World War II, and the percentage of women graduating from college, doing postgraduate work, and entering professions actually declined.

By the early 1960's a number of other forces were converging, however. The first concerns of ecologists about natural resources and the impact of overpopulation were voiced; numbers of adult women in the full-time occupation of motherhood were no longer needed or even welcome, as pressure for fewer children grew. Increased longevity and the prospect of vigorous health for another lifetime after childrearing years are over, and the near impossibility for a middle-aged woman to develop new skills or update old ones, emerged as serious concerns. With effective and widely available contraception in women's hands, alternatives to accepting biology as destiny were on the scene, and women began to question what their options might be. Feminists are now demanding changes in social definitions of approved characteristics and behaviors for both sexes. Their concerns transcend sexual identity, precedents imposed by culture, and existing limitations in the economic system. These aims are highly idealistic and are directed to achieving changes in society that will permit optimal freedom for individual personal growth and fulfillment in every man and woman. Rossi (1964) offers the hypothetical case of a woman who is reared and lives out her life under the changed social conditions modern feminists propose.

> She will be reared, as her brother . . . with a combination of loving warmth, firm discipline, household responsibility, and encouragement of independence and self-reliance. She will not be pampered and in-

dulged, subtly taught to achieve her ends through coquetry and tears. . . . [and] will view domestic skills as useful tools to acquire, some of which . . . [have] their own intrinsic pleasures, but most of which are necessary [and] best . . . done as quickly and efficiently as possible. She will be able to handle minor mechanical breakdowns in the home as well as her brother can, and he will be able to tend a child, press, sew, and cook with the same easy skills and comfortable feeling his sister has. . . .

Marriage for our hypothetical woman will not mark a withdrawal from the life and work pattern that she has established. . . . [but] an enlargement of her life experiences, the addition of a new dimension to an already established pattern. . . . She will marry and bear children only if she deeply desires a mate and children, and will not be judged a failure as a person if she decides against either. . . .

When [the children] are grown and establish adult lives of their own . . . her own independent activities will continue and expand. She will be neither an embittered wife, an interfering mother-in-law, nor an idle parasite, but together with her husband she will be able to live an independent, purposeful and satisfying third act in life [pp. 647-649].

Psychoanalytic Contributions to a Psychology of Women

The most vehement leaders in the new feminist movement seem to be united in blaming male domination from earliest to latest times for the relative economic poverty and the mental and emotional debasement of women in even the richest countries in the world. Past this point of general agreement, however, their concepts of the psychology of women are unclear and their formal ideas about the place of women in society are divided. Mitchell (1971) designates the ideologically different groups as Radical Feminists and Abstract Socialists. She summarizes the arguments on either side (pp. 94-95). Radical Feminists: Men are the oppressors; all societies have been male supremacist; everything starts with a psychological power struggle which men win; socialism has nothing to offer us (women); socialist countries oppress women; what we want is all women to unite against men and male-dominated society; we want to liberate men from male oppression. Abstract Socialists: Men are not the oppressors—it's the system; capitalism oppresses women; everything starts with private property;

we've got to discover "our relationship to socialism; the scene isn't
too good in socialist countries for women—but that's because women's
liberation wasn't part of the revolutionary struggle; it's most necessary
to convince men of the importance of our struggle. They are oppressed
by their roles, too; all people are alienated under capitalism. We want
to liberate everyone to become 'whole people.' "

Mitchell believes that "There is nothing inevitable about the form
or role of the family, any more than there is about the character or
role of women. It is the function of ideology to present these given
social types as aspects of Nature itself" (pp. 99-100). Mitchell earlier
(1966) stated her conviction that the biology of women has to be taken
into account, but she presents this in terms of the family and women's
relegation to functions in the family. She does not consider the question of hormonal differences and whatever role these may play in the
psychology of women. She is concerned with patriarchy and questions
its inevitability. Her argument, expressed in a variety of ways by other
feminists, is that technology and modern medicine have enabled women
to surmount the limitations of their entrapment by reproductive functions and their inferior size and strength.

Shainess (1970, 1972) has suggested that there is *no* psychological
difference between the qualities of being penetrating for a man and
being receptive for a woman. Shainess says that ideas of feminine
passivity as health must be jettisoned if women are really to be helped
to mature and attain reasonably satisfactory lives. Mastery over their
own bodies and reproductive lives is essential for women's emotional
health and emancipation. And again, as with all human beings, women
must be helped to become as free from anxiety as possible and to learn
collaborative modes of relationship as equals.

There is no question about the impact of the so-called new feminism on contemporary society. The movement has leaped barriers of
geography, language, and even sex, so that women and men, adherents of feminist goals, are meeting, talking, and writing in all countries
of the free world. There has been a veritable explosion in research
literature pertaining to women. An overview of studies relevant to the
psychology of women (Seiden, 1976a) notes recent research on gender
differences in behavior and on women's sexual and reproductive lives,
including various aspects of menstruation, menopause, coitus, rape,

childbearing, fertility, and contraception. A second section of this same study (1976b) surveys the changing role of women in the family, community, work, and psychotherapy. One psychoanalytic psychotherapist has published a comparison of women she treated in the 1950's with women patients treated in the 1970's. She finds that twenty years ago the typical complaints of women in therapy included frigidity, finding husbands, and difficulties in rearing children. Today, women patients bring conflicts about personal identity, professional goals, divorce, and extramarital sexual relationships. Some regard marriage as a trap, and many are not sure they want children. The new freedom has brought both expanded opportunity and new problems. Women entering new jobs may experience conflict about self-assertion and successful performance in a man's world. The sexual demands of "liberated" women produce anxiety in men and may result in impotence or other sexual symptoms (Moulton, 1977). My own clinical experience, spanning the same time and including children as well as adults, supports in general Moulton's observations. She points out that, "The new feminism, while opening up new paths for both sexes and loosening up sex-role stereotypes, has also unleashed new anxieties" (p. 5).

It is my impression that one major anxiety is shared alike by the "new woman" and those to whom she turns for help. One stark revelation of the current attempts at understanding women is that we do not at this time have an adequate theory of the psychology of women. The attempt Freud and a very few other psychoanalysts made, only some 40 years ago, was the first scientific one in history. Apart from the work on hysteria done with Breuer, Freud wrote only three papers devoted specifically to theoretical issues in the psychology of women (1925b, 1931, 1933). Additional references are scattered throughout his writings and in published letters. A close reading of this material makes it clear that Freud was working on a theory, not sharing a revealed truth. His opening remarks in the 1925 paper were to the effect that he had decided to publish his ideas at that time because he felt his time for more work was limited and he could not wait for his observations to be confirmed. He said, "An eager crowd of fellow-workers is ready to make use of what is unfinished or doubtful, and I can leave to them that part of the work which I should otherwise have done myself. On this occasion, therefore, I feel justified in publishing something which stands in urgent need of confirmation before its value or lack of value can be decided" (1925b, p. 249). The tenor of his comments was speculative and indicated recurrently a tentative approach.

In 1905 he wrote "[The erotic life of men] alone has become accessible to research. That of women . . . is still veiled in an impenetrable obscurity" (p. 151). More than twenty years later he still found "The sexual life of women . . . a 'dark continent' for psychology" (1926, p. 212). Although many of his early ideas about infantile sexuality derived from his work with female patients, he acknowledged that his formulations were "obtained from the study of men and the theory deduced from it was concerned with male children" (1925c, p. 36). Notations throughout his papers anticipated many of the objections raised by feminist critics today, for example, "I am inclined to set some value on the considerations I have brought forward upon the psychical consequences of the anatomical distinction between the sexes. I am aware, however, that this opinion can only be maintained if my findings, which are based on a handful of cases, turn out to have general validity and to be typical. If not, they would remain no more than a contribution to our knowledge of the different paths along which sexual life develops" (1925b, p. 258). About passivity, he said, "It is perhaps the case that in a woman, on the basis of her share in the sexual function, a preference for passive behaviour and passive aims is carried over into her life to a greater or lesser extent, in proportion to the limits, restricted or far-reaching, within which her sexual life thus serves as a model. But we must beware in this of underestimating the influence of social customs, which similarly force a woman into passive situations. . . . The suppression of women's aggressiveness which is prescribed for them constitutionally and imposed on them socially favours the development of powerful masochistic impulses. . . . Thus masochism, as people say, is truly feminine" (1933, pp. 115-116). Of "psychical peculiarities of mature feminity" he said, " . . . nor is it always easy to distinguish what should be ascribed to the influence of the sexual function and what to social breeding" (1933, p. 132). In closing his final paper on the subject, he said, "That is all I had to say to you about femininity. It is certainly incomplete and fragmentary and does not always sound friendly. But do not forget that I have only been describing women in so far as their nature is determined by their sexual function. It is true that that influence extends very far, but we do not overlook the fact that an individual woman may be a human being in other respects as well. If you want to know more about femininity, enquire from your own experiences of life, or turn to the poets, or wait until science can give you deeper and more coherent information'' (1933, p. 135).

In addition to Freud's own caveat, there were some objections to his theories from other psychoanalysts. Jones (1927, 1933) suggested that girls might be more basically feminine than analysts thought. He believed that penis envy might be defensive, a response to fear of femininity rather than a primary stage. Horney (1926) suggested that small girls have perception of the vagina and that fear of vaginal injury rather than awareness of being castrated and wounded characterized girls. Josine Muller (1932), who was a pediatrician before becoming an analyst, reported vaginal masturbation in girls between the ages of three and five. Müller-Braunschweig (1926) questioned the concept that the original sexuality of the girl is the same as that of the boy; his observation was that she possesses a deep sense of her femininity and has at least unconscious knowledge of the vagina. Quite early, Horney (1926, 1933) had a great deal to say about the interaction of psychic and social factors, stressing that the complex development of each person's character involves not only innate propensities but experience in a given situation. Somewhat later Clara Thompson (1942, 1943, 1950) and Zilboorg (1944) noted that classical psychoanalytic theory dealing with the psychological differences between men and women did not address the function of cultural pressures in determining femininity. Zilboorg found it surprising that psychoanalysis, which was so inquisitive and iconoclastic in every other area and had revolutionized psychology while influencing new approaches in social science, had abandoned discussion of the phenomenology and genesis of the psychological differences between the sexes without any resolution of most of the issues raised by clinical evidence. A review of psychoanalytic literature vividly confirms this observation.

Freud himself (1925b, 1931) responded briefly to the dissident theories of Jones and Horney on penis envy, dismissing them as not tallying with his impressions. Other influential analysts published views that were on the whole merely elaborations of Freud's. Abraham (1922) endorsed the term "castration complex" as appropriate for both sexes and cited clinical evidence to prove that every girl believes she once had a penis. Marie Bonaparte (1953) formulated origins of female character traits, in particular feminine masochism, as the inevitable consequence of the girl's discovery of her anatomic difference (thus inferiority) from boys. Helene Deutsch, whose work culminated in the monumental two-volume *The Psychology of Women* (1944-1945), agreed with Freud that all children are biologically destined to want a penis and that the girl inevitably feels defective when she discovers she lacks one. In fact, Deutsch went further than Freud, categorically equating femininity with passivity, masculinity with activity. She said, "While fully recognizing that women's position is subjected to external influence, I venture to say that the fundamental identities 'feminine-passive' and 'masculine-active' assert themselves in all known cultures and races, in various forms and various quantitative proportions" (1944, p. 224).

A number of reasons have been put forward to explain why Freud's early theories so quickly became dogma. Apparently he did not expect this. In 1909 he wrote to Jung, "Your notion that after my retirement from the ranks my errors may come to be worshipped as relics amused me a good deal, but I don't believe it. I believe on the contrary that the younger men will demolish in my heritage everything that is not absolutely solid as fast as they can" (McGuire, 1974, p. 277). Nevertheless, whatever the causes and despite a never quite extinguished undercurrent of dissent from a few psychoanalysts and others (cf. Kinsey et al., 1953) Freud's original propositions about the female castration complex, penis envy, feminine masochism, and feminine character development have remained the cornerstone of the only formulated psychology of women. His case studies are brilliant, detailed reports of the complex interaction of the individual and her environment. For example, his observations about female sexuality display clearly the internal conflicts mingled with the cultural pressure of a girl growing up in Europe during the early years of this century. That his theories, formulated on the clinical evidence, do not differentiate observed reality from immutable, universally applicable natural law is neither here nor there. Theories are made to be tested against new data and revised. Freud revised his own theories often—in fact he took a stab at modifying his psychology of women to include the lifelong influence of the girl's active preoedipal tie to the mother. As he predicted, he left the work unfinished, and the justified quarrel of the feminists is with his successors, who have not pursued thinking about women beyond the initial speculations of early analysts.

A summary of the controversial issues in Freud's concept of the psychology of women will highlight the sources of feminist outrage and focus on work to be done by contemporary analysts.

Freud thought that the development of girls and boys is essentially the same until the phallic stage, when the interest of both sexes in the external genital organs is heightened. At this time, a little girl, seeing a penis, is confronted with the fact that she does not have such an organ and concludes that she has been castrated. Lacking this organ which is ''the superior counterpart of their own small and inconspic- uous organ [she] from that time forward fall[s] a victim to envy for the penis'' (1925b, p. 252). Freud thought ''The difference between the sexual development of males and females at the stage we have been considering is an intelligible consequence of the anatomical dis- tinction between their genitals and of the psychical situation involved in it; it corresponds to the difference between a castration that has been carried out and one that has merely been threatened'' (1925b, pp. 256-257). Therefore, the psychology of the woman is derived from the fact that she began to develop thinking she was like a boy, was confronted with the fact that she had no penis, i.e., had been castrated, and thus was doomed to inferiority, and must, as well as she can, adapt to this situation. Freud felt that feelings about being castrated propelled girls into turning away from their mothers, who were blamed for the castration, toward their fathers. Then they hoped for a baby from father as compensation for castration. Especially they could hope for a male child who would have the special organ. In girls, Freud said, the motive for giving up the oedipal attachment to the father is lacking because the castration so feared by the boy is already a fact. Consequently, the superego, formed in the boy when paternal prohibitions are internalized under pressure of castration anx- iety, is not so inexorable. To this he attributed character traits which critics of every epoch have brought up against women: "that they show less sense of justice than men, that they are less ready to submit to the great exigencies of life, that they are more often influenced in their judgements by feelings of affection or hostility. . ." (1925b, pp. 257-258). The solutions Freud postulated for the inevitable penis envy of girls are all discouraging to women. One option is to renounce all sexuality, but this requires severe repression and leads to neurosis. Another is to deny the fact of being without a penis and adhere to the fantasy of having one or the hope of regaining it, but this gives rise to a masculinity complex expressed by maintaining the habit of clitoral masturbation, otherwise abandoned by the girl out of disgust for her inadequate genital. And the masculinity complex may lead to homo-sexual object choice, or, if the penis envy is sufficiently sublimated, the woman may carry on an intellectual profession. The path to mature femininity, Freud thought, was reached when the girl gave up clitoral masturbation and with it a certain amount of activity. The ensuing passivity "clears the phallic activity out of the way, smooths the ground for femininity. If too much is not lost in the course of it through repression, this femininity may turn out to be normal" (1933, p. 128). Even so, he said, the lot of women is hard. They have difficulty in maturing, never reach the heights of creative work or contributions to civilization that men attain. They have little sense of justice, are prone to envy, and are weaker in their social interests, with less capacity for sublimating their instincts. And finally, Freud said, "A man of about thirty strikes us as a youthful, somewhat un-formed individual, whom we expect to make powerful use of the possibilities for development opened up to him by analysis. A woman of the same age, however, often frightens us by her psychical rigidity and unchangeability. Her libido has taken up final positions and seems incapable of exchanging them for others. There are no paths open to further development; it is as though the whole process had already run its course and remains thenceforward insusceptible to influence—as though, indeed, the difficult development to femininity had exhausted the possibilities of the person concerned" (1933, pp. 134-135).

Given this bold statement of the best-known and hitherto unques-tioned view of the nature of femininity, it is not surprising that, with a few notable exceptions, the radical feminists have denounced Freud and his followers as advocates of the very male supremacy that has undermined feminism and contributed heavily to a narrow, biologically defined psychology of women. Rossi (1964, p. 613) says, "Our society has been so inundated with psychoanalytic thinking that any dissatisfaction or conflict in personal life is considered to require solution on an individual basis. . . . American women have increasingly resorted to psychotherapy, the most highly individualized solution of all, for answers to the problems they have as women. In the process the idea has been lost that many problems, even in the personal family sphere, cannot be solved on an individual basis, but require solution on a societal level by changing the institutional contexts within which we live." Rossi asserts that the widespread influence of psychoanalytic ideas and conservatism in the social sciences has dampened intellectual dialogue on sex equality as a goal, and that it has provided a quasi-scientific basis for educators, marriage counselors, mass media, and advertising researchers who have partly created and reinforced the withdrawal of American women from the mainstream of work in our society.

This attitude is fairly representative of the feminist objection to psychoanalytic theory, and the point is well taken. Freud's early concepts, often vulgarized, have indeed pervaded all thinking about women, even the ideas of those who do not know his theories per se and do not consider themselves "Freudian." It is nevertheless unfortunate that so much feminist anti-Freudian literature is polemical. Irate feminists, fighting the well-documented social and economic inequality of women, have too often erupted in sweeping *ad hominem* denunciations of Freud as a male chauvinist product of his culture, equating his personality and life style with his attempts to formulate some understanding of the development of women. Only from a handful of feminists have come more considered points of view and a focus on still unanswered questions about the nature of femininity. Lazarre (1975), writing from the experience of a personal analysis with a male Freudian analyst, describes her acquisition of insight into the personal sources of her unsatisfactory relationships, based on a neurotic need to please men. She set out to see what impact the women's movement's classic feminist questions on penis envy, passivity, and masochism, social versus psychic causality, and the mother-child relationship have had on the psychoanalytic establishment. She notes, "Whatever sexism these analysts evidence as men and products of their time was not bolstered by any simple notion of female biological inferiority." She continues, "I have never met a woman who expressed phallic envy on the Freudian model. What I do see everywhere, expressed in social gatherings and political movements, acted out in love affairs, and dramatized for me whenever men suddenly enter a group which was previously all women, what is confessed over and over in women's groups . . . attesting to the bastion-like strength of traditional social roles, is female passivity in the presence of men, and its more virulent unconscious cousin, 'masochism' " (p. 76).

Elizabeth Janeway (1974) suggests that Freud's statement that girls are castrated cannot be taken seriously, as no woman can be deprived of something she never had, unless one understands the symbolic meaning of the penis: power and freedom. She comments on his understanding of the difficulty women have in achieving satisfactory adult sexual relationships in a culture that prohibits sexual knowledge and feelings in girls before marriage.

Shulamith Firestone, author of *The Dialectic of Sex* (1970), one of the most-quoted feminist books, defends Freud's ideas as "poetic rather than scientific; . . . more valuable as metaphors than as literal truth" (p. 52).

Most pertinent of all, Juliet Mitchell (1971) supports the value of psychoanalysis as a science. She says, "Psychoanalysis, exploring the unconscious and the constructs of mental life, works on the terrain of which the dominant phenomenal form is the family. In studying women we cannot neglect the methods of a science of the mind, a theory that attempts to explain how women become women and men, men. The borderline between the biological and the social which finds expression in the family is the land that psychoanalysis sets out to chart" (p. 167). Mitchell believes that post-Freudian empiricism has trapped Freud's tentative analyses of sexual differences into rigidity. She, too, thinks the concept of penis envy does not imply a wish to seize the object itself, but a much more complex notion of the power of the image of the phallus in human society. She rejects the radical feminist postulate of a primary psychological demand for power by men as the original source of the oppression of women, but she also rejects the post-Freudian psychoanalytic ideology of inherent inferiority of women. This, she says, "is pernicious to women and should be forcefully combated. It is also pernicious to psychoanalysis" (p. 164). Mitchell points out that feminist authors deny the unconscious itself, but she interprets the Oedipus complex as an expression of the patriarchal structure of society, culturally determined. Her conclusion is that oppression of women will end when the nuclear family and its economic system are destroyed (Mitchell, 1974), so she, too, attributes the psychology of women to cultural influence.

Toward a New Psychology of Women

The Freudian propositions about female psychology which have been the target of feminist attack—anatomy is destiny, the female castration complex, penis envy, feminine passivity, and masochism—are issues undergoing the liveliest discussion in psychoanalysis today. From Schafer (1974, p. 332) has come a ringing challenge to Freudian analysts:

> . . . psychoanalysts who genuinely appreciate ego psychology will not shrug off the current great discussion of the making, warping, and exploitation of women in our society. In this discussion, fundamental Freudian propositions about psychological development are being challenged from all sides while the entire psychoanalytic enterprise is being widely discredited as the child and now the servant of the male-dominated social order. Simply interpreting these criticisms as militant rationalizations of penis envy being put forth by neurotic females and their male supporters is a flagrant instance of reductionism and intellectual isolationism and is equivalent to shrugging off this discussion which, it should be noted, concerns the allegedly distorted development of men as well as women.

Schafer advocates rethinking the concept as well as the role of penis envy in female development: "It is legitimate to begin by limiting the discussion to Freud alone. One warrant for doing so is that much of the current criticism is directed specifically against Freud and relies heavily on allegedly representative quotations from his writings. Another warrant is this: although many major theoretical and technical

advances beyond Freud have been made by his psychoanalytic des-
cendents, his basic assumptions, indeed the very mode of his thought,
are very much with us in modern psychoanalysis" (p. 333). Schafer
comments further that Freud emphasized how little he finally understood female development, and he did speak to the girl's active preoedipal attachment to her mother. But, as Schafer points out, Freud
never did change his patriarchal viewpoint—that viewpoint, to quote
Schafer again, " . . . from which female development appears to be
both second best and second-rate in the judgment of patriarchal
spokesmen of civilization at large. . . . From this fact follow many
of the problems in [Freud's] psychology of women" (1974, p. 333).

The influx of information about human development from biology,
the behavioral sciences, and the elaboration of psychoanalytic developmental psychology has presented complex theoretical and technical
problems for analysts. I will not undertake here a review of accu-
mulating data now emerging, more and more of it from the ranks of
Freudian analysts themselves. This has been set forth exhaustively in
recent literature, which also points out how classical theory is being
questioned and altered as additional knowledge accrues (e.g., Moore,
1976). Some tendency to restate earlier views, with the flavor of old
wine in new bottles, still continues (Nagera, 1975), but it does appear
that a new psychoanalytic psychology of women is in the making.
Brief references to the most significant new data and new points of
view should illustrate the point.

Modern research in endocrinology (Gadpaille, 1972) has revealed
that anatomical sexual dimorphism comes about with the production
of androgen at the critical period when the fetal reproductive system
is forming. At first, both sexes are under the influence of female sex
hormones *in utero*. With the introduction of androgen the male genital
tract and, some researchers believe, also certain male circuits in the
brain develop. There are some data to suggest that testosterone is
related to levels of assertiveness, and other findings show how sex-
related physiological variables influence mood, sensoriperceptual responses and activity levels in human beings. Behavior and affect evoke
responses from the environment, which in turn tend to accentuate or
inhibit behavior patterns in the growing child. Medical research documents the fact that males have increased vulnerability to a number

of diseases, explained, in theory, by the more complex process of male fetal differentiation. Apparently there are some innate fundamental differences, determined by physiology, between the sexes. However, from the work of Hampson and Hampson (1961), Money and Ehrhardt (1972), and Stoller (1968a, b), it appears that the parental designation of sex and the attitudes and expectations of parents toward children of each sex are the major factors in determining ultimate gender identity.

Systematic direct observation of children and clinical work with children provide knowledge of early experience. This newer knowledge refutes Freud's theory that both sexes pass through the early stages of libidinal development in the same manner, and that the original sexuality of the little girl is of a wholly masculine character. Gender identity is firmly established before the phallic stage, having been consolidated in the separation-individuation process (Kleeman, 1971; Stoller, 1964, 1968a, b). Furthermore, Freud's belief that clitoral sensitivity, identified as masculine, must be transformed into vaginal sensitivity in order to achieve a feminine character in puberty is untenable. Masters and Johnson (1966) have established that orgasm is orgasm regardless of the site or means of stimulation. Their work demonstrated the precise structure and function of the clitoris as an organ system totally limited to initiating or elevating levels of sexual tension. No such organ exists in male anatomy. This, plus the fact that the clitoris is anatomically a true homologue of the penis and that it has long been called "the female phallus" have confused understanding its functional role. The clitoris is not, as Freud thought, an inferior substitute for a penis. It serves as an erotic focus for genital stimulation. This capacity is a biological given, manifest in the preoedipal girl, never entirely lost in normal latency, reinforced in adolescence, and retained in mature women as an integrated part of the genital apparatus (Clower, 1975, p. 129).

Curiosity and excitement about the genital area of the self and others is clear in both sexes by about eighteen months (Kleeman, 1975; Galenson and Roiphe, 1974, 1977). The discovery of the genital difference between the sexes provokes a wide range of responses from mild and transient to severe and disruptive. The behavior of girls in this situation is interpreted variously: Galenson and Roiphe (1974) describe evidence of penis envy and believe this is a major element in the girl's turning away from mother to father. This is in line with Freud's theory, but at an earlier time in development. Galenson and Roiphe (1977) stress that a satisfying relationship with the mother mitigates the experience. Earlier experience which has interfered with an adequate sense of the self and bodily integrity increases vulnerability to object loss, and an unusually severe castration response may ensue, since the genitals are not securely integrated in the self-representation this early. Perhaps girls are more vulnerable because their genitals are less available for stimulation and comforting reassurance than the penis of the boy. Kleeman (1971) doubts whether genital sensations and awareness are as important as learning, imitation, and identification with significant objects.

The impact of discovering anatomical differences in the sexes is determined by the narcissistic vulnerability of the girl. Galenson and Roiphe (1977) and Schafer (1974) concur in this. Grossman and Stewart (1977) point out that penis envy may become a metaphor: a concrete explanation for dissatisfaction from a variety of sources. They believe that there are two phases in penis envy: first, an early stage in which the task of differentiation from the mother and the establishment of self-esteem are the critical developmental issues. If the girl has difficulty in resolving these conflicts at the same time that she is faced with her sexual difference, she may blame her feelings of being inadequate and unloved on her "castration." In a later stage when the girl is disappointed in wishes for a sexual relationship with father, she may resort to fantasies of having a penis as a solution to the oedipal conflict. Formal and informal discussion among analysts today emphasizes the fact that very few any longer believe that persistent penis envy is inevitable or healthy in female psychology. It is understood more as an outcome of inadequate mothering and faulty resolution of early developmental conflicts. The role of the mother and the father in accepting and appreciating the girl as a girl is seen as much more important than actual anatomical difference.

Furthermore, there are reports of little girls who show definite heterosexual interest, genital sensuality, and manifest wishes to have their own baby before reaction to sexual difference (castration complex) appears. Parens et al. (1977) demonstrated that "normal-enough" girls enter the Oedipus complex under the same impetus as the boy: *"to gratify and comply with the first and powerfully expressed heterosexual genital impulses in the libido as well as the child's gender-related ego dispositions"* (p. 104). Kleeman (1977) and Stoller (1977) also doubt that penis envy is the initiator of feminine gender identity.

The concept of masochism as a universal normal psychobiological component in the human female has been more difficult to address. Feminists protest that analysts are all chauvinists who brainwash women into accepting inferiority and subservience. Analysts, on the other hand, report that women themselves continue to identify femininity with being long-suffering, and that women are fearful of success, and unable to be appropriately aggressive in competitive situations even when opportunity arises (Horner, 1972). This tendency can be a problem in analytic treatment as a transference resistance with male or female analysts. The newer theoretical position of analysts has been described by Blum (1977), who concludes that masochism is not healthy in either sex and that mature femininity involves not masochistic renunciation but the capacity for loving care and sublimation. Nevertheless, the adaptive function of masochism in our society continues to support and conceal pathology in women. It is not surprising that, at a recent discussion group of the American Psychoanalytic Association, the unanimous choice of a topic for first consideration was the modern problem of feminine masochism.

Psychoanalysts today are sensitive to the effects on women of our changing culture. The function of motherhood as a stage in development has been discussed repeatedly, most recently by Kestenberg (1977) and Blum (1977). Ticho (1977) has described the pressures on young women who now often leave the parental home much earlier than in the past, and must establish autonomy and make important decisions and choices while working through a final separation phase as young adults.

Conclusions

The feminist movement and modern psychoanalysis share the conviction that a new psychology of women is required today. Feminist work for alleviation of derogation and exploitation of women has begun to change many established cultural stereotypes, and we already see the effects on women as they reassess themselves in the light of shifting expectations and opportunities. What we may hope to see more clearly in the future is more exactly what the unique aspects of femininity may be. To this end it is regrettable that most feminist leaders have contented themselves with attacks on a male-dominated society. With few exceptions they write as if there were no significant biological substratum in human beings, as if all mental mechanisms were conscious, and as if all perception of the self and the environment were learned. Feminist literature is replete with references to history, sociology, and anthropology whose accuracy I cannot always judge, but the references to psychoanalytic formulations reveal an incomplete grasp of the original theories and an almost total ignorance and disinterest in what psychoanalysts are thinking and saying today. Not only is the scholarship poor, in many instances the writing is so imprecise as to obscure lines of reasoning and conclusions. A recent critical review by Barglow and Schaefer (1977) of current influential books from the women's liberation movement supports my conclusion that the feminist version of a new psychology of women is that femininity evolves from cultural conditioning; *ergo*, changing the culture will change characteristics of women.

Neither as a woman nor as a scientist have I ever been able to believe that femininity is derived from castrated maleness. But no more can I accept the premise that female infants are so amorphous and so lacking in inherent capacity for development into women that they will be shaped exclusively by environmental influences which force crippling adaptation to a male culture. No psychoanalyst, and most certainly no psychoanalyst who works with mothers and children, will discount the formative contribution of the environment. But, whatever the infant may be, it is a participant in interacting with its environment, mediated through the mother, from birth. Every human being, male or female, is an individual from conception, with innate capacities determined by chromosome inheritance. The unborn child is not only potentially male or female, but has cognitive *Anlagen* and a readiness for responsiveness to selective stimuli which may be partly sex-linked and may be individual in ways determined by more subtle and complex factors still undefined.

The girl, no less than the boy, has species-specific inborn drives with their later mental representations. Her maturation of drive and ego capacities unfolds on an epigenetic scheme, which produces new abilities and resulting developmental conflicts at every step. The environment can enhance and constructively direct drives and developing ego capacities, or it can inhibit and distort them: it can never create them out of nothing. So, the little girl is born female with psycho-biological attributes related to her unique fitness for maturation into a woman who can conceive, bear, and suckle offspring. The extent to which these capacities are mentally represented and at what age they are cognitively perceived is not certain. Recent work indicates an earlier age than analysts formerly thought. It is clear that the girl's self-esteem, her freedom to explore and enjoy her own body, to experience genital pleasure, and to think positively about her nonsexual personal qualities such as intelligence and talent depend heavily on her childhood experiences with her own parents. First, the mother must be autonomous and stable enough to foster separation and individuation, being neither so unavailable nor so over protective as to interfere with the child's differentiation (Mahler, 1968). In the course of this process, the girl must identify with the mother in her femininity, her nurturing of the child, and her relationship with the father. Some of this may be accomplished via intuitive response to sensations in the clitoral-vaginal area, and by small quantities of hormones, but much is learned by close association with the parents and incorporation of the mother into the ego ideal. This parallels the move from dyadic to triadic object relationships, making the father an important object of libidinal investment. In my opinion, this dual step in development can account for the libidinal shift from mother to father. It has been my observation that girls who repudiate their mothers entirely out of narcissistic injury are not in a good position to establish heterosexual relationships. The girl who enters the oedipal conflict by identification with the mother and thereby becomes a rival for father can be very hateful to and mobilize a great deal of aggression toward mother. She is not, however, the same girl who has not optimally separated from mother and whose hostility is based on feelings of being uncared for and of missing something. Such girls are propelled into the oedipal stage by the developmental process, but they are not able to resolve it satisfactorily, lacking a firm identification with a good mother. They may blame their dissatisfaction on not being a boy, especially if they had male siblings. However, their real complaint is of a more basic deprivation at the hands of mother, and it is not a penis they want.

The normally developing girl is affirmed in her femininity, first established by about age three, in the oedipal conflict not only by her mother but by her father. If he is able to appreciate and enjoy his daughter's sexuality without being either seduced or frightened away, she will have another experience of herself as feminine. It is especially important that the father be able to recognize and enjoy the ego capacities of his daughter as well. The girl who is fortunate enough to have a father who likes her being a girl, and at the same time neither overidealizes nor underestimates her as a person, has a model for future relationships with men as friend, colleague, lover, and husband.

The wish for a child which appears early in childhood fantasy and doll play as an identification with the mother may never disappear entirely during latency. It is often expressed in love for animals and interest in the reproduction of pets when the girl is too old for doll play. In adolescence, with the establishment of menstruation, the specific wish for a baby with a specific love object—who may not have been found yet—is quite conscious. This involves both the reinstitution of the oedipal conflict and the rivalry with mother, and the strengthening of the feminine identification with the idealized mother.

Needless to say, no human being develops without pressures and frustrations from his own capacities, his object relationships, and the opportunities and limitations of his environment. Psychoanalysis sheds a great deal of light on this process and also demonstrates that the finished product then changes very little, no matter what happens outside. This fact is crucially significant both for the analysts who seek to understand and help women and the feminists who would change the world for them. While analysts revise the theory that woman is the product of a piece carved out of Adam, feminists must get past harping on what Adam has done to women. Freud's great contribution to women's liberation was to expose not only that women are devalued and oppressed in a male chauvinist society, but that both boys *and* girls reared in such a society regard women as basically inferior. Women have unconsciously identified themselves as altogether deficient because of their genital difference. Whether expressed by forthright derogation or by pity and overprotection, the message has been the same, handed down from parents to daughters. This will not stop until mothers and fathers regard their girl children as whole individuals with individual abilities and capacities, including those uniquely female. When this happens, women in succeeding generations will be faced with the clarification of their own contributions to maintaining a patriarchal society. It does not stand to reason that male needs alone could form and sustain a culture without some conscious or unconscious acquiescence from the other half of the population. It has been my observation that many of the mothers who suffer· exploitation at the hands of acknowledged or unwittingly male chauvinistic husbands are rearing sons to be just such men and daughters to be like themselves. We do not know whether some basic feminine needs have been satisfied, even if at great cost, by patriarchy. We do not know, for example, how fundamental the wish for a baby is and how necessary this experience may be in the formation of mature feminine character, even as fulfillment of ego potential is necessary for all human maturity. As women are freed from long periods of uncontrolled reproduction and have access to other modes of creativity and personal satisfaction, we may define these issues better.

It is a matter of grave concern to clinicians even now. We are seeing young women who elect to have no children, or who postpone having them until it may be biologically or practicably impossible. It is often hard to say whether such a decision may be soundly based on mature choice and capacity to sublimate, or whether it is a neurotic attempt to resolve an infantile conflict (see chapter 5, this volume). After all, a baby is a baby, and the experience of conceiving, delivery, and nursing one is like nothing else. Ideally it should be possible for any woman to choose freely whether she will be a mother and it should be possible for those who do not or cannot bear a child to deal with the reality and find compensation in other ways. But the timetable for childbearing is limited, and the limit is irrevocable.

We do not know exactly how indispensable the mother alone is in direct care of the child for a prolonged time. The feminist assertion that fathers, nurseries, and daycare centers are adequate substitutes, perhaps even desirable alternatives, to an intense long-term relationship with the mother is supported by some studies (cf. Spurlock and

Rembold, 1976). This thesis needs careful investigation. Most likely there is no one pattern for separation and individuation that is equally appropriate for every infant and mother. It seems to me very probable that the process may differ in each sex as the individuation of the boy involves a "disidentification" with the mother (Greenson, 1968; Person, 1974), whereas the girl's identification with her mother strengthens her gender identity.

We do not know how early and in what profound ways the anatomical configuration of her body and the rhythmic hormonal ebb and flow, totally unlike anything male, contributes to the girl's body image and her sense of the kind of human being she is. Margaret Mead points out that women's bodies are prepared for lengthy participation in the creation of a human being, and she wonders if this may make females—even those who bear no children—more prone to take their own bodies as the theater of action. "Feminine interaction," she says, "may only be the result of having been the girl child of a mother who was alert to her child's slightest need; but girls continue to be born from their mother's bodies . . . so that alertness to tiny cues may continue to be transmitted from mother to daughter, and inhibited in sons, even if both boys and girls come to be reared equally by both parents from birth" (1974, p. 105). Erikson's poetic and widely quoted "Womanhood and the Inner Space" (1968) has been hotly rejected by feminists as a latter-day statement of "anatomy is destiny." Erikson asked whether the identity formation of women may differ because their somatic design harbors an "inner space." In a later elaboration of this proposition (1974) he reiterates unanswered questions: " . . . whether a person or a generation can simply choose to disregard as inconvenient or unnecessary any part of the instinctuality essential to man's bodily existence. In other words, on the way to liberate genitality but to restrict procreation, are we about to repress yet another 'basic drive'? Or *is* it 'yet another'?" (p. 337).

It is apparent that no one field alone can study comprehensively enough the data that may eventually yield valid assumptions about the basic differences between the sexes. There are anatomical, physiological, and psychological facts. There are historical, social, and behavioral facts. Men and women are different from each other in some or all ways in these spheres, and individuals differ from each other in ways that are not determined primarily by sex. An adequate theory of the psychology of women must take all these elements into account, although analysts still do not agree on the value of information from other disciplines in revision of psychoanalytic theory. The obstacle of translating findings from biology and behavior into psychology is monumental.

But this task must be accepted. We are in a new world today, with many aspects of human existence changed utterly by technology and cultural upheaval. The status of women will never again be what it has been traditionally. Women are no longer set apart either on pedestals or as slaves, but as wives and colleagues of men, mothers of future generations, informed and active citizens, and contributors to the economy, they have to redefine themselves. Increasing numbers of women are responsibly insisting on this re-evaluation of their unique nature, their capacities and limitations, and their function in the world at large. Their contributions to further elucidation of the psychology of women are indispensable to anyone who would understand and work to alleviate the social and psychologic ills of mankind.

CHAPTER 15

Social Factors in Symptom Choice:
The New Dynamics of Impotence

WILLIAM A. FROSCH,
GEORGE L. GINSBERG,
and THEODORE SHAPIRO

When we examine objects from the tomb of Tutankhamen, we cannot but be impressed with the immediacy and humanness of gesture, the intimacy of glance, the awareness of love, which testify to the continuity of human experience, to the similarities—perhaps even sameness-of human relationships and feelings across generations and cultures. Counter to this is the observation, usually voiced as a complaint, that the world is changing, the old order crumbling. The complaint is as old as the history of civilization and is usually voiced by the older generation. Certainly, there has been change, some progressive, some cyclic. Progressive change is most obvious in technological developments; we now wheel and fly as well as walk and run. Cyclic change is clearest in fashion: women's skirts rise and fall; men's ties narrow and widen; we dance touching or apart. These cyclic changes appear to come with increasing and at times bewildering rapidity, undoubtedly speeded by technological change in travel and communication. In addition, the swelling number of adolescents, coupled with their economic privilege and power, may permit them to foster and utilize change in their struggle for independence.

Lifton (1971), Toffler (1970), and others agree with Wallerstein (1973) that this relatively recent increase in the rate of change requires that we rethink our assumptions in our attempts to understand behav-

ior. Freud and other Victorian and post-Victorian psychologists assumed a relatively stable world as a background to the complex interplay
of psyche and society, an unchanging "average expectable environment."[1] Despite this, Freud's earliest formulation was that neuroses
stemmed from a real adult seduction of the child. With the discovery
of the important role of fantasy, attention turned from actuality as an
interpersonal happening to the inner world. Psychoanalytic psychology
became a depth psychology seeking universals of mind, and only
partially returned to consideration of the real world with the introduction of the structural theory and with Anna Freud's delineation of
defenses directed against anxiety due to instinctual conflict with the
demands of reality. Hartmann's adaptational view completed this swing:
". . . social factors must also be described psychologically in such
a way as to demonstrate their selective effects . . . in what manner
and to what degree does a given social structure bring to the surface,
provoke, or reinforce certain instinctual tendencies, or certain sublimations, for instance?" (1944, p. 27). At yet another juncture, Hartmann, Kris, and Loewenstein (1951) wrote that individual societies
provide differing discharge channels for the drives and that the proper
focus of psychoanalysis ought to remain on how man's inner life is
given permission or distorted by these variations.

In 1972 (Ginsberg, Frosch, and Shapiro), we suggested that changing public attitudes toward sexuality and a widening definition of
acceptability of practice were affecting symptom complexes of patients
who came to therapists requesting help. In the recent past our culture's
mythology divided women into the good, who were either asexual
prior to marriage or, if sexual, certainly did not engage in intercourse;
and the bad, who were actively sexual, considered promiscuous, and
who lost the respect of their elders and peers, both male and female.
Such a world provided men who feared the female genitals or the
ultimate sexual act with a ready rationalization for avoiding intercourse. Such men, although they undoubtedly were suffering from
neurotic inhibitions, were able to avoid recognizing their own difficulties. They (consciously) thought that the only available women

[1] It is of interest that the social and economic theorists of the same era (Marx and Engels,
for example) were postulating an everchanging society on the bases of conflict and struggle.

were the bad ones, infected and infecting (unconsciously castrating), to be eschewed if possible. On the other hand, the good women were to be protected, if necessary from their own wishes, by masculine self-restraint. This very restraint, though couched in terms of altruism, served as a poor cover for perverse pregenital aims which might be practiced instead of coitus. If these men were aware of subjective distress, they might express it as sexual unrest or dismay at yielding to masturbation, but not as performance anxiety or incompetence. Their vocabulary of complaint referred to the real world, as though the external world of women and societal rules imposed their lack of fulfillment. Less inhibited men were able, in the context of a relationship with a "good girl," to recognize her sexual interest and work together with her toward the gradual dissolution of barriers without loss of the idealized image of the beloved. The march from double dating through going steady and a long engagement permitted and encouraged this learning process. Similar more or less neurotic interlocking fantasies and behaviors in women could also be observed.

More recently the old mythology is being displaced, in part stimulated by the central role of sexuality in psychoanalytic theory, recurrent world turmoil with accompanying social disruption, and also by medical advances, which include improvements in contraception, infection control, and safety of abortion. The mythology has been replaced by increased understanding of feminine needs and wishes, both sexual and otherwise, greater openness of sexual and affectional expression, changes in sex-role stereotypes, and diminished sexual discrimination. While we are confident that a new equilibrium will provide new culturally syntonic defenses for the neurotic, some of the old structures that sustained us are no longer available. Sexually demanding women are no longer seen as bad, nor are they to be avoided. The refuge that used to be culturally approved is no longer available. Men now are forced to confront their inhibition as a symptom even as women had been forced for years to inhibit their sexuality and not see the inhibition as a symptom. The following cases are illustrative of the difficulties impotent men present in our "new" culture.

Case 1. A nineteen-year-old college student complained that fear of losing his erection had resulted in severe social inhibition with women. Following a period of pleasurable sexuality which included petting, his girl friend had suggested that their sexual practices were immature and that coitus was more appropriate. He ejaculated prematurely and then was impotent. He had formerly been more comfortable in his voyeurism because "the female is never responsible for compliance, for she doesn't even realize I am looking." Masturbation or fellatio was acceptable because "my penis is the center of attention," and he did not feel "used and appreciated as a tool." Coitus was difficult because he saw it as "doing something for her"; he had been potent when he did not feel "compelled to continue [to coitus] by social pressure," when he was reassured that he was cared for, and when he felt loved. He did not, however, find it easy to give love.

Case 2. A man in his mid-thirties was referred for therapy after urologic examination had failed to reveal any organic basis for his impotence. He sought both consultations because his wife threatened divorce: she was unsatisfied by sexual practices limited to foreplay. The patient felt that his problems resulted from lack of experience. Driven to excel in order to impress his powerful and effective father, he had thrown himself into campus politics and then into the family business. He claimed inadequate time to develop a longer or lasting relationship with a "good girl," one that might have led to sexual involvement. Instead he sought out prostitutes whom he saw as dirty and diseased. Justifying his insistence on fellatio rather than coitus, he said that not only did he thus avoid infection [sic] but it was quicker, permitting prompt return to the major pursuits of his life. He finally married in his early thirties because he felt it was expected of him. Until his wife's insistent demand that he perform sexually, he was able to avoid his anxiety at confronting the female genitals and his own castration anxiety.

Case 3. A man in his early twenties entered treatment because of concern about recent impotence. He had met a young woman whom he liked. After the first two dates he felt that she expected him to approach her sexually. When she responded vigorously to his advance, he interrupted with the excuse that her roommate might return. He then felt no longer able to avoid the expected sexual contact and was obliged to invite her to his room. When he attempted coitus he ejaculated immediately after intromission and apologized. A second attempt that same evening ended because he could not sustain an erection.

When the failure was repeated on their fourth date, his partner suggested there was something wrong and berated him for his failure. In addition, she was unable to achieve orgasm when he tried to practice masturbation on her. She claimed this was unusual and tacitly blamed his insufficiencies. Despite his friends' commiserations concerning her impatience, he became increasingly inhibited, depressed, and aware of his retaliatory rage.

A similar failure in a European brothel at age seventeen had not been disturbing; he had been able to rationalize that a friend had chosen the prostitute for him and that she was indifferent and mechanical. The psychological features of his current difficulty were the same: although he had not actively chosen to perform, performance was expected, and he did not feel desired "for himself."

These young men, and others, sought consultation with the complaint of potency difficulty, inability to maintain an erection in the presence of a sexually responsive and, in their eyes, demanding woman. The social transition can be seen with particular clarity in Case 2. Somewhat older than most of our cases, he had for many years been able to postpone awareness of his coital inhibition. His wife, considerably younger and clearly imbued with the awareness of her wishes and their acceptability, made them clear to her husband, which in turn resulted in the decreased effectiveness of his rationalizations as a defense and the development of anxiety. Perhaps in an earlier decade she would have joined him in neurosis by silent acceptance of her frustration, or, if more neurotic, shown gratitude at not having to submit or deny him his marital rights.

Such men are in particularly difficult straits if their partner is not merely responsive or demanding but is also struggling with control of aggression. Women's sense of exploitation often results in retaliatory rage. When this exploitation is generational as well as personal, the group and historical coincidence lends support and justification to the anger. Conscious or unconscious transmission of feminine revenge by an aggressive manner and overassertiveness may enhance a man's castration anxiety with consequent fear of the vagina. The visibility of the difficulty in maintaining erection makes it a social interpersonal embarrassment as well as an internal failure. "Whereas a man's impotence is obvious, a woman's frigidity can be hidden" (Fenichel,

1945, p. 174). Inhibited nonorgastic women can, if they choose, often hide or disguise their lack of response, but men without erect penises cannot feign intromission. This will often compound the failure and compound its psychic consequences as "examination anxiety," and at times precipitate attack by a disappointed partner, thus adding insult to humiliation. On the other hand, a tolerant female partner, sympathetic and understanding, may permit some men to suffer initial failure and overcome it. This was seen in another patient.

Case 4. A 24-year-old single man came for analysis consciously wishing to avoid military service because he was unable to urinate in public toilets. His limited sexual contacts had been marked by impotence or premature ejaculation. His excellent academic performance had deteriorated; he was in danger of not completing his current year of professional school. He lived a monastic existence and only ventured forth from his cluttered, dirty, shade-drawn apartment to go to work.

He was initially impotent with his fiancée and attempted to drive her away by confessing his difficulties. Her sympathetic and understanding response, at variance with the demanding attitude of other women he had known, allowed him to tolerate the failure. His symptom reflected inhibition of tremendous rage due to his fear of retaliation. He partially gratified both the wish and the defense in not giving the woman what she wanted, while protecting himself by refraining. He also pre-empted the expected retaliation by confession. "How better to take your anger out on a woman—it doesn't matter what the cause is—she has to feel there is something wrong with her—fear will do it, anger will do it [impotence]—but, ever since I've been able to love her, sex is fun."

It is clear that these men had significant neurotic conflict antedating their impotence, which was handled by inhibition, rationalization, and projection. The women they met were not responsible for their impotence except as an environmental precipitant. The change in socially expected sexual behavior transmuted inner conflict into a manifest loss of function: what had been hidden became visible and undeniable. For these men the new sexual freedom was not liberating; it only induced different symptoms, a trade-off from within. Whereas they had formerly paraded their sexual prowess in pregenital activity, they now had to perform at a more advanced level and were not prepared to risk the action with so uncertain a partner, a partner who wanted, perhaps without loving or without giving.

Lowenfeld and Lowenfeld (1970) focus on the decrease in control of aggression rather than on sexuality: " . . . sexual freedom has, in accordance with Freud's conception of repression, considerably transformed the manifestations of the neuroses; . . . [it has produced] . . . new neurotic constellations. . . . The task of 'reconciling man to civilization' is not made easier through the liberation of drives'' (p. 607).

These changes in the way neuroses present themselves are not restricted to sexual symptoms or to men. Moulton (1977) recently reviewed the impact of the new feminism on women's symptoms by comparing 50 patients, half of whom were treated between 1953 and 1956, and half between 1973 and 1976. She described four major overlapping syndromes as striking because of their increasing frequency. These are: "(1) reentry anxiety to the point of panic or avoidance when a long-homebound woman returns to work in the outer world, (2) performance anxiety, such as a woman's difficulty asserting herself in public or her fear of success when she does, (3) the 'good girl's' difficulty holding her own or fighting for her rights when faced with hostility, as typified by battles for academic tenure, and (4) conflict between a woman's sense of personal identity and her professional identity, in which marriage is often seen as a threat to autonomy'' (p. 1). Moulton suggests that, although the newly available approved options for women may offer promise of greater happiness in the future, they do not necessarily emerge in the present. Moulton attributes part of the origin of our sex-role stereotypes and their self-perpetuation to the need to devalue "mother" and denial of dependency, to avoid the child's experience of "deep feelings of envy, fear, rage, and shame about their helpless dependency on mother'' (p. 5).

Although the changes described clearly imply greater sexual freedom for women, this freedom may induce greater sexual difficulties for certain women. We have seen a number of women in consultation who present with a variety of nonsexual complaints—problems at home, with the children, at work, with the boss, etc. On inquiry, they describe active gratifying sexual lives. Later we hear of their shame at being anorgastic or not multiply responsive, or, perhaps more commonly, we discover previously denied guilt concerning their sexual involvements. This in turn may result in a secondary loss of orgasmic response. The old freedom to say no has now become the freedom, indeed the demand, to say yes. For those in conflict concerning intercourse, avoidance is less possible and alternative defenses are brought into play: regression, denial, etc. If the reader recognizes in this new array of symptoms a parallel to the new presenting symptoms of men, (s)he is correct: what is so for the gander similarly has affected the goose. Moulton describes "a few 'liberated' women whose extreme pursuit of sexual freedom for its own sake, while lifting many old inhibitions, had . . . [led to their being] . . . depressed and dissatisfied when they entered treatment. Some realized that they had been punishing men; others had dreaded commitment and marriage; still others had been trying to prove their sexual prowess" (1977, p. 5).

Clearly, for some and, it is to be hoped, soon for many, the new feminism and the change in sexual mores brings greater individual fulfillment. Rapid cultural change, however, disturbs the previous equilibrium, disrupts the use of previously culturally syntonic defenses and attributions. It is clear that social learning affects the ways people define their complaints as well as the ways they seek care (Mechanic, 1972). The social acceptability of certain types of complaint may determine the nature and site of reference for the verbalized complaint. It may be that just as denial of impotence by avoidance is now more difficult, declaration of impotence as a means of seeking help may be culturally more available. Certainly, verbalization of sexual difficulties in the consultation room seems easier now than it used to be. Thus, our perception of an increase in the frequency of impotence, if true, may result from a number of forces, intrapsychic and social, impinging on a single final common pathway.

Anthony Burgess recently wrote (1976), "In 1960, I published a novel that had the sentence: 'He looked him up and down from his niggerbrown shoes to his spinsterishly tightset lips and then said quietly: '—— off.' In the new edition of 1975, the shoes and the lips are more generally and less offensively characterized, and the dirty word is set out in full. One semantic area has been freed from taboo; two others have been freshly enslaved by it. There is a lesson here: Human history does not depict the progressive throwing off of chains, merely the exchange of one set of chains for another, or two others.'' Social change appears to do no better than semantic change. While symptoms may vary, conflict and conflict resolution remain, one misery exchanged for another. This is so, intraindividual as well as between individual and society or between one social order and another. Our experience suggests that change is not simply progressive, but dynamic, causing shifts in equilibrium that eventuate in changing adaptations. Some of these may not be purely beneficial or at least not beneficial to all.

In closing it should be noted that social change has affected many other areas of our lives. Lifton (1971) has described the development of a new personality style particularly suited to such turbulent times. His "Protean Man" is characterized by effortless, rapid, and radical shifts in life styles, identifications, and belief systems. How jarring such a view of man is to the wishes we used to have for steady, stable paternal caretakers. For less flexible characters, the loss of external structure and ritual may prove difficult (Gushin et al., 1978; Whisnant and Zegans, 1975). Presumably, a new equilibrium will provide new forms to guide behavior into styles that will be both ego- and culturally syntonic.

CHAPTER 16

Sexual Deviance, Psychoanalysis, and Society

EDWARD M. LEVINE

The proliferation of commentary, contentions, and controversy centering on the subject of sexual deviance over the past decade, focusing primarily on homosexuality, has created a great deal of confusion in the minds of many adults and youth, most of all the latter. Inasmuch as young people are probably inclined to be more receptive to the views of those in or near their age group, they are inclined to doubt the more traditional views of their parents and other adults about whether deviant sexual behavior is normal or abnormal.

At any rate, the traditions which have so unequivocally defined homosexuality as a deplorable and unacceptable form of sexual behavior have so weakened or vanished as to be lost to youth as signposts in their efforts to determine what is proper, healthy sexual behavior. On the other hand, youth are sufficiently sophisticated to realize that traditions are not necessarily based on reason, but are more often a reflection of the ways of the past, a past with which they have little connection and which has ever-less meaning for them. Small wonder, then, that they are so uncertain about knowing what to believe about sexual deviance, or that they, as well as numbers of adults, are inclined

I wish to express my appreciation to the *American Journal of Psychiatry* for permitting me to include portions of articles it has published: "Male Transsexuals in the Homosexual Subculture," (1976), v. 133, and "Sexual Dysfunctions and Psychoanalysis," (1977), v. 134, co-author, Nathaniel Ross, M.D.

to accept the assertions of those who claim that it is a natural form of
sexual behavior.

On the other hand, it is easy for well-trained, thoughtful professionals to deplore how popularized misconceptions and misrepresen-
tations of sexual deviance have so quickly gained widespread
acceptance among the public. The more optimistic among them tend
to assume that if life has gone slightly awry, it is no more than a
disconcerting phase in the cycle of history, which will sooner or later
be replaced by a positive one. That is, people will gradually regain
their senses, the age of sensationalism will play out its energies, and
society will recapture its bearings. In this not-too-distant future, sexual
deviants will probably be treated with more humanity, but their numbers will have diminished, their voice will have lost its influence, and
their sexual behavior will again be regarded as deviant. For reasons
that follow, such developments are not at all likely to occur.

My purpose here is to discuss the principal factors which have
been responsible for the transformation in recent years of the social
standards and attitudes concerned with sexual deviance, especially
with homosexuality. This will entail examining the humanist ideology,
whose fundamental value is the dignity of the individual, and how
humanism has been misconstrued and improperly modified by those
attempting to legitimatize sexual deviance; the social science relativization of the social norms determining sexually deviant behavior; the
role of the mass media of communications; and the animated controversy in which psychoanalysis find itself increasingly on the defensive
as nonprofessionals' opinions have gained dominance (though not scientific validity) among the public—with the result that sexual deviance
is considered less a form of psychopathology, and its forms are regarded as natural and legitimate sexual expressions.

Humanism's Legitimatization of Sexual Deviance: An Ideological Misconstruction

The striking changes in the moral standards judging sexual behavior which have occurred in recent years are largely responsible for the
public's having become immensely more familiar with and accepting

of sexual deviants and the views they advance about their sexual preferences. While it is not possible to examine here all the important factors involved in this transformation of standards, the one which is probably the most important, and which appears to have affected all the others, is the modification of the humanist[1] ideology, which fundamentally opposes any infringement on individual dignity.

The basic importance of this ethical standard is evidenced in its serving as the foundation of our Constitution. Without it, it is unimaginable that the host of reform movements and social welfare legislation which have become the signposts of political progress would have been undertaken. It also served as the moral bulwark for the abolitionists' struggle to end slavery, and the Civil Rights Movement has been and remains the central moral standard in the struggle to win equal rights for women, and is the very basis of free speech and justice in democratic societies.

In the present context, this social standard has been drawn on to oppose the discriminatory attitudes and practices as well as the harsh social stigma which sexual deviants almost universally experienced until recently. Expressed positively, the moral dictates of humanism vigorously and completely support their right and wish to be judged and dealt with on the basis of their abilities, rather than in terms of their deviant sexual behavior. However, the humanist ideology is now frequently used improperly (however compassionate and genuine the intent) to legitimatize sexual deviance as behavior which is as proper, acceptable, normal, and natural as heterosexuality.

In past generations, the humanist perspective was much more limited in influence and scope, for it shared the moral terrain with a variety of religious, cultural, and class traditions, norms, and values. The influence of the latter over sexual behavior and attitudes used to be dominant and seldom openly challenged, but has declined substan-

---

[1] The word "humanist" can be misleading in that more than a few professionals, including Albert Ellis, and laymen openly advocate sexual behavior that is essentially dehumanizing —dissociating, as it does, sex from love, from the fundamental individuality of the partners. And there are those who take this to its extreme in advocating (not merely stating) that love between children and parents, between spouses and their close friends, legitimately involves sexual behavior which, it is claimed, is the completion of the expression of their love for each other.

tially since the 1960's. A major reason for this has been the gradual but steady erosion of cohesive cultural communities and their traditional secular and religious values. Intermarriage, assimilation, advanced education, the prevalence of the nuclear family, and social, geographic, and occupational mobility have resulted in their attrition (Bettelheim, 1962; Gans, 1962; Gordon, 1964; Levine and Shaiova, 1971; Parsons, 1964; Riesman et al., 1950). The decline of these values and traditions resulted in the growing dominance of the humanist ideology.

The modifications of humanism occurred as a result of two important developments in contemporary thought. The first has been a marked change in the meaning of one of its fundamental tenets—respect for the rights of others to their opinions. In general, this standard has meant that in such matters as preferences, tastes, and life style, one outlook is as valid as another. In recent years, however, this meaning has been modified by growing numbers of individuals who conclude that knowledge, particularly that bearing on social behavior, is essentially opinion, and is no more convincingly grounded in evidence than opinion, which, as DeTocqueville noted, is based on the daily, practical experience of individuals, and not on deliberation. The humanist ideology has thus taken on a relativistic emphasis, with questionable consequences ensuing with regard to the public's understanding of homosexuality. That is, by focusing on the fundamental rights of homosexuals (and other sexual deviants) to social acceptance as sexual *deviants*, their sexual deviance itself tends to become legitimatized.

Indeed, it is difficult to see how this change in perspective could have been averted, for relieving homosexuals from the social stigma attached to homosexuality is not really possible so long as their sexual behavior—which is their primary social identity—is considered deviant. Therefore, to insist that they are merely different from heterosexuals and should therefore be regarded as acceptable as they are is the logical culmination of this view. And many who share the humanist concern about human rights because of their conviction in its moral correctness have accepted this redefinition of homosexuality. This view, of course, lies at the core of the voluminous publications and public statements by homosexuals in their continuing and vigorous efforts to eliminate the various kinds of discrimination and prejudice they experience, and particularly in their attempts to gain public acceptance of their deviant sexuality.

Social Science Interpretations of Sexual Deviance

Another major reason for the growing public acceptance of homosexuality and other forms of sexual deviance is found in the influence of the social sciences (particularly sociology and anthropology), which have properly used a value-free and relativistic approach for the purpose of identifying and objectively attempting to understand differences in human values and behavior.

Unlike psychoanalysis, however, these disciplines do not have standards or concepts identifying and defining emotional disturbances and their causes. Nevertheless, studies of primitive societies have been drawn on to indicate the functional roles which emotionally disturbed individuals have performed in them (Malinowski, 1927; Mead, 1935). The inferences or conclusions of such studies are that, by having socially valued roles to perform, such individuals were much less stigmatized or were altogether unburdened by their being deviant sexually (or otherwise). Later, as sociologists began to investigate problems of mental health, the emphasis turned to epidemiological studies in urban areas and the sociological variables significantly associated with emotional disturbances (Clark, 1969; Hare and Shaw, 1965; Hollingshead and Redlich, 1958; Phillips and Segal, 1969; Schur, 1965). Sociological researchers also studied mental institutions, focusing on the lack of proper care or the ways in which formal and informal institutional requirements and social norms have exacerbated the problems of institutionalized patients (Fletcher, 1969; Goffman, 1959, 1961; Gove, 1970).

In recent years, a new sociological approach emerged when a number of sociologists turned to the study of sexual deviants (primarily homosexuals) chiefly to examine their problems and life styles. Underlying this body of research are exclusively sociological interpretations of the etiology of homosexuality, which have not only been extremely influential in changing the views of students, but which also have had special significance for parenting and, thus, for the gender and ego development of children. These investigators contend that, first, the cause of homosexuality is the individual's *learning* this sex role from others (Gagnon and Simon, 1969, 1973; Henderson, 1975), or that the individual's need to acquire the support and good will of significant others who are sexual deviants results in their becoming sexually deviant (role acquisition). Homosexuality (and other forms of sexual deviance) are therefore the outcome of purely voluntary choice or of associations taken on because of what are said (but never shown) to be appreciable dependency needs.

In these terms, it is difficult to regard sexual deviance of any kind as psychopathologic or as aberrant sexual behavior. Instead, it is viewed as a sexual posture related to experiences and psychosocial needs. Consequently, homosexuality cannot be in any way related to the psychodynamics of parent-child relationships during any phase of the process of ego formation, including one so basic as the oedipal. It is noteworthy, however, that the advocates of these views characteristically fail to indicate why only *some* persons "learn" to become homosexuals, or why only *some* individuals have such vulnerable dependency needs so that they choose to socialize with sexual deviants, a relationship which somehow results in their becoming sexually deviant. Nor, for that matter, do they account for the existence of the first sexual deviant. It need only be noted that none of the components or the psychodynamics of the learning process are either identified or discussed by those who advance these views.[2]

Still another approach in recent sociological investigations of sexual deviance dwells largely on the various adversities which burden the lives of homosexuals (Reiss, 1964; Schur, 1965). By concentrating on the numerous problems with which homosexuals must cope, it is evident that objective inquiry has been conscientiously (if unconsciously) guided by the ideology of humanism. In stressing the plight of sexual deviants, however, such studies have then tended to depict homosexuality (and, increasingly, other forms of sexual deviance) as

---

[2]In his examination of certain fundamental studies of an often underemphasized aspect of parenting, Ross (1975) notes the way in which the male child's strong, early identifications with the mother's childbearing and nurturing functions are gradually transformed, for the most part, not into homosexuality, but into his effective functioning as a father. (See also chap. 6, this volume.) The various disturbances occurring in the early stages of gender development which result in distortions of gender identity have been thoroughly discussed by Socarides (1968a), Bieber et al. (1962), and others.

sexual behavior that is merely and unfairly socially criticized and condemned—that is, as personally proper but socially judged as improper. Thus, the only problem such persons have is that they are "victimized" by society. A companion argument frequently made is that sexual behavior is relative to the culture;[3] inasmuch as certain kinds of sexual deviance have not been condemned in some cultures (e.g., the Athens of Plato), condemning it or understanding it as psychopathologic in ours is then judged to be inaccurate or biased.

Some women, perhaps mainly professionals, have created a special variation of the homosexuals' and the sociologists' "victimization" theory of homosexuality by identifying men as the underlying cause of female homosexuality. According to a report in the *Chicago Sun-Times* of June 22, 1975, Sec. 2, pp. 1-2, Marilyn Grossman, a psychologist, has said that when women stop judging themselves as they believe men do, begin to make their decisions independently, and realize that their emotional involvement is in activities with women, the next logical step is to engage in homosexual activity. Pauline Bart, a sociologist, stated that the experiences and increased self-awareness of some women in the women's movement make it more difficult for them to have relationships with men. The result is that women become more important to these women, which is the reason for their becoming homosexuals. Jane Lever, also a sociologist, remarked that some women become homosexuals due to their commitment to other women because of their antipathy to men, while others are forced to become homosexuals since they are accused of being less than committed to the women's movement because they are sleeping with men.

These assertions raise the question why only very few women become homosexuals for the reasons alleged. None of these approaches to the study of homosexual behavior deals with the question whether it is sexually deviant or psychopathologic. They fail to take into account vicissitudes of ego development, virtually never referring to the voluminous literature on the subject from Freud to the present. Nor do they mention the role of repressed emotional conflicts or the unconscious.

In an age when genuine concern for those in want and those subjected to discrimination because of religion, color, sex, or cultural

[3]In an excellent article synthesizing the extending research in biology, physiology, ethology, and psychoanalysis, Gadpaille (1972) has shown the relativist position to be without validity.

background is so evidently among the highest priorities of youth with advanced education, it is not surprising that many young people have also become much more tolerant and accepting of sexual deviance upon learning how widely homosexuals have encountered discrimination and prejudice. Indeed, there are surprisingly large numbers of undergraduate students who believe that bisexual behavior is essentially an expression of curiosity or adventurousness, a trend of the times, and is not really sexually deviant. Furthermore, there is a growing tendency stemming from the relativistic perspective that prompts students to equate knowledge with opinion; those who do read well-substantiated research and thoughtfully reasoned, if at times tentative conclusions dealing with the etiology of sexual deviance (e.g., Gadpaille, 1972; Money, 1965; Socarides, 1968a; Stoller, 1968b, 1975b) regard this literature not as evidence, but only as opinions.

The Impact of the Media

With the proliferation of problems during the past decade, the media of mass communication have drawn more and more frequently on the novel and sensational developments of the times in their competition for audience attention. The popularity of sociology during the 1960's, as well as the Civil Rights Movement, established a precedent for giving concentrated and extensive coverage to individual rights. Television and radio panel shows have increasingly been candidly and unperturbedly airing virtually all aspects of homosexual attitudes, values, and behavior, with homosexuals (and, more recently, transsexuals) frequently being the only panelists.[4] Not unexpectedly, they speak with the purpose of informing the public about the sanctions and inhibitions with which they have had to live in order to escape detection and discrimination.

Having described their plight, however, they then proceed to ad-

----

[4]Responses from major television stations in Chicago to requests for information concerning the number of local and national shows featuring sexual deviance as a subject, the number of sexual deviants who participated, and the number of individuals who questioned the advocacy of "normality" of sexual deviance were essentially rationalizations for presenting programs of this kind. Specific requests to one local and one national television program for "equal representation" resulted in no answer from the former, a form reply from the latter.

vocate homosexuality—that is, to argue that it is justified as another, entirely natural, and unquestionably legitimate sexual expression. The extremes to which they carry their views are illustrated by the growing, adamant advocacy of homosexual foster-parenting for teenage male homosexuals without parents, and of the equally insistent contention that it is as proper for lesbians to adopt children as it is for heterosexual married couples. It is noteworthy that with only extremely rare exceptions do such television panel discussions include a heterosexual layman or professional, with the result that there is almost never any thoughtful, extended questioning of the homosexual point of view.[5] Nor, of course, are there panels featuring heterosexuals discussing why heterosexuality is the norm.

Some psychotherapists have expressed serious concern about this trend. They strongly believe that middle-class male adolescents who do not have heterosexual males as a general presence in their lives with whom they can identify as emotionally positive figures can become extremely confused by the continuing statements in the media that homosexuality is merely an alternative to heterosexuality, and that it does not involve emotional disturbances.

Also instrumental in bringing sexual deviance to the forefront of public attention and keeping it there are journalists, newspaper columnists, feature writers, and social scientists. Many have written about the difficulties troubling sexual deviants, thus helping to establish them as a proper subject of public interest. These individuals have added their influence to the humanist-relativist perspective by stressing the need to free homosexuals from social stigma and prejudice. Yet, as with the other media, they have not dealt with its causes or sought to determine whether or not homosexuality is deviant sexual behavior.

Last but not least are the pornographic films and magazines, which exploit sexual deviance by presenting it as desirable.

It is not possible, of course, to provide irrefutable statistical evidence demonstrating a clear and appreciable causal relationship between the influence of the modified humanist ideology, the social

[5]The claim that any form of sexual deviance is a freely chosen "life style" stands in contradiction to the extensively documented findings of psychoanalysis, which show that the most decisive psychic processes operate at an unconscious level. Consequently, this contention constitutes a direct attack upon the scientific validity of psychoanalytic studies.

sciences, and the mass media of communications, and a substantial increase in the public's acceptance and tolerance of sexual deviants and their behavior. Carefully designed, administered, and interpreted national surveys of this kind remain to be undertaken.

A Different View of Male Transsexuals

Attesting to the fact that the previously unimaginable is currently commonplace is that transsexuals have become widely known to the public in only the past two or three years. As with homosexuals, they have gained recognition chiefly due to the efforts of the media of mass communications to feature them for their novelty value. Thus, although their numbers are substantially less than those of homosexuals, transvestites, and bisexuals, their newfound recognition and prominence as sexual deviants calls for some discussion, as does the equally surprising suddenness with which numbers of people have come to regard them as people who *are* women (or men).

The transsexuals to be discussed here differ in certain very important ways from the vast majority of those discussed in the psychoanalytic literature. The latter outwardly live normal lives, unknown as transsexuals to their associates at work or to their acquaintances where they reside. Moreover, they completely avoid all contact with other sexual deviants. The public's awareness of them has been limited to an occasional sensational piece of news played up by news telecasts or the newspapers, such as the Christine Jorgenson case or that involving Renée Richards.

I have recently conducted interviews (Levine et al., 1975, 1976) that indicate that growing numbers of male transsexuals live in the homosexual subculture. And, contrary to the images they present on television and in the newspapers, there is evidence which unequivocally refutes the contentions that transsexualism is pleasant, acceptable, or desirable— or that, save for the public's prejudices, transsexuals would lead personally gratifying lives.

The transsexuals I interviewed had passed through a homosexual phase prior to their becoming full-time, cross-dressed transsexuals. Because of this, it may be correct to identity them as "secondary" transsexuals, which Person and Ovesey (1974b) consider more accurate—individuals who have a less than complete transsexual identity.

What is also generally unknown about transsexuals living in the homosexual subculture is that certain aspects of their relationships with homosexuals and bisexuals are extremely demeaning. Those discussed here, for example, originally thought they "must" be homosexuals because they found heterosexual male roles and feelings to be increasingly uncomfortable, and because they were unfamiliar with transsexualism. In their late teens they were befriended by homosexuals who introduced them to the homosexual subculture. But the personal relations between them became strained as their transsexual identity crystallized and was more deeply sensed. Consequently, the transsexuals withdrew from homosexuals who rejected and derided them for being "women," although their animosity also stemmed from their being in competition with the transsexuals for bisexuals as sexual partners.

It is common for such transsexuals to have bisexual boyfriends or lovers out of the need for companionship, to share living expenses, and for sexual gratification (more eagerly sought by the bisexuals). Furthermore, bisexuals provide transsexuals with the façade of femaleness, for the latter are inclined to claim during the early phase of these relationships that their lovers are heterosexual males—who alone, they contend, can confirm their claim to be women.

In their living arrangements, however, the bisexuals dominated them, obliging the transsexuals to attend to all household tasks. Some openly indulged themselves in sexual activities with women and homosexuals, and further humiliated the transsexuals by inducing them to turn to prostitution (to which all had resorted independently when living alone) in order to supplement their incomes. While these relationships were not long-lived, they held together largely because of the transsexuals' exceptional dependency needs.

Further intensifying the unpleasantness of the lives of transsexuals living in the homosexual subculture is that their social life is sparse and limited. They seldom socialize with other transsexuals except at bars and female-impersonator and homosexual strip-tease lounges. Their self-chosen isolation from each other appears to be attributable to their deep sense of emotional insecurity, which was revealed in their depreciating remarks during interviews about other transsexuals. All gratuitously expressed strong reservations about the authenticity of the others' transsexuality, adding cutting remarks about their lack of femininity (Levine et al., 1975).

If such individuals have a less stable self-system, as seems likely (Levine et al., 1976), they will probably be denied authorization for sex-change surgery, and will forever be destined to live in a psychosocial limbo as anatomical males with female gender identities. Needless to say, this tragic aspect of their lives goes unmentioned in newspaper and magazine articles and during panel-show discussions.

Much more could be added about the troubles and bleakness which envelop so great a part of the lives of transsexuals, as well as about the emotional turmoil which also denies them any real happiness, but these and other related matters are beyond the scope of this discussion. However, it is pertinent to note that the assertions and public presentations that depict transsexuality as merely another form of sexual behavior do so without awareness of the realities discussed above. To talk with them at their apartments and chat with them at bars is to know their great frustrations, distress, and unhappiness. And this awareness is more than reason enough to suggest that it is timelier than ever to stress the prevention of the development of this form of sexual deviance, all the more so for those, perhaps the great majority, who will not seek or who will be denied sex-reconstruction surgery.

The Implications of Changing Attitudes Toward
Sexual Deviance for Psychoanalysis

The trend to attempt to legitimatize sexual deviance by humanistically regarding all its forms as acceptable and the weakening, discarding, and relativizing of sexual standards, have created a problem of fundamental importance for psychoanalysis. The assertion that sexual deviance is not psychopathologic directly and adamantly opposes and claims to have invalidated a central part of the theoretical foundation of psychoanalysis. That is, the contributions of scholars from Freud to the present who have demonstrated the paramount role of the libidinal drive in the various stages of ego development, and of its constant interplay in the establishment of emotional well-being, are being vigorously challenged and summarily rejected by sexual deviants and substantially increasing numbers of youth and young adults. Should these unfounded contentions come to prevail, all those who are concerned with the emotional health of growing children—of which heterosexuality is a basic expression—will find the values underlying their efforts to facilitate the sound emotional development of their children persistently undermined. As a result of gradually losing societal support for these values, the signs that would indicate to parents that their youngsters are incipient homosexuals may very well come to be only faintly perceived or viewed with indifference by adults who consider homosexuality as "valid" an outcome as heterosexuality.

Thus, if parents come to consider it unimportant or normal for a child to grow up to become a homosexual (transvestite, bisexual, or transsexual), they need not be concerned about this, let alone consider having their child enter treatment. And when the symptoms are evident as early as the phallic stage, the opportunity for them to resolve this developing sexual conflict, when such children are more amenable to treatment, would be lost. Furthermore, appropriate attentiveness to effective parenting before and during the oedipal stage as well as during later stages of development may be lacking if heterosexuality is no longer regarded as a basic cultural value. Then, too, with both parents and children increasingly confused or in disagreement about the normality of heterosexuality and the fundamental importance of gender differentiation for sound emotional development—or unconcerned about it, as some are—sexually deviant youth will very likely become more numerous in the years ahead.

This challenge to psychoanalysis stems from yet another source, the powerful belief that popular views are correct and are therefore the proper standards by which to judge the pressing social issues of the day. While the influences of the majority have clearly contributed to vastly improved conditions of life for countless people, they have also elevated public opinion to a position which frequently enables it and those who misuse the humanist ideology to gain a position of primacy for their moral judgments (Kristol, 1974).

The threat that this problem presents to psychoanalytic knowledge and, more generally, to human well-being occurs in yet other ways.

One of these is that psychotherapists with commanding professional qualifications, as well as others with less persuasive credentials, have added their voices on behalf of those who argue that homosexuality is not abnormal. Not only has the vote of 56 percent of the members of the American Psychiatric Association resulted in its officially adopting a position to remove homosexuality from the category of emotional disorders (thereby providing the proponents of this view with substantial support for their contentions), but there are equally disturbing signs elsewhere.

The APA position apparently emboldened numbers of its homosexual members sufficiently to hold a caucus at the organization's annual conference in 1976, partly to bolster the feelings of those wanting to be able to present themselves openly as homosexuals. The caucus was publicized with placards in the convention hall and drew an audience of nearly a hundred. The major purpose was to establish and legitimatize the claim that homosexual psychiatrists were no different from heterosexual psychiatrists except for their sexual behavior, which was just as acceptable as that of the latter.[6] The success of their aspirations to form committees to undertake the tasks involved was not determined at this session.

At the conference, homosexual organizations had a booth in the same general area as book publishers where they distributed literature and spoke with individuals who sought information, attempting to proselytize when the occasion arose. Thus, they took full advantage of the APA policy statement on homosexuality.

Other indications of the trend to attempt to convince the public that homosexual behavior is normal are found among psychologists. One clinical psychologist with a private practice who conducts encounters for all-male groups has written an article stating that homosexual activity in the course of such group encounters would occur

---

[6]In order to determine how inclusive the claim of normality for sexual deviance was among homosexual psychiatrists, I asked several of those who attended the caucus whether they thought a transsexual who had the requisite training would be qualified to practice psychiatry. Except for two of them, they were hesitant and uncomfortable with the question and did not really offer an answer. However, one rather quickly and awkwardly said he thought they were qualified. The other said, "If he has enough peace with himself, if his ego is intact, why shouldn't he?" Those knowledgeable about the psychic structure of transsexuals realize how weak and distorted their psychic structures are, and how preposterous a response this is for a psychiatrist.

spontaneously were it not for the inhibiting effects of cultural norms (Clark, 1972). This alone scarcely attests to a widely shared belief in this view among such practitioners, but indications are that growing numbers of psychologists believe that homosexuality and other forms of deviant sexuality are merely different from heterosexuality, not perversions of it.

It should be added that many of those conducting various kinds of encounter groups assert that homosexuality (and any other form of sexual deviance) is a problem *only* if the homosexual says it is a problem. The shortcoming of this assertion is that it assumes that the individual knows what an emotional conflict is, how it interferes with his behavior, and whether or not he or she is so encumbered. A variation of this view is used occasionally by homosexuals attempting to prove that their sexual behavior is as normal as that of heterosexuals. They state that they do not have emotional problems, but that numbers of heterosexuals obviously do have such problems, so that homosexuality is therefore not psychopathologic.

Most of what has been said to this point has a direct bearing on the ways in which sexual deviants are likely to perceive and define their sexuality, as well as on certain fundamental aspects of psychoanalytic knowledge concerning the dynamics of ego development and ego states. For example, if homosexuality (or any other form of deviant sexuality) comes to be generally understood and regarded by homosexuals as genuinely natural sexual behavior, if this outlook becomes the dominant one for them which they then use to affirm the self-imputed legitimacy of their sexual preference and behavior, then they will experience their homosexuality more easily as ego-syntonic. That is, having less reason to consider the nature and appropriateness of their sexuality, let alone to question it, homosexuals will consider their sexuality consonant with the rest of their character structure. And those who find that their homosexuality is ego-dystonic because of intrapsychic tensions which disturb them (as does and will occur), the likelihood is that they will then view their sexuality as ego-dystonic in a special way. That is, they will be apt to sense their sexual problems as those of maladjustment vis-à-vis those whose homosexuality is ego-syntonic, and not in relationship to heterosexuality. Thus, they would be prone to consider themselves as parallel to heterosexuals with sexual problems who compare themselves to sexually functioning heterosexuals. As a result, ego-dystonicity may lose its meaning and relevance for them.

While this may seem to be an academic point, it is well to remember that (as many analysts who treat or who have treated homosexuals can verify) there are presently numbers of homosexuals who feel that their sexuality is ego-syntonic. For them, treatment for their sexuality is virtually impossible; and some respond to the recommendation that they seek treatment as a grossly insensitive suggestion. That they have become some of the most vocal and strident critics of psychoanalysis is largely the result of their changing conception of their sexuality.

Another aspect of this problem is that psychoanalytic knowledge, like the basic knowledge in other scientific disciplines, does not—and can not—receive its validation from majority *views* or *opinions*. Nor is its knowledge limited (relative) to specific historical or cultural settings. Yet, because psychoanalytic knowledge is complex and deals with phenomena not readily understood by those not well acquainted with its literature, it can not be easily conveyed to the public or readily understood by it. This is particularly the case for the enormous numbers of people reached by the mass media, which must necessarily simplify highly technical and complex information so as to avoid losing the attention of mass audiences. Understandably, therefore, they abbreviate, modify, and fragment—and thereby distort—the meaning of such knowledge. Consequently, the little reliable information they do present about sexual deviance can scarcely be considered to be adequately detailed, logically developed, or concentrating upon the fundamentals of a subject which is so relentlessly and heatedly disputed by sexual deviants and the growing numbers of those who have come to share their views.

Insofar as all signs indicate that public opinion will continue to doubt, dismiss, and oppose the centrality of the libidinal drives in attaining emotional well-being, and deny that its being thwarted is a major cause of emotional disturbances, there is a very real likelihood that psychoanalysis will exist as an ever-weakening intellectual oasis in the midst of powerful currents of social change. These are disturbing signs for the profession and the public. Indeed, such developments have already begun to jeopardize its public status and its prospects for contributing its knowledge for the purpose of furthering human well-being. In view of the popularization and relativization of sexual deviance, including its broadening base of influence within the homosexual subculture, perhaps a key question to ask at this time is whether the psychoanalytic profession will decide to devote the time, attention, and activity necessary to counteract these trends. Perhaps, in other words, it is now necessary for the analyst to become the activist.

CHAPTER 17

Overview of New Sex Therapies

TOKSOZ B. KARASU,
MAJ-BRITT ROSENBAUM,
and INEZ JERRETT

The treatment of sexual dysfunction has undergone a radical change in attitude, clinical approach and practice over the past decade. Until recently, prevailing psychiatric opinion, influenced by psychoanalytic theory, viewed a sexual dysfunction as an expression of deepseated psychological conflict, rooted in the vicissitudes of aggressive and sexual drive development.

When Masters and Johnson (1970) published *Human Sexual Inadequacy*, which describes their direct, directive, time-limited, and symptom-oriented approach to the treatment of sexual dysfunctions, they set into motion a landslide of new treatment modalities for sexual difficulties. Masters and Johnson are regarded as *the* innovators of "sex therapy." It is important to note, however, that "sex therapy" did not begin with them. Rather, they built on, and borrowed freely from the work and tradition of a long series of thinkers and professionals, who, in various ways, attempted to deal with sexual problems. We may even include in their ranks the Roman poet, Ovid, who, 2,000 years ago, presented his suggestion for "sensate focus":

> . . . nor will the left hand lie idle on the bed. Their fingers will find what to do in those parts where love plies his weapons unperceived. . . Believe me, love's bliss must not be hastened, but gradually lured on by slow delay. When you have found the place where a woman loves to be touched, let not shame prevent you from touching it. You will see her eyes shooting tremulous gleams, as the sun often glitters in clear water [*Art of Love*].

And many hundred years later, in the mid-18th century, a British physician, Sir John Hunter (cited in Comfort, 1965), described a treatment for impotence that is almost identical with the Masters and Johnson approach. Masters and Johnson also built on previously reported behavioral procedures (Wolpe, 1958; Lazarus, 1963; Brady, 1966; Tyler, 1975) as well as on specific treatment approaches such as urologist Semans' (1956) ''squeeze technique'' for the relief of premature ejaculation. We can even note that one of Masters and Johnson's basic premises—that the marital relationship is the patient—is none other than the basic premise evolved over the years by family therapists and conjoint marital therapists. The references (e.g., to Ackerman, Haley, Hoffman, etc.) do appear in the bibliography of *Human Sexual Inadequacy*, but are not clearly cited by the authors. The borrowing from other sources is not evident to the general reader, despite the extensive bibliography: ''No attempt has been made to cite these references in the text . . . such citing would have been a herculean task with minimal return, other than an impressive maze of essentially valueless numbers strewn throughout the text'' (Masters and Johnson, 1970, p. 393).

As Rittenberg and Wyman (1977) point out, ''the authors have begged off from a fundamental requirement of scientific scholarship, which is to clarify, through documented references, the relationship between present and previous work.''

Masters and Johnson's contribution lies in their particular integration of various treatment approaches with some of their own findings from their extensive physiological research into the human sexual response. They may be credited with ''packaging'' the treatment into one practical format. Especially important is the fact that they systematically applied this treatment format to a large number of patients and assessed the effectiveness of their approach with an extensive follow-up program. They should also be given credit for publicizing their approach and being trail blazers by providing a more practical, educative view of a common human problem. In their wake has followed a multitude of slightly different approaches, some of which tend to emphasize various aspects of the original protocol—others that have developed further along sidelines or tangents, and still others that have used one or more components of Masters and Johnson's model, integrating them with other approaches.

Masters and Johnson Program

In order to best discuss the role of the new sex therapies, which are increasingly claiming their place as one of the psychotherapies, let us begin by discussing some of the common denominators—some of the main tenets of Masters and Johnson's treatment program. When Masters and Johnson had completed the first part of their research program related to human sexuality, namely, the studies of the physiology of human sexual response (1966), they embarked on the second aspect of their research, which was to take eleven years, a controlled clinical study with the aim of developing a rapid treatment of human sexual dysfunction, which is described in detail in their book (1970).

According to Masters and Johnson, the critical components are as follows:

1. A sexual dysfunction in a marital unit is the responsibility of both partners. The logical corollary is that both spouses have to be seen in therapy; perhaps even more correctly, both partners have to voluntarily take part in, as well as take equal responsibility for, both the problem and the therapy. In a sense, the relationship is the patient.

2. Sexual problems are not always the result of deep-seated neurotic conflicts. They are also the products of faulty experiential learning, as well as social and parental attitudes. Masters and Johnson never tire of stating that "sex is a natural function," implying that it is not only necessary, but impossible to "teach" a man to have an erection or a woman to lubricate. The sexual responses, however, unlike other physiological processes (breathing, for example) can be delayed and inhibited even for a lifetime. Therapy, which is heavily laden with education and information, is only aimed at progressively removing the psychosocial roadblocks that impede the normal, natural expression of this bodily function.

In addition to providing education, information, support, and reassurance, Masters and Johnson focus on some of the more "superficial causes" for sexual anxiety that hinder normal sexual expression —e.g., performance anxiety, fear of failure, and excessive need to please the partner.

3. Sexual interaction depends on the capacity to communicate in ways other than directly sexual. There is thus a heavy emphasis in the treatment program on enhancing the communication between the part-

ners—utilizing educational and directive modes of implementing it.

4. The dual sex-therapy team is one of the integral aspects of the Masters and Johnson approach. They feel that there are specific advantages inherent in using both a male and a female therapist in the treatment of a couple. The main purpose is to provide full and fair clinical representation for both the man and the woman, based on the assumption that no man or woman will ever fully understand the other gender's sexual function or dysfunction. Also, each patient is supplied with his or her "friend in court" and with the same-sex therapist with whom to identify.

5. The basic treatment approach is a directive and behaviorally oriented one. A key ingredient is the assignment of progressive tasks, behavioral prescriptions that are carried out by the patients in private and that are fully debriefed and discussed with the therapists before proceeding to the next one.

The main dysfunctions that Masters and Johnson treat are: premature ejaculation, ejaculatory incompetence, and primary and secondary impotence in the man; primary and secondary orgasmic dysfunctions, vaginismus, and painful intercourse in the female. In addition to the general behavioral tasks used by all patients, specific experiential techniques were developed for dealing with each of the dysfunctions. For instance, for the treatment of premature ejaculation, the "squeeze technique" is used (Semans, 1956); for vaginismus, dilators of gradually increasing size are employed.

The Master and Johnson treatment program, used at the Reproductive Biology Research Foundation in St. Louis, consists of a two-week phase of rapid education and treatment aimed at symptom reversal plus a five-year follow-up period. All couples in the acute phase of the treatment program are seen daily. Since 90 percent of the units treated by Masters and Johnson live outside the St. Louis area, the daily treatment plan requires a two-week "vacation" for most couples. This imposed isolation from everyday demands is advantageous in that it provides the opportunity for a rekindling of communication between the marital partners without external intrusions. Another advantage of the daily conference is that it allows for immediate discussion of sexual events and feelings instead of permitting mistakes to go uncorrected or fears to escalate.

The therapy typically starts with a detailed history for each individual separately, taken first by the same-sex therapist and then by the opposite-sex therapist. The purpose of the history is to establish communication and to elicit the attitudes, expectations, and experiences of the patients in order to understand their sexual value systems. In addition, each patient receives a specific medical examination in the presence of the spouse and both members of the therapy team. This serves to educate the unit and remove the "cloak of mystery" and misinformation around the sex organs. The therapists attempt to clarify misconceptions, encourage questioning, and promote an acceptance of the genital area as natural and potentially pleasurable.

Following history-taking and medical examination, the marital unit and co-therapists join in a "roundtable" discussion in which the therapists interpret and relate the individual and marital histories to the presenting dysfunction. An important therapeutic technique used by the sex team is that of "reflective teaching," whereby the therapists restate in objective terms what the problems are and how the couples are failing to communicate with each other. By holding up the "mirror of professional objectivity" to reflect the marital unit's sexual attitudes and practices, the therapists can aid the couple in understanding what it reveals. Masters and Johnson feel that the nonjudgmental attitude of the therapists, in addition to the continual focus on the marital unit as the patient, rather than a particular partner, helps the unit to accept constructive criticism in a nondefensive manner. One of the principal aims of the therapy is to identify and lessen the impact of the "spectator role" that is so often assumed by dysfunctional individuals who are incapacitated by fear of inadequacy and fear of failure—and who become spectators to their own sexual performance—standing by the bedside monitoring every stroke, every thrust, anxiously watching for the rise and fall of the penis. Realizing that performance fears cannot be removed by simply exhorting against them, a highly structural behavioral conditioning approach, referred to as "sensate focus," was developed. The sensate-focus exercises are designed to permit a gradual learning or relearning of sensual and sexual feeling under authoritative direction. The goal is to break the maladaptive patterns of sexual response and to replace them with more pleasurable patterns.

Sensate focus involves a hierarchy of behavioral prescriptions in the form of mutual body exercises. First, the partners are instructed to take turns pleasuring each other by caressing, touching, massaging each others' bodies—avoiding the genital areas and refraining from intercourse. The focus is continually on the *process* and not the *goal*, which serves to decrease performance anxiety, for there is essentially no possibility for failure. Next, the partners are instructed to give feedback to each other, to indicate their preferences about the kind and location of touch desired. Experiences, mistakes, feelings, and reactions are discussed in detail during the sessions with the therapists the following day. When one step has been successfully negotiated, the next step is introduced—and gradually, as the couples progress, and according to the therapists' clinical judgment, they move into more extensive genital and sexual stimulation. Then the specific techniques for various sexual dysfunctions are introduced.

The treatment period was limited to two weeks regardless of symptomatology or improvement. Masters and Johnson decided that it would be impossible to establish treatment successes when statistically evaluating the efficacy of the treatment. They decided to give their results in terms of treatment failures. They also felt that symptom reversal during the acute phase of therapy was relatively unimportant—and established that a patient must maintain or continue progressive improvement after termination. They therefore added the concept of a five-year follow-up. They report an initial failure rate of 18.9 percent and a five-year follow-up failure rate of 20 percent. Although this rate is only suggestive, insofar as all five-year follow-ups have not as yet been completed, the numbers are quite impressive!

Because of these impressive results, the treatment method was quickly adopted for use in hundreds of clinics, centers, and private practices throughout the country. Because of the special setting that the "Foundation" in St. Louis provided, the treatment program has undoubtedly lost considerably when transplanted to other clinics and locales—as well as gained a number of new variables depending on the new setting. The criticisms of the Masters and Johnson program have to be seen in this light, because there is no quarreling with the fact that the original results reported will rival any results achieved through psychosocial interventions. And as Jules Masserman is quoted as saying in *Human Sexual Inadequacy*, "Psychotherapy is anything that works" (Masters and Johnson, 1970, p. 23).

The main criticisms of the Masters and Johnson program are:

1. The expense involved, due not only to the commitment of spending two weeks in St. Louis, but also to paying for the services of two therapists, limits the accessibility of this particular treatment to all but a select affluent population (McCarthy, 1973; Obler, 1975).

2. A biased sample has been seen as one of the reasons for the impressive results. The patients treated at the Foundation had to be highly motivated in order to go to the lengths required. They were also participants in a special undertaking, having made the pilgrimage to the oracles in St. Louis surrounded by the aura of a new magical cure. In addition, they were selected on the basis of their relative freedom from psychopathology, a sizeable proportion of them having completed psychodynamic psychotherapy (Lansky and Davenport, 1975; Mann, 1975).

Another difficulty is that the program is designed for married couples who have relatively stable and secure relationships and who are willing to work together. This omits all single individuals with sexual dysfunction and those with partners who refuse to participate in treatment, an omission compounded by the fact that a large proportion of individuals with sexual problems are single or have unstable relationships (Obler, 1975; Zilbergeld, 1975). Because these latter would not be accepted for treatment in a Masters and Johnson program, a sampling bias is in a sense operating.

3. The two-week time commitment in Masters and Johnson's original approach is difficult, not only because of the expense, but, perhaps more important, has been questioned in terms of efficacy: Do results obtained in the ideal climate of a vacation atmosphere carry over into the everyday existence of a couple, with all the stresses and demands of their regular lives?

4. The need for two therapists has not been established. Although Masters and Johnson (1970) believe that dual therapy teams are necessary, they never proved the need for them (Kaplan, 1974). A number of investigators have pointed out that one skilled therapist is quite adequate (Duddle, 1975; Kovel, 1976; Kaplan, 1974; McCarthy, 1973; Obler, 1975).

5. From the psychodynamic viewpoint, Masters and Johnson have been criticized for not allowing sufficient time for the assimilation of character or intrapsychic change. To the extent that an individual has

neurotic and character problems, there is concern about backsliding when the co-therapists are no longer present. Further, it is argued that there are limitations on the degree of emotional and physical rehabilitation that can occur as a result of the two-week treatment, since the inner conflicts of the individual are not dealt with (Meyer, 1975).

6. Other criticisms are concerned with the evaluative aspects of the program. These criticisms include the lack of careful controls in investigating the efficacy of the methods (Obler, 1975), the lack of specificity in the degree of improvement among nonfailures (Meyer et al., 1975), and the lack of information concerning treatment failures (Lansky and Davenport, 1975).

Modifications of the Masters and Johnson Program

In view of some of the criticisms we have described, many modifications of the Masters and Johnson program have been developed at various treatment centers. Before discussing in more detail the contributions of different investigators and clinicians in the field, we can summarize the most important modifications as follows: (1) Tailoring the time allotted for therapy to fit the needs of individual patients —contracting or expanding the time commitment as deemed necessary for optimal results. One of the first modifications was to see patients in weekly or biweekly visits (Sallie Schumacher at the Human Sexuality Center at Long Island Jewish-Hillside Medical Center in New York) and to be more flexible in deciding on the length of treatment (usually ten to twenty sessions). (2) Making the therapy available to patients in their home community, allowing for continuous integration of the treatment experience with the everyday life of the individuals. (3) Developing methods for working with the single patient if necessary—either on an individual basis or in a group setting. (4) Using a single therapist instead of the dual sex-therapy team approach. (5) Making the therapy available to low-income populations and special-patient populations. And finally, perhaps most important, (6) integrating the specific "sex therapy" techniques with other forms of therapy—with virtually the whole range of available psychosocial and medical therapies. This covers the spectrum from behavioral to psychodynamic therapies, including medical and even surgical interventions when indicated.

We are not aware of any program which has not, at least to some degree, modified their treatment approach to include, for example, the use of a single therapist or to change the original two-week treatment format to a more flexible schedule, as well as to include the single patient or the disadvantaged (either economically, physically, or psychologically) patient. Certain programs have added other interesting features.

Hartman and Fithian (1974) depart from the traditional Masters and Johnson approach in many ways. First, they themselves or any other therapist team participate actively in the sexual training procedures. During the "sexological" examination given to all patients at the onset of therapy, the therapists stimulate the patients' body parts, specifically the genitals, to determine the nature of the sexual response elicited. In addition, the patients are requested to carry out foot, face, and body-caress exercises in the presence of the therapists. The rationale is that the therapists can observe the couples' physical interactions, instead of relying solely on their verbal reports. In addition, it allows the therapists to teach the couple more effective techniques by direct "coaching" and demonstrations.

Second, in contrast to Masters and Johnson, Hartman and Fithian strongly emphasize the use of body-imagery work to raise the patient's low self-concepts. The patients inspect their nude bodies before a triple mirror in the presence of the therapists and are instructed to touch each part of the body, from the head down, focusing on both the touch and their feelings about each part. The therapist's role is to confront the patients with their negative feelings and help them focus on their positive ones. The technique is designed to aid the patients in resolving their feelings of shame and insecurity stemming from the negatively viewed body parts. Hartman and Fithian's technique is more faddish and controversial than most. Their active participation in sexual exercises, such as in the sexological examination, although potentially beneficial, leaves open the opportunity for exploitation of the patients. In addition, since success rates as well as any other types of assessment are not reported, it is difficult to determine if their methods do in fact contribute anything to therapeutic success. It appears that, at the very least, a careful evaluation is needed to ensure the efficacy of this program as well as its ethical and legal implications.

Lobitz and Lo Piccolo (1972) have fused the general program of Masters and Johnson with behavior techniques developed by Wolpe and others. The result is a program with several clinical innovations as well as an ongoing built-in evaluation process.

First, ongoing data on the patients' sexual activities are continuously and systematically collected. Patients are asked to fill out a daily record form detailing their sexual activities, including duration, pleasure and arousal ratings, and subjective comments. These records provide the therapists with feedback and enable them to adjust the program to fit the specific needs of the clients. Second, safeguards are included to insure that the patients carry out the homework assignments which are an integral part of this program as well as a number of other therapy programs. The couples meet with the dual-sex therapy team once a week for fifteen weeks and are assigned a series of homework exercises to be carried out between the visits. Patients are motivated to do their homework exercises by a series of arithmetically progressing fines. After six violations, the treatment is terminated.

A third innovation is the inclusion of a nine-step masturbation program designed to enhance the couple's arousal toward each other, building on progressively more comfortable autoerotic experiences. The final steps differ slightly, depending on the presenting dysfunction. In general, just prior to orgasm by masturbation, the patient is instructed to switch his or her focus to fantasies of sexual activity with the partner. This allows for pairing of responses of sexual arousal and orgasm with the previously neutral stimulus of sex with the partner.

Although the sample size is small, Lobitz and Lo Piccolo (1972) report good results from their treatment program, with success rates that equal or exceed those reported by Masters and Johnson (McGovern et al., 1975). However, they do report less successful results for women with secondary orgasmic dysfunction. It is possible that these women require a greater emphasis on psychotherapeutic techniques than is provided by this program.

Using a more psychodynamically oriented framework, Kaplan (1974) has expanded on the Masters and Johnson method at the Cornell

Medical Center. Her approach involves a combination of prescribed sexual exercises and psychotherapeutic sessions, designed to alter unconscious blocks to sexual functioning and create a free and healthy sexual expression. According to Kaplan this new sex therapy is a ".... task-centered form of crisis intervention which presents an opportunity for rapid conflict resolution. Toward this end the various sexual tasks are employed, as well as the methods of insight therapy, supportive therapy, marital therapy, and other psychiatric techniques as indicated" (p. 199).

Kaplan's treatment approach is very flexible, the sequence of exercises tailored to fit the needs of the particular unit. Sensate focus exercises and medical examinations are prescribed only when indicated. Although the dual-sex therapist approach may be used on occasion for training purposes, individual therapists of either gender are the norm in Kaplan's program. Only skilled psychotherapists are accepted for training. In general, the therapists are dynamically oriented and have experience with psychoanalytic psychotherapy and marital therapy, as well as behavior therapy. Therapy is conducted on an outpatient basis, and the spacing between visits allows the couple time to carry out the prescribed exercises and discuss their reactions and feelings. Further, there is no time limit on the duration of treatment. Therapy is completed when the specific difficulty is relieved.

Probably the most significant difference between Kaplan's approach and the programs previously described lies in the conceptualization of the therapeutic process. Although the primary goal of therapy is to improve sexual functioning, Kaplan's treatment is conducted within a psychodynamic framework. An attempt is made to understand the causes of the problem and to relate these to the treatment plan. Psychodynamic and transactional material are, in general, only discussed to help remove obstacles to effective sexual functioning. Psychodynamic intervention and interpretations are confined to those aspects of the patient's behavior which are defenses against sexuality or resistances to treatment.

The reported results of this therapy program are comparable to those given by Masters and Johnson (1970) and compare well to conventional psychodynamic therapies in terms of both symptom reversal and overall psychic effects (Kaplan, 1974; Kaplan and Kohl, 1972).

It is the flexible integration of analytic and behavioral techniques that characterizes Kaplan's approach and is said to contribute to its success.

Behavior Therapy

The behaviorally oriented therapies merit some additional consideration in this context, for they have greatly influenced the development of the more specific sexual dysfunction therapies. Theoretically, they are based on a model diametrically opposed to the psychodynamic model. The behavior techniques are based upon the assumption that human sexual behavior is learned and that sexual dysfunction results when anxiety is evoked by sexual situations because of past pairings of negative affect and unpleasant sexual experiences. The rationale is similar to Masters and Johnson's (1970) conceptualization of ''fear of performance'' as the greatest deterrent to effective sexual functioning. It is argued that sexual arousal is counteracted by intense anxiety because arousal and anxiety are antagonistic (parasympathetic vs. sympathetic, respectively) nervous system functions (Obler, 1975). Hence, behavior techniques generally focus on decreasing or desensitizing the sexually related anxiety and building up a new and more effective set of sexual responses.

One of the most widely used behavior techniques in the treatment of sexual dysfunction is systematic desensitization, an attempt to eliminate anxiety by replacing it with a stronger, incompatible response, usually relaxation, with the object of extinguishing the association between anxiety and sexual situations. The first step is to create a list of sexually-related situations which elicit increasing degrees of anxiety. The subject is then trained in relaxation, either by instruction, hypnosis or drugs. When the patient is in deep muscular relaxation, he is asked to visualize the least anxiety-producing scene (e.g., going on a date). The desensitization procedure is continued up the hierarchy until the most intensely disturbing scene (e.g., intercourse) can be visualized while the patient is relaxed. In many cases, *in vivo* systematic desensitization exercises are introduced so that the patient can actually function sexually without anxiety.

Desensitization techniques have been reported to be successful for premature ejaculation (Dengrove, 1967; Ince, 1973); frigidity (Brady,

1975; Glick, 1975; Ince, 1973); impotence (Dengrove, 1973; Glick, 1975) and vaginismus (Husted, 1975). Kockott et al. (1975), however, have reported that a Masters-and-Johnson-type approach is superior to systematic desensitization in the treatment of impotence. Other comparisons have not been made, and the literature is sparse in this area.

A modified systematic desensitization technique, used within a multivariate behavior approach, has been described by Obler (1975). Because it was found that some patients are unable to imagine situations that cause extreme anxiety, Obler (1975) has substituted erotic films and slides protraying intense anxiety experiences for the imagined sequences. In addition, biofeedback information was included, enabling patients to determine their levels of anxiety in response to specific situations and to provide continuous feedback during desensitization. When patients no longer experienced anxiety in the presence of the films and slides, in vivo desensitization methods were used. After a barrage of assertive training, confidence therapy, and role-playing exercises, patients were directly exposed to their most intense sexual fears "under conditions essentially equivalent to real life circumstances" (p. 57). While success was defined as the ability to confront the circumstances with a minimal level of recorded tension, the final cure was the elimination of the sexual dysfunction. This multivariate behavior approach claimed an initial success rate of 80 percent and no symptom reversals within the one-and-half-year follow-up period.

An even more extensive multivariate behavior approach has been described by Sayner and Durrell (1975). In addition to systematic desensitization, assertion exercises, and biofeedback, this approach uses a variety of other techniques such as cue analysis, orgasmic role-playing, masturbation, and body-imagery work.

By means of paper and pencil surveys, a systematic assessment is made of those aspects of the environment which either facilitate or inhibit sexual arousal. These cues are then clarified during an interview with the therapist, and the couple is instructed to use those cues which elicit sexual arousal (e.g., soft music) as a regular procedure. Cues that have repeatedly been associated with failure, such as particular positions or the bedroom itself, are to be avoided.

Anorgasmic women are instructed to pretend to reach orgasm with their partners present, with exaggerated screams and thrashes. Orgasmic role playing is particularly useful for women who are ashamed and embarrassed about the contractions and involuntary noises that accompany orgasm. Another technique used with anorgasmic women is a "fading out" method. Women are instructed to reach orgasm by means of a vibrator, which is successful 96 percent of the time. Then, using a backward fading technique, the vibrator is removed, first at the point of orgasm and then earlier and earlier in the sequence. Manual stimulation is substituted, first by the woman and then by her partner, until the woman can achieve orgasm by her partner's manual stimulation alone.

Because a large number of individuals with sexual dysfunctions also have body-image problems, a technique combining masturbation and fantasy is used to condition positive feelings to stimuli of disliked body parts. The patient is instructed to use erotic fantasy and self-stimulation to reach orgasm. Just prior to orgasm, the patient is asked to switch his or her focus to the offending body part. It is felt that repetitive pairings of intensely pleasant feelings with a negatively viewed body part will result in more positive feelings about that part.

A somewhat different use of masturbation exercises has been reported by Lo Piccolo and Lobitz (1972) in the treatment of orgasmic dysfunction. In the case of a primary anorgasmic woman who has never experienced an orgasm from any source of stimulation, it is felt that masturbation is especially therapeutic because it is one of the techniques that is most likely to produce orgasm. Kinsey et al. (1953) reported that the average woman reaches orgasm in more than 95 percent of her masturbatory attempts. In addition, it is thought that frequent orgasms increase vascularity, which in turn enhances orgasm potential. The nine-step masturbation program follows a graduated-approach model to desensitize the client to masturbation. The exercise begins with the woman exploring her body, proceeds to manual self-stimulation, and finally ends with the woman engaging in intercourse, during which time her partner manually stimulates her genitals. Although this technique is said to be very successful (Kohlenberg, 1974; Lobitz and Lo Piccolo, 1972; Lo Piccolo and Lobitz, 1972), this is an adjunctive procedure and the data do not warrant its use without the backdrop of an adequate counseling program (Kohlenberg, 1974).

In addition to the action-oriented, overt behavior methods, a number of imagery-based techniques have been used in the treatment of sexual dysfunction (Flowers and Booraem, 1975; Nims, 1975; Wisk, 1975). The imagery techniques are adjuncts and most useful either when the patient has a deficit of sexual fantasy, has a fear of failure that is so intense that he cannot participate in *in vivo* exercises, or when a cooperative partner is unavailable. Flowers and Booraem (1975) describe a graded thirteen-step imagination exercise that involves active patient participation, accurate feedback, and reward for behavioral change. The patient is asked to visualize and fantasize from a series of scenes that are increasingly sexual in nature. First, paintings and written material are used, but gradually the patient must create his own fantasies. At the successful completion of each step, the patient reinforces his own behavior, while the final reward is improved sexuality. Other adjunct imagery-based techniques include thought-stopping, covert assertion, and covert conditioning. These techniques are based upon the assumption that imagery or thoughts are behavior—that is, covert behavior. By pairing fantasies of sexual encounters with positive stimuli (covert conditioning) and negative self-defeating thoughts with thought-blocking stimuli, such as the word "STOP" (thought-stopping), the individual can gradually experience arousal in response to sexual stimuli and be able to stop obsessive ruminations about the sexual dysfunction.

Two other adjunctive techniques merit attention. The first is the use of videotape feedback to assess particular areas of difficulty as well as to correct and reinforce other behaviors. Serber (1974) found that patients were often unable to accurately report the specific details of their difficulties. The videotape serves to provide the therapist with an actual sample of the couple's behavior, allowing him to point out specific aspects that warrant discussion and/or change. The use of immediate video feedback during sexual activity has not yet been investigated, and more research is needed to assess its effectiveness (Serber, 1974).

The second adjunct is hypnosis. This technique has been used to treat a variety of problems with widely varying results. Hypnosis is used in the treatment of sexual dysfunction by suggesting relaxation and/or loss of inhibition in response to sexual situations. Hypnotherapy has been used alone and in conjunction with other techniques (Tyler, 1975). Kratochavil (1968) has reported success in treating frigidity by posthypnotic suggestion. Combining hypnosis with desensitization techniques, Fuchs and co-workers (1973) have reported an 85 percent success rate in the treatment of vaginismus, with no cases of symptom reversal within a five-year follow-up period. As with videotape feedback, more information is needed to make an adequate assessment.

In general, the efficacy of behavior therapy alone is not comparable to the outcome of the couple therapies described by Hartman and Fithian (1974), Kaplan (1974), and Masters and Johnson (1970), all of which do in fact include behavior techniques. In summary, it can be said that although the behavior techniques are useful in modifying specific aspects of sexual behavior, they do not in themselves constitute a complete therapy. Not only is there a failure to appreciate the deeper problems and roots of the sexual dysfunction, but, further, behavior therapy completely neglects the social environment in which the dysfunctions developed and flourished and fails to take the individual or couple into consideration (Kaplan, 1974). The behavior approach to the treatment of sexual problems appears most valuable when it is included in an eclectic framework.

Cognitive Therapy

Integrating the behavior approach with cognitive and emotive methods in a systematic framework, Ellis (1975b) has described the Rational-Emotional approach (RET) to sex therapy. The main premise of RET is that humans feel disturbed and act dysfunctionally, in sexual as well as in other areas, when they escalate any desire or wish into an absolute "should," "ought," or "must." To exemplify this, Ellis (1975b) has described the A-B-C's of emotional disturbance. "A" is the activating experience (e.g., a sexual failure), and 'C'' is the emotional consequence (e.g., feelings of shame, depression, and self-downing). The mediating "B" is the belief system which consists of rational and irrational beliefs (e.g., How awful that I failed!). The aim of RET is to dispute these irrational beliefs and remove the individual's guilt about sex. The cognitive aspect of RET is designed to change the individual's "awfulizing" and "absolutizing" philosophies so that he can think and act differently. The emotive aspect of RET aims at changing irrational beliefs by altering emotions. This is accomplished by unconditional acceptance by the therapist, shame-attacking exercises, risk-taking exercises, and emotive feedback. The behavior phase includes assertion training, homework assignments, and operant conditioning in an attempt to improve sexual functioning by training procedures.

As described, RET encompasses a variety of techniques used by other known programs. It appropriately stresses the desirability of cognitive, emotional, and behavioral change. Because information concerning the success of this approach is not presented nor are any outcome comparisons made between this and other therapies, the utility of this approach is difficult to ascertain.

Group Therapy

In addition to individual and couple sex therapy, a number of group approaches to the treatment of sexual dysfunction have been developed. Therapy conducted within the group milieu offers a safe atmosphere for change and provides an *in vivo* setting in which patients can experiment, role-play and receive feedback (Sadock and Spitz, 1975). Further, group treatments are generally less expensive than are individual or couple therapies and therefore are available to a broader population.

The use of group therapy for the treatment of sexual dysfunction is not a new concept. As early as 1950, Stone and Levine reported the use of group sessions for women with orgasmic difficulties. Discussions centered on the underlying causes of the difficulties and what measures could be taken to correct them. The group technique was considered both useful and feasible, and a number of women showed marked improvement.

In a more sophisticated approach, Powell et al. (1974) have described a program integrating the principles of Masters and Johnson (1970) into a group-therapy framework. The program, designed for couples, incorporates dual-sex therapy teams, self-administered questionnaires to shorten intake, and group techniques in an intense two-

and-a-half day sexual workshop. After the initial intake, each individual couple meets with the cotherapists for a round table discussion, where the specific problems are crystallized and the details of the workshop are explained. Several couples meet together with the therapist team at the workshop, where audiovisual slides as well as movies are shown and explicit instructions are given for homework exercises. After practicing the exercises, the couples meet again the next day for group discussions, and share their feelings, attitudes, and experiences. In general, these discussions serve to facilitate great progress since "success in the group is contagious" (Powell et al., 1974, p. 93).

Using a more homogenous theme for group meetings, Kaplan et al. (1974) have treated couples for whom premature ejaculation was the chief complaint. The group treatment is based on the analytic plus behavior approach previously described by Kaplan (1974). Although the results reported were excellent, the sample size was far too small ($n=4$) to be definitive.

Another couple-group-therapy approach has been described by Lo Piccolo and Miller (1975). The interesting aspect here is that the design is to teach basic sexual skills to "normal," nondysfunctional couples who, despite the absence of specific dysfunctions, join the group because they are dissatisfied with their sexual lives. Both encounter-group techniques and specific behavioral exercises are used. Each group consists of three patient couples plus a dual-sex therapy team and meets for three, three-hour exercises. Between the sessions, the couples carry out their homework exercises. Using a no-treatment control group, the authors reported significant gains in sexual interaction for the couples, as measured by the Sexual Interaction Inventory. Since most other therapy programs deal with specific dysfunctions and use the presence or absence of symptoms as outcome measures, it is difficult to compare the efficacy of this method to the other approaches. However, it is notable that an objective measuring instrument is used to determine the efficacy of the program.

Other couples' groups described in the literature have included time-extended therapy in resort settings (Reckless et al., 1973), nude marathons (Bindrim, 1968), and sexual attitude restructuring groups (Mann, 1975; Vandervoort and Blank, 1975). The information on these groups is vague, however, and the results are not described fully.

As can be seen, the major emphasis of sex therapy has been on couples. It has become increasingly apparent that sexually dysfunctional individuals without partners or those with uncooperative partners constitute a large and neglected population seeking relief of sexual symptoms (Zilbergeld, 1975). In many cases, the sexual problems or fears associated with them may contribute to the difficulty in forming intimate relationships. It is, therefore, often not feasible to expect these people to wait until they have found a new and/or cooperative partner to enter sex therapy. It was from this context that group treatments for individuals without partners emerged. Groups have been conducted for men and women separately, as well as for "mixed singles."

Zilbergeld (1975) has described a behaviorally oriented group treatment of men without partners. The major techniques include masturbation exercises, homework assignments, self-disclosure, assertiveness training, relaxation training, and re-education. As with most other approaches, the goals of the group are to correct the presenting dysfunction as well as to help the patient understand the problem and develop the skills necessary for effective sexual functioning. Zilbergeld reports two-thirds of the patients completely achieved their goals by the end of the therapy, while most of the remaining third showed some degree of success. Further, a large proportion of the patients showed continued progress when followed up a year later.

An analagous group for "preorgasmic" women has been described by Barbach (1974; Wallace and Barbach, 1974), which utilizes a modified version of the nine-step masturbation program described by Lobitz and Lo Piccolo (1972), assigned for "homeplay." In addition to group discussions, film and sex-education lectures are also included. Results indicate that almost 92 percent of the women were orgasmic with masturbation by the end of ten sessions. The women also reported improvement in ratings of happiness, relaxation, and communication as well as in sexual activities. Further, the stability of outcome was reported as high over an eight-month period (Wallace and Barbach, 1974).

Barbach (1974) attributes the reversal of orgasmic dysfunction to several factors: the supportive and permission-giving aspect of the group; the therapist's ability to deal with the woman's resistance; the

woman's assuming responsibility for the orgasm; and the use of masturbation exercises as the major technique. Although the sample was
small, the results appear to be promising. Using the step-by-step masturbation exercises developed for the group, Barbach (1975) has written a popular guide to orgasmic response. The book, which describes
the exercises in great detail, also provides a wealth of physiological
information and psychological support. It is particularly useful for
anorgasmic women who are unable to enter any type of sex therapy,
and is widely used as an adjunct to direct therapy.

Kaufman and Krupka (1973) describe a co-ed sexual therapy group
program for young men and women. They see the nonstructured and
experiential group as recreating a family and providing the members
with a means of re-enacting the dynamics of both early and current
relationships, with the therapists acting as role models for healthy
adult relationships. The innovative aspect of this approach is that it
is a preventive group that enables young people to integrate sexuality
in their personal experience.

The group approach to the treatment of sexual dysfunction offers
several advantages over individual or couple treatment. First, it is less
expensive. Second, the group offers peer understanding in a group
atmosphere of mutual support and encouragement. A third advantage
is that the group provides for vicarious learning from the successes
and failures of others (Zilbergeld, 1975). One final advantage lies in
the impetus supplied when other group members resolve their problems. Success is often contagious. Many individuals, however, are
unable or unwilling to participate in a group session because of inhibitions, shame, or embarrassment. Others may need more individual
attention and support than the group offers.

Psychodynamic Techniques

To close the circle, we would like to return to the role of psychodynamic therapies in the treatment of sexual dysfunction. Although
''the new sex therapy'' may have started as a diverging form of treatment for the sexual dysfunctions, the experience of many of the professionals in the field has led us to reconsider the place that the
psychoanalytically oriented approach still has in the totality of the

therapeutic armamentarium to this personal and interpersonal problem.

The basic assumption held by psychodynamically oriented therapists is that a sexual symptom is always an expression of a deeper conflict. We have come to see that this is not always the case—that many sexual difficulties are more easily treated than hitherto assumed—and are probably rooted in more superficial sources for anxiety and inadequacy, such as ignorance, misinformation, rigid attitudes, and faulty experiential learning. However, it would be naïve to think that all sexual dysfunctions are easily treated by the symptom-oriented, directive approaches described above. One of the challenges of the field is to learn to distinguish between the many different categories of problems that present as sexual dysfunctions and to learn to assess which ones are best treated by what method, by whom, and for how long. Many problems do not respond to the brief sex therapies—and require the traditional psychodynamic approaches, which are still the treatments of choice when the sexual problems have a neurotic or characterological basis (Meyer, 1975). Levay (1976) suggests that sex therapy can be seen as a series of useful diagnostic tests. The assignment of tasks and the couple's reaction and experience in relation to carrying them out are often diagnostic of hidden psychopathology either in the individual or in the marital dyad. Clinical manifestations such as symptom formation, resistances, and idiosyncratic ways of handling the assigned tasks are almost like fingerprints, indicating what is going on at a deeper layer, and may clearly show the necessity for further psychotherapeutic intervention.

Unfortunately, years of applying the psychodynamic techniques as the sole means of treatment of sexual dysfunction has often failed to provide relief (Ellis, 1975a; Kaplan, 1974; Renshaw, 1975b). The data on the treatment results of psychotherapy are sparse (O'Connor and Stern, 1972), but what is available indicates that the psychodynamic approaches to the treatment of sexual dysfunction are often not adequate in themselves. There are several possible reasons for this. First, psychotherapy cannot limit itself to the specific area of sexual dysfunction, and it is too ambiguous to deal with the problem (Kovel, 1976). Second, the majority of psychotherapists are nondirective and, as a result, cannot give direct sexual information or prescribe and supervise the sexual exercises that have overwhelmingly been found to be essential ingredients in the relief of sexual dysfunction (Ellis, 1975a; Tyler, 1975). Finally, therapist characteristics, specifically the therapist's comfort with sexuality and his definition of what is ''normal,'' are probably more critical factors in psychodynamically oriented therapies than they are in the more ritualized treatments such as Masters and Johnson's (1970) or the strictly behavioral therapies (Tyler, 1975).

Outcome

It is very difficult to compare the efficacies of the various sex therapies. Aside from incomplete or nonexistent reports of results, there is a lack of well-defined criteria in terms of the operational definition of ''success'' or ''failure.'' For example, while certain therapies accept changes in attitudes and improved general sexual functioning as ''success,'' although the specific complaint (e.g., orgasmic dysfunction) may still exist (Bieber, 1974; Lo Piccolo et al., 1975), others, such as those described by Hartman and Fithian (1974) or Kaplan (1974), consider only symptom reversals ''success.'' Further, it is difficult to compare the rates of time-limited therapies, where success or failure is determined at the end of the specified treatment program (e.g., Hartman and Fithian, 1974; Masters and Johnson, 1970) with the rates of programs where treatment ends when either there is a symptom reversal or the patient ends therapy (Kaplan, 1974). Finally, there is a lack of criteria to differentiate varying degrees of presenting symptom severity from varying degrees of success or failure at the termination of treatment.

Aside from the effect of the definition of ''success'' or ''failure'' on outcome rates, a number of other factors influencing outcome have been discussed in the literature. One is concerned with the motivation and commitment of the patients to finding relief of sexual symptoms as opposed to their resistance to change (Kaplan, 1974; Tyler, 1975). Kaplan and Kohl (1972) have pointed out that sexual symptoms, as any other symptoms, often have a defensive function, and clients may be unable or unwilling to give them up. Further, a partner's overt attempts to sabotage treatment or covert unwillingness to help is directly related to the failure of the couple to reverse the dysfunction.

Another variable related to outcome is the presence of psychopathology. A number of investigators (Kaplan, 1974; Kaplan and Kohl, 1972; Lansky and Davenport, 1975; O'Connor and Stern, 1972) have reported a poor outcome for patients or couples with a psychiatric diagnosis. Although most sex therapy programs screen their patients for major psychotic illness, there is still a relatively high incidence of psychopathological disturbances among patients in sex treatment.

In addition to patient variables, therapist characteristics have also been reported to influence outcome (Tyler, 1975). Each therapist brings his own sexual attitudes and anxieties into the treatment. It is necessary for the therapist to accept his own sexuality and avoid using his own sexual functioning as an ideal index (Renshaw, 1975a). As Masters and Johnson (1972) have stated: "It is vital that psychotherapists dealing directly with clinical symptoms of sexual distress react from a sense of confidence and comfort in their own sexuality and sexual functioning. . . . Any failure to maintain perspective has grave potential for undermining the effectiveness of the professional's therapeutic approach to the patient's complaint of sexual inadequacy" (p. 560).

It appears that, regardless of the type of therapy, the efficacy depends largely upon the ability of the therapist to instill a sense of confidence and give the client "permission" to have a more enjoyable sex life (Kovel, 1976; Lassen, 1976).

Other factors related to poor prognosis are excessive vulnerability to stress, the structuring of sex therapy so that other decisions, such as divorce, are contingent upon it, and intense anxiety (Kaplan, 1974). It should also be noted that certain dysfunctions, such as premature ejaculation and vaginismus, have a better prognosis than others (e.g., secondary orgasmic dysfunction).

Problems and Controversies

One of the major problems of sex therapy involves the appropriate screening or selection of patients (Fordney-Settlage, 1975). This has been partially ameliorated by requiring prospective patients to have psychiatric assessment or by requiring patients to be referred from a clinician who presumably knows the patient well. Most sex therapy programs attempt to accept patients who are free of psychosis or other major psychopathology. However, the screening processes are not always adequate, and some psychiatric difficulties are too subtle to detect at first (Kaplan and Kohl, 1972). The danger is that the rapid removal of the sexual dysfunction may precipitate an acute psychiatric disturbance when either the symptomatic patient or spouse is suffering from an underlying psychiatric disturbance and the symptom serves as a defense (Kaplan and Kohl, 1972).

Probably the chief controversy concerning sex therapy is the lack of quality control and licensure requirements for sex therapists (Holden, 1974; Kaplan, 1974; Renshaw, 1975b). Kaplan (1974) reports that a number of "therapists" have engaged in sexual practices with patients, conducted group sexual experiences, and employed prostitutes under the guise of "trained sex therapists." Moreover, a few "sex therapists" have been reported to use sadomasochistic practices and homosexual seduction (Holden, 1974).

On a less dramatic level but still a problem is the widespread occurrence of poorly trained therapists who charge substantial fees and offer nothing more than a variety of gimmicks and pornographic films (Holden, 1974). Some confusion prevails as to what constitutes proper training for sex therapists, and what is needed is a system containing standards for accreditation and licensing in addition to methods for evaluating therapeutic competence and treatment techniques (Sadock et al., 1975).

Another problem is the high cost and, thus, unavailability of treatment to a large segment of the population. In general, sex therapy is limited to middle-class heterosexual couples (Obler, 1975). Although group sex therapy has helped increase the range of people that can be treated by lowering the cost and including individuals without available partners, this still remains a problem. Sex therapy groups are not that widespread, and fees, although lower, are still charged. In addition, many people are not able or willing to participate in and share their problems with a group.

Another issue that deserves mention is the paucity of research in the area of sex therapy. More specifically, there is a lack of adequate comparisons of the efficacies of the various treatment techniques, as well as a lack of control group comparisons (treatment vs. no-treatment groups) for a particular method. This last comparison is particularly important insofar as it has been suggested that merely applying for therapy results in symptom reduction (Obler, 1975). What is needed are careful controls to study the outcomes of the different treatment approaches, holding a wide variety of variables constant, and comparisons of intervention vs. no intervention groups (Fordney-Settlage, 1975).

Although the methods and theories of sex therapy vary greatly, the one thing they have in common is that they do work. Nevertheless, widespread prevention programs must be instituted since so many sexual problems result needlessly from misinformation or anxiety stemming from performance fears. Moreover, the incidence of sexual dysfunction is pervasive. Masters and Johnson (1970) estimate that nearly 50 percent of married couples suffer from sexual problems that significantly affect their relationship. Therefore, it appears necessary for adolescents and young adults, or any individuals for that matter, to receive appropriate sex education and therapeutic intervention, when necessary, to prevent the development of disabling sexual dysfunction.

References

Abelin, E. L. (1971), The Role of the Father in the Separation-Individuation Process. In: *Separation-Individuation: Essays in Honor of Margaret S. Mahler*, ed. J. B. McDevitt & C. F. Settlage. New York: International Universities Press, pp. 229-252.

——— (1975), Some Further Observations and Comments on the Earliest Role of the Father. *Internat. J. Psycho-Anal.*, 16:293-302.

Abraham, K. (1922), Manifestations of the Female Castration Complex. In: *Selected Papers on Psychoanalysis*. New York: Basic Books, 1953, pp. 338-369.

Acton, W. A. (1871), *The Functions and Disorders of the Reproductive Organs*, 3rd Amer. ed. Philadelphia.

Adams, C. R. (1963), Sexual Responsiveness of Certain College Wives. In: *Sexual Behavior and Personality Characteristics*, ed. M. F. De Martino. New York: Citadel Press.

Ainsworth, M. D. (1974), Infant Behavioral Correlates to Maternal Attachment. In: *The Competent Infant: Research and Commentary*, ed. L. J. Stone, H. T. Smith & L. B. Murphy. New York: Basic Books, pp. 1161-1168.

Alper, P. (1977), Help! I've Missed the Sexual Revolution. *Med. Economics*, pp. 80-84.

Anon. (n.d.), *Onania, or the Heinous Sin of Self-Pollution*. London.

Anthony, E. J. (1970), The Reactions of Parents to the Oedipal Child. In: *Parenthood*, ed. E. J. Anthony & T. Benedek. Boston: Little, Brown, pp. 275-288.

Arlow, J. A. (1963), Conflict, Regression and Symptom Formation. *Internat. J. Psycho-Anal.*, 44:12-22.

Augustine, Saint, Bishop of Hippo. *Confessions*, trans. R. S. Pine-Coffin. Baltimore: Penguin Books, 1961.

Bak, R. (1953), Fetishism. *J. Amer. Psychoanal. Assn.*, 1:285-297.

——— (1956), Aggression and Perversion. In: *Perversions, Psychodynamics and Therapy*, ed. S. Lorand & M. Balint. New York: Random House, pp. 231-240.

——— (1968), The Phallic Woman: The Ubiquitous Fantasy in Perversions. *The Psychoanalytic Study of the Child*, 23:15-36. New York: International Universities Press.

——— (1971), Object-relationships in Schizophrenia and Perversion. *Internat. J. Psycho-Anal.*, 52:235-242.

371

Baldessarini, R. J. (1975), The Biogenic Amine Hypothesis in Affective Disorders. In: *The Nature and Treatment of Depression*, ed. F. F. Flach & S. C. Draghi. New York: John Wiley, pp. 347-387.

Barbach, L. G. (1974), Group Treatment of Preorgasmic Women. *J. Sex & Marital Ther.*, 1:139-145.

———— (1975), *For Yourself: The Fulfillment of Female Sexuality*. New York: Doubleday.

Barglow, P. & Schaefer, M. (1977), A New Female Psychology? In: *Female Psychology*, ed. H. P. Blum. New York: International Universities Press, pp. 393-438.

Bateson, G. (1958), *Naven*. 2nd ed. Palo Alto: Stanford University Press.

de Beauvoir, S. (1953), *The Second Sex*. New York: Knopf.

Bell, A. I. (1964), Bowel Training Difficulties in Boys: Phallic and Prephallic Considerations. *J. Amer. Acad. Child Psychiat.*, 3:577-590.

Benedek, T. (1959), Parenthood as a Developmental Phase. *J. Amer. Psychoanal. Assn.*, 7:389-417.

———— (1970a), Fatherhood and Providing. In: *Parenthood*, ed. E. J. Anthony & T. Benedek. Boston: Little, Brown, pp. 167-183.

———— (1970b), Parenthood During the Life Cycle. In: *Parenthood*, ed. E. J. Anthony & T. Benedek. Boston: Little, Brown, pp. 185-206.

Benjamin, H. (1953), Transvestism and Transsexualism. *Internat. J. Sexol.*, 7:12-14.

———— (1966), *The Transsexual Phenomenon*. New York: Julian Press.

———— & Ihlenfeld, C. L. (1970), The Nature and Treatment of Transsexualism. *Med. Opin. & Rev.*, 6.

Bergler, E. & Kroger, W. S. (1954), *Kinsey's Myth of Female Sexuality*. New York: Grune & Stratton.

Berman, E. M. & Lief, H. I. (1976), Sex and the Aging Process. In: *Sex and the Life Cycle*, ed. W. W. Oaks, G. A. Melchiode & I. Ficher. New York: Grune & Stratton, pp. 125-134.

Bernstein, I. (1962), Dreams and Masturbation in an Adolescent Boy. *J. Amer. Psychoanal. Assn.*, 10:289-302.

Bernstein, W. C. (1972), Sexual Dysfunction Following Radical Surgery for Cancer of the Rectum and Sigmoid Colon. *Med. Aspects Hum. Sexual.*, 6:156-163.

Bettelheim, B. (1954), *Symbolic Wounds*. Glencoe, Ill.: The Free Press.

———— (1962), The Problem of Generations. In: *The Challenge of Youth*, ed. E. H. Erikson. New York: Basic Books, 1965, pp. 64-92.

Bibring, G., Dwyer, T. F., Huntington, D. S., & Valenstein, A. F. (1961), A Study of the Psychological Process in Pregnancy and of the Earliest Mother-Child Relationship. *The Psychoanalytic Study of the Child*, 16:9-72. New York: International Universities Press.

Bieber, I. (1974), The Psychoanalytic Treatment of Sexual Disorders. *J. Sex & Marital Ther.*, 1:5-15.

———— et al. (1962), *Homosexuality: A Psychoanalytic Study of Male Homosexuals*. New York: Basic Books.

Biller, H. (1974), Paternal Deprivation, Cognitive Functioning, and the Feminized Classroom. In: *Child Personality and Psychopathology*, ed. A. Davids. New York: Wiley, pp. 11-52.

———— & Meredith, D. (1974), *Father Power*. New York: McKay.

Bindrim, P. (1968), A Report on a Nude Marathon. *Psychother. Theory, Res. & Pract.*, 5:180-188.

Birchall, E. & Gerson, N. (1974), *Sex and the Adult Woman*. New York: Pocket Books.

Blos, P. (1962), *On Adolescence: A Psychoanalytic Interpretation*. New York: Free Press of Glencoe.

———— (1967), The Second Individuation Process of Adolescence. *The Psychoanalytic Study of the Child*, 22:162-186. New York: International Universities Press.

Blum, H. P. (1977), Masochism, the Ego Ideal, and the Psychology of Women. In: *Female Psychology*, ed. H. P. Blum. New York: International Universities Press, pp. 157-191.

Boehm, F. (1930), The Femininity Complex in Men. *Internat. J. Psycho-Anal.*, 11:444-469.

Bonaparte, M. (1953), *Female Sexuality*. New York: International Universities Press.

Bowlby, J. (1951), *Maternal Love and Mental Health*. New York: Schocken Books, 1966.

———— (1969), *Attachment and Love*. New York: Basic Books.

Brady, J. P. (1966), Breviatal Relaxation: Treatment of Frigidity. *Behav. Res. & Ther.*, 4:71-77.

———— (1975), Behavior Therapy of Sexual Disorders. In: *Comprehensive Textbook of Psychiatry*, Vol. II, ed. A. M. Freedman et al. Baltimore: Williams & Wilkins, pp. 1824-1831.

Brazelton, T. B. (1969), *Infants and Mothers: Differences in Development*. New York: Delacorte.

———— Dixon, S., Yogman, M., Tronick, E., Adamson, M. S., & Als, H. (1976), Early Social Interaction of Infants with Parents and Strangers. Presented at the American Academy of Pediatrics Meeting, Child Development Section, Chicago. Unpublished.

Brinton, C. (1959), *A History of Western Morals*. New York: Harcourt, Brace & World.

Brownmiller, S. (1975), *Against Our Will: Men, Women and Rape*. New York: Simon & Schuster.

Bullough, V. (1976), *Sexual Variance in Society and History*. New York: Wiley.

Burgess, A. (1976), Dirty Words. *The New York Times Magazine*. Guest Observer, August 8.

Burnap, D. W. & Golden, J. S. (1967), Sexual Problems in Medical Practice. *J. Med. Ed.*, 42:673-681.

Busse, E. W. (1966), Longitudinal Reseach—the Duke Study. *Proceedings of the 7th International Congress of Gerontology*, Vienna, pp. 283-288.

Butler, R. N. & Lewis, M. I. (1973), *Aging and Mental Health*. St. Louis: C. V. Mosby.

Buxbaum, E. (1970), *Troubled Children in a Troubled World*. New York: International Universities Press.

Calder-Marshall, A. (1959), *The Saga of Sex: A Life of Havelock Ellis*. New York: Putnam.

Calderone, M.S. (1970), Sex and Sexuality—Emerging Concepts. *Reiss-Davis Clinic Bull.*, 7:19-25.

Caldwell, D. O. (1949), Psychopathic Transsexualism. *Sexology*, 16:274-280.

Calleja, M. A. (1967), Homosexual Behavior in Older Men. *Sexology*, 34:46-48.

Campbell, I. W. & Clarke, B. F. (1975), Sexual Dysfunction in Diabetic Men. *Med. Aspects Hum. Sexual.*, 9:157-158.

Caplan, G. (1964), *Principles of Preventive Psychiatry*. New York: Basic Books.

Carden, M. (1974), *The New Feminist Movement*. New York: Russell Sage Foundation.

Carver, J. R. & Oaks, W. W. (1976), Sex & Hypertension. In: *Sex and the Life Cycle*, ed. W. W. Oaks, G. A. Melchiode, & I. Ficher. New York: Grune & Stratton, pp. 175-178.

Chauvin, R. (1977), *Ethology: The Biological Study of Animal Behavior*, trans. J. Diamanti. New York: International Universities Press.

Chess, S., Thomas, A., & Cameron, M. (1976), Sexual Attitudes & Behavior Patterns in a Middle-Class Adolescent Population. *Amer. J. Orthopsychiat.*, 46:689-701.

Chez, R. A. (1971), Movies of Human Sexual Responses as Learned Aids for Medical Students. *J. Med. Ed.*, 46:977-981.

Christenson, C. V. & Gagnon, J. H. (1965), Sexual Behavior in a Group of Older Women. *J. Gerontol.*, 20:351-356.

———— & Johnson, W. (1973), Sexual Patterns in a Group of Older Never-Married Women. *J. Geriat. Psychiat.*, 6:80-98.

Clark, D. (1972), Homosexual Encounters in All-Male Groups. In: *New Perspectives on Encounter Groups*, ed. L. Solomon & B. Berzon. San Francisco: Jossey-Bass.

Clark, R. (1969), Psychosis, Income, and Occupational Prestige. *Amer. Soc. Rev.*, 34:4, 533-541.

Clower, V. (1975), Significance of Masturbation in Female Sexual Development and Function. In: *Masturbation: From Infancy to Senescence*, ed. I. Marcus & J. J. Francis. New York: International Universities Press, pp. 107-143.

Cole, W. G. (1966), *Sex in Christianity and Psychoanalysis*. New York: Oxford University Press.

Comfort, A. (1970), *The Anxiety Makers*. New York: Dell.

Crist, T. (1971), Contraceptive Practices Among College Women. *Med. Aspects Hum. Sexuality*, 5:168-178.

Degler, C. (1964), Revolution without Ideology: The Changing Place of Women in America. *Daedalus*, 93/2:653-670.

Dengrove, E. (1967), Behavior Therapy of Sexual Disorders. *J. Sex. Res.*, 3:49-61.

—— (1973), The Mechanotherapy of Sexual Disorders. *Current Psychiat. Ther.*, 13:131-140.

Deutsch, H. (1942), Some Forms of Emotional Disturbance and their Relationship to Schizophrenia. In: *Neuroses and Character Types*. New York: International Universities Press, 1965, pp. 262-281.

—— (1944-1945), *The Psychology of Women*, Vol. 1 & 2. New York: Grune & Stratton.

Dickes, R. (1977), Chapters on Adult Sexuality. In: *Understanding Human Behavior in Health and Illness*, ed. R. C. Simons & H. Pardes. Baltimore: Williams & Wilkins, #20-26, pp. 213-283.

Dubin, L. & Amelar, R. D. (1971), Urologic Disease and Sexual Function. *Med. Aspects Hum. Sexual.*, 5:108-117.

Duddle, C. M. (1975), The Treatment of Marital Psycho-sexual Problems. *Brit. J. Psychiat.*, 127:169-170.

Easley, E. B. (1974), Atrophic Vaginitis & Sexual Relations. *Med. Aspects Hum. Sexual.*, 2:32-47.

Edgecumbe, R. & Burgner, M. (1975), The Phallic-Narcissistic Phase: The Differentiation Between Preoedipal and Oedipal Aspects of Development. *The Psychoanalytic Study of the Child*, 30:161-180. New Haven: Yale University Press.

Eichenlaub, J. E. (1969), *The Marriage Art*. New York: Dell.

Ekstein, R. (1970), Dialogue on Sex: Distance versus Intimacy. *Reiss-Davis Clinic Bull.*, 7:38-48.

Ellis, A. (1975a), An Informal History of Sex Therapy. *Counseling Psychologist*, 5:9-13.

—— (1975b), The Rational-Emotive Approach to Sex Therapy. *Counseling Psychologist*, 5:14-21.

Ellis, H. (1936), *Studies in the Psychology of Sex*. New York: Random House.

Engel, I. M., Resnick, P. J., & Levine, S. B. (1976), The Use of Programmed Patients and Videotape in Teaching Medical Students to Take a Sexual History. *J. Med. Ed.*, 51:425-427.

Erikson, E. (1959), *Identity and the Life Cycle. Psychological Issues*, Monogr. 1. New York: International Universities Press.

—— (1963), *Childhood and Society*. New York: Norton.

—— (1964), *Insight and Responsibility*. New York: Norton.

—— (1968), *Identity, Youth and Crisis*. New York: Norton.

—— (1969), *Gandhi's Truth*. New York: Norton.

—— (1974), Once More the Inner Space. In: *Women and Analysis*, ed. J. Strouse. New York: Grossman, pp. 320-340.

Escalona, S. (1963), Patterns of Infantile Experience and the Developmental Process. *The Psychoanalytic Study of the Child*, 18:197-244. New York: International Universities Press.

Esman, A. H. (1972), Adolescence and the Consolidation of Values. In: *Moral Values and the Superego Concept in Psychoanalysis*, ed. S. C. Post. New York: International Universities Press, pp. 87-100.

———— (1977), Changing Values: Their Implications for Adolescent Development & Psychoanalytic Ideas. In: *Adolescent Psychiatry*, 5, ed. S. C. Feinstein & P. L. Giovacchini. New York: Jason Aronson, pp. 18-34.

Esquirol, J. Quoted in Comfort (1970).

Farber, L. H. (1966), *The Ways of the Will*. New York: Basic Books.

Fenichel, O. (1930), The Psychology of Transvestitism. In: *Collected Papers*, First Series. New York: Norton, 1953, pp. 167-180.

———— (1945), *The Psychoanalytic Theory of Neurosis*. New York: Norton.

Finkle, A. L. (1973), Emotional Quality and Physical Quantity of Sexual Activity in Aging Males. *J. Geriat. Psychiat.*, 6:70-79.

———— Moyers, T.G., Tobenkin, M., & Karg, S. J. (1959), Sexual Potency in Aging Males with Frequency of Coitus Among Clinic Patients. *JAMA*, 170:1391-1393.

———— & Thompson, R. (1972), Urologic Counseling in Male Sexual Impotence. *Geriatrics*, 27:67-72.

Finkle, P. S. & Finkle, A. L. (1975), Urologic Counseling Can Overcome Male Sexual Impotence. *Geriatrics*, 30:119-129.

Firestone, S. (1970), *The Dialectic of Sex: The Case for Feminist Revolution*. New York: William Morrow.

Fisher, C. (1966), Dreaming and Sexuality. In: *Psychoanalysis: A General Psychology*, ed. R. M. Loewenstein, L. M. Newman, M. Schur, & A. J. Solnit. New York: International Universities Press, pp. 537-569.

Fletcher, R. (1969), Measuring Community Mental Health Attitudes by Means of Hypothetical Case Descriptions. *Soc. Psychiat.*, 4:152-156.

Flowers, J. V. & Booraem, C. D. (1975), Imagination Training in the Treatment of Sexual Dysfunction. *Counseling Psychologist*, 5:50-51.

Ford, C. & Beach, F. (1951), *Patterns of Sexual Behavior*. New York: Ace Star.

Fordney-Settlage, D. S. (1975), Heterosexual Dysfunction: Evaluation of Treatment Procedures. *Arch. Sex. Behav.*, 4:367-387.

Foucault, M. (1961), *Histoire de la Folie*. Paris: Librairie Pion.

Frazer, J. G. (1959), *The New Golden Bough*. New York: Criterion Books.

Freud, A. (1951), Observations on Child Development. *Writings*, 4:143-162. New York: International Universities Press, 1968.

———— (1958), Adolescence. *Writings*, 5:136-166. New York: International Universities Press, 1969.

———— (1965), Normality and Pathology in Childhood. *Writings*, 6. New York: International Universities Press.

Freud, S. (1887-1902), *The Origins of Psychoanalysis*. New York: Basic Books, 1954.

————, (1905), Three Essays on the Theory of Sexuality. *Standard Edition,* * 7:125-243.

———— (1908), On the Sexual Theories of Children. *Standard Edition*, 9:207-226.

*All references are to *The Complete Psychological Works of Sigmund Freud*. London: Hogarth Press, 1953-1974.

————— (1909a), Analysis of a Phobia in a Five-Year-Old Boy. *Standard Edition*, 10:3-147.

————— (1909b), Notes upon a Case of Obsessional Neurosis. *Standard Edition*, 10:153-249.

————— (1910a), Five Lectures on Psycho-Analysis. Fourth Lecture: Infant Sexuality and Neurosis. *Standard Edition*, 11:40-49.

————— (1910b), "Wild" Psycho-Analysis. *Standard Edition*, 11:220-227.

————— (1912a), Totem and Taboo. *Standard Edition*, 13:1-161.

————— (1912b), On the Universal Tendency to Debasement in the Sphere of Love (Contributions to the Psychology of Love). *Standard Edition*, 11:178-190.

————— (1914), On Narcissism: An Introduction. *Standard Edition*, 14:69-102.

————— (1918), From the History of an Infantile Neurosis. *Standard Edition*, 17:3-122.

————— (1920), Beyond the Pleasure Principle. *Standard Edition*, 18:3-64.

————— (1921), Group Psychology and the Analysis of the Ego. *Standard Edition*, 18:67-143.

————— (1923a), The Ego and the Id. *Standard Edition*, 19:3-66.

————— (1923b), The Infantile Genital Organization: An Interpolation into the Theory of Sexuality. *Standard Edition*, 19, 141-145.

————— (1925a), Negation. *Standard Edition*, 19:235-242.

————— (1925b), Some Psychical Consequences of the Anatomical Distinction Between the Sexes. *Standard Edition*, 19:243-258.

————— (1925c), An Autobiographical Study. *Standard Edition*, 20:3-74.

————— (1926), The Question of Lay Analysis. Standard Edition, 20:179-258.

————— (1927), Fetishism. *Standard Edition*, 21:149-157.

————— (1930), Civilization and its Discontents. *Standard Edition*, 21:57-145.

————— (1931), Female Sexuality. *Standard Edition*, 21:223-243.

————— (1933), New Introductory Lectures on Psycho-Analysis. Femininity (Lecture 33). *Standard Edition*, 22:112-135.

————— (1937), Analysis Terminable and Interminable. *Standard Edition*, 23:216-254.

————— (1940a), An Outline of Psycho-Analysis. *Standard Edition*, 23:141-207.

————— (1940b), Splitting of the Ego in the Process of Defence. *Standard Edition*, 23:271-278.

Friedan, B. (1963), *The Feminine Mystique*. New York: Norton.

Friedemann, M. W. (1966), Reflections on Two Cases of Male Transvestitism. *Amer. J. Psychother.*, 20, 270-283.

Fuchs, K., Hock, Z., Paldi, E., Arbramovich, H., Brandes, J. M., Timor-Tritsch, I., & Kleinhaus, M. (1973), Hypno-desensitization Therapy of Vaginismus. *Internat. J. Clin. Exper. Hypn.*, 21:144-156.

Gadpaille, W. J. (1972), Research into the Physiology of Maleness and Femaleness. *Arch. Gen. Psychiat.*, 26:193-207.

————— (1976), A Consideration of Two Concepts of Normality as it Applies to Adolescent Sexuality. *J. Amer. Acad. Child Psychiat.*, 15:679-692.

Gagnon, J. & Simon, W. (1969), Psychosexual Development. *Trans-Action,* March.
—— —— (1973), *Sexual Conduct: The Social Sources of Human Sexuality.* Chicago: Aldine.
Galenson, E. (1971), A Consideration of the Nature of Thought in Childhood Play. In: *Separation-Individuation,* ed. J. B. McDevitt & C. F. Settlage. New York: International Universities Press, pp. 41-59.
—— Miller, R., & Roiphe, H. (1976), The Choice of Symbols. *J. Amer. Acad. Child Psychiat.,* 15:83-96.
—— & Roiphe, H. (1971), The Impact of Early Sexual Discovery on Mood, Defensive Organization, and Symbolization. *The Psychoanalytic Study of the Child,* 26:195-216. New York: Quadrangle.
—— —— (1974), Emergence of Genital Awareness Druring the Second Year of Life. In: *Sex Differences in Behavior,* ed. R. C. Friedman, R. M. Richart, & R. L. Van de Wiele. New York: Wiley.
—— —— (1977), Some Suggested Revisions Concerning Early Female Development. In: *Female Psychology,* ed. H. P. Blum. New York: International Universities Press, pp. 29-58.
—— —— Miller, R., Drucker, J., & Shapiro, C. (in prep.), Normal Development During the Second Year.
—— Vogel, S., Blau, S., & Roiphe, H. (1975), Disturbance in Sexual Identity Beginning at 18 Months of Age. *Internat. Rev. Psycho-Anal.,* 2:389-397.
Gans, H. (1962), *The Urban Villagers.* New York: The Free Press.
Gessa, G. L. & Tagliamonte, A. (1975), Role of Brain Serotonin and Dopamine in Male Sexual Behavior. In: *Sexual Behavior, Pharmacology & Biochemistry,* ed. M. Sandler & G. L. Gessa. New York: Raven Press, pp. 117-128.
Gillespie, W. H. (1956a), The General Theory of Sexual Perversion. *Internat. J. Psycho-Anal.,* 37:396-403.
—— (1956b), The Structure and Aetiology of Sexual Perversions. In: *Perversion: Psychodynamics and Therapy,* ed. S. Lorand & M. Balint. New York: Random House, pp. 28-41.
Ginsberg, G. L., Frosch, W. A., & Shapiro, T. (1972), The New Impotence. *Arch. Gen. Psychiat.,* 26:218-220.
Glenn, J. (1978), The Analysis of Prelatency Children. In: *Child Analysis and Therapy,* ed. J. Glenn. New York: Jason Aronson.
Glick, B. S. (1975), Desensitization Therapy in Impotence and Frigidity: Review of the Literature and Report of a Case. *Amer. J. Psychiat.,* 132:169-171.
Goffman, E. (1959), *The Presentation of Self in Everyday Life.* Garden City, N.Y.: Doubleday Anchor.
—— (1961), *Asylums.* Chicago: Aldine.
Gonick, P. (1976), Urologic Problems and Sexual Dysfunction. In: *Sex and the Life Cycle,* ed. W. W. Oaks, G. A. Melchiode, & I. Ficher. New York: Grune & Stratton, pp. 195-196.
Goodwin, F. K. (1971), Behavioral Effects of L-Dopa in Man. *Seminars in Psychiat.,* 3:477-492.

Gordon, M. (1964), *Assimilation in American Life*. New York: Oxford University Press.

Gove, W. (1970), Societal Reaction as an Explanation of Mental Illness: An Evaluation. *Amer. Soc. Rev.*, 35:873-874.

Green, R. & Money, J. (1969), *Transsexualism and Sex Reassignment*. Baltimore: Johns Hopkins Press.

Greenacre, P. (1950), Special Problems of Early Female Sexual Development. *The Psychoanalytic Study of the Child*, 5:122-138. New York: International Universities Press.

——— (1953), Certain Relationships between Fetishism and the Faulty Development of the Body Image. In: *Emotional Growth*. New York: International Universities Press, 1971, pp. 9-30.

——— (1955), Further Considerations Regarding Fetishism. In: *Emotional Growth*. New York: International Universities Press, 1971, pp. 58-66.

——— (1957), The Childhood of the Artist: Libidinal Phase Development and Giftedness. In: *Emotional Growth*. New York: International Universities Press, 1971, pp. 479-505.

——— (1958), Early Physical Determinants in the Development of the Sense of Identity. In: *Emotional Growth*. New York: International Universities Press, 1971, pp. 113-127.

——— (1960a), Considerations Regarding the Parent-Infant Relationship. In: *Emotional Growth*. New York: International Universities Press, 1971, pp. 199-224.

——— (1960b), Further Notes on Fetishism. In: *Emotional Growth*. New York: International Universities Press, 1971, pp. 182-198.

——— (1966), Problems of Overidealization of the Analyst and of Analysis: Their Manifestations in the Transference and Countertransference Relationship. In: *Emotional Growth*. New York: International Universities Press, 1971, pp. 743-761.

——— (1968a), Personal Communication, April 23.

——— (1968b), Perversions: General Considerations Regarding Their Genetic and Dynamic Background. In: *Emotional Growth*. New York: International Universities Press, 1971, pp. 300-314.

——— (1969), The Fetish and the Transitional Object. In: *Emotional Growth*. New York: International Universities Press, 1971, pp. 315-334.

——— (1970), The Transitional Object and the Fetish. In: *Emotional Growth*. New York: International Universities Press, 1971, pp. 335-352.

Greenson, R. R. (1964), On Homosexuality and Gender Identity. In: *Explorations in Psychoanalysis*. New York: International Universities Press, 1978, pp. 191-198.

——— (1966), A Transsexual Boy and a Hypothesis. In: *Explorations in Psychoanalysis*. New York: International Universities Press, 1978, pp. 289-304.

——— (1968), Disidentifying from Mother: Its Special Importance for the Boy. In: *Explorations in Psychoanalysis*. New York: International Universities Press, 1978, pp. 305-312.

Grossman, W. I. (1976), Discussion of Freud and Female Sexuality. *Internat. J. Psycho-Anal.*, 57:301-305.

———— & Stewart, W. (1977), Penis Envy as Metaphor. In: *Female Psychology*, ed. H. P. Blum. New York: International Universities Press, pp. 193-212.

Gurwitt, A. R. (1976), Aspects of Prospective Fatherhood. *The Psychoanalytic Study of the Child*, 31:237-270. New Haven: Yale University Press.

Gushin, S. R., Shillman, J., & Frosch, W. A. (1978), On Sitting Shivah: The Use of Ritual to Facilitate and Control Mourning. In: *Advances in Thanatology*, Vol. 1. New York: Arno Press.

Haller, J. & Haller, R. (1974), *The Physician and Sexuality in Victorian America*. Urbana: University of Illinois Press.

Hamburger, C. (1953), The Desire for Change of Sex as Shown by Personal Letters from 465 Men and Women. *Acta Endocr.*, 14:361-375.

———— Stürup, G. K., & Dahl-Iversen, E. (1953), Transvestitism: Hormonal, Psychiatric and Surgical Treatment. *JAMA*, 152:391-396.

Hampson, J. L. & Hampson, J. G. (1961), The Ontogenesis of Sexual Behavior in Man. In: *Sex and Internal Secretions*, 3rd ed., ed. W. C. Young. Baltimore: Williams & Wilkins, 1967.

Hare, E. (1962), Masturbatory Insanity: The History of an Idea. *J. Ment. Sci.*, 108:1-25.

———— & Shaw, G. (1965), *Mental Health on a New Housing Estate*. London: Oxford University Press.

Harlow, H. F. & Harlow, M. K. (1965), Affectional Systems. In: *Behavior in Non-Human Primates*, ed. A. M. Schrier, H. F. Harlow, & F. Stollnitz. New York: Academic Press, pp. 287-334.

———— ————, Dodsworth, R. D., & Arling, G. L. (1966), Maternal Behavior of Rhesus Monkeys Deprived of Mothering and Peer Associations in Infancy. *Proc. Amer. Phil. Soc.*, 110:58-66.

Hartman, W. E. & Fithian, M. A. (1974), *Treatment of Sexual Dysfunction*. New York: Jason Aronson.

Hartmann, H. (1939), *Ego Psychology and the Problem of Adaptation*. New York: International Universities Press, 1958.

———— (1944), Psychoanalysis and Sociology. In: *Essays on Ego Psychology*. New York: International Universities Press, 1964, pp. 19-36.

———— Kris, E., & Loewenstein, R. M. (1951), Some Psychoanalytic Comments on "Culture and Personality." In: *Psychoanalysis and Culture*, ed. G. Wilbur & W. Muensterberger. New York: International Universities Press, pp. 3-31.

Hastings, D. (1969), Inauguration of a Research Project on Transsexualism in a University Medical Center. In: *Transsexualism and Sex Reassignment*, ed. R. Green & J. Money. Baltimore: The Johns Hopkins Press.

Hawkes, J. (1976), *Atlas of Early Man*. New York: St. Martin's Press.

Hayes, H. R. (1965), *The Dangerous Sex: The Myth of Feminine Evil*. New York: Pocket Books.

Hellerstein, H. K. & Friedman, G. H. (1969), Sexual Activity and the Post-Coronary Patient. *Med. Aspects Hum. Sexual.*, 3:70-96.

Henderson, B. (1975), *Human Sexuality: An Age of Ambiguity.* Boston: Little, Brown.

Hendin, H. (1975), *Youth in Crisis.* New York: Norton.

Hirschfeld, M. (1910), *Die Transvestiten.* Berlin: Pulvermacher.

Hite, S. (1976), *The Hite Report.* New York: Dell.

Hoenig, J. & Torr, J. B. B. (1964), Karyotyping of Transsexualists. *J. Psychosom. Res.,* 8:157-159.

Hoffer, W. (1950), Development of the Body Ego. *The Psychoanalytic Study of the Child,* 5:18-23. New York: International Universities Press.

———— (1954), Defence Process and Defence Organization: Their Place in Psychoanalytic Technique. *Internat. J. Psycho-Anal.,* 35:194-198.

Holden, C. (1974), Sex Therapy: Making it as a Science and an Industry. *Science,* 186:330-334.

Hollingshead, A. & Redlich, F. (1958), *Social Class and Mental Illness.* New York: Wiley.

Horenstein, S. (1976), Sexual Dysfunction in Neurologic Disease. *Med. Aspects Hum. Sexual.,* 10:6-31.

Horner, M. (1972), Toward an Understanding of Achievement—Related Conflicts in Women. *J. Soc. Issues,* 28:157-175.

Horney, K. (1926), The Flight from Womanhood. *Internat. J. Psycho-Anal.,* 7:324-339.

———— (1933), The Denial of the Vagina. *Internat. J. Psycho-Anal.,* 14:57-70.

Hunt, M. M. (1959), *The Natural History of Love.* New York: Knopf.

———— (1974), *Sexual Behavior in the 1970's.* New York: Dell.

Husted, J. R. (1975), Desensitization Procedures in Dealing with Female Sexual Dysfunction. *Counseling Psychologist,* 5:30-37.

Ince, L. P. (1973), Behavior Modification of Sexual Disorders. *Amer. J. Psychother.,* 27:446-451.

Isakower, O. (1938), A Contribution to the Pathopsychology of Phenomena Associated with Falling Asleep. *Internat. J. Psycho-Anal.,* 19:331-345.

J. (1969), *The Sensuous Woman.* New York: Lyle Stuart.

Jacobson, E. (1964), *The Self and the Object World.* New York: International Universities Press.

JAMA (1969) Editorial. *JAMA,* 210:717.

Janeway, E. (1974), On "Female Sexuality." In: *Women and Analysis,* ed. J. Strouse. New York: Grossman, pp. 57-70.

Jenkins, E. (1958), *Elizabeth the Great.* New York: Coward McCann.

Johnson, A. B. (1975), Drifting on the God Circuit. In: *The Psychology of Adolescence: Essential Readings,* ed. A. H. Esman. New York: International Universities Press, pp. 524-534.

Johnson, A. M. (1949), Sanctions for Superego Lacunae of Adolescents. In: *Searchlights on Delinquency,* ed. K. R. Eissler. New York: International Universities Press, pp. 225-245.

Jones, E. (1927), The Early Development of Female Sexuality. In: *Papers on Psychoanalysis,* 5th ed. Baltimore: Williams & Wilkins, 1948, pp. 438-451.

—— (1933), The Phallic Phase. *Internat. J. Psycho-Anal.*, 14:1-33.
—— (1955), *The Life and Work of Sigmund Freud*, Vol. 2. New York: Basic Books.
Josselyn, I. M. (1970), Sex Education—Is It Wise? *Reiss-Davis Clinic Bull.*, 7:26-37.
Jucovy, M. E. (1976), Initiation Fantasies and Transvestitism. *J. Amer. Psychoanal. Assn.*, 24:525-546.
Kafka, F. (1919), *Letter to His Father*. New York: Schocken Books, 1953.
Kaplan, H. S. (1974), *The New Sex Therapy*. New York: Brunner/Mazel.
—— & Kohl, R. (1972), Adverse Reactions to the Treatment of Sexual Problems. *Psychosomatics*, 13:185-190.
—— —— Pomeroy, W. B., Offitt, A. K., & Hogan, B. (1974), Group Treatment of Premature Ejaculation. *Arch. Sex. Behav.*, 3:443-452.
Karacan, I., Hirsch, C. V., & Williams, R. L. (1972), Some Characteristics of Nocturnal Penile Tumescence in Elderly Males. *J. Geront.*, 27:39-45.
Karlen, A. (1971), *Sexuality and Homosexuality: A New View*. New York: Norton.
Kauffmann, I. (1970), Biologic Considerations of Parenthood. In: *Parenthood*, ed. E. J. Anthony & T. Benedek. Boston: Little, Brown, pp. 3-55.
Kaufman, G. & Krupka, J. (1973), Integrating One's Sexuality: Crisis and Change. *Internat. J. Group Psychother.*, 23:445-464.
Kernberg, O. F. (1966), Structural Derivatives of Object Relationships. *Internat. J. Psycho-Anal.*, 47:236-253.
—— (1967), Borderline Personality Organization. *J. Amer. Psychoanal. Assn.*, 15:641-685.
—— (1972), Early Ego Integration and Object Relations. *Ann. Acad. Sci.*, 193:233-247.
—— (1975), *Borderline Conditions and Pathological Narcissism*. New York: Jason Aronson.
—— (1976), *Object Relations Theory and Clinical Psychoanalysis*. New York: Jason Aronson.
—— (1977), Boundaries and Structure in Love Relations. *J. Amer. Psychoanal. Assn.*, 25:81-114.
Kestenberg, J. (1956), On Development of Maternal Feelings in Early Childhood. *The Psychoanalytic Study of the Child*, 11:257-291. New York: International Universities Press.
—— (1968), Outside and Inside; Male and Female. *J. Amer. Psychoanal. Assn.*, 16:456-520.
—— (1975), *Children and Parents*. New York: Jason Aronson.
—— (1977), Regression and Reintegration in Pregnancy. In: *Female Psychology*, ed. H. P. Blum. New York: International Universities Press, pp. 213-250.
Kinsey, A. C., Pomeroy, W. B., Martin, C. E., & Gebhard, P. H. (1948), *Sexual Behavior in the Human Male*. Philadelphia: W. B. Saunders.
—— —— —— —— (1953), *Sexual Behavior in the Human Female*. Philadelphia: W. B. Saunders.
Klaus, M. (1975), Issues of Parent-Infant Attachment. Proceedings sponsored by the

Univ. Wash. School of Nursing and Maternal and Child Health Services. Battelle Seattle Research Center, May 4-6, pp. 29-34.

———— Jerauld, R., Kreger, N., et al. (1972), Maternal Attachment: Importance of the First Post-Partum Days. *New Eng. J. Med.*, 286:460-463.

———— & Kennell, J. H. (1976), *Maternal-Infant Bonding.* St. Louis: C. V. Mosby.

———— Leger, T., & Trause, M. A. (1975), *Maternal Attachment and Mothering Disorders: A Round Table.* Princeton, N.J.: Johnson & Johnson.

Kleeman, J. (1965), A Boy Discovers His Penis. *The Psychoanalytic Study of the Child,* 20:239-266. New York: International Universities Press.

———— (1966), Genital Discovery During a Boy's Second Year: A Follow-up. *The Psychoanalytic Study of the Child,* 21:358-392. New York: International Universities Press.

———— (1971), The Establishment of Core Gender Identity in Normal Girls. *Arch. Gen. Psychiat.,* 1:103-129.

———— (1975), Genital Self-Stimulation in Infant and Toddler Girls. In: *Masturbation from Infancy to Senescence,* ed. I. M. Marcus & J. J. Francis. New York: International Universities Press, pp. 77-106.

———— (1977), Freud's Views on Early Female Sexuality in the Light of Direct Child Observation. In: *Female Sexuality,* ed. H. P. Blum. New York: International Universities Press, pp. 3-27.

Klein, G. (1975), *Psychoanalysis: An Exploration of Essentials.* New York: International Universities Press.

Klein, M. (1946), Notes on Some Schizoid Mechanisms. *Internat. J. Psycho-Anal.,* 27:99-110.

Knorr, N. J., Wolf, S. R., & Mayer, E. (1968), The Transsexual's Request for Surgery. *J. Nerv. Ment. Dis.,* 147:517-524.

Kockott, G., Pittman, F., & Nosselt, L. (1975), Systematic Desensitization of Erectile Impotence. *Arch. Sex. Behav.,* 4:493-500.

Kohlberg, L. (1967), *Psychosexual Development in Children.* New York: Holt, Rinehart & Winston.

Kohlenberg, R. J. (1974), Directed Masturbation and the Treatment of Primary Orgasmic Dysfunction. *Arch. Sex. Behav.,* 3:349-356.

Kohut, H. (1971), *The Analysis of the Self.* New York: International Universities Press.

Komisar, L. (1971), *The New Feminism.* New York: Franklin Watts.

Kovel, J. (1976), *A Complete Guide to Therapy: From Psychoanalysis to Behavior Modification.* New York: Pantheon.

Kozol, H. L., Cohen, M. I., & Garofilo, R. F. (1966), The Criminally Dangerous Sex Offender. *New Eng. J. Med.,* 79:275.

Krafft-Ebing, R. (1892), *Psychopathia Sexualis.* New York: Putnam, 1965.

Kramer, H. & Sprenger, J. (1486), *Malleus Maleficarum,* trans. M. Summers. London: Pushkin Press, 1928.

Kratochavil, S. (1968), Hypnotherapy in Frigidity. *Symposium Sexuologicum Progense.*

Kristol, I. (1974), Taxes, Poverty, and Equality. *The Public Interest,* Fall, 3-28.

Kubie, L. & Mackie, J. (1968), Critical Issues Raised by Operations for Gender Transmutation. *J. Nerv. Ment. Dis.*, 147:431-443.

Lamb, M. (1975), Fathers. *Hum. Devel.*, 18:245-266.

Lampl-de Groot, J. (1927), The Evolution of the Oedipus Complex in Women. In: *The Development of the Mind*. New York: International Universities Press, 1965, pp. 3-18.

Lansky, M. R. & Davenport, A. A. (1975), Difficulties in Brief Conjoint Treatment of Sexual Dysfunction. *Amer. J. Psychiat.*, 132:177-179.

Lassen, C. L. (1976), Issues and Dilemmas in Sexual Treatment. *J. Sex. & Marital Ther.*, 2:32-39.

Lazarre, J. (1975), What Feminists and Freudians Can Learn From Each Other. In: *Women in a Changing World*, ed. U. West. New York: McGraw-Hill.

Lazarus, A. A. (1963), The Treatment of Chronic Frigidity by Systematic Desensitization. *J. Nerv. Ment. Dis.*, 136:272-278.

Leboyer, F. (1974), *Birth without Violence*. Paris: Editions Seuil.

Leror-Gourhan, A. (1975), Abstract of article in *Science News*, November 8, 1975. Washington, D.C.: Science Service.

Levay, A. N. (1976), Modifications of Sex Therapy. American Psychiatric Association Meeting, Miami, Florida. Unpublished.

Levenson, A. J. & Croft, H. (1977), Patients' Sexual Problems: Aspects of Physician's Qualifications and Management. *J. Repro. Med.*, 18:27-31.

Levine, E. (1976), Male Transsexuals in the Homosexual Subculture. *Amer. J. Psychiat.*, 133:11-13.

———— Gruenewald, D., & Shaiova, C. (1976), Behavioral Differences and Emotional Conflict Among Male-to-Female Transsexuals. *Arch. Sex. Behav.*, 5:1.

———— & Shaiova, C. (1971), Equality and Rationality v. Child Socialization: A Conflict of Interests. *Israel Ann. Psychiat. & Relat. Discipl.*, 9:107-116.

———— ———— (1974), Biology, Personality, and Culture: A Theoretical Comment on the Etiology of Character Disorders in Industrial Society. *Israel Ann. Psychiat. & Relat. Discipl.*, 12:10-28.

———— ———— & Mihailovic, M. (1975), Male to Female: The Role Transformation of Transsexuals. *Arch. Sex. Behav.*, 4:2.

Levine, J. (1976), *Who Will Raise the Children: New Options for Fathers*. Philadelphia: Lippincott.

Lewis, L. & Brissett, D. (1967), Sex as Work. *Soc. Problems*, 15, No. 1:8-18.

Lewis, M. D. (1963), A Case of Transvestitism with Multiple Body-Phallus Identification. *Internat. J. Psycho-Anal.*, 44:345-361.

Licht, H. (1932), *Sexual Life in Ancient Greece*. London: The Abbey Library.

Lichtenstein, H. (1977), Identity and Sexuality. In: *The Dilemma of Human Identity*. New York: Jason Aronson, pp. 49-126.

Lief, H. I. (1969), Sex Education of the Physician. *Human Sexual Function and Dysfunction*, ed. P. J. Find & V. O. Hammett. Philadelphia: F. A. Davis.

———— (1970), New Developments in the Sex Education of the Physician. *JAMA*, 212:1864-1868.

———— & Karlen, A., Eds. (1976), *Sex Education in Medicine*. New York: Spectrum Books.

———— & Reed, D. M. (1967), Normal Psychosexual Functioning. In: *Comprehensive Textbook of Psychiatry*, ed. A. M. Freedman & H. I. Kaplan. Baltimore: William & Wilkins, pp. 258-265.

Lifton, R. J. (1971), Protean Man. *Arch. Gen. Psychiat.*, 24:298-304.

Lindenmann, E. (1941), Observations of Psychiatric Sequelae of Surgical Operations in Women. *Amer. J. Psychiat.*, 98:132.

Lobitz, W. C. & Lo Piccolo, J. (1972), New Methods in the Behavioral Treatment of Sexual Dysfunction. *J. Behav. Ther. & Exper. Psychiat.*, 3:265-271.

Loewald, H. (1951), Ego and Reality. *Internat. J. Psycho-Anal.*, 32:18-19.

———— (1960), The Therapeutic Action of Psychoanalysis. *Internat. J. Psycho-Anal.*, 41:16-33.

Lo Piccolo, J. & Lobitz, W. C. (1972), The Role of Masturbation in the Treatment of Sexual Dysfunction. *Arch. Sex. Behav.*, 2:163-171.

———— ———— & Miller, V. H. (1975), A Program for Enhancing the Sexual Relationship of Normal Couples. *Counseling Psychologist*, 5:41-45.

Lorand, A. (1925), *Old Age Deferred*. New York: F. A. Davies.

Lord, J. W., Jr. (1973), Peripheral Vascular Disorders and Sexual Function. *Med. Aspects Hum. Sexual.*, 7:34-43.

Lorenz, K. (1952), *King Solomon's Ring*. New York: Crowell.

Lowenfeld, H. & Lowenfeld, Y. (1970), Our Permissive Society and the Superego: Some Current Thoughts About Freud's Cultural Concepts. *Psychoanal. Quart.*, 39:590-608.

Lundberg, F. & Farnham, M. (1947), *Modern Woman: The Lost Sex*. New York: Grosset & Dunlap.

M. (1971), *The Sensuous Man*. New York: Lyle Stuart.

McCarthy, B. W. (1973), A Modification of Masters and Johnson Sex Therapy Model in a Clinical Setting. *Psychother. Theory, Res., & Pract.*, 10:290-293.

McGovern, K. B., Stewart, R., & Lo Piccolo, J. (1975), Secondary Orgasmic Dysfunction. I. Analyses and Strategies for Treatment. *Arch. Sex. Behav.*, 4:265-275.

McGuire, W., Ed. (1974), *The Freud/Jung Letters*. Princeton, N.J.: Princeton University Press.

Mahler, M. S. (1963), Thoughts About Development and Individuation. *The Psychoanalytic Study of the Child*, 18:307-324. New York: International Universities Press.

———— (1965), On the Significance of the Normal Separation-Individuation Phase: With Reference to Research in Symbiotic Child Psychosis. In: *Drives, Affects, Behavior*, 2, ed. M. Schur. New York: International Universities Press, pp. 165-169.

———— (1966), Notes on the Development of Basic Moods: The Depressive Affect. In: *Psychoanalysis—A General Psychology: Essays in Honor of Heinz Hartmann*, ed. R. M. Loewenstein, L. M. Newman, M. Schur, & A. J. Solnit. New York: International Universities Press, pp. 152-168.

———— (1968), *On Human Symbiosis and the Vicissitudes of Individuation*. New York: International Universities Press.

———— (1975), Discussion of ''Healthy Parental Influences on the Earliest Development of Masculinity in Baby Boys'' by R. J. Stoller. *Psychoanal. Forum*, 5:244-247.

———— & Furer, M. (1966), Development of Symbiosis, Symbiotic Psychosis, and the Nature of Separation Anxiety. *Internat. J. Psycho-Anal.*, 47:559-560.

———— & Gosliner, B. J. (1955), On Symbiotic Child Psychosis: Genetic, Dynamic, and Restitutive Aspects. *The Psychoanalytic Study of the Child*, 10:195-212. New York: International Universities Press.

———— & La Perriere, K. (1965), Mother-Child Interaction During Separation-Individuation. *Psychoanal. Quart.*, 34:483-497.

———— Pine, F., & Bergman, A. (1975), *The Psychological Birth of the Human Infant*. New York: Basic Books.

Malinowski, B. (1927), *Sex and Repression in Savage Societies*. New York: Harcourt, Brace.

Mann, J. (1975), Is Sex Counseling Here to Stay? *Counseling Psychologist*, 5:60-63.

Marcus, I. M. (1956), Psychoanalytic Group Therapy with Fathers of Emotionally Disturbed Preschool Children. *Internat. J. Group Psychother.*, 6:61-76.

———— (1971), The Marriage-Separation Pendulum. A Character Disorder Associated with Early Object Loss. In: *Currents in Psychoanalysis*, ed. I. M. Marcus. New York: International Universities Press, pp. 361-383.

———— & Francis, J. J. (1975), Masturbation: A Developmental View. In: *Masturbation: From Infancy to Senescence*, ed. I. M. Marcus & J. J. Francis. New York: International Universities Press, pp. 9-51.

Marcus, S. (1964), *The Other Victorians*. New York: Basic Books.

Marquis, J. N. (1970), Orgasmic Reconditioning: Changing Sexual Object Choice Through Controlling Masturbation Fantasies. *J. Behav. Ther. Exper. Psychiat.*, 1:263-271.

Marshall, D. S. & Suggs, R. C., Eds., (1971), *Human Sexual Behavior*. New York: Basic Books.

Martin, P. A. & Lief, H. I. (1973), Resistances to Innovation in Psychiatric Training as Exemplified by Marital Therapy. In: *Psychiatry: Education and Image*, ed. G. Usden. New York: Brunner/Mazel.

Maslow, A. H. (1942), Self-Esteem (Dominance-Feeling) and Sexuality in Women. *J. Soc. Psychol.*, 16:259-294.

———— (1954), *Motivation in Personality*. New York: Harper & Bros. Abridged as Love in Self-Actualizing People in *Sexual Behavior and Personality Characteristics*, ed. M. F. De Martino. New York: Citadel Press, 1963.

———— (1972), *The Farther Reaches of Human Nature*. New York: Viking Press.

Masserman, J. (1973), *Theory and Therapy in Dynamic Psychiatry*. New York: Jason Aronson.

Masters, W. H. & Johnson, V. E. (1966), *The Human Sexual Response*. Boston: Little, Brown.

———— ———— (1970), *Human Sexual Inadequacy*. Boston: Little, Brown.

———— ———— (1972), The Rapid Treatment of Human Sexual Dysfunction. In: *Progress in Group and Family Therapy*, ed. C. Sager et al. New York: Brunner/Mazel, pp. 553-563.

May, G. (1930), *Social Control of Sex Expression*. London: Allen & Unwin.

Mead, M. (1928), *Coming of Age in Samoa*. New York: Morrow.

———— (1935), *Sex and Temperament in Three Primitive Societies*. New York: Morrow.

———— (1974), On Freud's View of Female Psychology. In: *Women and Analysis*, ed. J. Strouse. New York: Grossman, pp. 95-106.

Mechanic, D. (1972), Social Psychologic Factors Affecting the Presentation of Bodily Complaints. *New Eng. J. Med.*, 286:1132-1139.

Meyer, J. K. (1974), Clinical Variants Among Applicants for Sex Reassignment. *Arch. Sex. Behav.*, 3:527-558.

———— (1975), Individual Psychotherapy of Sexual Disorders. In: *Comprehensive Textbook of Psychiatry*, Vol. II, ed. A. M. Freedman et al. Baltimore: Williams & Wilkins, pp. 1545-1556.

———— (1977), Sex Reassignment: Follow-up. Presented at the 130th Annual Meeting of the American Psychiatric Association. Unpublished.

———— Knorr, N., & Blumer, D. (1971), Characterization of a Self-Designated Transsexual Population. *Arch Sex. Behav.*, 1:219-230.

———— Schmidt, C. S., Lucas, M. J. & Smith, E. (1975), Short-term Treatment of Sexual Problems: Interim Report. *Amer. J. Psychiat.*, 132:172-176.

Mitchell, J. (1966), Women: The Longest Revolution. *New Left Review*, 40:11-37.

———— (1971), *Women's Estate*. New York: Pantheon Books.

———— (1974), *Psychoanalysis and Feminism*. New York: Pantheon Books.

———— (1976), Review of *The Transsexual Experiment: Sex and Gender*, Vol. 2 by R. J. Stoller. *Internat. J. Psycho-Anal.*, 57:357-360.

Money, J. (1965), *Sex Research: New Developments*. New York: Rinehart & Winston.

———— (1971), Pornography and Medical Education. *Macy Conference on Family Planning, Demography, and Human Sexuality in Medical Education*, ed. V. W. Lippard. New York: Joshua Macy Jr. Foundation, pp. 98-109.

———— (1974), Intersexual and Transsexual Behavior and Syndrome. In: *The American Handbook of Psychiatry*, Vol. 3, ed. S. Arieti & E. B. Brody. New York: Basic Books, pp. 334-351.

———— & Ehrhardt, A. A. (1972), *Man and Woman, Boy and Girl*. Baltimore/London: Johns Hopkins Press.

Moore, B. (1976), Freud and Female Sexuality: A Current View. *Internat. J. Psycho-Anal.*, 57:287-300.

———— & Fine, B., Eds. (1968), *A Glossary of Psychoanalytic Terms and Concepts*. New York: American Psychoanalytic Association.

Moulton, R. (1977), Some Effects of the New Feminism. *Amer. J. Psychiat.*, 134:1-112.

Müller-Braunschweig, C. (1926), The Genesis of the Feminine Superego. *Internat. J. Psycho-Anal.*, 13:362-368.

Mueller-Heubach, F. (1972), Prolapse of the Uterus: Its Effects on Sexual Behavior. *Med. Aspects Hum. Sexual.*, 6:114-120.

Muensterberger, W. (1962), The Creative Process, Its Relation to Object Loss and Fetishism. *The Psychoanalytic Study of Society*, 2:161-185. New York: International Universities Press.

Muller, J. (1932), The Problems of the Libidinal Development of the Genital Phase in Girls. *Internat. J. Psycho-Anal.*, 13:361-368.

Nagera, H. (1975), Female Sexuality and the Oedipus Complex. New York: Jason Aronson.

Newman, G. & Nichols, C. R. (1960), Sexual Activity and Attitudes of Older Persons. *JAMA*, 173:33-35.

Newman, L. E. & Stoller, R. J. (1971), The Oedipal Situation in Male Transsexualism. *Brit. J. Med. Psychol.*, 44:295-303.

Nims, J. P. (1975), Imagery, Shaping and Orgasm. *J. Sex. & Marital Ther.*, 1:198-203.

Nunberg, H. (1947), Circumcision and the Problems of Bisexuality. *Internat. J. Psycho-Anal.*, 28:145-179.

—— & Federn, E., Eds. (1962), *Minutes of the Vienna Psychoanalytic Society, Vol. 1, 1906-1908*. New York: International Universities Press.

—— —— (1967), *Minutes of the Vienna Psychoanalytic Society, Vol. 2, 1908-1910*. New York: International Universities Press.

Oaks, W. W. & Moyer, J. H. (1972), Sex and Hypertension. *Med. Aspects Hum. Sexual.*, 6:128-137.

Obler, M. (1975), Multivariate Approaches to Psychotherapy with Sexual Dysfunction. *Counseling Psychologist*, 5:55-60.

O'Brien, C. B., DiGiacomo, J. N., Fahn, S., & Schwartz, G. A. (1971), Mental Effects of High Dosage Levodopa. *Arch. Gen. Psychiat.*, 24:61.

O'Connor, J. D. & Stern, L. O. (1972), Results of Treatment in Functional Sexual Disorders. *N.Y. State J. Med.*, 72:1927-1934.

Offer, D. (1971), Attitudes Toward Sexuality in a Group of 1500 Middle-Class Teenagers. *J. Youth & Adoles.*, 1:81-91.

—— Sabshin, M., & Offer, J. L. (1969), *Psychological World of the Teenager*. New York: Basic Books.

Olin, B. M. & Pearlman, A. (1972), Sex After Ileostomy or Colostomy. *Med. Aspects Hum. Sexual.*, 6:32-43.

Ostfeld, A., Smith, C. M., & Stotsky, B. (1977), The Systemic Use of Procaine in the Treatment of the Elderly: A Review. *J. Amer. Geriat. Soc.*, 25:1-20.

Ovesey, L. & Person, E. (1973), Gender Identity and Sexual Psychopathology in Men: A Psychodynamic Analysis of Homosexuality, Transsexualism, and Transvestitism. *J. Amer. Acad. Psychoanal.*, 1:53-72.

—— —— (1976), Transvestitism: A Disorder of the Sense of Self. *Internat. J. Psychother.*, 5:219-235.

Page, L. B. (1975), Advising Hypertensive Patients About Sex. *Med. Aspects Hum. Sexual.*, 9:103-104.

Panel (1952), Psychodynamics and Treatment of Perversions, J.A. Arlow, reporter. *Bull. Amer. Psychoanal. Assn.*, 8:315-327.

—— (1954), Perversion: Theoretical and Therapeutic Aspects, J. A. Arlow, reporter. *J. Amer. Psychoanal. Assn.*, 2:336-350.

—— (1957), Problems of Identity, D. Rubinfine, reporter. *J. Amer. Psychoanal. Assn.*, 6:131-142.

—— (1962), On Masturbation, I. M. Marcus, reporter. *J. Amer. Psychoanal. Assn.*, 10:91-101.

—— (1973), The Experience of Separation-Individuation in Infancy and Its Reverberations Through the Course of Life: 2. Adolescence and Maturity, I.M. Marcus, reporter. *J. Amer. Psychoanal. Assn.*, 21:155-167.

—— (1975), Parenthood as a Developmental Phase, H. Parens, reporter. *J. Amer. Psychoanal. Assn.*, 23:154-165.

—— (1977), The Psychoanalytic Treatment of Male Homosexuality. E. C. Payne, reporter. *J. Amer. Psychoanal. Assn.*, 25:183-199.

—— (1978), The Role of the Father in the Preoedipal Years, R. C. Prall, reporter. *J. Amer. Psychoanal. Assn.*, 26:143-161.

Parens, H. et al. (1977), On the Girl's Entry into the Oedipus Complex. In: *Female Psychology*, ed. H. P. Blum. New York: International Universities Press, pp. 79-107.

Parsons, T. (1964), *Social Structure and Personality*. New York: Free Press.

Pauly, I. (1965), Male Psychosexual Inversion: Transsexualism. *Arch. Gen. Psychiat.*, 13:172-181.

—— (1968), The Current Status of the Change of Sex Operation. *J. Nerv. Ment. Dis.*, 147:460-471.

—— & Goldstein, S. G. (1970), Physicians' Perception of their Education in Human Sexuality. *J. Med. Ed.*, 45:745-754.

Pearman, R. D. (1972), Insertion of Penile Prosthesis for Treatment of Organic Sexual Impotence. *J. Urol.*, 107:802-806.

Peplau, L. (1977), Quoted in *Psychiatric News*, 12, Feb. 4, 1977, pp. 32-33.

Person, E. (1974), Some New Observations on the Origins of Femininity. In: *Women and Analysis*, ed. J. Strouse. New York: Grossman, pp. 250-261.

—— (1976), Discussion: Initiation Fantasies and Transvestitism. *J. Amer. Psychoanal. Assn.*, 24:547-551.

—— & Ovesey, L. (1974a), The Transsexual Syndrome in Males. I: Primary Transsexualism. *Amer. J. Psychother.*, 28:4-20.

—— —— (1974b), The Transsexual Syndrome in Males. II: Secondary Transsexualism. *Amer. J. Psychother.*, 28:174-193.

Pfeiffer, E. & Davis, G. C. (1972), Determinants of Sexual Behavior in Middle and Old Age. *J. Amer. Geriat. Soc.*, 20:151-158.

—— Verwoerdt, A., & Davis, G. C. (1972), Sexual Behavior in Middle Life. *Amer. J. Psychiat.*, 128:1262-1267.

—— —— & Wang, H. S. (1968), Sexual Behavior in Aged Men and Women. I. Observation on 254 Community Volunteers. *Arch. Gen. Psychiat.*, 19:641-646.

—— —— —— (1969), The Natural History of Sexual Behavior in a Biologically Advantaged Group of Aged Individuals. *J. Geront.*, 24:193-198.

Phillips, D. & Segal, B. (1969), Sexual Status and Psychiatric Symptoms. *Amer. Soc. Rev.*, 34:58-72.

Piaget, J. (1945), *Play, Dreams and Imitation in Childhood*. New York: Norton, 1951.

—— (1970), *Structuralism*. New York: Basic Books.

Pine, F. & Furer, M. (1963), Studies of the Separation-Individuation Phase: A Methodological Overview. *The Psychoanalytic Study of the Child*, 18:325-342. New York: International Universities Press.

Pomeroy, W. B. (1966), The Masters-Johnson Report and the Kinsey Tradition. In: *An Analysis of Human Sexual Response*, ed. R. Brecher & E. Brecher. New York: Signet Books.

—— (1968), *Boys and Sex*. New York: Delacorte.

—— (1969), *Girls and Sex*. New York: Delacorte.

Powell, L. C., Blakeney, P., Croft, H., & Pulliam, G. P. (1974), Rapid Treatment Approach to Human Sexual Inadequacy. *Amer. J. Obstet. Gynecol.*, 119:89-97.

Pruyser, P. W. (1975), What Splits in Splitting? *Bull. Menninger Clin.*, 39:1-46.

Ralske, N. N., Aronson, M. J., Kay, P., Sarnoff, C. A., & Scharfman, M.A. (1971), Report of the Long Island Psychoanalytic Society Community Psychiatry Committee on Sex Education in the Schools. Unpublished.

Rangell, L. (1970), The Return of Repressed "Oedipus." In: *Parenthood*, ed. E. J. Anthony & T. Benedek. Boston: Little, Brown, pp. 325-334.

Ray, G. R. (1975), Potency After Radiation Therapy of Prostatic Carcinoma. *Med. Aspects Hum. Sexual.*, 9:132.

Reckless, J., Hawkins, D., & Fauntleroy, A. (1973), Time-extended Group Therapy Sessions in a Remote Setting. *Amer. J. Psychiat.*, 130:1024-1026.

Reiss, A. (1964), The Social Integration of Queers and Peers. In: *The Other Side*, ed. H. Becker. New York: The Free Press.

Reiss, I. (1960), *Premarital Sexual Standards in America*. New York: The Free Press.

—— (1967), *The Social Context of Premarital Sexual Permissiveness*. New York: Holt, Rinehart & Winston.

Renshaw, D.C. (1975a), Sex Therapy in the 1970's. *Psychiat. Opinion*, 12:6-11.

—— (1975b), Sexual Problems in Stroke Patients. *Med. Aspects Hum. Sexual.*, 9:68-74.

Riesman, D., Glazer, N., & Denny, R. (1950), *The Lonely Crowd*. New Haven: Yale University Press.

Rittenberg, S. M. & Wyman, H. M. (1977), Masters and Johnson and the Sexual Revolution. Unpublished.

Robinson, I. E., King, K., & Balswick, J. O. (1972), The Premarital Sexual Revolution Among College Females. *Fam. Coord.*, 6:189-195.

Rogow, A. (1970), *The Psychiatrists*. New York: Putnam.

Roiphe, H. (1968), On an Early Genital Phase. The Psychoanalytic Study of the Child, 23:348-365. New York: International Universities Press.

——— (1973), Some Thoughts on Childhood Psychosis, Self, and Object. *The Psychoanalytic Study of the Child*, 28:131-145. New Haven: Yale University Press.

——— & Galenson, E. (1972), Early Genital Activity and the Castration Complex. *Psychoanal. Quart.*, 41:334-347.

——— ——— (1973a), The Infantile Fetish. *The Psychoanalytic Study of the Child*, 28:147-166. New Haven: Yale University Press.

——— ——— (1973b), Object Loss and Early Sexual Development. *Psychoanal. Quart.*, 42:73-90.

——— ——— (1975), Some Observations on Transitional Object and Infantile Fetish. *Psychoanal. Quart.*, 44:206-231.

Root, N. M. (1962), Some Remarks on Anxiety Dreams in Latency and Adolescence. *J. Amer. Psychoanal. Assn.*, 10:303-332.

Ross, J. M. (1974), The Children's Children: A Psychoanalytic Study of Generativity and Nurturance in Boys. Unpublished.

——— (1975), The Development of Paternal Identity: A Critical Review of the Literature on Nurturance and Generativity in Boys and Men. *J. Amer. Psychoanal. Assn.*, 23:783-817.

——— (1977), Toward Fatherhood: The Epigenesis of Paternal Identity During a Boy's First Decade. *Internat. Rev. Psycho-Anal.*, 4:327-347.

——— (in press), The Forgotten Father. In: *Self-In-Process Series*, Vol. 2, ed. Ikenberry & Coleman.

——— & Dunn, P. B. (in press), Notes on the Genesis of Pathological Splitting. *Internat. J. or Rev. Psycho-Anal.*

Ross, N. (1960), Rivalry with the Product: A Specific Form of Inhibition in Creative Activity. *J. Amer. Psychoanal. Assn.*, 8:450-463.

——— (1975), Affect as Cognition: With Observations on Mystical States. *Internat. Rev. Psycho-Anal.*, 2:79-93.

Rossi, A. (1964), Equality Between the Sexes: An Immodest Proposal. *Daedalus*, 93/2:607-652.

——— Ed. (1974), *The Feminist Papers: From Adams to de Beauvoir*. New York: Bantam Books.

Rush, B. (1812), *Medical Inquiries and Observations upon the Diseases of the Mind*. Philadelphia.

Sachs, H. (1923), On the Genesis of Sexual Perversion. *Internazionale Zeitschrifte f. Psychoanalyse*, 9:172-182. Trans. H. Freud Bernays. In: *Homosexuality*, C. W. Socarides. New York: Jason Aronson, 1978.

Sachs, L. J. (1962), A Case of Castration Anxiety Beginning at 18 Months. *J. Amer. Psychoanal. Assn.*, 10:329-337.

Sadock, B. J. & Spitz, H. I. (1975), Group Psychotherapy of Sexual Disorders. In: *Comprehensive Textbook of Psychiatry*, Vol. 2, ed. A. M. Freedman et al. Baltimore: Williams & Wilkins, pp. 1569-1575.

Sadock, V. V., Sadock, B. J., & Kaplan, H. I. (1975), Comprehensive Sex Therapy Training: A New Approach. *Amer. J. Psychiat.*, 132:858-860.

Sagan, C. (1977), *The Dragons of Eden: Speculations on the Evolution of Human Intelligence*. New York: Random House.

Sarnoff, C. A. (1975), *Latency*. New York: Aronson.

Sayner, R. & Durrell, D. (1975), Multiple Behavior Therapy Techniques in the Treatment of Sexual Dysfunction. *Counseling Psychologist*, 5:38-41.

Schafer, R. (1974), Problems in Freud's Psychology of Women. In: *Female Psychology*, ed. H. P. Blum. New York: International Universities Press, 1977, pp. 331-360.

Schmidt, G. & Sigusch, V. (1972), Changes in Sexual Behavior Among Young Males & Females Between 1960-1970. *Arch. Sex. Behav.*, 2:27-45.

Schur, E. (1965), *Crimes Without Victims*. Englewood Cliffs, N.J.: Prentice-Hall.

Scott, F. B., Baarley, W. E., & Timm, G. W. (1973), Management of Erectile Impotence: Use of Implantable Inflatable Prostheses. *Urol.*, 2:81-82.

Segal, M. M. (1963), Impulsive Sexuality: Some Clinical and Theoretical Observations. *Internat. J. Psycho-Anal.*, 44:407-418.

——— (1965), Transvestitism as an Impulse and as a Defence. *Internat. J. Psycho-Anal.*, 46:209-217.

Segall, P. E., Miller, C., & Timiras, P. S. (1975), Aging and CNS Monoamines. *Abstracts, 10th International Congress of Gerontology*, 2:87.

Seiden, A. (1976a), Overview: Research on the Psychology of Women. Part I: Gender Differences and Sexual and Reproductive Life. *Amer. J. Psychiat.*, 133:995-1007.

——— (1976b), Overview: Research on the Psychology of Women. Part II. Women in Families, Work and Psychotherapy. *Amer. J. Psychiat.*, 133:1111-1128.

Semans, J. H. (1956), Premature Ejaculation: A New Approach. *Southern Med. J.*, 49:353-357.

Serber, M. (1974), Videotape Feedback in the Treatment of Couples with Sexual Dysfunction. *Arch. Sex. Behav.*, 3:377-380.

Shainess, N. (1966), A Re-assessment of Feminine Sexuality and Erotic Experience. In: *Science and Psychoanalysis*, ed. J. Masserman. New York: Grune & Stratton, pp. 56-71.

——— (1970), Is There a Separate Feminine Psychology? *N.Y. State J. Med.*, 70:3007-3009.

——— (1972), Toward a New Feminine Psychology. *Notre Dame J. Ed.*, 4:293-299.

Shanas, E. (1969), Living Arrangements and Housing of Old People. In: *Behavior and Adaptation in Late Life*, ed. E. W. Busse & E. Pfeiffer. Boston: Little, Brown.

Shapiro, E. R., Zinner, J., Shapiro, R. I., & Berkowitz, D. A. (1975), The Influence of Family Experience on Borderline Personality Development. *Internat. Rev. Psycho-Anal.*, 2:399-412.

Shengold, L. & McLaughlin, J. T. (reporters) (1976), Plenary Session on "Changes in Psychoanalytic Practice and Experience." *Internat. J. Psycho-Anal.*, 57:261-274.

Simon, W., Berger, A. S., & Gagnon, J. J. (1972), Beyond Anxiety and Fantasy: The Coital Experience of College Youth. *J. Youth & Adoles.*, 1:203-222.

Simons, R. C. & Pardes, H., Eds. (1977), *Understanding Human Behavior in Health and Illness.* Baltimore: Williams & Wilkins.

Singer, I. (1973), *The Goals of Human Sexuality.* New York: Norton.

Skae, D. (1863), *The Classification of the Various Forms of Insanity.*

Small, M. P., Carrion, H. N., & Gordan, J. J. (1975), Small-Carrion Penile Prosthesis—New Implant for the Management of Impotence. *Urol.*, 5:479-486.

Smith, B. H. (1976), Peyronie's Disease. *Amer. J. Clin. Path.*, 45:670-678.

Socarides, C. W. (1959), Meaning and Content of a Pedophiliac Perversion. *J. Amer. Psychoanal. Assn.*, 7:84-94.

———— (1960), The Development of a Fetishistic Perversion. *J. Amer. Psychoanal. Assn.*, 8:281-311.

———— (1968a), *The Overt Homosexual.* New York: Jason Aronson, 1978.

———— (1968b), A Provisional Theory of Etiology in Male Homosexuality: A Case of Preoedipal Origin. *Internat. J. Psycho-Anal.*, 49:27-37.

———— (1969a), The Desire for Sexual Transformation: A Psychiatric Evaluation of Transsexualism. *Amer. J. Psychiat.*, 125:1419-1425.

———— (1969b), The Psychoanalytic Therapy of a Male Homosexual. *Psychoanal. Quart.*, 38:173-190.

———— (1970), A Psychoanalytic Study of the Desire for Sexual Transformation ('Transsexualism'): The Plaster of Paris Man. *Internat. J. Psychoanal. Psychother.*, 51:341-349.

———— (1973), Sexual Perversion and the Fear of Engulfment. *Internat. J. Psychoanal. Psychother.*, 2:432-448.

———— (1974), The Demonified Mother: A Study of Voyeurism and Sexual Sadism. *Internat. Rev. Psycho-Anal.*, 1:187-195.

———— (1975), Discussion of "Healthy Parental Influences on the Earliest Development of Masculinity in Baby Boys" by R. J. Stoller. *Psychoanal. Forum*, 5:241-243.

———— (1977a), Considerations on the Psychoanalytic Treatment of Overt Homosexuality. Part IV: A Provisional Classification and Differentiating Criteria of the Homosexualities. Presented at the American Psychoanalytic Association, December. Unpublished.

———— (1977b), Transsexualism and the First Law of Medicine. *Psychiat. Opin.*, 14:20-24.

———— (1978), *Homosexuality.* New York: Jason Aronson.

Solecki, R. S. (1975), Abstract of article in *Science News*, November 28, 1975. Washington, D.C.: Science Service.

Sorensen, R. C. (1973), *Adolescent Sexuality in Contemporary America.* New York: World.

Speers, R. W. & Lansing, C. (1965), *Group Therapy in Childhood Psychosis.* Chapel Hill: University of North Carolina Press.

Sperling, M. (1963), Fetishism in Children. *Psychoanal. Quart.*, 32:374-392.
——— (1964), The Analysis of a Boy with Transvestitic Tendencies. *The Psychoanalytic Study of the Child*, 19:470-493. New York: International Universities
   Press.
Spitz, R. A. (1952), Authority and Masturbation. *Psychoanal. Quart.*, 21:490-527.
——— (1945, 1946a), Hospitalism: An Inquiry into Psychiatric Conditions in Early
   Childhood. *The Psychoanalytic Study of the Child*, 1:53-74; 2:113-117. New
   York: International Universities Press.
——— (1946b), The Smiling Response. *Genet. Psychol. Monogr.*, 34:57-125.
——— (1959), *A Genetic Field Theory of Ego Formation*. New York: International
   Universities Press.
——— (1965), *The First Year of Life*. New York: International Universities Press.
——— & Wolf, K. M. (1949), Autoerotism: Some Empirical Findings and Hy-
   potheses on Three of its Manifestations in the First Year of Life. *The Psychoan-
   alytic Study of the Child*, 3/4:85-120. New York: International Universities
   Press.
Spock, B. (1963), Should Mothers Work? *Ladies Home Journal*, February.
Spurlock, J. & Rembold, K. (1976), A Reappraisal of Psychodynamic Theories as
   Related to Evaluation and Treatment of Children and Their Parents. Unpublished.
Starr, C., Ed. (1971), *Anthropology Today*. Del Mar, California: CRM Books.
Stearns, G. L., MacDonnell, J. A., Kaufman, B. J., Padja, R., Lucman, T. S.,
   Winter, J. S., & Faiman, C. (1974), Declining Testicular Function with
   Age—Hormonal and Clinical Correlates. *Amer. J. Med.*, 57:761-766.
Stoller, R. J. (1964), A Contribution to the Study of Gender Identity. *Internat. J.
   Psycho-Anal.*, 45:220-226.
——— (1965), The Sense of Maleness. *Psychoanal. Quart.*, 34:207-218.
——— (1966), The Mother's Contribution to Infantile Transvestitic Behavior. *Internat. J. Psycho-Anal.*, 47:384-395.
——— (1968a), The Sense of Femaleness. *Psychoanal. Quart.*, 37:42-55.
——— (1968b), *Sex and Gender*. New York: Science House.
——— (1973a), Male Transsexualism: Uneasiness. *Amer. J. Psychiat.*, 130:536-539.
——— (1973b), The Male Transsexual as 'Experiment'. *Internat. J. Psycho-Anal.*,
   54:215-225.
——— (1975a), Healthy Parental Influences on the Earliest Development of Masculinity in Baby Boys. *Psychoanal. Forum*, 5:232-262.
——— (1975b), *The Transsexual Experiment: Sex and Gender*, Vol. 2. London:
   Hogarth Press & the Institute of Psychoanalysis.
——— (1977), Primary Femininity. In: *Female Psychology*, ed. H. P. Blum. New
   York: International Universities Press.
Stolorow, R. & Atwood, G. (in press), *Faces in a Cloud*. New York: Jason Aronson.
——— ——— & Ross, J. (1978), The Representational World in Psycho-Analytic
   Therapy. *Internat. Rev. Psycho-Anal.*, 5:247-256.
Stone, A. & Levine, J. (1950), Group Therapy in Sexual Maladjustment. *Amer. J.
   Psychiat.*, 107:195-202.

Street, R. (1959), *Modern Sex Techniques*. New York: Lancer Books.

Suggs, R. (1966), *Marquesan Sexual Behavior*. New York: Harcourt, Brace & World.

Tagliamonte, A., Tagliamonte, P., & Gessa, G. L. (1969), Compulsive Sexual Activity Induced by P-Chlorophenylalanine in Normal and Pinealectomized Rats. *Science*, 166:1433-1435.

Taylor, G. R. (1954), *Sex in History*. New York: Vanguard.

——— (1958), *The Angel Makers*. London: Heinemann.

Thomas, E. B., Leiderman, P. H., & Olson, J. P. (1972), Neonate-Mother Interaction During Breast-Feeding. *Devel. Psychol.*, 6:110-118.

Thompson, C. (1942), Cultural Pressures in the Psychology of Women. *Psychiatry*, 5:331-339.

——— (1943), Penis Envy in Women. *Psychiatry*, 6:123-125.

——— (1950), Some Effects of the Derogatory Attitude Towards Female Sexuality. *Psychiatry*, 13:349-354.

Ticho, G. (1977), Female Autonomy and Young Adult Women. In: *Female Psychology*, ed. H. P. Blum. New York: International Universities Press, pp. 139-155.

Tissot, S. (1760), *Onania*. Lausanne: Chapuis.

Toffler, A. (1970), *Future Shock*. New York: Random House.

Tolpin, M. (1971), On the Beginnings of the Cohesive Self: An Application of the Concept of Transmuting Internalization to the Study of the Transitional Object and Signal Anxiety. *The Psychoanalytic Study of the Child*, 26:316-354. New York: Quadrangle.

Trehowan, W. (1965), The Couvade Syndrome. *Brit. J. Psychiat.*, 3:57-66.

Trilling, L. (1954), An Analysis of the Kinsey Reports. In: *An Analysis of the Kinsey Reports*, ed. D. Geddes. New York: New American Library.

Tyler, E. (1970), Introducing a Sex Education Course into the Medical Curriculum. *J. Med. Ed.*, 45:1025-1031.

——— (1975), Sexual Incapacity Therapy. In: *American Handbook of Psychiatry*, Vol. 5, ed. S. Arieti. New York: Basic Books, pp. 408-423.

Ueno, M. (1963), The So-Called Coition Death. *Jap. J. Legal Med.*, 17:330-340.

Van der Leeuw, P. J. (1958), The Preoedipal Phase of the Male. *The Psychoanalytic Study of the Child*, 13:352-374. New York: International Universities Press.

Vandervoort, H. E. & Blank, J. E. (1975), A Sex Counseling Program in a University Medical Center. *Counseling Psychologist*, 5:64-67.

Van de Velde, T. H. (1930), *Ideal Marriage*. New York: Random House.

Vanggaard, T. (1972), *Phallós*. New York: International Universities Press.

Verwoerdt, A., Pfeiffer, E., & Wang, H. S. (1969a), Sexual Behavior in Senescence. I. Changes in Sexual Activity and Interest of Aging Men and Women. *J. Geriat. Psychiat.*, 2:163-180.

——— ——— ——— (1969b), Sexual Behavior in Senescence. II. Patterns of Sexual Activity and Interest. *Geriatrics*, 24:137-154.

Vieth, I. (1965), *Hysteria: The History of a Disease*. Chicago: University of Chicago Press.

Vincent, C. E., ed. (1968), *Human Sexuality in Medical Education and Practice.* Springfield, Ill.: Charles C Thomas.

Volkan, V.D. (1974) Transsexuals: A Different Understanding. In: *Marital and Sexual Counseling in Medical Practice,* ed. D. W. Abse, E. Nash, & L. Louden. New York: Harper & Row, pp. 383-404.

——— (1975), Who are Transsexuals and Should They Be Subject to Surgical Intervention? *Tip Dünyasi* (Istanbul, Turkey), 48:165-176.

——— (1976), *Primitive Internalized Object Relations.* New York: International Universities Press.

——— & Berent, S. (1976), Psychiatric Aspects of Surgical Treatment for Problems of Sexual Identification (Transsexualism). In: *Modern Perspectives in the Psychiatric Aspects of Surgery,* ed. J. G. Howells. New York: Brunner/Mazel, pp. 447-467.

——— & Bhatti, T.H. (1972), Dreams of Transsexuals Awaiting Surgery. *Compr. Psychiat.,* 14:269-279.

——— & Kavanaugh, J. (1977), A Nine-Year-Old Transsexual Boy and his Family. Presented at the spring meeting of the Neuropsychiatric Society of Virginia, Williamsburg.

Wall, S. & Kaltreider, N. (1977), Changing Social-Sexual Patterns in Gynecological Practice. *JAMA,* 237:565-568.

Wallace, D. H. & Barbach, L. G. (1974), Preorgasmic Group Treatment. *J. Sex. & Marital Ther.,* 1:146-154.

Wallerstein, R. S. (1973), Psychoanalytic Perspectives on the Problem of Reality. *J. Amer. Psychoanal. Assn.,* 21:5-33.

Weber, M. (1947), *The Theory of Economic and Social Organization.* New York: Free Press.

Weinberg, M. S. (1969), The Aging Male Homosexual. *Med. Aspects Hum. Sexual.,* 3:66-72.

Weitzman, E. L., Shamoian, C. A., & Golosow, N. (1971), Family Dynamics in Male Transsexualism. *Psychosom. Med.,* 33:289-299.

Wendt, H. (1972), *From Ape to Man: The Search for the Ancestry of Man.* Indianapolis: Bobbs-Merrill.

Whiskin, F. E. (1970), The Geriatric Sex Offender. *Med. Aspects Hum. Sexual.,* 4:125-129.

Whisnant, L. & Zegans, L. (1975), A Study of Attitudes Toward Menarche in White Middle-Class American Adolescent Girls. *Amer. J. Psychiat.,* 132:809-814.

Wilson, E. O. (1975), *Sociobiology, The New Synthesis.* Cambridge, Mass.: Belknap Press of Harvard University Press.

Winnicott, D. W. (1953), Transitional Objects and Transitional Phenomena. *Internat. J. Psycho-Anal.,* 34:89-97.

——— (1957), *The Child and the Outside World.* New York: Basic Books.

——— (1958), *Collected Papers. Through Pediatrics to Psychoanalysis.* New York: Basic Books.

——— (1963), Psychiatric Disorders in Terms of Infantile Maturational Processes.

In: *The Maturational Processes and the Facilitating Environment*. New York: International Universities Press, 1965, pp. 230-241.

———— (1965), *The Maturational Processes and the Facilitating Environment*. New York: International Universities Press.

Winokur, G., Auze, S. & Pfeiffer, A. (1959), Developmental & Sexual Factors in Women. *Amer. J. Psychiat.*, 115:1097-1100.

Wisk, P. A. (1975), The Use of Imagery-Based Techniques in the Treatment of Sexual Dysfunction. *Counseling Psychologist*, 5:52-54.

Wollstonecraft, M. (1792), *A Vindication of the Rights of Woman with Strictures on Political and Moral Subjects*. New York: Norton, 1967.

Wolpe, J. (1958), *Psychotherapy by Reciprocal Inhibition*. Palo Alto: Stanford University Press.

Yankelovich, D. (1974), *The New Morality*. New York: McGraw-Hill.

Yazmajian, R. V. (1966), The Testes and Body-Image Formation in Transvestitism. *J. Amer. Psychoanal. Assn.*, 14:304-312.

Zelnik, M. & Kantner, J. F. (1971), Sex and Contraception Among Unmarried Teenagers. In: *Toward the End of Growth*, ed. C. F. Westcoff. Englewood Cliffs, N.J.: Prentice-Hall.

———— ———— (1977), Sexual and Contraceptive Experience of Young Unmarried Women in the United States 1976 and 1971. *Fam. Plan. Perspect.*, 9:55-71.

Zilbergeld, B. (1975), Group Treatment of Sexual Dysfunction in Men Without Partners. *J. Sex & Marital Ther.*, 1:204-214.

Zilboorg, G. (1941), *A History of Medical Psychology*. New York: Norton.

———— (1944), Masculine and Feminine. *Psychiatry*, 7:257-296.

Zinner, J. & Shapiro, R. (1974), The Family Group as a Single Psychic Entity: Implications for Acting Out in Adolescence. *Internat. Rev. Psycho-Anal.*, 1:179-186.

Name Index

Subject Index